R.W. Kilmp

Philosophy, Literature, and Politics

Philosophy, Literature, and Politics

Essays Honoring Ellis Sandoz

Edited by
Charles R. Embry
and Barry Cooper

University of Missouri Press
Columbia and London

Copyright © 2005 by the Curators of the University of Missouri
University of Missouri Press, Columbia, Missouri 65201
Printed and bound in the United States of America
All rights reserved
5 4 3 2 1   09 08 07 06 05

Library of Congress Cataloging-in-Publication Data

Philosophy, literature, and politics : essays honoring Ellis Sandoz /
edited by Charles R. Embry and Barry Cooper.
    p. cm.
  Summary: "Festschrift honoring Ellis Sandoz, director of the Eric
Voegelin Institute for American Renaissance Studies and editor of Collected
Works of Eric Voegelin. Essays explore philosophy, literature, and politics,
and focus on Xenophon, Natsume, Freud, Robert Penn Warren, and George
Santayana"—Provided by publisher.
  Includes bibliographical references and index.
  ISBN 0-8262-1592-0 (alk. paper)
  1. Voegelin, Eric, 1901–   I. Embry, Charles R., 1942–   II. Cooper,
Barry, 1943–   III. Sandoz, Ellis, 1931–
  B3354.V884P45 2005
  190—dc22   2005005401

∞™ This paper meets the requirements of the American
National Standard for Permanence of Paper for Printed Library Materials,
Z39.48, 1984.

Designer: Jennifer Cropp
Typesetter: Phoenix Type, Inc.
Printer and binder: The Maple-Vail Book Manufacturing Group
Typefaces: Minion and Cocktail

*The University of Missouri Press offers its grateful
acknowledgment to the Earhart Foundation, the LSU
Alumni Association, and the Office of the Dean of
Graduate Studies and Research at Texas A&M
University–Commerce for generous contributions
in support of the publication of this volume.*

Contents

Publisher's Note vii
Beverly Jarrett

Preface xi
Charles R. Embry and Barry Cooper

I. Philosophy

1. The Turn toward Existence as Existence in the Turn 3
David Walsh

2. Hunting and Political Philosophy:
An Interpretation of the *Kynegetikos* 28
Barry Cooper

3. The (Anti-)Eschatological Perspective in
Sigmund Freud's Psychoanalysis 54
Gilbert Weiss

4. Eric Voegelin's Defense of Human Dignity 74
Glenn Hughes

5. Eric Voegelin and a New Science of Politics 91
James L. Wiser

6. The Big Mystery:
Human Emergence as Cosmic Metaxy 102
Brendan Purcell

II. Literature

7. A Discipline of the Mind and Heart:
Voegelin and Santayana as Philosophers of Experience 129
Elizabeth Corey

8. Compactness, Poetic Ambiguity,
and the Fiction of Robert Penn Warren 146
Steven D. Ealy

9. Biographies of Consciousness:
Péter Nádas and Eric Voegelin 170
Charles R. Embry

10. Imagining Modern Japan:
Natsume Soseki's First Trilogy 188
Timothy Hoye

III. Politics

11. The Concept of "the Political" Revisited 209
Jürgen Gebhardt

12. Eric Voegelin on the Nature of Law 223
Timothy Fuller

13. A Classical Prince:
The Style of François Mitterrand 234
Tilo Schabert

14. Common Sense and the Rule of Law:
Returning Voegelin to Central Europe 258
Martin Palous

15. Civilizational Conflict and Spiritual Disorder 285
Michael Franz

16. Voegelin's Puritan Gnosticism
and Bacon's *Great Instauration* 302
Stephen A. McKnight

17. History as Open Horizon:
Eric Voegelin's Search for a Post-Imperial Order 325
Thomas Hollweck

Contributors 341
Index 345

 Publisher's Note

Intrepid. If I were obliged to select a single word to describe Ellis Sandoz, that's the word I'd choose: *Intrepid.* Throughout the thirty-some years I've known him, and in all the kinds of work we've done together, this unique scholar has never faltered in any task he confronted. As teacher, as scholar, as friend, Ellis Sandoz is one of those special individuals who will walk the extra mile with you and for you.

With considerable assistance from Ellis Sandoz, I had the privilege of serving as copyeditor for Eric Voegelin's last three publications: *The Ecumenic Age* (1974), *In Search of Order* (1987), and *Autobiographical Reflections* (1989). It was during this fifteen-year period that I first came to know Ellis Sandoz, who recorded and then transcribed *Autobiographical Reflections,* and who aided me and Voegelin's widow, Lissy, as we readied *In Search of Order* for posthumous publication.

In the years following Voegelin's death in January 1985, Sandoz led the editorial board and me as we laid out plans for publication of the thirty-four-volume *Collected Works of Eric Voegelin.* Any scholar who has ever participated in such a gargantuan project knows of the many difficulties the editors and publishers have confronted. This is not the place to itemize all those difficulties.

It is, however, appropriate to record the fact that Ellis Sandoz was the one human who worked hardest to assure that *The Collected Works* was not allowed to falter. Whether it was volume editors, translators, a dedicated publisher, or money that needed to be secured, it was Ellis Sandoz who worked tirelessly to locate those necessities.

I can speak only as publisher—both originally at LSU Press and finally at the University of Missouri Press—regarding the invaluable service of Sandoz in seeing that *The Collected Works* came to a meaningful end. In order for Missouri's press to complete the work begun at LSU Press, funds to supplement the purchase of the LSU Press volumes were provided by the Eric Voegelin Institute that Sandoz had established. In addition, each volume published by Missouri has been subsidized by the Eric Voegelin Institute.

When one volume editor couldn't, for one reason or another, complete the editorial work, Sandoz located another. When deadlines weren't met, Sandoz helped move the work along. Whatever struggles individual volume editors confronted, Sandoz helped to solve them—with money, coeditors, translators, copyeditors. We at the University of Missouri Press have had the distinct pleasure of working with a scholar who believed in the value of *The Collected Works of Eric Voegelin* and who helped us at every stage. Always optimistic, never succumbing to defeat or delay, Sandoz deserves ultimate credit for our success in getting so many important books published expeditiously, making them available to a large audience.

In addition to the immeasurable service Sandoz has provided for the successful publication of the Voegelin volumes, he has befriended numerous young scholars in a broad range of intellectual inquiry. He is a dedicated teacher, one who excites youngsters as they begin their studies (my eldest grandson, Matthew Jarrett Gibson, among them). And he has aided more advanced scholars as they produced dissertations and later works that merited publication. Too many established scholar/teachers lose interest in what younger thinkers are doing. Not Ellis Sandoz; he stays in touch with new thinkers—both his own students and those coming from other universities. He encourages and guides them as they locate publishing homes for their own work.

The accomplishments of Ellis Sandoz as editor and teacher have in no way diminished his own academic achievements. This volume of essays honoring Sandoz is divided into three sections—philosophy, literature, and politics—because those are the three large areas within which Sandoz has worked himself. His early book on Dostoyevsky remains a classic. His massive compendium, *Political Sermons of the American Founding Era,* serves the community of scholars investigating early American history, just as *A Government of Laws* provides a profoundly knowledgeable interpretive investigation of the American founding. Sandoz provided the first and best introduction to Eric Voegelin with his *The Voegelinian Revolution.* And Ellis Sandoz is still hard at work, with a new volume on "republicanism and religion" expected next year.

The distinguished scholars who have contributed to this volume honoring Ellis Sandoz know they are celebrating a hero. All of us know how large have been his contributions to academic discourse. It is the University of Missouri Press's honor to publish these tributes to Ellis Sandoz.

To end on a somewhat personal note, I must say that but for Ellis Sandoz I'd never have been introduced to Eric Voegelin. I would not have had the joy of getting acquainted with Lissy Voegelin, a magnificent lady who understood her husband and his work better than some have given her credit for. Nor would I have come to know and respect the many individuals who have edited specific volumes in *The Collected Works* or those whose books in political philosophy came to Missouri because Sandoz steered them that way. All of these people have enriched my life in publishing, and Ellis Sandoz, most especially, has helped me continue to know how important is the work of a university press.

An outstanding philosopher, literary critic, student of politics—not to mention a splendid human being—Ellis Sandoz has been and continues to be a scholar whose gifts as teacher, student, and friend make him the very deserving honoree for whom this book was prepared. I join the essayists in celebrating his place in our lives.

Beverly Jarrett

P.S. And he makes a mean jar of fig preserves!

 Preface

We are pleased to present this set of essays to Professor G. Ellis Sandoz, Hermann Moyse Jr. Distinguished Professor of Political Science and founding director of the Eric Voegelin Institute for American Renaissance Studies at Louisiana State University, an institution devoted to research and publication in the fields of political philosophy and constitutionalism. He is a native of Louisiana, whose family first came to the state in 1829 from Switzerland, and a veteran of the U.S. Marine Corps. He was educated at LSU, the University of North Carolina, Georgetown, Heidelberg, and the University of Munich, where he was the sole American to complete a doctorate under the supervision of Eric Voegelin.

Ellis Sandoz has plowed, sowed, pruned, and harvested the groves of academe for more than forty years. He has served three different universities—Louisiana Tech University, Texas A&M University–Commerce (formerly East Texas State University), and Louisiana State University in Baton Rouge. He is a specialist in American, European, and Russian political philosophy, and he has written extensively on public policy from the perspective provided by his study of the great works in political science. He has done his duty as a department head, served as a leader on the Editorial Board for the publication of the Collected Works of Eric Voegelin, raised financial support for the Collected Works, the Eric Voegelin Institute, and the Eric Voegelin Institute Series in Political Philosophy (University of Missouri Press). Most important, he has encouraged and supported the work of other scholars.

President Ronald Reagan appointed him to the National Council of Humanities in 1982 for a six-year term. In 1987 he was appointed by the Board of Foreign Scholarships as Fulbright 40th Anniversary Distinguished American Scholar to represent the United States in Italy and to lecture on the American Constitution during the bicentennial year. After the Velvet Revolution in 1989 he conducted a series of conferences in the new Czech Republic on Anglo-American constitutionalism, liberty, and Western political philosophy. He lectured as well in Slovakia and Poland. For these educational activities in the former East Bloc countries he was awarded the University Medal and Rector's Certificate by Palacky University at Olomouc, Czech Republic, and in 1995 he received an honorary doctorate from Palacky.

Amid all this activity Ellis Sandoz executed a substantial and variegated research agenda. He has authored and edited more than a dozen books, including *Political Apocalypse: A Study of Dostoevsky's Grand Inquisitor; Conceived in Liberty; A Government of Laws; The Voegelinian Revolution: A Biographical Introduction;* and *The Politics of Truth and Other Untimely Essays: The Crisis of Civic Consciousness.* His work as general editor of *The Collected Works of Eric Voegelin* does not begin to indicate the effort he has expended in animating this enormous publication project. He recruited editors and then kept them, more or less, to an agreed-upon timetable. He edited and introduced several of the volumes himself. It is altogether fitting that he was awarded a chair in political science endowed by Hermann Moyse Jr., a member of the first class taught by Eric Voegelin at LSU. All of us represented in this collection have been beneficiaries of his support, generosity, and friendship. We hope that this collection will not only acknowledge his manifold contribution to contemporary political science but give him enjoyment in the reading thereof.

Each of us has his or her own story to tell about Ellis. But one of the perquisites of editorship is that we get to tell our stories and hope they will stand as exemplary for others.

Charles Embry first knew of Ellis in 1962 while enrolled as a history major at Louisiana Tech University. All history majors were required to take two political science courses: American Government and Comparative European Government (the latter taught by Professor Sandoz). I had heard through the student grapevine that one should postpone taking Sandoz until the eleventh hour because he was impossibly difficult. Foolishly I followed the mass. By the spring of 1964 the Louisiana Legislature had passed a law that all college students must take a one-hour course entitled "Americanism vs. Communism," and Ellis had been assigned this course. So as a graduating senior I had my first two classes with him at Louisiana Tech. Ellis lectured (in both courses) on political theory, testing us both on his lectures and on the required readings, which he did not overtly cover in class. His inspiring lectures introduced me both to the perennial questions that humans ask and to the ways in which philosophers and political theorists grapple with these questions. Near the end of the semester, Ellis persuaded me to enter graduate school in political science, even though I had taken only two political science courses. It was not a hard sell. To help rectify my lack of work in political science, he suggested a list of books for me to read during the summer before graduate school in the fall.

There were eight or so books on the list, including Aristotle, John Hallowell's text on political philosophy, and two of Voegelin's books: *The New Science of Politics* and *Plato and Aristotle*. I will always be grateful to Ellis for introducing me to the grand tradition of political philosophy, in general, and to the remarkable work of Eric Voegelin, in particular. When in 1968 I was offered a teaching position at East Texas State University, where Ellis had become head of the department of political science, I was again grateful—this time to become the colleague of my mentor.

Barry Cooper first met Ellis Sandoz in Atlanta at Emory University in 1967 when Eric Voegelin delivered his Walter Turner Candler lectures. My supervisor at Duke, John Hallowell, suggested that it would be a splendid opportunity to see Voegelin in action. It was, though I recollect being baffled at the time by the subject matter of his talks, "The Drama of Humanity." Fortunately Gregor Sebba, his friend of many years, organized a seminar in the afternoon while Voegelin napped, and people who actually understood Voegelin did their best to explain him to a group of twenty-something graduate students. Ellis led. I was astonished not simply with his command of Voegelin's political science but at his ability to present it in a way that we found intelligible. I was in the presence of a master of Socratic rhetoric.

Over the years we would meet at the annual American Political Science Association meetings. Once I recall luring him to the Canadian Political Science Association. It was not until the 1980s, with the establishment of the Eric Voegelin Society, that we met regularly. And then I discovered that his greatest accomplishment was not his scholarship, impressive though that remains, but that he was a crack wing shot. For several years during the fall he visited either the University of Calgary or the University of Saskatchewan in Saskatoon, where Jene Porter taught for many years. His official purpose, of course, was to attend a scholarly conference or to deliver guest lectures. In addition, as soon as his duties were performed we would repair to a rustic motel or hotel in Stettler, Alberta, or Rose Valley, Saskatchewan, to commence what we called "field work."

There is a magnificence as well as an excitement that comes from huddling in a goose pit as a flight of greater Canada geese set their wings to glide toward your hiding place. Just before they land they are the size of B-52s. But that is not why political scientists hunt. It is for the conversation. Visualize driving through the cold prairie night with Ellis in a pickup, discussing Voegelin's political science. What could be better? About the only thing comparable in my experience is driving from his goose blind in the Louisiana delta to hunt quail in the Texas panhandle.

Michael Oakeshott uses the image of a conversation to express what is essential concerning our humanity. It is a great blessing to have been able to converse with Ellis on so many, many questions over the years.

The editors wish to express their thanks to Carolyn Andres, University of Calgary, who transformed the many different essays into one uniform text for the University of Missouri Press, and to Julie Schorfheide, copy editor, for excellent work in preparing this book for publication. Charles Embry also wishes to thank the following persons at Texas A&M University–Commerce, who in various ways provided time from teaching duties that permitted him to complete work on this project:

>President Keith McFarland and Dr. Joyce Scott, provost and vice-president for academic affairs, for approval of my Faculty Development Leave grant;
>the Faculty Development Leave committee, for recommending my leave application for approval;
>Ben Doughty, interim dean of arts and sciences, for approval of release time;
>Paul Lechner, professor and head of political science, for recommending release time and for his continual support of my research activities.

I
 Philosophy

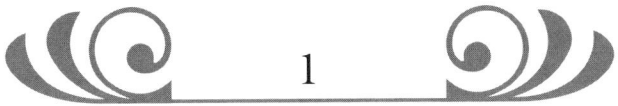

The Turn toward Existence as Existence in the Turn

David Walsh

The crisis of meaning that has confronted modernity is inseparable from the drive to technology. Not only can nature no longer provide a guide when we subject it to universal dominion, but even the coherence of nature as a concept begins to fall apart. Nature may be the means by which we dominate nature, but the boundary between the natural and the artificial can then scarcely be maintained. All becomes raw material for homogenization and manipulation. Nothing is simply given as a fixed or permanent form; everything is drawn into the process of transformation. The dream of universal mastery finds no limit except one. Mastery cannot master itself. In the end the vast expansion of power is itself unmastered because it is left without purpose or guide. Technology has no goal. But in this realization our philosophical reflection has at the same time illuminated the self-limitation of all instrumentality. Nothing can really be an instrument unless it somehow serves a goal that is not instrumental. Just as in each case the object pursued is regarded as a relative end, so the scheme of instrumentality as such can only function if it is embedded in an order of things that limits its expansion. The process cannot continue indefinitely. It is only from the overwhelming power of technological development that we gain the impression of its omnivorousness. The reality is that the whole structure quickly crumbles unless it is sustained by an order of limits that define and guide it. Formal rationality may seem to exercise unchallenged dominance, but without a substance of ends it falls apart. The pursuit of means is always structured by ends.

Correlative with this philosophic critique of instrumentalization is the growth of the alternative by which it is judged. The still incompletely realized revolution in modern philosophy consists in the progressive articulation of substantive reason. Modern science may have succeeded by virtue of its restriction to the world of phenomena, but modern philosophy has correspondingly found itself within a reality that it knows from within. Technology too is ultimately known from the inner perspective of participation, and this in turn is what enables our philosophical reflection to escape the realm of technique. Unlike the superficial expectation that a technical solution may be found to all the problems of technology, our philosophical meditation unfolds at the heart of the technological project. Refusing to be limited to the realm of appearance, the philosophical penetration of the underlying reality is an opening toward being as such. It is a disclosure of reality from within, in contrast to the illusion of domination from without. In place of the subject standing over against a world of objects, we expand the meditative knowledge of our participation within existence. Illusory superiority is replaced by submission to truth. This is the shift of perspective that has been under way in modern philosophy as it struggled against the subject-object model whose dominance has been so great that the countermovement has scarcely been noticed.

To really comprehend the far-reaching implications of this philosophic revolution, a revolution that does indeed return us to the very beginning of philosophy, we must be prepared to follow out the many threads by which it is unfolded. All that can be attempted here is a sketch, but it cannot be only a sketch. In keeping with the existential shift in philosophy itself we cannot avoid an actual beginning. Philosophy can no longer be talked about; it can only be discussed from within. A non-philosophic account of the movement of modern philosophy would be like describing an event of which we had no experience. No doubt much useful information could be assembled by such a strictly historical approach, but it would miss the core that alone justifies attention to the periphery. Philosophy can only be understood by participating in it. This is a principle that increasingly informs and identifies the philosophic revolution of the modern period. Once we become self-conscious in our discourse attention turns toward the conditions of philosophical reflection itself. Among the conditions that cannot be overleaped is the existence of the philosopher himself. It is in this way that philosophy returns to its classical conception as a way of life. But merely recognizing the indispensability of the existential perspective does not mean that a thinker will fully recognize the implications of the shift. Indeed one of the patterns we will discern is that the modern philosophic revolution is often characterized by the struggle, not always successful, to remain true to itself. If we are to uncover the full dimensions of this movement we cannot remain at the level of intellectual formulations. We must reach beyond what was said to the dynamic of questioning that in many cases yielded developments never fully acknowledged and sometimes even distorted by the thinkers themselves. Given the inconclusive state of much contemporary philosophical discussion the notion that a unifying pattern exists at all is a claim requiring justification. For now all we can do is prepare the way by taking note of the fundamental condition for perceiving its plausibility. We must be prepared to exist within the mode of philosophy. To understand those who worked toward this new way of conceiving philosophy we must place ourselves within the same dynamic. We must be prepared to philosophize about philosophy.

The recognition of this necessity is slow to emerge in the history of modern thought but it clearly antedates the so-called "existentialists" of the twentieth century. A persuasive case can be made that Kant marks the beginning of the return of philosophy, more explicitly than with the classical thinkers, to the primacy of existence. The shift is proclaimed in Kant's assertion of the superiority of practical reason for the disclosure of being.[1] God, the immortality of the soul, and the reality of human freedom are postulates of the moral life, and Kant is very careful to emphasize that this provides no theoretical knowledge of their truth. Since all of our knowledge comes through our sensible intuitions, that of which we can have no experience can never become an object of knowledge. This is the famous end of metaphysics in the sense of a claim to know entities that exist in some abstract realm apart from all possibility of experience. Kant inaugurates the liberation from unreal entities that Nietzsche continues to celebrate. Relief from the burden of unreality is seen as a break from a long imposition dating to Plato. Yet as every reader of Kant can recognize, he does not thereby abandon his concern with faith or metaphysics, for he brings them to a deeper level. This is not merely a haunting of the past. Both in tone and in substance Kant displays the new seriousness about getting at the real truth of things, even to the extent of proclaiming his own search for the pure a priori of reason to be the only adequate metaphysics. What makes him sanguine about the possibility of thereby bringing about a fundamental advance in philosophy is his conviction that the critique of pure reason, both theoretical and practical, puts us in touch with the thing in itself. It is reality known from within, knowledge of the noumenon rather than the phenomenon. In reflecting on the a priori of pure reason, whether in its theoretical or practical

---

1. This is a view of Kant that is gradually coming into focus. See Richard Velkley, *Freedom and the End of Reason: On the Moral Foundation of Kant's Critical Philosophy* (Chicago: University of Chicago Press, 1989).

mode, we are no longer apprehending the appearance of what is intended but know it as it is. This means that what is discovered in this noumenal reflection of the self on itself carries with it a force of reality that breaks through the barrier of the phenomenal. We still have no phenomenal basis for our assertions concerning God, immortality, or freedom, but we are profoundly convinced of their reality. As "postulates" of practical reason, they are the indispensable continuities from the reality that is most powerfully evident in our own existence. To the extent that Kant struggles to heighten the human dignity that realizes itself exclusively through the exercise of self-responsibility, he at the same time intensifies the awareness of the dimensions of reality into which human being extends.

    This is the excitement that took hold of philosophy in the movement known as Idealism. A whole generation of thinkers looked on the completion of Kant's philosophical revolution as their project. They understood that Kant had placed the subject, the transcendental ego, at the center of reality and had thereby resolved the gulf that seemed irresolvable within all correspondence theories of knowledge. By making knowledge of the world derive from the subject he had redefined the nature of the problem. Knowledge now meant the categories we impose on sensible institutions, which removes entirely the mystery of how they connect us with the world outside ourselves. Rather than conceive knowledge as something that comes from a source outside, he showed that it is essentially the order we impose on the world of our experience. That left, of course, the great problem of truth. If knowledge consists of the imposition of categories on data, how do we know if our imposition is true in some sense? What does truth mean in this context? These are the questions with which Kant himself struggled in his last great critique, *The Critique of Judgment,* which was the point of departure for the Idealists. Comprehension of reality by means of our categories is true only if our reason is itself continuous with the structure of reality itself. Recourse to a postulate of teleology is again the way in which Kant formulated this derivation, but the Idealists made the existential leap to grasp that this is no longer a claim about knowledge but about human being. Our categories can comprehend reality, not because we can bridge the separation of subject and object, but because our being is already the unity of the two. Human existence is never simply a fact within a world of other discrete facts, but is already that which can see facts as facts. The way to understand reality, the Idealists concluded from Kant, was not to contemplate it as a whole outside of the subject but to recognize that the subject was already the whole or the point through which its self-disclosure took place most completely. They saw that it is practical reason that holds the key to theoretical reason, and they turned their attention to the process of history in which the self-realization of man unfolds into the self-disclosure of reality.

When human self-consciousness occupied such a pivotal role, the temptation to claim possession of absolute knowledge proved, of course, irresistible. But this distortion should not devalue the philosophic shift toward existence that lies behind it. Before Hegel's claim to absolute knowledge could be rendered plausible there had to be the prior recognition of man's openness toward the absolute. It is not our knowledge that makes this relationship possible, but our participation in the absolute mode of being that makes the knowledge of it possible. Hegel gave voice to the turn toward existence as the mode of knowing by his insistence that knowledge could no longer be apprehended as a result.[2] Propositions had to be replaced by the movement that catches truth as it discloses itself in the unfolding movement of reality. We know ourselves, not by contemplating the self objectively, but by the process of self-realization. Truth is in the movement, never in the dead result. It is unfortunate that this profound insight, which sought to restore philosophy to its original understanding of the love of wisdom, was overshadowed by the counter pull within Hegel to bring the movement to its completion within his system. He is thus the first of the ironic exemplars whose intention of countering the objectifying tendency of thought is subverted by his own inclination to commit the same mistake. Nevertheless, Hegel does stamp the history of philosophy with the discovery of its dynamic quality. Reality is not a fixed condition but one that discloses itself through its movement. This is the turning point in which philosophy becomes historical. The entire empirical course of events becomes material for philosophic reflection because it is in this existential course that the truth of being emerges. Correcting for the Hegelian distortions, while it has taken much of the succeeding two centuries, does not entail a rejection of his fundamental project.

It was his colleague Schelling who first separated what is living from what is dead in Hegel. While never bringing his own project to a satisfactory conclusion, Schelling directed single-minded attention to the point from which he departed from Hegel. It is an issue of fundamental importance that utterly eliminates the possibility of philosophy collapsing back into the deadness of a system, and the real point of departure for the history of contemporary philosophy. Schelling has quite rightly been hailed as the source both for the existential turn and for the postmodern emphasis on the dynamic.[3] He is the one

---

2. See in particular the preface to the *Phenomenology of Spirit*.
3. A useful account in this regard is Andrew Bowie, *Schelling and Modern European Philosophy* (New York: Routledge, 1993), while Schelling's own self-location is probably best indicated by his lectures *On the History of Modern Philosophy,* trans. Andrew Bowie (New York: Cambridge University Press, 1994). The centrality of freedom in Schelling's thought is the core of his refusal of systematization. See his *Philosophical Inquiries into the Nature of Human Freedom,* trans. James Gutman (La Salle, IL: Open Court, 1936).

who insists that reality always escapes speculation. No matter how comprehensive the speculative grasp may be it cannot include the reality from which it itself is derived. As soon as it makes an attempt to include that wherein it itself stands, it has merely rendered its own ground as no longer its ground, only the marker of where the ground had been. Speculation that attempts to include the living process in which it exists is left only with the dead remains. Living life always escapes the attempt to capture it; to the extent it is captured it is no longer living. Schelling understood that this had been the tragic flaw of Hegel's temptation to yield to the definitiveness of system. Existence always lies outside of that which it has created. Philosophy must therefore bow to this necessity and concede that it can be no more than the love of wisdom. While Schelling did not embrace the full existential implications of this recognition, and thereby proved both an inspiration and a disappointment to Kierkegaard, he did demonstrate the inability of speculation to overleap the boundary that includes itself. The best that philosophy could do then was to turn to life, to catch the disclosure of being in act, and to respect the narrative of myth, which is the mode of discourse concerning what is beyond all discourse.

The priority of existential knowledge is inescapable. Unlike the conventional notion that we recognize ourselves in a mirror by seeing our reflection, it is doubtful that we would know who it is we see there unless we had a prereflective knowledge of the self. We cannot claim to have seen ourselves before, since it is precisely that claim to self-recognition that is in question. At best the image we contemplate in the mirror is only an image. It is never the self that does the contemplating, which remains radically beyond the boundary. This is what the infinite means. It can never be fully unfolded into its creations. Schelling saw this truth with a blinding clarity, while Hegel periodically lost sight of it. Where Hegel allowed the possibility of self-consciousness reaching its culmination, Schelling insisted that the goal could never be attained. This is why Schelling could insist that history can never be reduced to the inner dynamics of consciousness. There is always the irreducible beyond of the process. The ironic consequence is that this preserves history, while the attempt to draw everything into history abolishes it. Now existence is not merely a phase in the production of the end, but an irreplaceable expression of what can never be fully expressed. History as the trace of the infinite renders all existence as a luminous sign. The possibility that human consciousness could capture that by which it is held is an utter impossibility. Only the movement of existential disclosure, responding to the invitation of being, reveals what is contained from the beginning. Schelling's insistence on the unsurpassability of the order in which human consciousness is embedded is the point at which the primacy of existential disclosure is established within modern philosophy.

Not all of the subsequent turn toward existence took its lead from Schelling. Much of the movement flowed directly from the reaction to the self-enclosure of the Hegelian system. Marx is the most famous among a very talented group of Young Hegelians who saw rather clearly that their master had comprehended everything except life itself. The scandal was that the great culmination of philosophy had not effected the slightest change in how men live. Philosophy had been seduced by the perfection of the system. Now the task was to make philosophy real again by engaging in the struggle to transform the conditions in which human beings found themselves. Rather than permit theoretical reconciliation to conceal the extent of real social and economic conflict, theory must now be directed toward the unremitting dialectic of history itself. No more would philosophy allow itself to be used as a tool of oppression. Unfortunately Marxist philosophy ended by legitimizing a far more extensive regime of oppression. The unmasking of ideology recurrently gives way to a more extreme ideology. When philosophy has embarked on an activist course, the relapse into systematization can prove deadly. So long as theory sought only a contemplative transfiguration of all things, the result was relatively harmless. Once the same drive was manifested among individuals bent on the real transfiguration of reality we end with the totalitarian nightmare. The theoretical impulse to master being ends in the activist drive to remake the world. But this perversion does not minimize the initial realization that theory had failed to transform reality. The totalitarian debacle simply reveals that there is also no reason to expect revolutionary action to accomplish the same goal.

We are thrown back on the only route of transformation that remains. The individual can work on himself and from there begin to effect some wider social change. This is the path of Marx's great unknown contemporary, Kierkegaard, who understood the problem so profoundly that he hoped his books would not become popular.[4] If they did then they would be swept up in a social movement and would no longer address their real target, the solitary individual. In many respects Kierkegaard had understood the modern condition of philosophy most completely. It had to remain a philosophy of existence, neither forgetting itself in the realm of concepts nor imagining its superiority through systems. Yet despite his unique position and, perhaps, because of it, Kierkegaard is the least understood of modern philosophers. He is familiar through a few slogans about the absurd and the leap of faith which, when one actually reads him, one fails to recognize. Even the ubiquitous three stages turn out not to

---

4. Kierkegaard, Appendix, "An Understanding with the Reader," in *Concluding Unscientific Postscript to Philosophical Fragments,* ed. and trans. Howard and Edna Hong (Princeton: Princeton University Press, 1992).

function as such within his thought. What Kierkegaard feared in his cultivated obscurity has indeed happened to him. By becoming popular he has become misunderstood. The first wave of that popularity was his identification with the twentieth-century existentialists. Once such a movement has taken shape it is inevitable that its members, including its putative antecedents like Kierkegaard, are all reworked to fit the mold. What they actually said becomes far less important. This has certainly been the fate of the pseudonymous Dane whose strategy of publishing under other names was intended to warn of the difficulty of understanding existential philosophy. Only now with the passage of time has he begun to be read more carefully and in his own right. The result has been a renewed appreciation of his status as a thinker that has placed him at the very center of the postmodern debate.

The failure to recognize the full measure of Kierkegaard's achievement curiously begins with Kierkgaard himself. His own focus on the existential, on the struggle of the individual to live the life of fidelity, tended to forget the implications of this new approach for philosophy. Socrates and Jesus both figure prominently in his writings, but the notion that he was setting both philosophy and Christianity on the course of renewing their foundations emerged only occasionally. Kierkegaard would no doubt have seen such a perspective as a temptation away from his existential task. To this extent, however, one might say that he did not fully understand his role. It was not simply to become a better person; that could have been accomplished without all the voluminous writings. It was surely to chart a path of meaning within the modern world, where the historical symbols of philosophy and Christianity had become opaque and modern men seemed capable of only constructing ever more horrific schemes of instrumentalization. Kierkegaard can rightly be regarded as the first postmodern thinker because he is the first to take up the challenge of meaning in a context where all meaning has collapsed. He knows that all talk of finding a beginning is not only interminable but is merely a way of deferring a beginning. There is no beginning for discourse or action because we have already begun. We are in existence. Our task is to remain faithful to the truth that discloses itself within the process and resist the pull of untruth. Among the latter is the temptation to control the process in which we find ourselves, to make it instrumental to our own purposes rather than to submit to its exigencies. Communication about this condition is itself one of the variants of the temptation. By talking we avoid doing. How can we talk about living without sidestepping what we want to communicate? How do we communicate that which cannot be communicated, which can only be shown, but really only discovered? A profound understanding of language lies behind Kierkegaard's extensive ruminations on how one talks about Christianity within a society of Christians.

The attempt to seize existence on the run is also what animated the other great nineteenth-century loner, Friedrich Nietzsche. It is well known that Nietzsche exalts life over its conceptualization. He abandoned art in the Wagnerian sense because, although it brought us closer to heroic life, it too served only as another form of escape. If he was going to arrive at truth it would have to be by living it. For this reason his *Zarathustra* can never be any more than a bridge toward the goal that lies beyond all writing. The best that literature can capture is the radiance from life, and for this Nietzsche developed the aphoristic style. We might view him, therefore, not as the theorist of nihilism by which he is conventionally identified, but (as he viewed himself) the first European to have gone beyond nihilism. The tortured quality of his thought arises as much from Nietzsche's own inability to understand the novelty of his project as from the failure to break through the boundary of the self. Nietzsche is left railing against truth in the objectivist sense while unable to recognize his own achievement of truth in the existential sense. It is because he cannot bring the tension between them to any resolution that he suffers the conflict so intensely and becomes, as a consequence, the paradigmatic figure of modern and postmodern philosophy. In retrospect we can see, as Heidegger observes, that Nietzsche had thought through a metaphysics beyond metaphysics.[5] The death of God had never really meant the death of God. It only meant that a spatially imagined divinity was no longer credible, not that Nietzsche himself was no longer held by a mysterious fullness of life. Indeed it is the contrast between the denunciation of truth and the living commitment to truth that attests the utterly existential character of his faith, a faith that would not even permit itself the luxury of acknowledging itself.

The same fear of betraying the existential quest marks the unremitting struggle of Heidegger to unfold the Nietzschean project. It is also unclear to what extent the obstacles are self-created, to what extent the very intensity of the battle each of them wages for fidelity to the luminosity of existence masks an unwillingness to follow the full logic of openness to which they have committed themselves. This inscrutability has made both of them notoriously difficult to interpret. But in another sense such contested interpretations remain beside the point. If we have learnt anything from either of them it is that the value of a thinker is not defined by where he ends up. It is where his thought leads. This is for us the primary concern, although it can be expected that extending the direction in which they move will provide a unique vantage point for an overall assessment of what they accomplished. It may indeed turn out that it

---

5. Heidegger, *Nietzsche,* vols. 1–4, trans. David Farrell Krell (San Francisco: Harper San Francisco, 1979–1987).

was the tenacity of their blind spots that accounts for the depth of the struggle in which they articulated the existential exigency of truth. A thinker with fewer personal hangups who reached the goal of existential disclosure more easily might have been less useful to us. In philosophy the results are best when they do not come readily. Those who present themselves to us with all of their often horrible flaws not only compel themselves to wrestle with the blockages but, more important, impose on us the obligation of extending their thought into regions they were themselves not always prepared to go.

This must surely be our attitude toward the great flawed genius of twentieth-century philosophy. Like it or not, Heidegger's towering presence arises from his extended meditation on what philosophy must be when it has definitively adopted the originary perspective of existence. Even in his earlier "existentialist" phase Heidegger shied away from the label, knowing that it still preserved too much of the isolated subject for whom the whole of being could become an object. Heidegger continuously worked to eliminate any such suggestion of subjectivity from his thought. It was at the core of his famous turn from the existential phenomenology of *Being and Time* to the meditative opening toward Being that made all reflection possible. It was the truth of Being, rather than the intentionality of the subject, that made human knowledge and existence possible. *Being and Time* could still suggest a self-contained subject who must anxiously project or decide the meaning of its existence without resort to any disclosure beyond the self. Later, Heidegger came to see that even the self-contemplating subject was never locked within itself. From the very beginning it stood within the opening of Being that made all contemplation possible. In order for us to become conscious of anything we must first be able to think about it as such, that is, as standing in the light of Being. Not only does everything that exists participate in being, without being Being, but it is that relationship that enables us to know what exists, as what is in being. Human being enjoys the special privilege not only of participating in being but of seeing that it does so. From this all of the special features of human existence follow. Animals may live in the world, exist in time, and end in death, but it is only for man that the world, time, and death exist. He alone confronts them as such because he alone beholds them in the light of Being.[6]

But this does not mean that man contains or comprehends the light of Being. Heidegger mightily opposes the tendency to objectify Being, which he regards as the fatal misstep within the history of philosophy, a derailment that begins

---

6. Heidegger, *The Fundamental Concepts of Metaphysics,* trans. William McNeill and Nicholas Walker (Bloomington: Indiana University Press, 1995), on the poverty of the animals' world.

almost as soon as the difference between Being and beings is first encountered. The modern revolution is to return to that first moment with a new self-consciousness of the imperative of resisting the assimilation of Being to beings. This so-called "ontological difference" becomes the core of Heidegger's project. In this way he sought to make the modern shift from intentionality to luminosity definitive. Not only would philosophy not revert to an objectivist metaphysics, but the modern crisis of meaning would have reached a decisive turning point. The enthronement of instrumental rationality, as confirmed by the technological success of the contemporary world, would no longer prevail unchecked. Man's capacity to dominate reality would be seen as itself dependent on the prior openness toward Being that enables him to contemplate things as they are. The great problem, of furnishing the regime of instrumentalization with an end that would not itself be instrumentalized, had been solved. Being, in Heidegger's articulation, could never be absorbed into the stream of beings available for manipulation and control because it was itself what made such processes possible. Technological rationality is itself a mode of being, and it is the history of man's engagement with Being that is being realized within this modern manifestation. History is, in this sense, not the history of man but the history of Being in which man is the point at which the process becomes self-conscious. Hegel had made the mistake of claiming that Being itself had become self-conscious, but Heidegger understood that it is only the participation of beings in Being that reaches luminosity.

Being itself cannot become self-conscious because it cannot be in the mode of a being. This is what turns Heidegger against all forms of onto-theology that assimilate Being to God. Of course this does not mean that Heidegger was an atheist. He could more accurately be described, as he occasionally admitted, as a negative theologian.[7] Out of faithfulness to God, we might say, he refuses to name him. If Being is that in the light of which everything else is seen, then Being itself cannot be illuminated. Being is what brings beings into unconcealment but remains itself in concealment; otherwise it would become a being. Heidegger resolutely struggles against the conventional understanding of revelation because he sought to understand how the transcendent could be known as transcendent once it had been mediated by the immanent. How can Being be revealed through a being? Being is what can never be revealed no matter how many beings come forward to disclose it. So how then do we know about

---

7. Heidegger appears to be underlining his agreement with Nietzsche when he remarks: "What Nietzsche is practicing here with regard to the world totality is a kind of 'negative theology,' which tries to grasp the Absolute as purely as possible by holding at a distance all 'relative' determinations, that is all those that relate to human beings." *Nietzsche*, 2:95.

Being at all? Our knowledge derives from the trace of Being that remains in beings, for they point beyond themselves. Only in man, however, does this directionality become knowledge. He alone not only points but is aware of it. It is for this reason that man plays a special role in relation to Being. He is the "shepherd" or "guardian" of Being because it is only in him that Being is disclosed and nowhere else in existence. All other beings provide a mute testament to Being, that by which they are disclosed, but only man can give voice to that awareness through language. This special relationship, however, is not made possible because man has the capacity for articulation; rather, he has the capacity for speaking because of his relationship with Being. This is a point that Heidegger struggled mightily to make clear as he sought to complete the shift from a self-contained subject to a subject already constituted by its openness toward Being.

The question of Being cannot be separated from the question of man. In his exploration of the dynamics of revelation, Heidegger shows, the "revelation" of Being is possible only because man is already constituted by the revelation of Being from the beginning. Problems arise for Heidegger we might say because of the very relentlessness of his pursuit of revelation in the originary sense. He cannot abide any of the stopping points along the way in what Judaism or Christianity call revelation. None of these satisfy the requirement that revelation must bend its efforts toward what cannot be revealed. The result is an intoxicating and disorienting pursuit of what cannot be reached. In the name of sustaining a tension that is unsustainable Heidegger loses all points of reference within existence. His notorious political misjudgments are not the cause of this; they are its symptom. Nor do the blunders represent only an occasional lapse. They seem to form a pattern that his best critics have discerned as the betrayal of his own fundamental impulse. It seems as if the refusal of all intermediaries makes the tension toward a revelation of Being that cannot be revealed so unsupportable that it collapses into some intramundane manifestations as an all too welcome substitute. The danger of apocalyptic thinking is that it tends toward various forms of an immanent apocalypse. It is for this reason, Heidegger's critics have suggested, that all of his strictures against the metaphysics of presence have not been enough to prevent him from falling victim to the same tendency.[8] The Being that lies perpetually beyond disclosure is increasingly burdened with the expectation of its disclosure. Once that pressure has mounted the danger of opting for a substitute becomes almost irresistible.

---

8. Jacques Derrida, *Of Spirit: Heidegger and the Question,* trans. Geoffrey Bennington and Rachel Bowlby (Chicago: University of Chicago Press, 1989).

The scandal of Heidegger's dalliance with Nazism has been the most notorious case. Apocalyptic thinking veers precipitously close to the pseudo-apocalypse. The fact that a Heidegger was repeatedly prepared to run the risk says something about the hold of such thinking on the modern imagination. In many ways the style of immanent apocalypse can be seen as the culmination of the modern drive for mastery. What, after all, could be more gratifying than to be the individual or the generation that extends its control over reality totally? Behind the urge for technical control lurks the dream of comprehensive domination. The impulse can be so overwhelming that it blocks out all other considerations, including the realization that the achievement of total control abolishes any further technological progress. A willingness to obliterate the very process from which science itself has derived is mirrored in the willingness to obliterate the planet in the name of the final transfiguration of all things. What is fascinating about Heidegger's case is not the banality of evil into which he was drawn but the fact that he was susceptible to the lure of the false apocalypse despite the contrary implications of his own thought. Public attention has naturally been drawn to the spectacle of his astonishing political collaboration with the worst totalitarian regime of the century, as if one more tale of human wickedness would somehow insulate us from the enormity of the events. The challenge by contrast is to understand how a man like Heidegger could yield, indeed cheer, the advent of evil despite his own ability to unmask it. It is surely not our place to sit in judgment on Heidegger, since we are not privy to his soul. We do, however, have access to his thought, where the task is more straightforward. It is to understand how even a philosophic mind that strains against the closure of existence can nevertheless succumb to precisely the same temptation. How was it possible for Heidegger to perceive the parousia of Being in the beings of the Third Reich?

The journalistic side of philosophy has been preoccupied periodically with Heidegger's failure as a man.[9] Philosophy itself has always needed to pursue the more indispensable question of the failure of his philosophy, for there it is our humanity that is at stake. If Heidegger represents the limit of philosophy we have to ask whether it is sufficient for the task it has set itself. Is the case of Heidegger merely the failure of the man or is philosophy itself implicated? This is the question with which philosophy has wrestled increasingly as it has come to recognize the stature of his achievement. It would hardly be an exaggeration to say that he has carried the modern philosophic revolution the furthest. The shift from subjectivity dominating a world of objects to the luminosity of

---

9. A useful updated account is Rüdiger Safranski, *Martin Heidegger: Between Good and Evil*, trans. Ewald Osers (Cambridge: Harvard University Press, 1998).

existence that never succeeds in grounding itself has been brought to its fullest realization in his thought. Many others have made the leap intuitively, but Heidegger, perhaps by dint of the obstinacy of his struggle with objectification, has made the transition to the perspective of participation inescapably articulate. This is why he is the defining philosophic mind of the century. Without displaying an extensive range of philosophic interests, Heidegger has nevertheless compelled us to recognize the necessity of moving from the contemplation of reality to the reality of contemplation. Prior to all knowledge there is the existence that therefore can never be fully known but can become luminous. How then was it possible for Heidegger to fall back into the claim of the primacy of knowledge? If we take seriously the direction on which he had set philosophy then we must take equally seriously the necessity of preserving philosophy from the pitfalls into which philosophers too may fall.

Instead of simply dismissing Heidegger as a "historicist" or a "decisionist," the most acute readers have acknowledged the necessity of going beyond him by going through him. The issue becomes that of carrying Heidegger's project beyond himself by mounting a critique from within. In this way the transformation of philosophy that had been under way is carried forward by arguing that Heidegger had not been Heideggerian enough. This is why the leading postmodern thinkers are both under the shadow of Heidegger and his most vigorous critics. They take him to task for capitulating, despite his protestations, to an immanent apocalypse. His talk of the concealment of Being that makes all unconcealment or truth possible still suggests the parousia of Being. In part this is an inevitable consequence of the language he employs, which is still very much tied to a metaphysics of presence, as if an object were present before the subject. For all of his efforts to resist subjectivity, Heidegger still thinks of philosophy in a contemplative mode that privileges the perspective of the contemplator, who is thus outside of Being. The consequence was not only the tilt toward the intramundane apocalypse of National Socialism, but the more profound closure toward existence once the tension toward Being had been abolished. When the eschaton is drawn into time there is no more possibility. Existence is closed by its completion. This totalizing tendency of even Heidegger is perceptively discerned by Lévinas and Derrida, both of whom in their respective ways insist on a non-attainable eschaton as the only adequate horizon for humanity. What an "apocalypse without apocalypse" means in its specifics may not always be clear from their formulations, but it does mark a definitive turn away from any possibility of revelation.

The apophatic quality of this orientation has often been viewed as merely inscrutable rhetoric. Such an accusation, however, misses the crucial advance that a thinker like Lévinas introduces into the theoretical complex delineated by Heidegger. Lévinas represents a shift toward a more decisively existential perspective. Where Heidegger had used the existential emphasis as a starting point for a philosophic meditation that ultimately remained contemplative, Lévinas insists that the extraction of a contemplative fruit constitutes a betrayal of the existential impulse. His famous formulation that he is prioritizing ethics over ontology captures the essence of the move. Lévinas leaves the philosopher no room for relaxation. There is never a moment of escape in which he would be free to calculate or contemplate, because there is never a point at which the debt of moral obligation has been satisfied. Wherever we construct a compound of privacy the face of the other is already there before us. Responsibility toward the other is the condition of our existence that can neither be abandoned nor abolished. Philosophy becomes therefore not a disclosure of existence; but rather existence is itself the disclosure of philosophy. There is no independent mode of philosophy apart from the imperative of living out the imperatives of our moral life. Lévinas thus brings the turn toward existence to its completion by showing that a merely theoretic philosophy has become impossible. It is no accident that the contemplative mode has derailed into the totalizing, because it has turned its back on the primordial structure that is there before all possibility of structure. In this sense we never find what we are looking for in philosophy, according to Lévinas, but are always on the way toward it. Even the way cannot be hypostasized because then it would cease to be the way and become a rest stop.[10]

To accuse Heidegger of such reification may be a bit disingenuous since he is the one who most emphasizes the dynamic character of philosophy, but the critique does call attention to the difficulty of maintaining the purity of the event. If even Heidegger could end by tilting toward an external perspective on it then the danger of dominating the other is very real. Lévinas finds a crucial safeguard against this tendency by going behind domination itself. The possibility of domination arises from its impossibility. We can dominate the other only because we are already in a relation of responsibility toward him; we can turn our backs on the person who calls us by turning away from the face. What we cannot do is eliminate the relation that makes domination possible. Without the priority of the face of the other, placing us under obligation before all

---

10. This is a line of reflection developed in his two great works, *Totality and Infinity,* trans. Alphonso Lingis (Pittsburgh: Duquesne University Press, 1969), and *Otherwise than Being or Beyond Essence,* trans. Alphonso Lingis (Pittsburgh: Duquesne University Press, 1998).

freedom, there would not be the possibility of rejection. Lévinas has thought through the primordial character of transcendence in a way that is more originary than Heidegger's explorations.

Where Heidegger had sought the openness toward Being by going through beings, Lévinas focused on the being of the other as the movement beyond Being. Now it may be that the difference between them is not large, and it may turn out that Lévinas's "otherwise than Being" overlaps with Heidegger's "Being beyond beings," but the dynamic of responsibility toward the other more adequately marks the existential character of the disclosure. Lévinas eliminates the possibility that we might withdraw to a viewpoint outside of Being by identifying the relationship as one of responsibility. We are already called to act on behalf of the other before we can even think of who we are. There is no self that is prior to the relation to the other.

It is the unsurpassability of this relationship that makes it impossible for domination to succeed. We can never get back to the point at which the self exists in splendid isolation, as if there could be a moment at which the demand of the other ceased to be. Is it ever possible to maintain we have given enough? Surely "enough" is measured by the need of the other rather than our inclination or capacity for sacrifice. Before and beyond any state from which domination could be imposed there is the face of the other. We are never free to dominate. That realization, however, is not reached from within some independent perspective, itself suggesting a superior starting point. Our involvement is rather disclosed within the movement in which we are already engaged. Existence, in which we are already related through the face of the other, will not leave us alone. The vantage point of theory on which Western metaphysics has been based for more than two millennia is permanently displaced. No higher viewpoint is available than the truth of ethics that, as Aristotle emphasized, takes priority over all general propositions. This is also the culmination of Heidegger's resistance to all forms of the metaphysics of presence. Being as Lévinas conceives it is nothing at all like a presence but is rather what draws us into presence. We do not behold a reality before us but are ourselves brought into a fuller reality than we are. Luminosity does not precede our existence but is its unfolding direction.

The effort to reverse a pattern of thought that assimilates Being to beings or that remains tied to a world of objects is in large measure a struggle against language. Metaphor is the trap that language sets for us. Perhaps no one has devoted more attention to the constrictions of language than Jacques Derrida. In many respects his preoccupation with the limits of semiology can be viewed as a continuation of the critique of a metaphysics of presence on which the conventional conception of language is based. Naming is the preeminent model from which this misdirection originates, for nothing seems more obvious than that denomination is a way of making present that which is not. It easily misleads us into thinking that the mere practice of naming conjures the reality to which it refers, rather than merely representing what can no longer present itself. The critique of language, especially of the privilege that the spoken word always seems to exercise over the written one, is a continuation of the assault on the objectification of Being. Derrida takes over the indications of Heidegger and Lévinas while giving their existential shift an essentially linguistic application. This is no mere sidetrack but an essential completion of the project of removing the centrality of the all-seeing subject. Without the linguistic instruments of its domination of reality the subject is left forlorn, longing for a presence that it can no longer make real because the very means of its control have betrayed it. Derrida shows that language, far from delivering on its promise of making present what is absent, is itself a response to the problem of absence. Nouns cannot provide the security we seek, for we are adrift in a sea of verbs and adverbs that moves us along. The final chapter for the dislocated subject is surely provided by Derrida's analysis of the incapacity of language to refer to what we thought it refers.

In place of reference he emphasizes *différance*, a neologism that combines the senses of difference and deferral.[11] That to which language refers is both different from it and deferred by it at the same time. This failure of intentionality to achieve its object is not, however, a sheer negative, for it also opens up the space for elaboration. Without the gap between signifier and signified there would, according to Derrida, hardly be room for an unfolding of the language relationship within reality. If the project of definition had succeeded, then discussion would cease. Absolute knowledge in the Hegelian sense has the perverse consequence of terminating the search for knowledge, and without the search for knowledge we no longer actually know. Derrida thus emphasizes the penultimate character of language as the indispensable openness that makes the search for knowledge possible. Of course many readers have concluded that he renders all knowledge ultimately inconclusive. His own style of reflection often suggests an interminable digressiveness that has come to typify "postmodern" thought, although this is surely a misimpression. It would be more accurate to say that Derrida's main concern had been with preserving the space for signification even at the cost of devaluing its provisional character. The

---

11. Jacques Derrida, *Margins of Philosophy,* trans. Alan Bass (Chicago: University of Chicago Press, 1982); *Writing and Difference,* trans. Alan Bass (Chicago: University of Chicago Press, 1978); *Of Grammatology,* trans. Gayatri Chakravorty Spivak (Baltimore: Johns Hopkins University Press, 1974).

difficulty, as many commentators have noted, is that he had to use language in order to discuss the limits of language. How could he refer to an absence in the language of presence? His project would have been better served if he had distinguished more clearly between the ordinary context of language that refers to the world of objects and the existential context in which that ordinary use occurs. The difficulty is at this point a long-standing one in the history of modern philosophy and is at the heart of the reorientation on which it has been engaged. Derrida's work is one more aspect of the multifaceted shift from intentionality to luminosity.

The central issue may be identified as the absence that makes all movement toward presence possible but which is itself neither an absence nor a presence. In his later work Derrida used the language of religion as the most suitable mode of discourse. He had always alluded to the theological parallels with deconstruction, declaring that it was a form of negative theology, but in the late work he adopted the full-blown language of revelation. Messianic, apocalyptic, and eschatological vocabularies figure prominently in his thought to such an extent that he might be regarded as a religious thinker. This is a strange turn for a thinker who acknowledged that he was not quite a believer, although certainly not a disbeliever. His was a religion without God, an apocalypse without apocalypse that was more than a substitutional piety. It is an attitude that arises when God is no longer believable as a projection of spatio-temporal imagination, yet remains indispensable as the assurance of possibility by virtue of its impossibility.[12] Without the unreachable horizon of transcendence the movement of *différance* could not even begin, but if the divine were reached the movement could no longer continue. Derrida himself remained puzzled by the status of his faith, and we see in this bewilderment the incompletely understood character of the existential turn in philosophy. Even a thinker of his theoretical acuity could not adequately locate his project so long as he remained tied to the understanding of presence as objective. His railing against objective signification did not save him from captivation by the same model.

Derrida had difficulty conceiving of a pleromatic mode of presence, that is, of a presence that is so complete that it draws all else into presence and cannot therefore be one of the things that become present. We cannot know about it as an object out there. Rather we are already constituted by its pull before we even begin to search for it. We are the ones who are differed and deferred until

---

12. Jacques Derrida, *Acts of Religion*, ed. Gil Anidjar (New York: Routledge, 2002); *The Gift of Death*, trans. David Wills (Chicago: University of Chicago Press, 1995). For a good overview of this phase of Derrida's prolific development see John Caputo, *The Prayers and Tears of Jacques Derrida: Religion without Religion* (Bloomington: Indiana University Press, 1997).

we have begun to attune our existence toward its luminosity. It is not absent; we are. This is the meditative unfolding articulated by the first existentialist, Saint Augustine. His development of the language of interiority was in response to the discovery that he had found himself only when he found himself in God. The process did not consist of the subject turning his light inward, although it provided the language of introspection, but of realizing that the interiority in which he was contained was not his own. "Where else, then, did I find you, to learn of you, unless it was in yourself, above me?"[13] The absence to which Derrida and Heidegger refer is not an absence as such but our inability to ever catch up with that which is so fully present we can never outrun it. This better explains how that which is absent can exert such a powerful pull toward presence, for if it were a sheer absence it could never exercise an endless fascination. Only that which is somehow more present than the things that are present can do this, as Heidegger's lifelong occupation with the mystery of Being attests. So while the transcendent cannot be present in the mode of a thing, or else reality would shrink into a black hole without movement or light, it cannot be so transcendent that it fails to draw all things toward itself. The only way to conceive of God is, not as lying outside of us, but as that outside of which we lie. God is not the problem; we are.

The theoretical dead-end into which deconstruction seems to lead modern philosophy arises from the search for a theoretical resolution. Once we realize that practice resolves what in theory remains impenetrable, the impasse is removed. This does not mean that practice has become an instrument for a theoretical goal, but rather the reverse, that in abandoning the insistence on achieving a theoretical solution we have opened the way for the luminosity of life itself. A profound revision of the prevailing primacy of theory is contained in such a move. We seem to be turning our backs on the contemplative life as it was exalted by the classics, in which *theoria* is alone pursued for its own sake, but the shift can also be regarded as a more profound appropriation of philosophy. In contrast to the conventional conception of philosophy as a result we begin to see that there is no philosophy apart from the appropriation of it. This is the direction of the modern existential revolution, to catch philosophy in living life, only now with the realization that this brings us back to the beginning. It is not, as Derrida suggests, that we expect to arrive at a beginning before philosophy, only that we recognize that philosophy has no beginning before itself. The theoretical enterprise that extends its reach to include the birth of philosophy itself is already a misstep. Philosophy is in act, not in theory. Plato

---

13. Saint Augustine, *Confessions,* trans. R. S. Pine Coffin (Harmondsworth: Penguin, 1961), x, 26.

and Aristotle both struggle in different ways to maintain the truth of action rather than the discursive movement away from doing. The life of virtue lies in activity rather than in discussion, which thus makes philosophy a mode of discussion that must constantly move beyond itself. Paradox is the structure of philosophy, not a modern discovery about it. The derailment into the supplementarity of theorizing is not an accidental development within the history of philosophy but the central danger against which the discourse must perpetually struggle if it is not to lose the existential direction it seeks to articulate.

The modern revolution in philosophy does not so much introduce something new as bring us back, in the manner of revolutions, to the point from which it began. Return is in this sense never simply a return to the beginning. It is a new beginning, a reappropriation, made all the more necessary by the defectiveness of the first beginning. A re-initiation of philosophy is a genuinely philosophical act. Derrida's famous remark, "nothing outside the text," leaves itself open to a number of possible interpretations. Among the most compelling is the existential one that insists there is no point of reference that would relieve us of responsibility or permit us to dominate the meaning it provides. We cannot abandon our existence to a totality that would enclose it, not without ceasing to exist entirely. It is not that we are, in the cruder formulation of Sartre, "condemned to be free," but that we are condemned to exist in openness because that is the mode of human existence. Not only is there nothing outside the text, we are not even outside of it. The text is our existence. We can only get outside of it by existing, that is, by extending the text of our lives. A resting point, a security nook, could only be a falling away from the task. Sleep interrupts our consciousness, but we can hardly regard it as anything more than a necessary and inevitable break in the endeavor of freely and humanly becoming who we are. There is no point before the beginning that would make the beginning happen and relieve us of the burden of beginning ourselves, just as there is no end point that will allow us to rest in the easy release from all effort by having become all that is possible. Human existence is a mystery or, rather, since it is not a thing, human existence is caught within a mystery that can be neither fathomed nor exhausted. For this reason there is nothing outside the text, since the text encompasses the unreachable whole. If it did not, then we would be constantly tempted, as indeed we are, to settle down in the satisfaction of achieving our goal. All that saves us from spiritual suicide is the impossibility of finding a definitive point of reference outside the text.

We are the text, as Kierkegaard insisted, and the effort to stand outside of it is the refusal of existence. He may not have explicated the full extent of the revolution in philosophy that this recognition implied, but he is probably the one who carried it out most completely in his own life. It may be that it was

Kierkegaard's willingness to think through the issues within Christian categories that saved him from the tentativeness that characterizes most of his successors, just as it is the same openly "religious" character of his thought that remains the principal obstacle to the appreciation of his philosophic achievement. But if Derrida, Lévinas, and Heidegger are correct in seeing philosophy as implicated in the drama of revelation, then Kierkegaard may be one of the most underappreciated contributors to the discussion. For Kierkegaard it was no scandal that revelation had occurred. This was what enabled him to surmount the obstacle that loomed so large for many others. A historical revelation seemed so absurd because it could not be assimilated within any conceptual scheme. Kierkegaard even embraced the category of the absurd to talk about revelation, although he thereby also left himself open to the longstanding misimpression that he regarded revelation as irrational. What he really meant was that revelation escaped the categories of human reason. It definitively demoted reason from its central theoretical role and made reason itself dependent on the opening toward what is beyond it. By acknowledging revelation, reason was saved from itself. In place of the illusion of a control that could be imaginatively projected over the whole of reality, reason now had regained the rationality of its ever incomplete capacity to comprehend reality. The key is the existential submission of reason itself. Only by abandoning the impulse to dominate could reason avoid its own distortions and obtain the only access to reality available to it.[14]

By accepting the participatory requirement of knowledge Kierkegaard overcame the obstacles that still stood in the way so long as thinkers held on to the model of theoretic intentionality. In the process he introduced a far-reaching revision in the language of philosophy that has still not been absorbed. It has proved more convenient to classify him as an "irrationalist," a "decisionist," or an "existentialist," rather than grapple with the profound changes he introduced. We still have not understood his insistence that we do not really live in time but that, for the most important relationships, our context is already eternity. While we conventionally imagine eternity as something other than time, Kierkegaard is already showing us that time is itself a derivative of eternity. A human being is not really a creature of time and its effects. In every important respect we are transacting an eternal reality, of which the temporal passage is just a series of attenuations. This is why Kierkegaard can assert that

---

14. Along with *Concluding Unscientific Postscript,* see *The Concept of Anxiety,* trans. Reidar Thomte and Albert B. Anderson (Princeton: Princeton University Press, 1980), *The Sickness unto Death,* trans. Howard and Edna Hong (Princeton: Princeton University Press, 1980), and *Eighteen Upbuilding Discourses,* trans. Howard and Edna Hong (Princeton: Princeton University Press, 1990).

there is no beginning before the beginning of decision itself, which often makes him sound like an advocate of arbitrary leaps. In reality what he is saying is that the leap has already taken place. The commitment to marriage, which seems so improbable from the perspective of creatures that are the contingent playthings of time, makes perfect sense when we see that the decision was never actually made in time. How can you make a commitment at a particular point in time to remain steadfast to what also dissolves with time? The task seems nonsensical and futile, as we daily acknowledge in facilitating "no fault" divorce. Yet we also insist on retaining the fig leaf of marriage as a lifelong commitment. The reason, Kierkegaard explains, is that we know that nothing that is done in time can be serious. It is only if we invest the resolution with eternity that it can encompass all that we are. We know that we live, in every dimension that matters, in eternity rather than in time. It is eternity that makes every present possible.[15]

Contingency is not itself contingent. Once we realize that what characterizes the flow of things does not necessarily, and cannot necessarily, be extended to the whole itself, we are no longer so lost in the cosmos. Kierkegaard, who was a great student of irony, would surely have delighted in the irony of the limits of irony.[16] There has always been an element of this recognition in the objection that skepticism depends on not extending to itself, but there is more to it than mere cleverness. A philosophical revolution of the kind that has been two millennia in the making does not result from a brilliant turn of logic. A far deeper meditation is involved in which we lay hold of the utterly non-contingent reality of our lives. When we acknowledge that the value of a human being outweighs all the progress of history we are not simply voicing an aspiration. We are giving expression to a reality that makes possible the whole of history in the inexhaustibility of each human being. Human beings have history because they are not historical. They are never captured by the finitude of history because they exist in relation to the eternal. However much they may forget that participation in the eternal, falling into the inauthentic amnesia of time, they cannot sever the remembrance of the pull that makes this awareness possible. Kierkegaard was the one who definitively eliminated the imaginary space and time that attached to the discussion of souls and their afterlife. He made it clear that the language of Christian spirituality had its source in the existential now. We could conceive of an afterlife only because we already live

---

15. Kierkegaard, *Either/Or,* parts 1, 2, trans. Howard and Edna Hong (Princeton: Princeton University Press, 1987), and *Stages on Life's Way,* trans. Howard and Edna Hong (Princeton: Princeton University Press, 1988).

16. His dissertation was *The Concept of Irony,* trans. Howard and Edna Hong (Princeton: Princeton University Press, 1989).

in relation to eternity. Human life, every human life, is crucial because it is the arena in which good and evil are irrevocably chosen. Reading Kierkegaard we experience a shudder of the numinous which, while it may have been reinforced by his personal sensitivities, finds a resonance in us because it is an inescapable dimension of every human existence. We know that what we do matters more than life.

What was an antinomy for Kant had become transparent for Kierkegaard. Kant struggled with the impenetrability of the opposition between human freedom and spatio-temporal causality. If human action was subject to the causal exigencies of everything within this world then it could not be free; yet the essence of human action is autonomous self-determination, which can never be subject to extraneous factors. He resolved it by maintaining that human freedom does not occur in space and time but has its locus in eternity. The decision to act in a certain way could not be subject to causal necessities because it had already occurred before or outside of that realm. Kant's problem, as most of his readers recognized, was that he had made the spatio-temporal realm so real that anything beyond it seemed peculiarly attenuated. Kierkegaard had reversed this emphasis by contemplating the relativity of the space-time continuum. By beginning from the perspective of eternity he had been able to see the conditionality of time. Without the overarching-never-moving context of eternity there would not even be time. Heidegger would later make a great deal of temporality as what can be grasped as such only from the perspective of nontemporality, but Kierkegaard had exemplified this understanding through his existence. In this sense Kierkegaard had leapt over the temptation, still present in Heidegger, to turn this conditionality of time into a new mode of presence. Without really explaining that this would be to make eternity another mode of time, Kierkegaard ignored the suggestion by virtue of his existential struggle to live out the meaning of eternity. Once we take seriously the revolutionary insight that there is no way of stepping outside of ourselves to view the whole in which we are, then we recognize that the only perspective available is through our participation in existence. Kierkegaard resolutely insists that that participation requires our all.

There can be no holding back, as if we might yet be able to secure a corner of detachment from which our contemplative domination could expand. We must not yield to the final temptation of doing the right thing for the wrong reason. Ever since Hegel the philosophic revolution has wavered around the possibility of turning the existential movement into a mode of absolute knowledge. It is no accident that Kierkegaard took Hegel as the great other of his struggle and consequently managed to extricate himself from the fascination more successfully than most who have tried. He acknowledged his debt to

Hegel by refusing to become a Hegelian. Absolute knowledge must remain absolute, even while it provides the possibility of all other knowledge. What makes possible the whole movement of existence cannot become an object of attention without ceasing to be the source of all. This is the key challenge within the modern philosophic shift away from the model of intentionality. Fidelity to the basic insight that the process cannot be apprehended from within it except through the movement itself requires a resolute avoidance of the attempt surreptitiously to reintroduce its objectification. Hegel had seen that what provides the possibility must be beyond the possible, but he persisted in dreaming that he nevertheless could comprehend it. It was because Kierkegaard's resolve was more wholehearted, informed less by the contemplative quest than by the need for existence, that he could prove the more exemplary figure of the modern philosophic revolution. By being less of a philosopher he became more of one. The existential shift means that philosophy itself must become something of an aftereffect. Kierkegaard shows that it is only by becoming a man that one can become a philosopher.

Of course it is possible that he also shows that the demand is too great. It may well be that the modern shift of primacy toward existence will therefore mean that the revolution will always remain incomplete. That would not be a surprising outcome, especially given that philosophy itself is peculiarly implicated in the eternal. We should perhaps be more cautious about attributing so temporal a metaphor to its movements and, as a consequence, entertain some second thoughts concerning the present sketch. The burden of demonstrating that there has been a revolution accomplished by modern philosophy is not the essential point. It is rather that philosophy in the modern era has set itself the task of revolutionizing itself. By shifting the burden to philosophy the task of scholarship is lightened. But this is in no way to insure the project against failure. Scholarship about philosophy cannot ultimately shrink from the challenge of philosophy and philosophy, as Kierkegaard and his collaborators have taught us, cannot absolve us of the obligation of being human. The revolution in philosophy is truly revolutionary, touching all aspects of the discipline. Even the account of the change cannot ignore the logic of what it contains. Once we have eliminated the possibility of contemplation furnishing the meaning in which we live, we undertake the task of living first in the meaning from which contemplation can follow. By acknowledging the primacy of existence we have accepted the impossibility of reflection apprehending it in advance. Philosophy can now only be a matter of catching reality on the wing. Participation means there is nothing living beforehand and nothing living afterward. We may be released from the millennial illusion that we could contemplate the whole from the perspective of God. But we now must move toward God as the only mode in which the whole is at all apprehensible. The security of meaning is traded for a meaning that seeks security. We may be animated by the bonds of faith and trust that support us, but we cannot reach any surety without giving ourselves to them. To the extent that the nature of philosophy has now coincided with the nature of human existence we may be sure only of one thing: the goal of each cannot be reached in time. This makes them both impossible and possible.

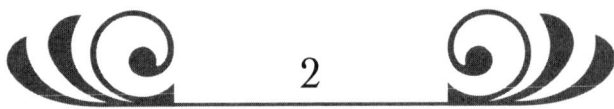

2

Hunting and Political Philosophy
An Interpretation of the *Kynegetikos*

Barry Cooper

> Perhaps only a country-bred man
> could comprehend loving the life he spills.
> —William Faulkner

Introduction

Xenophon, "slayer of foreigners," was not blessed by the gods either in his own day or in ours. He was exiled from Athens and was never at home in xenophobic Sparta. Today judgment is mixed. Guthrie, whose big book, *A History of Greek Philosophy,* attempted to gain a judicious balance, remarked: "Xenophon might be described as a gentleman in the old-fashioned sense of the term, implying as well a certain not ignoble type of character, a high level of education and general culture." But, using a metaphor appropriate to bookkeepers, Guthrie continued, "on the debit side we must put a certain literal-mindedness and tendency to prosiness, a pedestrian outlook which is sometimes frankly dull, and little sign of any capacity for profound philosophical thought."[1]

---

1. Proietti, *Xenophon's Sparta: An Introduction* (Leiden: Brill, 1987); W. K. C. Guthrie, *A History of Greek Philosophy* (Cambridge: Cambridge University Press, 1969), 3:334–35. This view was repeated in J. K. Anderson's semi-popular work, *Xenophon* (New York: Scribner's, 1974), 45.

Christopher Bruell, more circumspect than Guthrie, suggests something similar in his comparison of Xenophon and Plato. Werner Jaeger's magisterial work of a generation ago declared that "in spite of his pleasant style, [he] appear[s] to be intellectually trivial." Retreating further into the past we find Gomperz's pronouncement that "he remained for the whole of his life a dilettante in Goethe's sense of the word, that is, a man who is always venturing on tasks for which he is not fully equipped."[2] With few exceptions, respect for Xenophon's wisdom by the "higher critics" of the nineteenth century was similarly restrained. Some of them, as Leo Strauss has pointed out, allowed their judgments to be colored by their disapproval of Xenophon's apparent lack of patriotic sentiments.[3]

There appear to be two general reasons for this low estimation of Xenophon's intellectual power. The first is a consequence of modern attitudes toward the classical writers. Romanticism exalted philosophy so far beyond everyday life that it began to resemble Aristophanes' Phrontisterion. Moreover, the romantic notion that art is creation rather than imitation, which is what it was for Xenophon, almost inevitably devalued his art as "unoriginal." A related problem has been the invasion of philosophical discourse by language analysis and various kinds of subjectivism, providing philosophers with a highly technical linguistic mediating apparatus to study everyday life. Either way, discussion of ordinary matters in ordinary ways came to be viewed as "unphilosophic" at best, and more often as naïve or simple-minded. This is not to say that philosophy is simply ordinary language so much as it is to suggest that classical political philosophy at least began in an ordinary way with a commonsensical "it seems to me."

The second reason why Xenophon has fallen from the favor of modern academic opinion-leaders is a consequence of his rhetoric. In antiquity he was known as Xenophon the orator, in order to distinguish him from three other Xenophons. Now, rhetoric is an art that has fallen out of favor, and as Harry Neumann has observed, "Xenophon practices a rhetoric which refuses enlightenment to those whom it would only barbarize.... Obviously literary tastes

---

2. Bruell, "Xenophon," in *History of Political Philosophy,* ed. Leo Strauss and Joseph Cropsey, 3rd ed. (Chicago: University of Chicago Press, 1987), 91–92; Jaeger, *Paideia: The Ideals of Greek Culture,* trans. Gilbert Highet (New York: Oxford University Press, 1944), 3: 156; Theodor Gomperz, *Greek Thinkers: A History of Ancient Philosophy,* trans. G. G. Berry (New York: Scribner's, 1905), 2:118. A contemporary has opined that Xenophon was "a conceited lover of display, a hypocritical teacher of morality, an insincere historian, a flatterer of the strong man, a seeker of glory and apostate of his country, a self-centred individual," and nothing less than "the 'hippie' of the fourth century." E. M. Soulis, *Xenophon and Thucydides* (Athens: Privately printed, 1972 [Ph.D. thesis, University of Bristol]), 189.

3. Leo Strauss, *Xenophon's Socrates* (Ithaca: Cornell University Press, 1972), 179.

formed by the brutal sentimentality of contemporary moralities are poorly equipped to grasp the reason for Xenophon's sober rhetoric."[4] Sober rhetoric looked simple-minded to the higher criticism. For Xenophon, however, sober rhetoric served to catch potential philosophers by introducing them to the excitement of detecting the indirect communication of the meaning of a text. Because it was indirectly communicated, it was necessary to pay attention to small details. Once the hunt for meaning is on, the potential philosopher will have become an unreserved participant in the actual process of thinking, if not of "philosophizing" in a modern professional sense.

In recent years Xenophon has been studied again with some care. In 1957 Eduard Delebecque published a lengthy and careful study of Xenophon's life as it appeared through his writings. Ten years later a cautious revision of Xenophon's competence as a historian appeared; ten years after that, W. E. Higgins wrote a fine study centered on Xenophon's understanding of the relationship between the individual and the polis. There have also appeared a number of more focused studies on one or another aspect of Xenophon's work and several analyses of his relationship to the Persians.[5]

Political scientists have also turned their attention to Xenophon. Neal Wood introduced his study of leadership in Xenophon's writing with the remark that "nowhere is neglect of Xenophon more noticeable than in the history of political thought."[6] The most important student of Xenophon's political philosophy, and one who, so to speak, had nothing in common with Wood, was Leo Strauss. Strauss has left us several Xenophontic studies of Xenophon's texts, with the result that his work has been greeted with obloquy nearly equal to that gained by the original.[7] As most students of political philosophy know, Strauss was a careful reader. His interpretative principle, which I believe can be

---

4. Review of Leo Strauss, *Xenophon's Socratic Discourse* (Ithaca: Cornell University Press, 1971), in *Journal of the History of Philosophy* 9 (1971): 241.

5. Delebecque, *Essai sur la Vie de Xenophon* (Paris, Klinckseick, 1957); W. P. Henry, *Greek Historical Writing: A Historiographical Essay Based on Xenophon's Hellenica* (Chicago: Argonaut, 1966); Higgins, *Xenophon the Athenian* (Albany: State University of New York Press, 1977); Rainer Nickel, *Xenophon* (Darmstadt: Wissenschaftliche Buchgesellschaft, 1979); John Dillery, *Xenophon and the History of His Times* (London: Routledge, 1995); Godfrey Hutchinson, *Xenophon and the Art of Command* (London, Greenhill, 2000); Steven W. Hirsch, *The Friendship of the Barbarians: Xenophon and the Persian Empire* (Hanover, NH: University Press of New England, 1985); James Tatum, *Xenophon's Imperial Fiction: On the Education of Cyrus* (Princeton: Princeton University Press, 1989); Bodil Due, *The "Cyropaedia": A Study of Xenophon's Aims and Methods* (Aarhus: Aarhus University Press, 1989); Christopher Nadon, *Xenophon's Prince: Republic and Empire in the Cyropaedia* (Berkeley: University of California Press, 2001).

6. Wood, "Xenophon's Theory of Leadership," *Classica et Medievalia* 25 (1964): 38.

7. A fine example is by Terrence Irwin in the *Classical Review* 83 (1974): 409–13.

applied to Xenophon, was that "if in a given case he [Xenophon] apparently happens to do a bad job as a writer, or as a thinker, he actually does it deliberately and for very good reasons." Even commentators unsympathetic to Xenophon's rhetoric have suspected that there may be more to his "deceptions" and "false impressions" than meets the eye.[8]

The most obvious example: Xenophon's titles. In his introduction to the Loeb edition of the *Kyropaideia* (xi), Walter Miller wrote that the title of the book was misleading because it included "the whole life and career of the great conqueror," not just his education or formation. Similarly, the *Memorabilia* is not about memorable events in Xenophon's life but consists entirely in recollections about Socrates. The *Kyrou Anabasis* is not about the ascent of Cyrus, which terminated in book 1 with his going down at the battle of Kunaxa. But if Xenophon meant us to *think* about the appropriateness of his titles we might be led to consider that the life of Cyrus the Great was a continuous *paideia*, or that the most memorable events of Xenophon's life consisted in his being in the company of Socrates and not of his warrior associates or, indeed, that the *anabasis* in the *Anabasis* was Xenophon's, as told by an otherwise unknown author, Themistoges of Syracuse (*Anab.* 3.1.1–2). Strauss has shown, moreover, that "the *Constitution of the Lacedemonians*, far from being an encomium of Sparta, is actually a most trenchant, if disguised, satire on that city and its spirit."[9] A careful reading of the *Kyropaideia* in light of Plato's *Republic* would, I believe, show that the Great King and his *paideia* mocked much of Plato's account of the formation of the philosopher-king. At times, that is, Xenophon seems to be a comic writer. His sense of humor, however, is not always compatible with that of modern scholars who tend, by and large, to be very serious about comedy. Xenophon has also been called an ironic writer,[10] which is accurate enough if by irony one means a kind of double- or multiple-vision whereby the surface meaning of a statement is untrue but meant for the credulous and the implicit meaning, which must be discovered by interpretation, is true though not obvious.

Like many of Xenophon's texts, the *Kynegetikos* has suffered from neglect and from unsympathetic readers. A careful reading, however, indicates that it has been very skillfully composed. The assumption with which I begin but that can be justified only at the end of the analysis is that Xenophon was a philosophical writer of a stature comparable, if not equal, to that of Plato. At the

---

8. Strauss, "The Spirit of Sparta or the Taste of Xenophon," *Social Research* 6 (1939): 503; Gomperz, *Greek Thinkers*, 122.
9. Strauss, "The Spirit of Sparta," 528.
10. Strauss, *Xenophon's Socratic Discourse*, 114.

same time, however, he is also a writer who is more difficult to interpret, at least in one important sense. Plato is difficult, and he appears to be difficult; that is, Plato lets you know when you have not understood him because you remain puzzled. Xenophon is difficult, but he appears easy. But as Zeno said to Socrates (Plato, *Parm.* 128c), we must pick up the scent of his discourse like Laconian puppies. What the *Kynegetikos* says explicitly of hunting can be understood as an implicit account of *paideia* and, accordingly, of the relationship between philosophers and politics.

This essay begins with a summary of the classical understanding of the relation between hunting and *paideia*, followed by an analysis of several Platonic texts on the topic of hunting; Xenophon's writings other than the *Kynegetikos* provide the context for analysis of his discussion of the art of hunting. Some of these themes have been developed in conversation with Ellis Sandoz in goose pits outside Rose Valley, Saskatchewan, and Abbeville, Louisiana.

Hunting and Paideia

In Greek literature, hunting appeared in texts as early as those of Homer. Not surprising in a heroic age that praised physical courage, greater prominence was given to hunting dangerous lions, wolves, boars, and bulls than to hunting hares, the chief topic of Xenophon's study. There is only one mention of hare-hunting in the *Iliad* (10.360–62) but at least twenty-three references to big-game hunting. In the *Odyssey* (11.372), Orion engaged in posthumous hunting as a Homeric inhabitant of the happy hunting-ground. In Aristophanes' *Knights* (1832–33), hunting was considered part of training or education, *paideia;* thereafter hunting became a familiar topic for dispute, most notably by Isocrates, Plato, and Xenophon. Because hunting was discussed in connection with *paideia,* it was an activity surrounded by rules that diminished the efficiency of slaughter. In modern language, hunting was sport.[11]

The relationship of Plato and Xenophon, both of whom deeply admired Socrates, was complex. Stories of their rivalry began in Roman antiquity. So far as hunting is concerned, they held divergent, though not necessarily opposed, views. In the *Sophist,* Plato's discussion ended with the comic description of the angler as the practitioner of the secret and coercive kind of acquisitive art, namely, the daylight hunting of water animals of the fish kind by striking from below with a barb (219a–221c).

---

11. Consider the splendid work by Jose Ortega y Gasset, *Meditations on Hunting*, trans. Howard B. Wescott (New York: Scribner's, 1972).

In the *Laws* (822d–824c), hunting and similar pursuits were considered after the discussion of laws governing the topics of learning (*mathemata*) that are part of *paideia* had come to an end. What followed was concerned with *paideia* but not with *mathemata*. The regulations governing hunting would be drawn up with an eye to their ability to improve the souls of the young. There was a short diaeresis that divided game into things that moved by water, by wing, or by feet. Beasts that moved by feet were again divided into wild beasts and human beings. Human beings, in turn, might be hunted in war (cf. Arist., *Pol.* 1255b37–39, 1256b23–26) and in friendship (cf. Plato, *Sym.* 203d7), both of which may be praised or blamed. "And plunderings by robbers and armies against armies are hunts" (*Laws* 823b8–9). The exhortation of hunting that followed in the form of a prayer was intended to express in detail how to improve the souls of the young.

Hunting on the sea for water animals was blamed because it induced laziness; man-hunting by sea and piracy rendered the hunter cruel and lawless. Bird-hunting, which necessarily includes geese, because it relied upon craftiness, was unsuitable. Night-hunting of land animals was equally to be blamed because it was undertaken only intermittently and so also was an inducement to laziness. Similar problems arose with methods that relied on the use of nets and traps instead of upon victory gained directly by a toil-loving soul over the strength of wild beasts. Accordingly, only the hunting of four-footed beasts with horses, hounds, and the arms of the hunter himself, bringing down beasts by means of the hunter's own running, hitting, and throwing, would be praised. Only such hunting enabled divine courage to grow and was best for everyone. Young people (*neoi*) who practice such hunting are genuine and sacred hunters.

Following that lengthy prooimion, the law was drawn up: true or sacred hunters could hunt with hounds anywhere; night-hunters, snare-users, and net-users, nowhere. Bird-hunting would be allowed on mountains and fallow land but not in tilled fields or sacred places. Fish-hunters were forbidden from harbors and sacred places and could not use poisonous tinctures. This law finally ended all the laws on *paideia*. Ending the discussion of *paideia* in the *Laws* with hunting, rather than with dialectic or philosophy, as in the *Republic* (531d–e), was an indication of the different spiritual heights at which the two books aimed. In addition, it indicated a connection or continuity between hunting and philosophy. This connection was suggested in the *Laws* by an observation that the hunting of human beings under conditions of friendship as well as of war deserves thought (*axion ennoein*). Some of the friendly hunting of humans deserves praise, possibly because of the Athenian stranger's unusual appeal to go beyond mere obedience to the law (822d–823d). In the language of hunting, the Athenian stranger appealed to the hunters to be sportsmen.

Hunting was introduced several times in the *Republic;* on each occasion the significance seemed to be that it was both unavoidable and not fully to be desired. In book 2, after Glaukon, who owned hunting hounds and noble cocks (459a), objected to the true and healthy city as being a swinish city, a second and luxurious or feverish city came into existence. It was filled with chairs and couches for comfort, and new tastes, smells, and pleasures supplied by relishes, perfumes, and tarts (both *hetairai* and *pemmata*). Embroidery gave things a fancy look, which meant that other non-necessary things and occupations must already be in this city. Even before the poets, the first to be identified were "hunters and imitators" (373b3). Since Socrates and his companions never returned to the placid vegetarianism of the healthy city but rather reformed the feverish one, the implication was that harm to animals is connected to political justice, however undesirable such harming might be "in itself," or considered abstractly.

It is not immediately clear why hunters were joined with imitators. In the *Euthydemus* (209b–e), hunting was compared to the art of the general and of the geometer because they handed over what was gained by their art—game, victory, and knowledge—to others, the cooks, statesmen, and practitioners of dialectic, in order for the latter to use or use up what had been gained by the inferior art. Imitators may be akin to hunters in the sense that both depend on others for the exercise of their art to make sense. This may be true of other arts as well.

In book 3 of the *Republic,* once the outline of the *paideia* that breeds harmony by a proper mixture of music and gymnastic had been attained, there would be no need to practice the dances of citizens, nor hunts (*theras*), nor hunting with hounds (*kynegesia*), nor gymnastic contests, nor horse races. On the contrary, these methods of *paideia* would be modeled after music and gymnastics (412a–b).

Matters are never simple in the *Republic,* and just as the swinish healthy city was forgotten, so too the city modeled on musical and gymnastic harmony grew discordant in accord with the instability of the cosmos itself and the impossibility of perfectly just tuning (546a). The danger, however, seemed to be present even before the invocation of the muses to account for the decline or failure of *kallipolis* (527c) in book 8. After having established the contents of the philosophical *paideia*, Socrates and Glaukon turned to the question of distributing education among citizens. Philosopher-citizens must be courageous, especially in *mathemata,* because souls are more likely to be cowardly in that practice than in gymnastics; they must be lovers of toil (*ponos*) and have good memories, perhaps because the laborious *paideia* Plato had in mind exercised the memory (535b–d). Such people, Socrates said, would be genuine philosophers, not bastards. Glaukon asked him what he meant, and Socrates replied that the philosopher must not limp in his love of toil, loving only half, which is the case with the lover of gymnastics and the lover of the hunt, the *philotheros*. Both loved only toil connected with the body and were not lovers of *mathemata* or of listening and enquiring; on the contrary, they hated the toil associated with those things. Similarly, if one's love of toil was exercised exclusively in *mathemata*, listening and enquiring, one also would limp (535d). Love of hunting and gymnastics and of unnecessary bodily toil seemed to be a temptation to imbalance. And, of course, limpers make poor hunters.

The timocratic man, who in some respects resembled Glaukon (548d–e), gave in to the temptation. He was stubborn, a lover of music and speech but a poor musician and orator; he did not simply despise slaves as a gentleman would, but was harsh with them; he was tame with citizens and obedient to rulers. He loved ruling and honor and claimed his place on the basis of his deeds in war and his training for war, and not on speech. "He is a lover of gymnastics and a lover of the hunt, philotheric" (549a).

The place of hunting in Plato's philosophical *paideia* was, like war, ambiguous.[12] It was useful in training the body, but if not balanced by the toil connected with the soul, it would lead the philotheric man to injustice. According to Xenophon, the practice of hunting did not lead to injustice but induced piety. One may conclude, therefore, that in this respect Xenophon's teaching appears closer to Plato's teaching in the *Laws* than it is to the teaching of the *Republic*. Both Xenophon and Plato saw hunting as a part of *paideia*, but the former also considered hunting to be an image or *icon* of philosophy. Much of what Xenophon says explicitly about hunting is also an implicit discussion of philosophy and of politics or the relation of the philosopher to the polis.

Xenophon and Hunting

Texts, and especially dialogues, may be read from two contrasting interpretative stances. The dramatic perspective considers it as a work of art, a *poesis*, in which the speaker and the circumstances of the speech are important in understanding the significance of the discourse. In contrast, the primary concern of the analytical perspective is a technical critique of the content of the text "as it stands," namely, alone and without relation to "literary" matters.

---

12. See Leon Harold Craig, *The War Lover: A Study of Plato's* Republic (Toronto: University of Toronto Press, 1994).

Some texts seem to lend themselves to one approach more easily than to the other. Interpretation of a play or of a dialogue can hardly ignore the dramatic elements; interpretation of a treatise would seem to involve no more than a critical analysis. In interpreting Xenophon's discourse on hunting we must keep both perspectives in mind because his teaching was presented in both forms.

Xenophon wrote two dialogues and two treatises on the arts: the *Oikonomikos,* on the art (*techne*) of household management; the *Tyrannikos,* on the art of tyranny, which was a kind of expansion of the economic art to the polis; the *Hipparchikos,* on the art of the cavalry commander; and the *Kynegetikos,* on the art of hunting, chiefly with hounds. The topics considered in the dialogues were more obviously philosophical than those considered in the treatises because the form lent itself more easily to indirection. Hunting and matters related to hunting appeared in all these texts as well as in texts such as the *Anabasis* and the *Kyropaideia,* the literary genre of which is indeterminate. We begin analytically.

Xenophon's treatise on hunting has by tradition two titles, *Kynegetika* and *Kynegetikos.* The second is preferable not only because it is attested by ancient authorities but because the suffix, when joined to the implicit noun, *aner* (manly man), serves to classify the practitioner of an art, as in similar terms such as *politikos* and *hipparchikos.* The one who possesses the art of hunting is by that fact a good hunter. The feminine form, as in the title of Xenophon's treatise *Peri Hippikes* would refer to a *techne* without regard to its use. We conclude that hunting is, in Xenophon's view, akin to the arts of household management, of tyranny, and of cavalry command. Unlike horsemanship, therefore, and like the other arts, the art of hunting, we are meant to believe, is concerned chiefly with training men, perhaps even men in the guise of hounds (cf. *Rep.* 375e–376b).

The text of the *Kynegetikos* has a surface meaning that falls into three or perhaps four parts: (1) an introduction that considered the origin of hunting and its original heroic practitioners, (2) a "practical" account of contemporary hunting that dealt mostly with hunting hares with hounds and nets, and (3) a conclusion that explained the benefits of hunting, followed by an attack on sophists. The seemingly disparate topics in the several parts for a long time led classical philologists to doubt its authenticity.[13] Moreover, there are two ver-

---

13. Higgins still does; see *Xenophon the Athenian,* xiii. A review of the major points of dispute, which did not change during the twentieth century, is H. Richards, "The Cynegeticus," *Classical Review* 12 (1898): 285–92. See also: Gustav Koerte, "Zu Xenophons Kynegetikos," *Hermes* 53 (1918): 317–23; W. A. Baehrens, "De Kynegetiko Xenophonteo," *Mnemosyne* n.s. 54 (1926): 130–45.

sions of chapter 1, traditionally called Alpha and Sigma. Alpha is shorter and more elegant and was probably the later version.[14]

"First of the inventions due to the gods, Apollo and Artemis, was that of game and hounds." If one gives due weight to that "first," *proton,* the meaning of the first sentence is not simply that hunting was the first of the inventions of Apollo and Artemis but that hunting was the first thing the gods did to benefit man, this particular beneficence being the work of Apollo and Artemis. They gave the art to Cheiron, honoring him in this way because he was the most just of all the centaurs (*Il.* 11.832; cf. Pindar, *Nem.*3). This seems to imply that, at least for centaurs, justice is prior to the practice of hunting rather than a product of hunting. In any event, this half-brother to Zeus then gained as pupils in hunting and other fine (*kalon*) disciplines several heroes and demigods who were to the present day loved by the good and envied by the bad. They were made so fine by Cheiron's arts that they were able to rid cities and kings of any evil; they brought internal peace to the Greeks and triumph over the barbarians. Accordingly, "I myself charge the young men not to scorn the things connected with hunting nor any other *paideia*. For it is by them that young men become good in war and in other things, on the basis of which thinking, speaking, and doing are necessarily done honorably" (1.18). The use of the first person pronoun, *ego,* indicates both that Xenophon is speaking in his own name and that he is emphatic. He is also claiming a great deal. We wonder whether hunting can do so much, which may be an indication that Xenophon is also discussing greater things.

Closer inspection of the lives of the heroes indicates that something other than hunting is involved.[15] We are led to consider the details of the lives of exemplary heroes by a remark of Xenophon that indicated that there was nothing to be wondered at that most of them died (Sigma); in fact, they all died, many of them badly. Nor ought we wonder that they did not all live during the same time, Xenophon said, because Cheiron lived long enough to instruct them all, including Achilleus. In a book on hunting we may wonder whether Xenophon was from the start trying to put us off the scent by informing us that we have no cause to wonder. Of course, Cheiron and his pupils were necessary for the transmission of this art to humans, but at the very least, the composite nature of centaurs and the identification of them with barbaric practices,

---

14. A full discussion of this point is found in the critical edition in the Bude collection, edited by Edouard Delebecque, *Xenophon, L'Art de la Chasse* (Paris: Belles Lettres, 1970), 39 ff.

15. See the brief lives in the appendix to this chapter.

with rape and drunkenness, indicates that, as mediators of the divine inventions, they are of questionable status, like hunting itself.

One of the virtues taught by hunting was endurance, especially endurance of pain and toil, *ponos*. Cheiron, having been wounded in the knee by Herakles, agreed to give up his immortality in return for relief from the pain induced by Herakles' poisoned arrows. The "father of medicine," Asklepios, was taught by Cheiron, and Asklepios in turn taught his paired Homeric sons, Machaon and Podaleirios. None of these three is in any way connected with hunting. Two other pairs of heroes were also connected by Xenophon. Odysseus and Diomedes were linked to another hero, Palamades, because they murdered him. Castor and Pollux, the final pair, were connected to Theseus because of their piratical hunting ability in rescuing Helen from Athens. Theseus was connected to Hippolytos, his son, whom he killed; Nestor's son, Antilochos, was killed defending his father; Aeneas, the Trojan, was a good son, but one defeated in war. The other warrior son, Achilleus, was the son of a murderer, Peleus, who along with Telamon had killed their half-brother. The placing of Aeneas and Achilleus at the end of the catalogue of heroes enhanced the contrast between them.[16] Perhaps we were meant to compare Aeneas and Asklepios as well. Of the other warriors, Amphairos was a coward and Nestor and Menestheus were old soldiers filled with ineffective and obsolete opinions. In other words, honorable heroes are less associated with hunting than with healing. None of the others, so far as they are associated explicitly with hunting, are particularly honorable. Perhaps honorable hunting is a kind of healing, but no heroes practice it.

Turning to the heroes known chiefly as hunters, one finds similar problems. Kephalos's hunting skills enabled him accidentally to spear his wife, Prokris (cf. 13.18), and have his remarkable hound, Laelaps, turned to stone. Meilanion defeated a genuine hunter, Atalanta (cf. 13.18), by a trick and was later turned into an animal. Meleager, who organized the famous Calydonian boar hunt, which seven of the other heroes attended, was slain by one of the co-patrons of the hunters, Apollo, after his father offended the other, Artemis. In short, when one considers the obvious or external divisions of this list of heroes taught by Cheiron (that is, by looking at paired heroes, the relations of fathers and sons, or the actions of brothers), only Asklepios and his sons are unambiguously praised. And to repeat, they had nothing to do with hunting.

---

16. Alpha omitted Odysseus, Diomedes, and Menestheus. According to Delebecque, *L'Art de la Chasse*, 40–42, this was because Xenophon wished to diminish the stature of the heroes in order to exalt the gods Apollo and Artemis. This interpretation depends for its persuasiveness on accepting Delebecque's view of the relationship of Xenophon to Apollo and Artemis, indicated below.

The gods, Artemis and Apollo, were also paired, both being offspring of Titanic Leto. Artemis, "lady of wild beasts" (*Il.* 21.470), was mentioned or alluded to five times, which is not surprising. She was a pre-Hellenic earth or fertility goddess concerned chiefly with uncultivated parts filled with wild animals. In the *Kynegetikos* she was identified as the patron of hunters (13.18) and the protector of young hares (5.14). Her principal adventure was that she slew Orion, a gigantic and unsportsmanlike hunter, and the ex-lover of Eos, who "carried off" Kephalos, a euphemism for sudden death. Apollo was mentioned twice, each time along with Artemis. Although he was the father of Asklepios, it is not clear what his relationship to hunting might be. It is true that he killed the Python and Tityos, a giant who raped his mother, but he is mainly associated with music, medicine, the care of domestic animals, and archery, which was not a hunting technique.

Apollo did feature importantly in two episodes of Xenophon's early life, neither of them particularly praiseworthy. First, when his guest-friend, Proxenos, asked him to join the army of Cyrus the Younger, Xenophon asked the advice of Socrates. Socrates thought that Xenophon might be courting political trouble with the Athenians because Cyrus had supported Sparta in the war; but Socrates did not know the future (cf. *Apol. Soc.*, 29–31) and suggested that Xenophon enquire at Delphi. Xenophon then asked the oracle to what god he should pray and sacrifice in order to make the journey in the best and most successful way and to return safely after performing successful deeds. Apollo told him to what gods he must sacrifice (nothing was said of prayer). When Xenophon reported to Socrates, the old man found fault with him because he did not first ask whether he should go; he added that Xenophon must do what he was bid (*Anab.* 3.1.4–8). Immediately after recounting how he somewhat deceptively arrived in Asia, Xenophon remarked that Cyrus had deceived Proxenos by not indicating the true purpose of the expedition.

Deception was involved in the second episode as well. In the *Anabasis,* after the Greek army had successfully reached the seacoast, they stopped at Kerasountos to divide the booty they had gained, setting aside a tithe for Apollo and Artemis. Apollo had his share dedicated at Delphi, but Artemis did not receive hers until Xenophon had returned from Asia and was living in exile at Skillous. He built an altar and a temple at a spot appointed by Apollo and created a Hellenic game park, a *paradeisos* (cf. *Kyro.* 1.4.5–6). Each year at the festival, Xenophon and his guests would have a hunting expedition and a fine celebration (*Anab.* 5.3.7–13). Delebecque has interpreted the Kerasountos episode to suggest that Xenophon defrauded the two gods of their share of the spoils and thereafter continued to make honorable amends to the god of the hunt by conveniently associating brother and sister.[17] That interpretation may well be sound. What also seems true is that heroic hunting is not praiseworthy. The divine invention of hunting is most properly employed against animals and men by men and not by heroes. There is even, perhaps, a suggestion that hunting, which necessarily involves deception, can lead to impieties when the spirit of hunting directs human activity concerning the gods. Hunting, one may say, is a *paideia,* but one directed simply at the human and subhuman things and not at the heroic or divine things. In terms of the present interpretive hypothesis, that hunting as *paideia* is also an image of the relationship of philosophers to politics, the implication seems to be that this relationship must be worked out on the basis of arts given by the gods but not on the basis of divine intervention or of direct divine actions.

Xenophon began chapter 2 with another *proton,* this time less ambiguous than in chapter 1. This second *proton* marked the beginning of the ten chapters devoted to hunting properly speaking. *Ex hypothesi* it marked the beginning of his discussion of *paideia* philosophy, and politics. First of the things undertaken by a young man when leaving boyhood and entering upon adolescence is hunting with hounds, followed later by equally honored *paideiai.* Provided he can afford it, the young man should spend as much on hunting as possible because the benefits will be correspondingly great. If he has few means, he must spend more enthusiasm. Xenophon's point was that whatever was spent on hunting would be worth the value received, namely, the receipt of the most important *paideia.*

Xenophon began the description proper of hunting with an account of the necessary kit or tackle.[18] Included here were the net-keeper, the nets and stakes for setting them, a calfskin game bag, and two types of well-trained Laconian hounds (chaps. 2, 3). The preferred mobile tackle, the larger Castorian hound, was then described in more detail (4). Next Xenophon turned his attention to the quarry to be tackled, the hare, and how she was found (5).[19] In chapter 6 the tackle was put into motion and the quarry started. The central chapter dealt with the genesis of mobile tackle, that is, the breeding, raising, naming, and training of hounds (7). Because training hounds was similar to training sol-

17. Delebecque, *Essai,* 179.
18. The word used, *paraskeusis,* is often used to describe military equipment and armor. See *Ages.* 1.13; *Hell.* 5.2.33.
19. Possibly the most unusual information Xenophon imparted, at least for contemporary hunters, was that hares slept with their eyes open, which was one of the reasons why they had poor sight (5.11, 27), and that they steered themselves with the ears rather than by the tail, which, of course, was too short (5.32).

diers (*Kyro.* 1.6.19) or human beings (*Mem.* 4.1.3), the reason for its centrality seems plain. Moreover, there are obvious parallels in detail: some hounds speak or give tongue with no reason and try to make the false seem true, while others abandon the hunt from hatred of hunting, misotherony, or from love of humans, philanthropy (3.9–10). Likewise, the headstrong ought be praised sparingly, the philanthropic ones more, and the middle ones moderately (5.25).

Chapter 8 dealt with tracking the hare without hounds in snow. The next three chapters considered the hunting of animals other than the hare with hounds other than, or in addition to, the Laconian. Red deer (*elaphos*) required large Indian hounds with keepers, javelins (*akontia*), and great craft.[20] For hunting wild boars, the tackle was larger again. Cretan and Locrain hounds as well as Indian and Laconian were used along with nets and footsnares, long-shafted javelins and spears (*proboliaoi*) thick as a hardwood military spear (*kraneia*). Keepers were again required for the hounds, and there had to be several hunters to a party. The strategy was also more complex; the danger and excitement in facing the quarry, especially a boar, was correspondingly increased.[21] Less demanding methods, which relied more on nets and snares than on courage and a stout spear, were briefly explained (10.19–22). An even briefer account of how big cats and bears were captured (*aliskomai*) in foreign parts followed (11). It seems that Xenophon did not consider this last activity hunting at all, but capturing. Persian big-game expeditions were well known to him.[22] The brevity of his treatment of wild-boar hunting, his silence concerning the Persians, and his refusal even to use the verb *to hunt* with regard to what went on in foreign parts may indicate that Xenophon considered all the benefits of big-game hunting to be present in hare hunting.

Before turning to the third major section, on the benefits of hunting, we should consider the structure of this central section, chapters 2 through 11. The first subsection, chapters 2 to 4, dealt with static and mobile tackle; the second with the main quarry, the hare; the third combined the first two: the tackle was mobilized in pursuit of the quarry. The central part of this central section was concerned with the breeding, naming, training, and feeding of hounds. Matters of declining importance followed: hunting the hare without hounds,

---

20. Fawns might be captured where they lay and used to draw back the dam to be dispatched with a javelin, or footsnares might be employed.
21. The accusative Greek for the wild boar, *ton hun ton agrion*, is, in pronunciation, close to the "metaphysically dangerous" notion of the wild being, indicating thereby again the connection between hunting and philosophy. Immediately following the first mention of the boar (or being) is a complex and ambiguous numerical description of the nets and spears, a parody, perhaps, on what Plato called arithmetic or geometric thinking.
22. *Kyro.* 1.2.9, 4.2.10; *Anab.* 1.5.2–4, 1.9.6; Plato, *Alk.* 1, 121e; Hdt. 1.37.

hunting animals other than the hare, foreign (or barbaric) pseudo-hunting. If our interpretative hypothesis is sound, the following conclusions may be drawn. The philosopher-hunter must show the greatest care for his tackle, both inanimate nets, game bag, ropes, etc., and animate hounds. In some respects the animate tackle, because it is generated and trained by the philosopher-hunter, is more important. Ordinary hunting of hares amounts to ordinary philosophizing in the city. The philosopher relies on hounds to help him; these may simply be other citizens whom he helps to the truth or, as in the *Republic*, they may be guardians of the truth. But when the most dangerous or difficult quarry (or truth) is run to ground, namely, the wild boar (or being), the hunter must rely equally on hounds, net, and his own strength. Barbarians neither hunt nor philosophize.

The benefits for those who practice hunting diligently are many. To a large extent they are the benefits of philosophizing. For the individual, the most obvious advantages come to the body, which remains healthy. Sight and hearing improve, and the onset of old age is delayed (12.1). Other benefits to the individual are mediated through the benefits that hunting brings to the polis. First of all it is the best *paideia* for war. Victory in war, we know, is extremely important. It brings glory to the victor, and usually the gods grant happiness (*eudaimonia*) to victorious states. Accordingly, the disciplines (*askeses*) associated with it should be most practiced (*Hipp.* 8.7). In the *Kyropaideia*, war was the single thing to which Cyrus devoted himself (2.1.21), and hunting was its playful image.[23] Both activities were manifestations of a love of victory, a part of a man's nature so basic it could survive castration (*Kyro.* 7.5.64). A love of victory was perhaps even shared with horses (*P. Hipp.* 9.2, 10.14). Specifically, hunting accustomed men to travel with weapons, to sleep on the ground, and to attack and give orders at the same time (the hare hunter raced behind and directed the hounds). Hunting trained men in endurance and speed and accustomed them to work the woods and to travel over broken ground; in case of defeat in battle, this skill might enable them to save themselves honorably. Many times, in fact, a small number of fit and courageous men have rallied to defeat a larger enemy on difficult ground (12.2–5).

The chief benefits, however, combined physical training with spiritual virtues. In the old days men knew this and encouraged hunting among the young: "It makes them moderate (*sophronas*) and just because their *paideia* is in the truth" (12.7). To such men is owed victory in war and in other things, because

---

23. Compare *Kyro.* 1.6.39–40 with the hunting of the Armenian king, which used precisely the tactics employed in hare hunting (2.4.22–29).

effort (*ponos*) has removed what is shameful and hubristic from the soul and from the body and has replaced it with a desire for virtue. They are the true *aristoi* because they do not permit their polis to suffer injustice or wrong (12.8–9). The image here is not so elevated as that of a Platonic philosopher-king, which was not a serious possibility in any case, but was considerably more than rule by gentlemen. Like philosophers, Xenophon's guardians are educated in the truth through the *paideia* of hunting.

Politically speaking, justice and moderation may be said to be the most important virtues. Accounting for those virtues may be taken to be the mark of wisdom; taken by themselves and without appearing in speech, they are in one sense internal; but in another sense they appear as characteristic activities, especially war and politics. Xenophon gave several examples of how anger or a lack of moderation led to disaster in war. The Spartans were defeated by the Olynthians because of it (*Hell.* 5.3.6–7); Cyrus the Younger lost his life at Kunaxa because of it (*Anab.* 1.8.24–27); the stupidity of the Athenian demos in the trial of the generals victorious after Arginousai was also a consequence of their lack of moderation (*Hell.* 1.7.8–35). On the other hand, young Persians were taught to praise moderation, and hunting was an integral part of their *paideia* (*Kyro.* 1.2.10–11). They were so moderate that it was considered shameful to spit, to blow the nose, to break wind, or to be seen preparing to make water or anything similar (*Kyro.* 1.2.16). What was inside remained inside. Most of their bodily wastes, apparently, were sweated out invisibly (*Kyro.* 1.2.16; cf. 5.2.16). Indeed, when the Persians began again to spit and blow their noses, it was clear evidence of their degeneration following the death of Cyrus (*Kyro.* 8.8.8; cf. 8.1.42).

Xenophon's peculiar observation of the Persian habits concerning bodily discharges has sometimes been called a joke. Certainly Xenophon was fond of making jokes; indeed, some of what has been explicated in the present essay looks like a joke at Plato's expense. But if it is a joke, it is not, on the surface, very witty. Supposing, however, that spitting, farting, and so on is interpreted by analogy with being virtuous and accounting for virtue. If, then, what is inside comes out invisibly when the Persians are well ordered, this may mean only that the Persians do not account for what they are inside, namely, moderate and just through hunting. But then, barbarians never philosophize, which is a way of giving an account, even though they may be gentlemen. By nature the Persians cannot properly account for what they are, which is why the Greek Xenophon gave an account of them.

Xenophon was more tolerant of night hunting than was Plato. Night-hunters of animals, according to the Xenophontic Socrates, might instruct young men in astronomy sufficient to learn the time of night, the month, and the year, knowledge of which would be useful when planning a journey or setting a watch (*Mem.* 4.7.4). We note that this astronomical knowledge was practical and was learned from practical men. Moreover, it was learned from gazing upon the fixed stars and the pole of the ecliptic and not upon the wandering unstable planets or irregular comets. With such things, Socrates said, we have no need to be concerned. Rudimentary astronomy was useful; anything further was impious, not to say insane (*Mem.* 4.7.6).

The only night-hunter Xenophon discussed was also a human-hunter, the hetaira Theodote, who was also the only woman with whom the Xenophontic Socrates was directly reported as having conversed (*Mem.* 3.11). What Xenophon thought of her form of night hunting may have been indicated by the position of the account of her conversation in the *Memorabilia*. Earlier in the book Socrates' conversations and sayings with soldiers and politicians had been reported; they had conversed about military and political things. He also conversed with Glaukon and Charmides about political things. Xenophon alluded to the possibility of a conversation with Plato (*Mem.* 3.6.1) but reported a conversation with Aristippos, who was a philosopher but not of Plato's caliber. As Strauss pointed out, "the peak is missing," and the conversations reported subsequently are in the nature of a descent from a possible philosophic conversation.[24] Socrates then was reported as conversing with male artisans who imitated beauty but who were not themselves manly men (*andres*). Artisans made likenesses of things, especially of beautiful things, but for that reason were inferior to the best things, which came into sight only through speech (cf. *Kyn.* 12.19).

Socrates' conversation with Theodote was a conversation with a live model, a model imitated by artisans whose beauty was "beyond speech" as well as "god-given," as is indicated by her name. Like Socrates, Theodote lived on gifts given to her by friends; like Socrates, she would "be with" those who persuaded her; like Socrates, her "being with" people was erotic. As Socrates said, having looked upon her, he and his companions desired to touch what they had seen, and would leave her company secretly excited (*hypoknizomenoi*) and with longing for her.

Socrates then noticed the rich clothes and furniture nearby and her mother's jewelry and comely female attendants and concluded that a herd of friends was much more valuable than a herd of goats or sheep or oxen if they could fit her out so well. But Socrates wondered whether her friends settled on her like flies or whether she contrived like a spider. Theodote claimed ignorance of

---

24. Strauss, *Xenophon's Socrates*, 74.

friend hunting, and Socrates explained that it was much more complex than hare hunting.[25] Since hares were night eaters, specially trained night hounds were required for night hunting.[26] Theodote was likewise in need of a night-hunting hound who could drive wealthy men who loved beauty into her nets. She then asked Socrates to become her partner in friend hunting (cf. *Symp.* 3.10). Socrates agreed upon condition that she persuade him, but Theodote did not know how. Her sole attempt, "come and see me often," was dismissed by Socrates, a notorious *voyou,* on account of his being too busy. It would seem that Theodote's god-given beauty and her lack of technique in erotic things made her unable to account for her night hunting. We are, perhaps, meant to reflect on the relationship of silent erotic bodies and articulate erotic souls: relying overmuch on divine gifts, her beauty was beyond both speech and *techne.* Hunting of animals, it appears, is in the middle or is moderate, not given directly by the gods but indirectly, through Cheiron. It takes place in daylight, is practically articulate, and, being useful, is capable of persuasion. This specific interpretation adds weight to the general one, that hunting, for Xenophon, is an image of philosophizing.

Yet, hunting had its critics even in Xenophon's day. We have been prepared for them, however, by the knowledge that the *paideia* of hunting is in the truth and by the knowledge that most men do not walk the difficult trail of truth or that most men are not philosophers. Critics of hunting, we expect, will be in untruth or delusion.

One of the timeless criticisms, and so present even today, of those who love hunting, as well as of those who philosophize, is that they neglect their household affairs. Xenophon countered this remark first by declaring that those who care for the polis (and the hunters, those *aristoi,* certainly do) could not possibly neglect their domestic affairs because the polis was concerned with domestic prosperity. Second, even if they do seem to neglect their home life, it was justified by the great political service they rendered. Any criticism of hunting that ignored the larger political context was therefore worthless. Having in that way dismissed the critics as trivial, Xenophon turned to the attack: why, the hunter-philosopher asked himself, do some people attack the true *paideia*?

Many of those who talk badly of hunting are moved by envy (*phthonos*) and thoughtlessness and prefer to be ruined by their own baseness than be saved

---

25. The word for form, *eune,* is also the word for sleeping place or bed (cf. Plato, *Rep.* 415e); perhaps this is why Socrates found a similarity between hare hunting (the hare is caught most often when she returns to her form where the nets are set up) and Theodote's kind of nighttime friend hunting.

26. In *Kyro.* 1.6.40, nothing was said of night hounds for night-feeding hares.

by the virtue of others (12.12). Their baseness was specific and antithetical to hunting: they hate toil or effort, *ponos*. They are not merely unphilosophic but antiphilosophic.

Several times Xenophon remarked on the beneficial effects of toil in teaching virtue and especially in teaching moderation.[27] We are not surprised to learn, therefore, that most pleasures were base and that those who yielded to them were made worse in their words and in their deeds. Their baseness infected their children and friends; by their words they made enemies. Accordingly, they were useless to save the polis (12.13). Such base things would be shunned by one who followed the noble *paideia* Xenophon recommended, because that *paideia* taught obedience to the laws and the speaking and hearing of justice. For one who followed the strenuous *paideia* there was continuous toil; for the polis, however, there was salvation (cf. Plato, *Rep.* 621b–c). Those who avoided toil in order to pursue pleasure, on the other hand, were worst of all (*kakistoi*) because they obeyed neither the law nor good words. They were unable to discover virtue on their own because they were lazy and so were neither pious nor wise. "And being without *paideia* they greatly blame those who have gained *paideia*" (12.16). The tension between hunters and non- or antihunters is indistinguishable from the tension between the philosophers and the antiphilosophers. The truth of Xenophon's formula, that toil led to virtue, he said, had been shown in the example given earlier, of Cheiron's pupils.

It is certainly true that none of the heroes mentioned by Xenophon was lazy. In light of the fate of Cheiron's pupils, it may be questioned whether a *paideia* of toil alone led to virtue. All, however, love virtue, Xenophon said; but because the gaining of it required effort, it was not widely pursued. "For acquiring virtue by labor is unseen but the toils involved in the pursuit show forth" (12.19). Perhaps if the body of Virtue were visible to the eye, men would care more for her, knowing that they would be seen by Virtue as clearly as they see her, just as under the eye of a lover a man rises above himself and avoids what is base. But the lazy, who assume they are not seen by Virtue, do many base things. Yet, Virtue is immortal and present in every place and honors those who are good toward her and gets rid of the base. Accordingly, if men knew Virtue had her eye on them, they would gladly undertake the *ponoi* and the *paideia* by which, with difficulty, she may be won. And they would win her (12.20–22).

The discussion of Virtue reminds us of Socrates' account in the *Memorabilia* of Prodikos account of Herakles' *paideia* by Virtue (*Mem.* 2.1.21–34). According to Xenophon's version, Herakles was offered pleasure and ease by Vice,

---

27. *Mem.* 2.1.1–34; *Kyro.* 1.3.10–11, 4.2.38–45, 7.5.75–76, 8.1.30–32.

whom her friends call Happiness. Virtue told Herakles she hoped he would become a doer of good and noble things, provided he acted in the way the gods had disposed: "For of all good and noble things the gods give nothing to human beings without toil and effort" (*Mem.* 2.1.28). Vice and Virtue appeared to Herakles; the rest of mankind must make do with the ikon of Prodikos or with Xenophon's story. Virtue nonetheless is the common aim of hunters and philosophers.

Starting in chapter 12.10, Xenophon engaged the enemies of hunting in the general guise of "some persons" who tell lies about hunting. In chapter 13 they were flushed into the open: sophists.

"I wonder (*thaumazo*) at those who bear the fair name the wise ones (*hoi sophistai*)." His wonder was prompted by the observation that most of them say that they lead the young (*neoi*) to virtue but do the opposite. They have never caused a man to be good nor have they produced writings that might instruct men in how to be good; in fact, their books are frivolous, offering empty pleasures and teaching baseness. "I myself," said Xenophon, "am a private person, but I know the most important thing is to be taught what is good by [or from] nature, and second from men who truly know what is good and not from those who practice the art of deception" (13.2–5). In contrast to the deceivers, Xenophon tried to write plainly for those who seek *paideia* in virtue. Like the philosopher, the private person, Xenophon the hunter, minded his own business and lived according to nature.

Xenophon's first criticism of the sophists was that they were deceptive, "clever with words, not with thoughts," and concerned with seeming rather than being (13.6–7). Now, we know that hunting involves deception. This is emphasized, for example, in the book Xenophon devoted to the *paideia* of Cyrus who, as a young man, was taught only honesty (1.6.27–40). Likewise in war, to which hunting was closely allied, the great Spartan general Agesilaos was a master of deception (*Ages.* 1.17), for "nothing is more beneficial in war than deception" (*Hipp.* 5.9). Tissaphernes also practiced deception, but he did so by breaking his oaths, which is to say he deceived the gods; for that he gained their enmity (*Ages.* 1.13). Agesilaos never practiced deception upon his friends (*Ages.* 6.6; cf. *Oec.* 10); the first duty of a commander, Xenophon said, was to sacrifice to the gods (*Hipp.* 1.1; cf. 3.1) and his greatest mistake was to disregard omens (*Kyro.* 1.6.45). Xenophon's teaching about deception centered on friends and enemies, both human and divine. Cyrus, however, practiced a moderate deception on his subjects and his soldiers (*Kyro.* 7.1.10–20, 8.3.13–14). We are prepared, therefore, to learn that sophists are hunters who, like Tissaphernes, gained the enmity of the gods.

The many blame the sophists, Xenophon said, so it was important to distinguish them from the philosophers. The sophists speak in order to deceive and not for the sake of justice, for their own gain and not to be useful. This is why they hunt down rich young men, unlike the philosophers, who are friends to all and are indifferent to wealth (13.8–9; cf. Plato, *Soph.* 231d). Sophists are hunters of wealth who use empty words to instill baseness in the souls of young men; Xenophon, author of the *Kynegetikos*, would hunt them down. They are the most dangerous quarry, more dangerous even than the boar, because they are themselves deceptive, or rather, treacherous, hunters. Moreover, they go after the most valuable game, the souls of the young, and ruin them.

The result of sophistry is the production of men who seek to get more, who are infected with pleonexia (13.10; cf. Plato, *Rep.* 344a). The two types, one who pleonizes in private things and the other who does so in demotic things, are base even if they are successful; if they are not successful, they are still base. As Mencken said, if a bad thing is not worth doing, it is not worth doing well either. The pleonizers steal either private property or state treasure and, looking only to themselves, are useless for the defense of the polis. Since they avoid toil, they have bodies that are disgracefully unfit, and they make the greatest contrast with hunters: "the ones undertake to hunt game, the others their friends" (13.12). The appropriate personal qualities of these two kinds of hunter were then detailed: the game hunters were improved by their hunting, benefited the polis, and learned piety; the friend hunters were made worse, were bad for the polis, and were impious. "Old stories tell that the gods love those who undertake the work of game-hunting; they love to participate in such hunts and to look upon others hunting" (13.17). This is yet another reason, Xenophon said, to consider his words, follow his advice, and grow in piety, for a god sees what men do. If that is done, the young man will be good to his parents, good to the polis, and good to his friends and fellow citizens. "For not only have all those men who loved hunting been virtuous, so too have the females to whom the goddess [Artemis] has given this love, Atalanta, Prokris, and perhaps others" (13.18).

Urbane sophists claimed to teach *paideia* on the basis of words alone, but it cannot be done; they mislead the young with deceptions that camouflage their true appearance. At best the sophists would lead the young men to temporary success, the reward for which was no more than the envy of the unsuccessful. Xenophon, the country dweller, taught true *paideia* with hard deeds in the midst of nature and with plain words. His teaching of virtue in truth was not temporary but stable, everlasting, and irrefutable, like the law (13.7). In this respect he agreed with Plato and Isocrates on the detestability of sophists. Unlike Plato, however, he did not distinguish so sharply between body and soul. Hunting for Xenophon was also a moral art: a well-trained body would conform the soul. A body innured to toil showed evidence of self-rule and thereby was eligible to rule others. For these reasons, hunting was also a kind of philosophizing, or, rather, the consequences of hunting so far as the body and soul are concerned are the same as the political consequences of philosophizing.

Conclusion

The similarity of war and hunting seems to help sustain the charge of Laconism against Xenophon and justify Socrates' fears that he would be exiled by the type of Athenians he described in 12.15 as demotic pleonizers. In addition, Xenophon praised Laconian hounds and wrote the *Kynegetikos* for young men of good family and sufficient wealth (2.1) who were capable of remembering maxims (*gnomai*) not sayings (*onomata*) (12.5). The laconic Spartans were famous for their gnomic speech. If we ignore the fact that Prokris was skewered by her husband's spear and that Atalanta ended up as a wild beast, and if we interpret that last sentence of the text imaginatively, it could mean that Xenophon advocated that it would be good for females to hunt or at least to take physical training with men (cf. *Lak. Pol.* 1.4). Such an opinion, if indeed it was Xenophon's, could be interpreted as praise of Sparta.[28]

On the other hand, we may recall that in the *Oikonomikos* young girls were to be "watched," not exposed to *paideiai* (*Oec.* 7.5–7; cf. *Mem.* 1.5.2). In any case, we might wonder why Xenophon bothered to discuss sophists if he were concerned with Sparta, for that polis would prove barren ground for their hunting. Leaving aside Strauss's persuasive contention that the *Lakedaimonion Politeia* was a satire, we cannot help but notice that at the time of life when Xenophon thought that young men should be most fully engaged in hunting, at Sparta they were under the strictest control (*Lak. Pol.* 3.1–4). Despite the liberty to use other men's hounds (*Lak. Pol.* 6.3), the only people able to do so were "beyond the vigor of youth" (*Lak. Pol.* 4.7). For them, hunting was the finest occupation unless they had other public duty, which is to say that hunting was, in effect, a public duty for old men (cf. *Lak. Pol.* 10.4; 10.7). And old men are not very good at chasing hares. We suspect another Xenophontic joke.

What the suspicion of Xenophon's Laconism may indicate with more justification was that he was not a simple Athenian patriot. In the *Kynegetikos*, for example, he mentioned the words *homeland* or *polis* at least nine times, but never *Athens;* Theseus was identified by Xenophon with all Greece, not just

---

28. See, for example, Delebecque, *Essai*, 176.

Athens. Higgins argued forcefully that "Xenophon the writer is . . . not the man who hunted and farmed abroad in Skillous, much less the man who fought for Cyrus, but the returned Socratic advising his fellow Athenians (and anyone else who cared to read) what he thinks best for the city."[29] If we emphasize the ability of a "Socratic," or better, of a philosopher, to transcend the cares of the polis of his birth (cf. Plato, *Rep.* 592a–b), then Xenophon's depreciation of his fatherland was intelligible.[30] If virtue was the highest thing, then unless the fatherland was virtuous it could not properly expect to gain the undivided loyalty of the virtuous man (cf. Aristotle, *EN* 1129b12). And Xenophon's life was for many years, not all of them compulsory, the life of a *xenos,* a stranger, though hardly unconnected with politics. In this respect his life was not unlike that of Socrates.[31]

So far as the teaching of Xenophon, the philosopher, regarding hunting and *paideia* is concerned, one might say that hunting is necessary for true *paideia,* but it is not a complete *paideia.* In the *Kyropaideia,* Median justice, which Cyrus learned from his grandfather, depended only on the soul of the king and was unreliable, whereas Persian justice, being traditional and centered upon the practice of hunting, was upright and steady.[32] Only Cyrus could hold them together. His own soldiers, well schooled in the arts of hunting and of war, may have been overtrained, having lost the capacity for wonder (8.1.42). Too much self-discipline achieved only by enduring toil as proof of virtue would breed cynicism, a term derived from the Greek word for hound. It is hard to think that Xenophon would have had a fundamental disagreement with the opinion of Plato reported earlier (*Rep.* 549a). Accordingly, there is much to commend the suggestion of Delebecque that the *Kynegetikos* was written by Xenophon for his own sons; after they had learned its lessons they left Skillous for Athens. Politically, hunting may be a prophylactic against tyranny. One of the things that distinguished Agesilaos the king from Heiro the tyrant was that he kept hounds and Heiro did not (*Ages.* 9.6; *Heiro.* 2.2). Both kept horses, which was evidence only of their prosperity, not their virtue (*Poroi* 4.8), whatever the virtue of the horses (*Oec.* 11.3–6).

According to Strauss, one of the meanings of political philosophy is that it is "the political, or popular, treatment of philosophy, or the political introduction to philosophy—the attempt to lead the qualified citizens, or rather their

---

29. Higgins, *Xenophon the Athenian,* 132.
30. In the *Anabasis* (5.6.15–18), Xenophon was suspected of wanting to found a polis, as Plato said (*Rep.* 499c), "in some barbaric place."
31. Strauss, *Xenophon's Socrates* (Ithaca: Cornell University Press, 1972), 38.
32. Consider Cyrus's discussion with his mother over whether he should stay with her father, 1.3.13–18.

qualified sons, from the political life to the philosophic life."[33] Xenophon has taught that hunting is a practice of moderation. Being a hunter and a moderate man, being a philosopher as well, he has practiced political philosophy by practicing the art of moderate discourse. If the consequences of hunting are as Xenophon indicated, then for most human beings, including those whose souls are disposed toward philosophizing, the practice of hunting is a kind of philosophizing, and his study, the *Kynegetikos*, is an example of Socratic rhetoric, which sometimes involves deception.

One may also draw a conclusion useful for contemporary life. Herodotos distinguished Greeks and barbarians, among other ways, by emphasizing the homogenizing tendencies of the barbarians: what counted were numbers of bodies in standardized circles (Hdt. 7, 60). More philosophically, barbarians could see no difference between human and subhuman nature; or if they did, they would strive to ignore it. More philosophically still, barbarian consciousness exists in a cosmological order where the several realms of being are not, or are not sufficiently, differentiated. As they say, "The world is filled with gods." Contemporary sophistic barbarians who oppose hunting are similar to ancient barbarians in their lack of discrimination between human and subhuman. On the one hand, they degrade the human to the subhuman and speak about "ecosystems." On the other hand, they endow subhuman animals with what they call rights. In this way they identify themselves with the hunted, whom they call victims. It goes without saying that they have no notion of the superhuman, which is what redeemed the ancient barbarians. Nothing, so far as I can see, redeems the contemporary barbarians in their opposition to hunting, especially not their moralism.

Appendix: Biographic Allusions

Kephalos, Xenophon said, was abducted by a goddess; he was abducted by Eos. To be abducted was a euphemism for sudden death. Nothing was said of his hunting prowess nor of his remarkable tackle, a hound, Laelaps, that never lost its quarry, and a spear that never missed its target; nothing was said of the resentment of his wife, Prokris, nor how, as a result of it, she was accidentally speared by Kephalos. Xenophon was also silent about the fate of Laelaps when he encountered the uncatchable Cadmean vixen—Zeus turned both hound and fox to stone. As a result of hunting, Kephalos lost three things: his most famous quarry, his hound, and his wife.

33. *What Is Political Philosophy?* (Glencoe: Free Press, 1959), 93–94.

Asklepios in Sigma was able to raise the dead; in Alpha he was able only to cure the moribund. In Sigma he was a god and among men the possessor of immortal glory; in Alpha he was no longer a god. He was a pupil of Cheiron.

Meilanion was a lover of toil who eventually married Atalanta, who was a huntress. Xenophon did not mention that he did so only under compulsion from Aphrodite nor that he won her by trickery, nor that he did not fulfill his vow to Aphrodite and that as a consequence both he and Atalanta were turned into lions.

Nestor was so famous, Xenophon said, that he had no need to tell of his renown. The reason, perhaps, is that Nestor would do it himself (cf. *Il.* 23.624ff.).

Amphiaraos was a great warrior against Thebes; Xenophon is silent as to the fact that, foreknowing the outcome of the famous expedition against that polis, he declined to volunteer, was eventually compelled to fight, and then fled to be swallowed by a cleft in the earth made by Zeus's thunderbolt.

Peleus was admired by the gods for his self-control and other virtues; Sigma indicated as well that he married Thetis, mother of Achilleus. Nothing is said of the rejection of Thetis by Zeus and Poseidon because of a prophecy that her son would be greater than the father, nor of Peleus's betrayal on a hunt when his spear was stolen, nor of the subsequent attack by centaurs and his rescue by Cheiron, nor of his accidentally killing Eurytion, who had previously purified him after he and Telamon had killed his half-brother, Phocos, on a boar hunt. Nothing is said about Thetis leaving Peleus.

Telamon was praised for his virtue, his marriage to Periboea, and his being honored by Herakles. Nothing was said of his being the brother of Peleus nor of their joint murder.

Meleager was well known and famed, Xenophon said, and his misfortune was not his fault but the fault of his father, Oeneus. Oeneus neglected to sacrifice to Artemis, and she sent a wild boar to ravage the countryside. Meleager then collected a hunting party, which included Castor and Pollux, Atalanta, Amphiaraos, Peleus, Nestor, Telamon, and Theseus. Nothing was said of his death, of which there were two versions. In one he was killed by Apollo; in the other by his mother.

Theseus was admired, according to Xenophon, for enlarging the country controlled by his homeland and for single-handedly slaying the enemies of all the Greeks. No mention is made of the name of his homeland, which was the same as the homeland of Xenophon, the exile; nothing was said of his great hunts, nor of the more recent results of Athenian imperial hunting.

Hippolytos was honored by Artemis and spoke with her. In Sigma he was celebrated for his chastity and piety; in Alpha he was celebrated for his chastity.

Nothing was said of his betrayal by Phaedra to Theseus, who doubted his chastity, nor of Theseus's causing him to die.

Palamedes was described in Sigma as surpassing by far his contemporaries in wisdom, but being unjustly killed, he obtained from the gods an unprecedented revenge; in Alpha he obtained unprecedented fame. Nothing was said about how he died, nor what his revenge was; Xenophon seems to dispute the version that Odysseus was responsible for his death (but cf. *Mem.* 4.2.33).

Menestheus, through his love of hunting and his devotion to toil, was admitted by the first of the Greeks to be the best, except for Nestor who rivaled him. Menestheus was not identified by Xenophon as leader of the Athenians before Troy, nor was it pointed out that Nestor could challenge him only because he was far older and could do so only in drawing up soldiers and horses (*Il.* 2.552–56). Nothing was said of the effectiveness of these "Nestorian" tactics (cf., *Il.* 2.296–301).

There followed three pair of heroes:

Odysseus and *Diomedes* were famous for every deed; to them was owed the fall of Troy. Nothing was said of the deed of Palamades' murder.

Castor and *Pollux* in Sigma were immortal because they showed the Greeks the arts they learned from Cheiron; in Alpha they had lost their immortality and were remembered together. Nothing was mentioned of their hunting skills in recapturing Helen after Theseus kidnapped her nor of the hunting expedition with the Argonauts.

Machaon and *Polaleirios* were schooled in the healing arts taught by Cheiron. It was not mentioned that they were sons of Asklepios nor that they were the surgeon and physician of the Greek forces at Troy.

Antilochos was killed defending his father, Nestor, and received the name Philopator.

Aeneas according to Sigma gained renown for his piety by saving the paternal and maternal gods as well as his father; for that reason, alone of the Trojans, he was not stripped of his arms. According to Alpha, he gained a name for piety simply for saving his father, nothing being said of the penates.

Achilleus was brought up in this *paideia* so well that no one grows weary of hearing and telling of him.

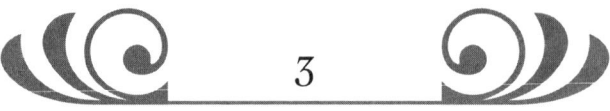

The (Anti-)Eschatalogical Perspective in Sigmund Freud's Psychoanalysis

Gilbert Weiss

Introduction

When Sigmund Freud's *Die Traumdeutung* came out in 1899, the scientific and philosophical discourse of the time was dominated by a configuration of ideas that could be described as aiming at the "discovery of the real reality." Epigrammatically stated, the purpose was to liberate reality from the confines and restrictions of reason that originated in German Idealism. It was intended to find the way back from the reality of absolute reason (*absolute Vernunftwirklichkeit*) to the reality of the natural world (*naturale Weltwirklichkeit*). As a result, a great variety of new phenomena were discovered: the economy, which lay behind spirit (Marx), the mortality of human existence, which lay behind speculation (Kierkegaard), the will, which lay behind reason (Schopenhauer), the will for power, which lay behind knowledge (Nietzsche), and biology, which lay behind history (Darwin). Sigmund Freud is part of this tradition of fin de siècle discovery. The new world he made accessible brought to light the unconscious, which lay behind consciousness, and the instinct, which lay behind culture.

What is common to all of these voyages of discovery is—as Eric Voegelin has pointed out—the turn to that sphere of human existence that in Classical and Christian ethics fell within the title of *passiones, concupiscentiae,* and *libidines.* The worldly immanent and natural existence of man was declared to be the "real reality." With this turn the speculative flights of fancy of German Idealism were provisionally grounded, but instead of continuing the unfettered search for reality that had become lost, new fetters were placed upon it: materialistic, naturalistic, psychologistic fetters. In short, the "escape from the noetic structure of reality"[1] continued. With Nietzsche, the revolt against God culminated in an explicit deicide. In this context, Sigmund Freud was an ally of Nietzsche. By attributing an illusionary character to religion, which the psychoanalytic method disclosed to be the *Urneurose der Menschheit,* he reached a climax of modern atheism.

For the philosopher Eric Voegelin, Freud belongs in a category with gnostic speculators such as Hegel, Marx, and Comte. In his view, the Freudian unconscious is an ideological deformation of human nature equal to Hegel's *Weltgeist,* Marx's *Produktionsverhältnisse,* or Comte's *physique sociale.*[2] Accordingly, Freudian psychoanalysis would present a gnostic construction of history that, as with all forms of modern Gnosticism, is characterized in its inner logic as an immanentist eschatology, that is, as an intramundane story of salvation.

In the following essay I will investigate whether this condemnation of Freud as a gnostic revolutionary is justified. Does Freudian psychoanalysis actually proclaim a worldly immanent redemption? Can it be classified according to its theoretical substance as an intramundane eschatology; or is it not rather the other way round, insofar as the Freudian man remains unredeemed and no social formation, neither historical nor utopian, is imaginable where this condition would change? Does Freud appear as a prophet? Does psychoanalysis fulfil the progressivistic hopes in a revolutionary transformation of human nature? Or is it not rather that Freud's analysis unmasks not only the religious message of salvation as an illusion but also the Marxist message along with every other chiliastic one? If so, what would be the political and social consequences of such an anti-eschatological conception?

In order to sketch possible answers to these questions—more cannot be achieved in the form of this paper—it is, first of all, necessary to indicate the key elements of the Freudian approach. These are: (1) the history of the individual (*Individualgeschichte*) as the mirror of the history of mankind (*Menschheitsgeschichte*), (2) *Sinnverstehen* as the analytical method, and (3) remembrance and recollection of the forgotten as the anamnetic principle of investigation. Then, to enter into the heart of the matter, one must consider Freud's last and philosophico-historically most important work, *Moses and Monotheism.* It is this book that shows the eschatological perspective of his theory of civilization

---

1. Eric Voegelin, "Reason: The Classic Experience," in *The Collected Works of Eric Voegelin* (hereinafter, *CW*), vol. 12, *Published Essays, 1966–1985,* ed. Ellis Sandoz (1990; available Columbia: University of Missouri Press, 1999), 278.
2. Cf. Eric Voegelin, "Immortality: Experience and Symbol," in *CW,* 12:69.

most clearly. Finally, I will briefly sketch the political and social consequences of this perspective in a somewhat pictorial way by referring to surrealism.

Individual Therapy and Theory of Civilization

Today, the work of Sigmund Freud presents itself in two ways: on the one hand as a therapeutic-clinical approach, as a specific technique for the medical treatment of psychic complaints, and on the other hand as a large-scale theory of culture and civilization. In the further development of psychoanalysis after Freud's death with the foundation of numberless schools these two aspects of his work have been widely separated from each other. The psychoanalytical orthodoxy, today represented primarily by the American Psychoanalytic Association, has devoted itself entirely to the therapeutic-clinical aspect and has more or less shelved the part of cultural theory. This has led to what may be called the phenomenon of "medicocentrism" within psychoanalysis. Furthermore, the peculiar union between psychoanalysis and Marxism, which became popular during the 1960s, did its part to evoke a certain not-unjustified skepticism against Freud as a cultural theorist, especially, in the academic world.[3]

For Freud himself, the psychoanalytical method as an instrument of cultural and historical analysis was of no less importance than its therapeutic-clinical application. One can even say that, with advancing years, Freud's interest turned more and more to culture and history. Thus, his most important late writings, from *Totem und Tabu* to *Moses,* are rather of a metapsychological nature and determined by the desire for theoretical universalism. There are several reasons for this change. Freud's medical pathos and sense of vocation were not particularly strong. Passages from his correspondence illustrate that very well. From the beginning he was opposed to the medicalization of the psychoanalytical method. In order to prevent the transformation of psychoanalysis into a "Spezialfach der Medizin,"[4] he also tried to keep the Wiener Psychoanalytische Vereinigung (founded in 1908) open to non-physicians, to "laymen," as he called

---

3. The union between psychoanalysis and Marxism was, above all, initiated by former members of the Frankfurter Institut für Sozialforschung, particularly by Herbert Marcuse. Although this union did not last long, because it was built on a dubious basis, it caused a kind of *allgemeiner Ideologieverdacht* that largely blocked serious scientific discussion of the sociological and philosophical implications of Freud's work. In the 1980s it came to a revival of Freud's ideas in the social sciences through structuralism and poststructuralism. Of course, the Freud that was presented there was mainly a Lacanian one.

4. Sigmund Freud, "Zur Frage der Laienanalyse," in his *Gesammelte Werke* (hereinafter, *GW*) (Frankfurt a. M.: S. Fischer, 1961), 14:289.

them. Before 1914, about a third of the group that came together for the famous Psychological Wednesday Evenings were non-physicians.[5]

Apart from the biographic fact that Freud lacked a therapeutic vocation, his turn to the questions of culture, society, and history had reasons that are to be found in the theoretical approach itself. Already in *Die Traumdeutung,* Freud discovered a phenomenon of grave consequence: the wishes that manifest themselves in dreams give not only information about the ontogenesis of the individual but also about the "phylogenetic childhood of mankind."[6] Not least because of the influence of Haeckel's biogenetics, Freud regarded the ontogenesis as the repetition of the phylogenesis, the individual as a mirror of the history of mankind. This phenomenon, applied to the structure of dreams, led to the immigration of phylogenetic elements into the individual unconscious and, therewith, to the assumption of universal symbolic constants.[7] These symbolic constants in the unconscious, the "seelischen Altertümer," that interested Freud most and, from his early days on, were his true passion.

With the individual as a mirror of history, as a deposit of generic sediments of mankind, the universal-historical perspective of psychoanalysis was already given at the very beginning of Freud's development. But only in his late writings, particularly in *Moses,* this perspective, as we will see below, finds its systematic formulation. In this regard an anecdote provided by Theodor Reik is quite illuminating: in one of the Wednesday evening discussions Reik took the view that the future of psychoanalysis would lie in the studies of history and anthropology and that, in the year 2000, the analytical therapy of neurotic and psychotic complaints would be considered as an antiquated enterprise. To the great astonishment of the people present, Freud entirely agreed with his statement.[8]

Sinnverstehen *as the Method of Psychoanalysis*

Freudian psychoanalysis, both as a clinical-therapeutic procedure and as metapsychological theory, uses, not a causal-scientific method, but rather a *geisteswissenschaftlich-verstehende* one, that is to say, of interpretative understanding. In spite of certain terminological borrowings from the natural sciences,

---

5. Among them, people such as Otto Rank, Theodor Reik, Hans Sachs, and Siegfried Bernfeld. Incidentally, Anna Freud was not a trained physician, but was originally a teacher.
6. Freud, *GW* 2/3:554: "die phylogenetische Kindheit . . . des Menschengeschlechts."
7. The notion "Symbolische Konstante" was first used with reference to Freud by Hans Blumenberg. See his *Die Lesbarkeit der Welt* (Frankfurt: Suhrkamp, 1986), 354.
8. See Theodor Reik, *Dreißig Jahre mit Sigmund Freud* (Munich: Kindler, 1976), 41.

which for reasons of acceptance in the scientific community at the turn of the century was unavoidable, its methodologically guiding principle was *Sinnverstehen,* that is, the interpretative understanding of psychic dispositions. Similarly to his great contemporaries Max Weber and Edmund Husserl, Freud regarded the decoding of processes of meaning to be the key to knowledge. For that reason he took as his starting point the dream, understood as a meaningful psychic disposition (*sinnvolles psychisches Gebilde*)[9] of which certain symptoms can be picked out. Strictly speaking, it was the seeming meaninglessness of the manifest contents of dreams (*manifester Trauminhalt*) that pressed Freud to search for their hidden quality of meaning. Freud always looked upon psychoanalysis as an "art of interpretation" (*Deutungskunst*)[10] that tried to "understand" the meaning of the psychic ambivalence of closure and disclosure, of covering and uncovering. A causal explanation of psychic life was not the goal, but rather the constitution of meaning as a process of communication between the analysand and the analyst. Accordingly, Freud did not write a book called *The Explanation of Dreams,* but instead wrote one with the title *The Interpretation of Dreams.* Philosophical criticism of psychoanalysis has repeatedly mistaken this point. Even a first-rate philosopher such as Karl Jaspers, who himself had come to philosophy from the field of psychopathology, misjudged the methodical principle of psychoanalysis. In his 1950 essay "Die Forderung der Wissenschaftlichkeit," Jaspers claimed that psychoanalysis is based on "kausalem Erklären" and not on "Sinnverstehen,"[11] which is a complete misinterpretation of the specific character of the psychoanalytical procedure. The significance of Freud's approach is, however, precisely the overcoming of the mechanistic nineteenth-century psychology, in which all psychic phenomena are explained by physiological causes. Thus, it is characteristic that in his writings Freud never used, for example, the term *hormone,* which, after all, had existed since 1902.[12] Radically resisting the materialism of the Helmholtz school (which he himself had passed through), he replaced the biochemical method of treatment of symptoms by a hermeneutic asking for the meaning-contexts of pyschic disorder. By searching behind the symptoms to the genesis of symptoms (*Symp-*

---

9. Freud, *GW,* 2/3:1.
10. "Jenseits des Lustprinzips," in *Das Ich und das Es: Metapsychologische Schriften* (Frankfurt: Fischer Taschenbuch 1992), 203.
11. "Sinnverstehen vollzieht sich in Gegenseitigkeit der Kommunikation, Kausalität ist sinnfremd." Karl Jaspers, *Vernunft und Widervernunft in unserer Zeit* (Munich: Piper, 1950), 18.
12. William Maddock Bayliss and Ernest Henry Starling, "The Chemical Regulation of the Secretory Process," *Proceedings of the Royal Society of London* ser. A, 73 (1904): 310–22.

tomgenese) and, finally, to the biography of the patient, he gradually uncoupled psychology from physiology.

We must imagine this process of uncoupling, not as an unproblematic or easy one, but rather as one conditioned by a good many internal and external obstacles to be overcome. The fact that Freud had the strength to overcome all those obstacles, the hostility of the Victorian-bourgeois environment, the dismissal of his ideas by the scientific establishment, and last but not least his own fears of the results of self-analysis—all that is attributable to an enormous will for knowledge (*Erkenntniswille*).

Remembrance of the Forgotten as the Anamnetic Principle of Investigation

In the language of Eric Voegelin we can say that psychoanalysis does not construct "causal connections" (*Kausalzusammenhänge*) but rather tries to understand "connections of symptoms" (*Symptomzusammenhänge*).[13] Symptoms are then to be regarded as formations of meaning that can be decoded by further inquiry into the biographical and cultural-historical contexts of their emergence. Freud is a genetic thinker; his method is "through and through historical."[14] In searching for displaced and repressed life-historical and cultural-historical origins, Freud's analysis does not essentially differ from other hermeneutic approaches of the time. His interpretation of the "texts" of the unconscious proceeds in a similar way as, for instance, Heidegger's interpretation of philosophical texts. In both cases the aim is to trace out the "unsaid" (*Ungesagte*) beyond the "said" (*Gesagte*), the "absent" (*Abwesende*) beyond the "presence" (*Anwesenheit*) of the text, and to save the forgotten from oblivion.[15] Both Freud and Heidegger strove for the remembrance of the forgotten, or, as the latter says, for the "Entbergung des Sich-Verbergenden."[16] Of course, there are still important differences between the anamnetic approach of psychoanalysis and that of *Daseinsanalyse,* but even so the basic attitude of interpretation as

---

13. Cf. Gilbert Weiss, *Theorie, Relevanz, und Wahrheit: Eine Rekonstruktion des Briefwechsels zwischen Eric Voegelin und Alfred Schütz (1938–1959)* (Munich: Wilhelm Fink, 2000), 158 f.
14. Jacob Taubes, "Psychoanalyse und Philosophie," in *Vom Kult zur Kultur: Bausteine zu einer Kritik der historischen Vernunft* (Munich: Wilhelm Fink, 1996), 360.
15. Martin Heidegger, *Was ist Metaphysik* (Frankfurt: Vittorio Klostermànn, 1943), 12.
16. See, for instance, *Einführung in die Metaphysik* (Tübingen: Niemeyer, 1953), 15 f., and *Was ist Metaphysik,* particularly the "Einleitung."

an act of uncovering (*Enthüllung*) shows significant parallels. In this connection, it is also worthwhile to consider Eric Voegelin's *Anamnesis*. In the *Vorwort* (1966), he describes his conception of the anamnetic process:

> A philosophy of order is the process through which we find the order of our existence as human beings in the order of consciousness. Plato has let this philosophy be dominated by the symbol of "Anamnesis," remembrance. Remembered, however, will be what has been forgotten; and we remember the forgotten—sometimes with considerable travail—because it should not remain forgotten. The culpably forgotten will be brought to the presence of knowledge through remembrance, and in the tension to knowledge oblivion reveals itself as the state of non-knowledge, of the *agnoia* of the soul in the Platonic sense. Knowledge and non-knowledge are states of existential order and disorder. What has been forgotten, however, can be remembered only because it is a knowledge in the mode of oblivion that through its presence in oblivion arouses the existential unrest that will urge toward its raising into the mode of knowledge. Oblivion and knowledge are modes of consciousness of which the first can be raised into the second through remembrance. Remembering is the activity of consciousness by which the forgotten, i.e., the latent knowledge in consciousness, is raised from unconsciousness into the presence of consciousness. In the *Enneads* (4.3, 30), Plotinus has described this action as the transition from non-articulate thinking to articulate thinking that perceives itself. Through an act of perceiving attention (*antilepsis*), the non-articulated knowledge (*noema*) is transformed into conscious knowledge; and this antileptic knowledge then becomes fixed through language (*logos*). Remembrance thus, is the process by which non-articulated (*ameres*) knowledge can be raised into the realm of language-images (*to phantastikon*) so that, through expression in the precise sense of becoming a thing in the external world (*eis to exo*), it will become linguistically articulated presence in consciousness.[17]

To be sure, the realm Voegelin's anamnesis opens differs radically from the contents of knowlegde Freud wants to make accessible. For the moment, however, let us consider solely the basic rhythm of the anamnetic process. In order to distinguish the two conceptions better from each other, I will in the following speak of Anamnesis (for Voegelin) and anamnesis (for Freud).

The goal of the Anamnesis is to "bring the culpably forgotten to the presence of knowledge through remembrance." Exactly the same also applies to Freud's anamnetic procedure. One could even say that Voegelin's sentence is one of the most concise summaries of the psychoanalytical method, especially

---

17. Eric Voegelin, *CW*, vol. 6, *Anamnesis: On the Theory of History and Politics*, trans. M. J. Hanak, ed. David Walsh (Columbia: University of Missouri Press, 2002), 36–37.

because it includes the aspect of guilt, which is of great importance for Freud. The problem of guilt in Freud will occupy us further below.

Following Voegelin's text, the next essential element is that oblivion is a "state of non-knowledge" that can only be realized in the "tension to knowledge." Hence, there has to exist a knowledge before we can speak of a non-knowledge. The next step is interesting: the forgotten is itself a knowledge, namely, one "in the mode of oblivion that through its presence in oblivion arouses an existential unrest." The forgotten, the absent, is still present in its absence; otherwise there would not be a problem. That this is a perfect description of what happens in the psychoanalytical anamnesis is instantly evident when we put in the Freudian terms (although, since the meaning remains the same, such changes are not even necessary): the *repressed* instead of the forgotten, the *unconscious* instead of knowledge in the mode of oblivion, *consciousness* instead of knowledge, and *neurosis* instead of the existential unrest.

Even more significant are the terminological equivalences in the following sentences: "Oblivion and knowledge are modes of consciousness of which the first can be raised into the second through remembrance." And further: "Remembering designates the activity of consciousness by which the forgotten, i.e., the latent knowledge in consciousness, is raised from unconsciousness into the presence of consciousness." In Freudian language this statement would be rendered famously: "Where the id ('it') was, there shall become ego" (*wo Es war, soll Ich werden*). The similarities between Freud and Voegelin are indeed significant, and they are not only linguistic—unconsciousness, latent knowledge, the metaphorics of raising—but also can be found in the categorial structure. Let us take, for instance, Voegelin's description of oblivion and knowledge as "modes of consciousness." For Freud, also, the unconscious is not a hinterworld; however it may be natured, it is not a something that hides itself *beyond* consciousness, but rather it is a mode of consciousness itself, a way consciousness *is*. That is why one can speak, as Freud does, of an *unconscious consciousness* or, as Voegelin does, of a consciousness in the mode of oblivion. This leads to a non sequitur only if we are not willing to take the step from the mechanistic idea of the unconscious as a dark world behind consciousness or even as a second consciousness toward the unconscious as a "mode of being" (*Seinsmodus*) of consciousness itself.

Voegelin's text draws the following conclusion: "Remembrance, thus, is the process by which non-articulated ... knowledge can be raised into the realm of language-images ... so that, through expression in the precise sense of becoming a thing in the external world ..., it will become linguistically articulated presence in consciousness." Nothing other happens in psychoanalysis.

All essential elements of the Freudian anamnesis are given by Voegelin, up to the necessity of the linguistic externalization of the forgotten or repressed. As we know, Freud's crucial progress in developing his therapeutic approach was the step from hypnosis to narration, that is, to the narrative method. In his studies on hysteria he realized that through hypnosis the hysteric symptoms disappear only temporarily. But in order really to dissolve them, the remembrance of the traumatizing event and its communication to the therapist are required. The patient has to *understand* why he has been repressing the traumatizing event, because the momentary ecstasy through hypnosis is not enough. And he can only understand by remembering and by linguistically articulating the remembered to the therapist. That is the only way that the forgotten can be brought to the presence of consciousness, the only way that the symptoms disappear. Remembrance (*Er-Innerung*) and linguistic externalization (*Ent-Äußerung*) are bound to each other in the Freudian anamnesis as well as in Voegelin's Anamnesis. The methodical rhythm is the same in both cases.

The foregoing remarks were solely intended to point to procedural parallels between Voegelin and Freud. The philosophical fundamentals of their approaches are of course quite different. Voegelin's *symptomatology* is based on the differentiation between knowledge and oblivion as conditions of "existential order and disorder." The criterion is not psychopathological, as in Freud, but *pneumopathological*. The state of oblivion represents, not a psychic illness in the narrow sense, but a *disease of spirit*. When consciousness falls back on the shadow plays of the cave, then its spiritual structure is eclipsed and man loses the center of his reality.

The clinical picture of neurosis that Freud describes and the Voegelinian diagnosis of a state of existential disorder have no more in common than the therapeutic necessity of anamnetic retrospection into the forgotten. They do differ from each other not only with regard to the evaluation of the diseased state but also concerning the sources and the therapeutic conclusions of the "illness." Whereas for Voegelin the essence of human nature lies in the noetic-pneumatic openness toward the transcendental ground of being, Freud looks upon man as a caveman with no chance of ever leaving the cave. Man is caught in the darkness of the cave. There is no way out. The darkness of human existence is characterized by boundless urges, fear, aggression, and destruction. Although there is some sort of reason that tries to maintain order in the jungle of instincts, it only "succeeds" to the degree that is necessary for man to survive. Its power of illumination is small. Like a flashlight, it provides only a minimum of light that perhaps lights up the corridors of the cave but never has the luminous power to show the way out of the cave. The man we encounter in Freud's writings is similar to the Hobbesian one, a creature caught in his own instincts. At best, he can tame his inborn disposition to evil but he can never overcome it. The cause of his suffering does not, as in Voegelin, lie in a deformation of human nature but rather in human nature itself. As a consequence, the dividing lines between pathology and normality, illness and sanity, become effaced. This is why a statement such as the following will come as no surprise:

> By demonstrating the part played by perverse impulses in the formation of symptoms in the psychoneurosis, we have quite remarkably increased the number of people who might be regarded as perverts. It is not only that neurotics in themselves constitute a very numerous class, but it must also be considered that an unbroken chain bridges the gap between the neuroses in all their manifestations and normality.... The conclusion now presents itself to us that there is indeed something innate lying behind the perversions but that it is something innate in everyone, though as a disposition it may vary in its intensity and may be increased by the influences of actual life.[18]

There is no doubt that Freud succeeds in de-demonizing mental illness; but, on the other hand, he does so by demonizing human nature. Ultimately his proclaimed goal—where the id was, there shall become ego—reveals itself as an illusion, a tragic illusion. The carnal forces of the unconscious are too powerful to be mastered by consciousness. The ratio is too weak to overcome man's inborn deficiencies, that is to say, the animal-like urges. All that can be achieved, under analysis, is a brief flickering of light in the everlasting darkness. The anamnetic process, after all, brings, not a real healing of the natural-born illness of man, but only a short-term soothing of his worst pain. Human nature remains imprisoned in the misery of its immanent existence. It is "groundless," in the sense of Voegelinian pneumopathology. Why this is so, will be shown in the final part of this paper.

Man and History in Freud: Eschatology or Anti-Eschatology?

As noted above, over the years Freud turned more and more from the clinical-therapeutic realm to the questions of culture, society, and history. The climax of this development is represented by his last work, *Moses and Monotheism.* It came out in 1939, one year after his emigration to London and just a few months before his death. Since 1913 he had been working on this book.

---

18. Freud, "Three Essays on Sexuality," in *The Standard Edition of the Complete Psychological Works of Sigmund Freud,* vol. 7 (London: Hogarth Press, 1953), 171.

It is not only his last book, but also his philosophical testimony. Nowhere else did he reach a similar philosophical depth.

Moses is, as is true of almost all the books of Freud, first of all a provocation. In this case, it results from the historical thesis that serves as the springboard of his argument. In summary his thesis says: Moses was not Jewish, but an Egyptian; he lived as a noble and high-ranking man at the court of Akhenaton (1375–1358 B.C.) who, originally, had been born as Amenothep VI and who subsequently threw off the official religion of his predecessor, the Amon-cult, and institutionalized with the sun-god of Aton the first monotheistic religion in the expanding Egyptian empire.[19] Akhenaton's reign, however, did not last long. Shortly after his death, the monotheistic religion was again abolished and former cults were re-established. Moses was a convinced adherent of the monotheistic Aton religion and refused to accept its abolition. Thus, he decided to realize his ideals in another people and to found a new realm with them. These people were the Jews. He introduced them to the Aton religion, left Egypt with them, made them holy by the mark of circumcision, and gave them laws. One day, the Jews, who "were headstrong and unruly towards their law-giver and leader, rose against him, killed him, and threw off the religion of the Aton which had been imposed on them, just as the Egyptians had thrown it off earlier."[20] Later they united with closely related tribes in the region between Palestine, the Sinai Peninsula, and Arabia; and under the influence of the Arabian Midianites, they took on a new religion, the worship of the volcano god Yahweh. Then they came to Canaan. Between the murder of Moses and the foundation of the new Midianitic religion, presumably fifty to sixty years elapsed. In this "latent period," the violent crime had been "repressed," but with the foundation of the Yahweh religion, the "great liberator Moses" was remembered again. They wanted to preserve this remembrance within the new religion along with the liberation from Egypt. Thus the Mosaic leadership—but not, of course, the later crime—was integrated into the Jewish historiography. Beyond that, substantial elements of monotheism and particularly the external mark of Mosaic religion, circumcision, were maintained.[21]

Thus went Freud's Moses thesis. There is not much to say about it beyond

---

19. In *The Political Religions* (1938), Voegelin, by the way, called Akhenaton "the first great religious individuality in world history." In *CW*, vol. 5, *Modernity without Restraint*, ed. Manfred Henningsen (Columbia: University of Missouri Press, 2000), 38.

20. "Moses and Monotheism," in *The Standard Edition of the Complete Psychological Works of Sigmund Freud*, vol. 23 (London: Hogarth Press, 1964), 60.

21. Cf. also Jan Assmann, *Moses the Egyptian: The Memory of Egypt in Western Monotheism* (Cambridge: Harvard University Press, 1997); René Girard, *Things Hidden since the Foundation of the World* (Stanford: University Press, 1987), 65.

the obvious fact that it is not historically tenable. This, however, is not decisive. As Jacob Taubes put it, the Freudian cultural-historical analysis is not founded on this thesis of Moses being an Egyptian, although it does use it as a support.[22] On the other hand, one cannot simply say that the "Egyptian Moses" is of no relevance for further analysis, as Taubes does in his reading of Freud. Freud's turning Moses into an Egyptian does indeed say something fundamental about his cultural-historical position in general and his relation with Judaism in particular: the genealogy of the people Israel whom Freud is calling into question by his Egyptianizing of Moses is, needless to say, his own people. For him, this genealogy, not least because of his bitter experiences of anti-Semitism, implies a danger of being excluded from European civilization. Since he considers Old Egypt to be the origin of European civilization, he by all means wants to show that his own roots as a Jew are Egyptian. As a consequence, he has to deny the convenant between God and the People Israel. it was not God who chose the Jews as His people, it was the man Moses, a human being, and not even a Jew. In a letter to Ernest Jones dating from 1939, Freud explicitly calls his Moses thesis a deliberate "denial of the Jewish-national myth" (*Sagengeschichte*).[23] His fear of being excluded from European/Egyptian civilization drove him into a genuine Egyptomania that found absurd expression in his huge collection of Egyptian symbols and statuettes, the so-called "Freudiana."

In recent years, many articles and books have been written about Freud's *Moses* and his Judaism. *Moses* has become a fashionable topic, as Peter Gay put it. Some authors, such as Y. H. Yerushalmi, in his most remarkable book *Freud's Moses: Judaism Terminable and Interminable,* have seen in Freud's late interest in Moses a return of psychoanalysis to the religious tradition. Others have been scandalized at his effort to dissociate himself from Judaism. And again others have considered Moses to be Freud's "*Ichideal*" and his work on the book as a "day-dream."[24] In one way or another all of these interpretations can claim some plausibility. Nevertheless, none of them gets the vital point of the Moses book. Its importance does not lie in Freud's attitude toward Judaism or Moses as a person, whatever this attitude may be, but rather in the fact that it is the most pronounced formulation of his cultural-historical and eschatological

---

22. Jacob Taubes, *Die politische Theologie des Paulus* (Munich: Wilhelm Fink, 1993), 123.
23. Sigmund Freud to Ernest Jones, in *The Complete Correspondence of S. Freud and E. Jones, 1908–1939* (Cambridge: Harvard University Press, 1993), 2:101.
24. Peter Gay, "Freud verstehen: Zu einem Essay von Ilse Grubrich-Simitis," *Psyche* 47 (1993): 973–83; P. Gay, *Freud: Eine Biographie für unsere Zeit* (Frankfurt: S. Fischer, 1989), 726 ff.; Ilse Grubrich-Simitis, *Freuds Moses-Studie als Tagtraum: Ein biographischer Essay* (Frankfurt: Fischer Taschenbuch, 1994).

perspective. In order to understand the essential feature of this perspective it is necessary to go beyond the provocative Moses thesis that has captivated so many interpreters. In doing so, I am following Jacob Taubes, whose reading of Freud, in my opinion, is far more illuminating than that of most psychoanalytic interpreters. Finally, we should remember the advice of Walter Benjamin, namely, that the late Freud had developed "his greatest ideas" more or less "in passing by" (*im Vorbeigehen*).[25]

At the core of *Moses and Monotheism* we find a profound discussion of the problem of guilt. This is anything but new in Freud. Since his early days he had been dealing with the question of repression and remembrance of guilt. But now he raised it in a more direct way than ever before by asking the question Is there hope of redemption from guilt, either actually or potentially? Can man ever free himself from the bondage of guilt? Freud's answer is definite: no, there is no liberation, no escape, not even a reconciliation through atonement. All that can be achieved is an acknowledgment of guilt, which is not much for the emancipatory hopes of modern man. Freud is a representative of so-called tragic humanism, for which not only is any hope of liberation illusionary but on the whole so is hope for the future. The future can only repeat the past, perhaps on a more conscious level, but in principle history is an everlasting recurrence of the same. Man cannot break this circular course of history, least of all by the imaginative construction of an "end of history."

In *Moses,* Freud adopted guilt as the universal category of history. In this way religion plays an important role in the genealogy of guilt. In his opinion, religion is not so much a matter of tradition in the sense of a *conscious* technique, as it is a matter of a memory of the *unconscious* psychic life or, to put it in a more spiritual way, a memory of the *seelischen Altertümer* of human history. In the words of Yerushalmi, the genealogical force of religion lies "in the recurrence of the repressed, in the activation of the unconscious reminiscences of real events of the distant past."[26] For Freud, all history is preceded by the prehistorical tragedy of the original crime: the murder of the primal father, the repentance, and the constitution of the brother-clan. From the very beginning, this original guilt as the primordial event casts a shadow over the historical process, a shadow that can never be shaken off. Human society is founded on the "primal father tragedy" in the forgotten prehistory. This prehistorical tragedy fatefully recurs in history, and it also does so in the assassination of

---

25. Walter Benjamin, *Gesammelte Schriften,* vol. 6, *Werkausgabe* (Frankfurt: Suhrkamp, 1980), 953.

26. Yosef Hayim Yerushalmi, *Freuds Moses: Endliches un unendliches Judentum* (Berlin: Wagenbuch, 1992), 58. (The translation back into English is my own.—G. W.)

Moses by the Jews: "Fate had brought the great deed and misdeed of primeval days, the killing of the father, closer to the Jewish people by causing them to repeat it on the person of Moses, an outstanding father-figure."[27]

With the murder of Moses there emerges a consciousness of guilt that as a constituent of the religious memory forces an incessant recurrence of the repressed crime, not only in the father-religion of Judaism but in the son-religion of Christianity as well. At this point, Saint Paul enters the Freudian scene and becomes the man Freud is most interested in. It is Saint Paul "in whose spirit the realization first emerged: 'the reason we are so unhappy is that we have killed God the father.'" For Freud, Saint Paul was "a man of an innately religious disposition: the dark traces of the past lurked in his mind, ready to break through into its more conscious regions." It was he who seized upon the Jewish consciousness of guilt fixed on the predominant father and "traced it back correctly to its original source."[28]

> He called this the "original sin;" it was a crime against God and could only be atoned for by death. With the original sin death came into the world. In fact this crime deserving death had been the murder of the primal father who was later deified. But the murder was not remembered: instead of it there was a phantasy of its atonement, and for that reason this phantasy could be hailed as a message of redemption (*evangelium*). A son of God had allowed himself to be killed without guilt and had thus taken on himself the guilt of all men. It had to be a son, since it had been the murder of a father."[29]

In order to elucidate the religion-historical dimension of the relation to the father, Freud is operating with analogies between neurotic dispositions and religious events, that is, he is transferring symptoms from the history of the individual to the history of civilization. Accordingly, the basic situation is that of the Oedipus complex: the son has a murderously ambivalent stand against the father. He feels guilty and gets more deeply involved in guilt through the dead father, who has an even more powerful effect on the son than the living one whom he wanted to kill:

> The ambivalence that dominates the relation to the father was clearly shown, however, in the final outcome of the religious novelty. Ostensibly aimed at propitiating the father god, it ended in his being dethroned and got rid of. Judaism had been a religion of the father; Christianity became a religion of the son. The old God the Father fell back behind Christ; Christ, the Son, took his place, just as

---

27. Freud, S., *Standard Edition*, 23:89.
28. Ibid., 135, 87, 86.
29. Ibid., 86.

every son had hoped to do in primeval times. Paul, who carried Judaism on, also destroyed it. No doubt he owed his success in the first instance to the fact that, through the idea of the redeemer, he exorcized humanity's sense of guilt; but he owed it as well to the circumstance that he abandoned the "chosen" character of his people and its visible mark—circumcision—so that the new religion could be a universal one, embracing all men.[30]

In integrating an implicit confession of guilt into the message of redemption, Saint Paul is establishing—through the idea of the original sin—a remarkable connection with the tragedy of primordial history. Although for him the confession is of secondary importance to the idea of redemption, the original guilt and the tragic starting point of human history become constitutionally anchored:

> Original sin and redemption by the sacrifice of a victim became the foundation stones of the new religion founded by Paul.... After the Christian doctrine had burst the framework of Judaism, it took up components from many other sources, renounced a number of characteristics of pure monotheism and adapted itself in many details to the rituals of the other Mediterranean peoples. It was as though Egypt was taking vengeance once more on the heirs of Akhenaton. It is worth noticing how the new religion dealt with the ancient ambivalence in the relation to the father. Its main content was, it is true, reconciliation with God the Father, atonement for the crime committed against him; but the other side of the emotional relation showed itself in the fact that the son, who had taken the atonement on himself, became a God himself beside the father and, actually, in place of the father. Christianity, having arisen out of a father-religion, became a son-religion. It has not escaped the fate of having to get rid of the father.[31]

No doubt, for Freud, the Pauline idea of redemption is an illusion. Basing itself upon atonement, the son-religion also blocks remembrance and thus remains caught in the trauma of the primordial crime and its endless recurrence in the historical spiral of guilt and atonement. That is why Christianity cannot escape the elimination of the father either. The eschatological doctrine of salvation by way of atonement only enlarges man's pain because guilt can never be atoned. It can only be admitted. This is the only chance of healing man's pain. It is important to point out: *healing*, not salvation. That means a soothing of pain, a therapeutic making-bearable of the tragic *conditio humana*, and nothing more. The eschatological idea of ultimate, transcendent, as well as immanent,

30. Ibid., 87 f.
31. Ibid., 136.

liberation is, however, an illusion. Man remains unredeemed. The way out of the cave is, and will always be, blocked.

To be sure, it is easy to criticize Freud's analytical approach to the monotheistic father- and son-religion. He has no sensibility for the pneumatic force of revelation. He is unable to understand religious experiences as *existential* experiences, for example, in the classical sense of *helkein* and *kinein*, not to mention that his linking of the individual with civilization is based on rather dubious phylogenetic speculations. Nevertheless, the crucial point of interest here is the eschatological perspective provided by Freud. With regard to the latter, the conclusion is that he does not present an innerworldly ersatzreligion; he is not a gnostic prophet, no secular *Religionsstifter*. As his correspondent Arnold Zweig once lapidarily said, he simply had not discovered *Zarathustra* but the psychoanalytic method.[32] Freud's conception of history is directed toward the past, not to the future. Not hope but guilt is the universal category. In contrast to his pamphlet on religion of 1927, in which he still spoke of the *Future of an Illusion,* in *Moses* he makes clear that the future in the sense of a progressive transformation of the past is itself an illusion.[33] There is no escape from the oppressive guilt of the past, least of all a revolutionary one. Marxism and every other chiliasm are as much illusionary projects as are the religious hopes of salvation. For Freud, the *paradise lost* is the tragic condition that cannot be overcome, neither today nor tomorrow. The therapeutic optimum that can be achieved through the anamnetic act is a temporary relief of pain through the acknowledgment of the constitutional guilt.

Résumé: Tragic Humanism, Thanatocracy, and Surrealism

As did many of his contemporaries, Sigmund Freud hoped to discover the *real reality*. And, as with many of his contemporaries, he did *not* discover it; on the contrary, reality became even more cloaked. True, the *naturale Weltwirklichkeit* came again to light behind the speculative *Vernunftwirklichkeit* of German Idealism. But at what price? What was claimed to be the real reality—in Marx, Comte, Schopenhauer, and Nietzsche as well as in Freud—turned out to be a dramatically reduced sphere of human existence: the domain of the carnal, the instinctive, the *libidines,* in the classical sense.

---

32. See Sigmund Freud and Arnold Zweig, *Briefwechsel,* ed. E. L. Freud (Frankfurt: Fischer Taschenbuch, 1984), 85.
33. Freud once called this pamphlet "his worst book." See Ronald W. Clark, *Sigmund Freud* (Frankfurt: Fischer Taschenbuch, 1981), 530.

What separated Freud from other voyagers of discovery such as Marx and Comte is that he did not replace the religious-transcendental message of redemption with a worldly immanent idea of pseudo-redemption. For Freud, man is not only unredeemed, but unredeemable. He did not construct an immanent message of salvation; indeed his theory is substantially anti-eschatological. As a representative of tragic humanism in its most radical form, he looks upon man as a miserable creature with no chance of being redeemed. It seems that Freud cannot be classified as a Gnostic in Voegelin's terms, since at least one criterion of Voegelin's category of Gnosticism is absent, namely, an immanentistic-eschatological element.

This, however, cannot be the final conclusion of a reading of Freud, because although the term *tragic humanism* refers to a certain image of man, it does not say much about the political and social consequences of that image—except that they are probably not similar to those of Marxism or Comtean progressivism. If Freud's anti-eschatological conception does not lead to progressivism, socialism, or another chiliasm, where does it then lead? What does the fateful impossibility of liberation from guilt mean for the social and political order of a society? Can man live without hope? Moreover, can he do so in a peaceful community with others? Is such a hopeless life worth living at all?

We find the answer in Freud himself: such a limited existence is not worth living; strictly speaking, it is only worth *dying*. To put it somewhat oversubtly, man is not a living being but a dying being. Accordingly, the organizing and structuring principle of human existence is not the "life urge" but the "death urge." This becomes most clear in Freud's essay from 1920, "Jenseits des Lustprinzips," which represents a turning point in his theoretical development. From this essay onward, the basic idea of analysis has changed from the "pleasure principle" to the "Nirvana principle," from the sexual urge to the death urge: "The goal of all life is death. . . . The lifeless was there before the living." Furthermore: "The roundabout ways to death . . . represent the phenomena of life, today. If the conservative nature of the urges is to be accepted"—and according to Freud it has to be accepted—"then one cannot come to another presumption concerning the origin and the goal of life."[34]

The meaning of human life, in spite of a large number of "diversions," is the approaching of death. Consequently, the "whole life of urges serves for the attainment of death."[35] Even the sexual urges, formerly introduced as original life urges, now become integrated into the death urges, which are also called

---

34. "Jenseits des Lustprinzips," in *Das Ich und das Es: Metapsychologische Schriften* (Frankfurt: Fischer Taschenbuch, 1992), 223 f.

35. Ibid., 224.

"satellites of death." There is no way but to "believe" in death.[36] Freud solves the puzzle of life by letting it disappear behind the ubiquity of death. The human beings he is talking about are no longer living souls but walking corpses. The world they are "living" in is a realm of the dead, a thanatocracy ruled by the demons of death.

Now, the cave in which the Freudian man is placed without any chance of ever leaving gains a more concrete form. It reveals itself as an Egyptian burial chamber, as a mystical residence for mummies. Freud, the Egyptian, the Egyptomaniac, following the jackal-headed god of the dead, Anubis, adopts the art of embalming as the highest art. The picture takes shape: the burial chamber is the place to which he had been drawn from the very beginning, the place where he had been hoping to find the "psychic relicts of the past." Already as a teenager he felt like being surrounded by an "Egyptian darkness."[37]

Freud's method of anamnetic recovery of the origins of man and mankind is a large-scale attempt to transform the cave into a burial chamber and man into a mummy, a colossal funeral ceremony, unprecedented in modernity. Thus was it said in *Moses*: "It was as though Egypt was taking vengeance on the heirs of Akhenaton." Indeed, Freud appears as avenger who is ascending from the Egyptian darkness to call the escaped and illuminated reason back into the tomb, who is trying to undo Moses' experience of the burning bush and the pneumatic opening of the human soul.

In order to sketch the social and political consequences of this universal mummification, it might be helpful to do so in a somewhat figurative way by taking a short look at the avant-garde movement of the twentieth century that more than any other movement of art has given symbolic expression to the Freudian realm of the dead, namely, surrealism. Let us, for instance, look at the mysterious paintings of Giorgio de Chirico with their timeless buildings, dark vaults, portals, arcades, statues. Appolinaire once characterized de Chirico's work as a sort of "dream writing." This dream writing, with its architectural and perspective of playfulness, produces the impression of loneliness, immobility, and torpidity. On de Chirico's squares, plunged in gloomy clair-obscure, we meet, not human beings, but beings of which we know not whether they are super- or subhuman, beings without faces leaning toward each other in secret meetings and performing obscure gestures. With regard to these images, Patrick Waldberg has spoken of "walking ghosts," "jointed dolls,"

---

36. See also "Zeitgemäßes über Krieg und Tod" (1915), in *Das Unbehagen in der Kultur: Und andere kulturtheoretische Schriften* (Frankfurt: Fischer Taschenbuch, 1994), 151.

37. Sigmund Freud, *Jugendbriefe an Eduard Silberstein, 1871–1881*, ed. W. Boehlich (Frankfurt: Fischer Taschenbuch, 1989), 45.

and "phantoms."[38] In the buildings, in these strange and timeless villas with their black apertures and facades, no human existence ever seems possible. What we find are statues and silhouettes living in their own shadows. These statues, with their threatening and long shadows, seem like mummies that have just emerged from their sepulchres. One of de Chirico's dream descriptions says:

> I am standing on a square of great metaphysical beauty now... on the one side, one can see arcades, above them—rooms with closed Venetian blinds and majestic balconies. On the horizon I perceive hills with villa. The sky is clear, white-washed through a thunderstorm; at the same time I notice that the sun is sinking because the houses and the few passers-by cast long shadows upon the square.... [T]he villas are white and somehow ceremonious; in front of the black curtain of the sky, they look like sepulchres.[39]

De Chirico's mysterious pictures are scenarios for the realm of the dead. There is a peculiar threat coming from his burial chamber–like villa and from the shadow-casting mummies who are their inhabitants. This threat is difficult to describe. It is similar to the threat produced by the death cult of communism. Think of the Lenin mausoleum, for instance. Its symbolic monstrosity lies in the exercise of power beyond death. The threat continues even if the threatener has already died. Moreover, only through the physical death of the threatener and his mummification it gains a special "religious" power. With the Lenin mausoleum we probably have the twentieth-century prototype of the installation of death as an absorbing instrument of power.

This totality of death, its extensive domination over life, is the defining characteristic of thanatocracy. Its power is based on a paradoxical principle: on the one hand, it declares death to be the overall principle of life; on the other hand, in order to be able to do so, it must make the dead appear as living. Processes of decay and putrification must give the impression of life. That is why the act of mummification is necessary. It helps to transform life into death and death into life. As a consequence, we cannot differentiate any more between living beings and dead ones. We are rather dealing with "un-deads." The statue-like figures in de Chirico's pictures are such un-deads who neutralize all differences between life and death.

In the *Surrealistic Papillons,* a coproduction of the group surrounding Breton, the following interrogative sentence is to be found: "*Is Surrealism the genius of*

---

38. P. Waldberg, "Die Entstehung de Metaphysik: Giorgio de Chirico," in *Der Surrealismus,* ed. R. Lebel, M. Sanouillet, and P. Waldberg (Cologne: Taschen, 1987), 8–33.

39. Giorgio de Chirico, "Erfolglos kämpfe ich: Eine Traumerzählung," in *Surrealismus in Paris, 1919–1939* (Leipzig: Reclam, 1990), 151. (The translation into English is my own.—G. W.)

communism?"⁴⁰ We could answer: yes, and psychoanalysis is the genius of surrealism. Freud is the *rêveur définitif* in Breton's sense. This, needless to say, does not mean that the Freudian pychoanalysis, surrealism, and communism shall be lumped together. In this essay, I have tried to show how eschatologically different, for instance, psychoanalysis and Marxism are. What all three of these movements, nevertheless, have in common is a more or less strongly pronounced aesthetics of thanatocracy. Let us listen to the surrealists again: "L'amour morte va embellir le peuple." This is the epigram of the death cult—in Freud as well as in the surrealistic staging of death and in the communist veneration of Lenin; unsurprisingly, it is found in the poem "Exquisite Corpses."⁴¹ Since love is the strongest force to overcome death, it is only logical that it has to be declared dead. When love is dead, then the triumph of the thanatocrats is absolute.

Freud is not a gnostic agitator like Marx or Comte. But he ends up where they do, in a *pneumopathological* vacuum where everything is possible. True, Freud does not construct a world-immanent message of redemption, but this does not alter the fact that he deprives man of the ground of his being. How shall man be able to stand this? Does the anti-eschatological tragic humanism not necessarily end up in a death ecstasy, be it a symbolic one like that of the surrealists, or a real totalitarian ecstasy that was so bitterly experienced during the twentieth century? The man who has been deprived of his ground has no *reason/ground* not to kill either: "Absorbed by the everlasting night and thrown to the other end of the cave," he ends up where "wild affinities [are] gnawn with nothingness, covered with murders."⁴²

Sigmund Freud, Viennese, Egyptian, genius of surrealism: if modernity were put in the dock, as required by Leszek Kolakowski,⁴³ Freud perhaps would not be convicted of gnostic agitation, but neither would he go unpunished.

---

40. De Chirico, "Surrealistische Papillons," ibid., 212.
41. De Chirico, "Erlesene Leichen," ibid., 210.
42. Tristan Tzara, "Annäherung an den Menschen," ibid., 386. (The translation into English is my own.—G. W.)
43. Leszek Kolakowski, *Die Moderne auf der Anklagebank* (Zurich: Manesse, 1991).

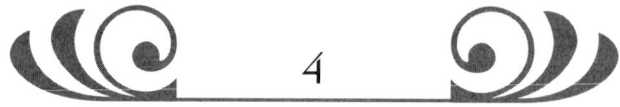

4

Eric Voegelin's Defense of Human Dignity

Glenn Hughes

Current political debate is permeated by references to a human dignity that is universal and inalienable. The term *dignity* is meant to convey a distinctive worth or value—specifically, the value of being a rational, free, and morally self-governing creature. All human beings are declared to be equal in their basic dignity, and so equal in their possession of certain fundamental rights and in their deserving of a range of political and legal protections. The Universal Declaration of Human Rights, adopted by the United Nations in 1948 partly in response to the systematized horrors of Nazi Germany, contains the most well-known political articulation of this idea: "Recognition of the inherent dignity and of the equal and inalienable rights of all members of the human family is the foundation of freedom, justice and peace in the world.... All human beings are born free and equal in dignity and rights. They are endowed with reason and conscience and should act towards one another in a spirit of brotherhood" (preamble, article 1).

In the half century since the Universal Declaration was written, references to this idea of innate human dignity have become ubiquitous in political debate, journalism, and everyday discourse. But there is little popular questioning and understanding of its origins. Just as one can protest the fact of one's free will with little grasp of what freedom ontologically is or what it morally implies, so one can insist upon an inherent and universal human dignity without any clear understanding of what it actually consists of and what its foundations must be. If we wish to credit the concept of human dignity pervading contemporary public discourse, we will want to have some understanding of its experiential and historical origins.

The most important modern source is the philosophy of Immanuel Kant. Kant ascribes *dignity* to human existence on the basis of "moral personality"—that is, on the freedom of a rational being to make moral law. The universality of such law morally binds the person who wills it, explains Kant, so that exercise of this capacity constitutes *moral autonomy,* or subjection to self-made law. It is this autonomy, grounded in rational freedom and regulated by conscience, he declares, that gives each person an intrinsic dignity, the term *dignity* denoting a value "infinitely above all price." A thing can be said to have a *price,* he writes, "if any substitute or equivalent can be found for it," but it has *dignity* only "if it admits of no equivalent." A rational being that can make moral law is of priceless and irreplaceable value, of "unconditional and incomparable worth," and should never be treated merely as a means to some end, because such a rational will constitutes an "end in itself." The law-making capacity of each human being, therefore, is due an appropriate "reverence."[1]

We should note Kant's use of the word *reverence.* It is suggestive of the two intertwining Western traditions that underlie and nourish his idea of dignity (although Kant's idea is distinctively modern, particularly in its emphasis on human autonomy). The first of these is the biblical tradition that has issued into Christian teaching, both Catholic and Protestant, on the dignity and sanctity of the human person as made "in the image of God," that is, as reflecting divine being insofar as a person is free, moral, and loving. The second tradition flows from Greek philosophy, with its conception of the human as a rational being, a being whose reason (*nous*) consists in participation in the divine Reason (*Nous*) that orders and governs the cosmos, making humans capable of both the rational apprehension of reality and the moral ordering of self and society.[2] Both of these traditions present an understanding of the human being as *imago Dei*—as manifesting a likeness to the divine through *participation* in the transcendent divine nature. Insofar as the created person in the Christian sense properly exercises her capacities for responsible freedom, reasoned self-governance, and love, she is attuned to and carries out God's will. Insofar as

---

1. Immanuel Kant, *Groundwork of the Metaphysic of Morals,* trans. H. J Paton (New York: Harper & Row, Harper Torchbook edition, 1964), 36, 102–3, 106–7.
2. On the Greek philosophical discovery of "reason" (*nous*) as constituting humanity through the human psyche's participation in divine *Nous,* see Eric Voegelin, "Reason: The Classic Experience," in Voegelin, *The Collected Works of Eric Voegelin* (hereinafter, *CW*), vol. 12, *Published Essays, 1966–1985,* ed. Ellis Sandoz (1990; available Columbia: University of Missouri Press, 1999), 265–91.

human *nous* orients personal existence through right action and wise contemplation, it concretely enacts the ordering wisdom of transcendent divine *Nous*. Human dignity is the value of the presence of the divine "form" of being in human consciousness.[3]

The Western conception of human dignity thus originated as, and remains, an inescapably spiritual conception, and the equality of human dignity is perforce a spiritual equality. Respect for human dignity, therefore, cannot be separated from a kind of reverence: the "unconditional and incomparable" worth of a person is his or her transparency for participation in the transcendent value of the divine nature. Any denial of the sacral quality of human existence, of the "mysterious principle" of divine presence at its core, would therefore constitute, however unintentionally, a repudiation of the foundations of the modern principles of equal human dignity and universal human rights.[4]

These observations suggest two further facts. A first is that there is something of a metaphysical paradox involved in a person's successful realization of dignity through reasoned judgment and responsible action. If dignity lies in exercising the rational freedom of moral autonomy, this is done precisely to the degree that freedom successfully attunes itself with the divine reason and love that is present to consciousness as its inspiration and ground. Rational *freedom*

---

3. On the biblical sources and meaning of the symbol of *imago Dei*, together with discussions of how that meaning was affected by the incorporation of Greek philosophy into Christian theology, Kant's view of dignity in this context, and political implications, see Robert P. Kraynak, "'Made in the Image of God': The Christian View of Human Dignity and Political Order," in *In Defense of Human Dignity: Essays for Our Times*, ed. Robert P. Kraynak and Glenn Tinder (Notre Dame: University of Notre Dame Press, 2003), 81–118. Kant's view does constitute in some respects an important break with earlier Western conceptions of human dignity. Distinctively modern is the way in which Kant isolates human autonomy, sharpening the representation of individual will as the ground of its own law separate from God, and grounding dignity and its rights exclusively in the individual's freedom and capacity to reason. From a traditional Christian perspective, this raises a concern both about an eclipse of the divine reality that bestows human freedom and about the dignity of those persons incapable of the significant exercise of reason. On Kant's idea of human dignity, see in the same volume Susan M. Shell, "Kant on Human Dignity," 53–80; for an evaluative comparison between the biblical (and medieval) view of human dignity, on the one hand, and the "Kantian-Christian" view, on the other, see Kraynak, "'Made in the Image of God,'" 107–15.

4. Gabriel Marcel, *The Existential Background of Human Dignity* (Cambridge, MA: Harvard University Press, 1963), 128: "To my mind, there can be no question of challenging the legitimate value of [Kant's] interpretation [of human dignity].... [Yet it] is my own profound belief that we cannot succeed in preserving the mysterious principle at the heart of human dignity unless we succeed in making explicit the properly sacral quality peculiar to it."

consists, paradoxically, in *obedience* to the divine ground made manifest in conscience.[5]

A second fact is that fulfilling one's dignity through actually developing habits of reasonableness and loving action is not that common an achievement. A distinction must be made, therefore, between dignity as a given, innate capacity of rational and spiritual consciousness—what might be called *elemental dignity*—and the dignity that consists in the realization of this capacity insofar as one actually *is* reasonable, responsible, and loving—what might be called *achieved dignity*. With this distinction in mind, we can understand how dignity in one sense may be viewed as innate and inalienable, while in another sense it may be regarded as something one can "win" or "lose." *Elemental dignity* is the divine presence in consciousness that establishes the aptitude for rational and loving thought and action, a presence that may be undeveloped, beleaguered, distorted, or abused, but still is always due reverence as an elemental "image of God." *Achieved dignity* is the enacted, performative "image of God," the dynamic fulfillment of the capacity for rational and loving freedom. Bearing this distinction in mind helps us to remember how it is that, whereas our free and rational capacities can be squandered and degraded, our elemental dignity as persons is inviolable and can never be taken away even by ourselves, consisting as it does in the gift of transcendent divine presence in consciousness.

Among twentieth-century philosophers, Eric Voegelin is one of the strongest defenders of this truth concerning human dignity. True, his writings include no extended analysis of the concept of dignity per se, no essay or chapter on the topic, and the word scarcely appears in the thirty-odd published indexes of the *Collected Works*. But important passages make clear Voegelin's commitment to the truth of human dignity as founded in the reality of humanity as *imago Dei*. These passages, together with appreciation of the centrality to Voegelin's work of a theory of consciousness at the core of which is a theoretical clarification of human consciousness as a participation in divine transcendence, encourage us to see his philosophy—indeed his life's work—as serving the recognition and protection of those truths upon which Western concepts of innate human dignity and universal rights are based. This facet of his work

---

5. This paradox helps to explain another, pertaining to personal identity. As a person, I become my distinctive self only through a "becoming one with" the divine absolute. Through uniting my intention with that of the divine absolute, my own self emerges with an absolutely individual identity. Paradoxically, then, to be a member of the human species is to be unique, one of a kind. Cf. Emmanuel Lévinas, "The Rights of Man and the Rights of the Other," in Lévinas, *Outside the Subject* (Stanford, CA: Stanford University Press, 1993), 117–18.

is well worth explicating, and by tracing a sequence of fundamental Voegelin themes it will be possible to delineate the distinctive features of Voegelin's defense of human dignity in a way that suggests its unusual power and scope. Such is the aim of the present essay, which begins with a look at Voegelin's affirmation of the notion of *imago Dei* and proceeds by considering pertinent aspects of his reflections on the obligation of the philosopher, on human consciousness as human-divine participation, on open versus closed existence, and on the value of philosophy as lamentation and witness.

Voegelin and Imago Dei

On the infrequent occasions in his writings when Voegelin focuses explicitly on the concept of dignity, he is emphatic about its core meaning: the distinctive dignity of human existence pertains to the fact that human consciousness shares in the divine form of existence. "The specific dignity of man," he writes, "is based... on his nature as *theomorphic,* as in the form and in the image of God."[6] In the proper functioning of human reason, moral self-determination, and love, conscious existence is transparent for the divine transcendence that grounds existence. This understanding of the human, Voegelin explains repeatedly in his writings, is central both to the Platonic-Aristotelian philosophical tradition and to the Christian vision of existence. The life of reason as understood by the philosophers is the effective presence of divine *Nous* in the ordering of existence; and the life of Christian existence is the effective presence in consciousness of the God revealed through Jesus and the prophets. The life of reason and the life of the spirit are the two means, the two modes, in the Western tradition, of human nature reaching its proper fulfillment or actualization; and not only should they be understood to be complementary, Voegelin explains, but should be regarded as functionally equivalent: "The practice of philosophy in the Socratic-Platonic sense is the equivalent of the Christian sanctification of man; it is the growth of the image of God in man."[7]

Still, Voegelin asserts, the Greek "theomorphic" understanding of the human is not equal to the Christian vision with respect to the degree of its differentiated insight into the character of divine transcendence. The Christian vision advances beyond the Platonic-Aristotelian field of conception, Voegelin states, in its recognition of the absolutely free, absolutely creative, and absolutely

---

6. Eric Voegelin, *CW,* vol. 31, *Hitler and the Germans,* trans. and ed. Detlev Clemens and Brendan Purcell (Columbia: University of Missouri Press, 1999), 87 (emphasis added).
7. Eric Voegelin, "On Hegel: A Study in Sorcery," in *CW,* 12:223.

loving nature of divine reality.⁸ The Christian vision liberates divine reality from all intrinsic and necessary association with pre-existing matter or limitations of "nature" and so liberates the idea of the human essence—of the divine "form" in human consciousness—from all value-determinations associated with natural structures, qualities, talents, or dispositions. Thus it is only the Christian vision of *imago Dei* that establishes the absolute spiritual equality of all human beings. This, writes Voegelin, is a unique achievement of Christianity: the recognition not just that "man is man insofar as he is *imago Dei*" but also that "insofar as he is *imago Dei* are all men *equal* as participating in the reality of God and thus united with God." Centered on the "experience of an extraordinary divine irruption in the existence of Jesus" and on the exegesis of the meaning of that experience as the climax of a "millennial process of revelation," Christianity taught the radical anthropological truth that later became foundational for Western political thought, that of "the equal spiritual dignity of all men."⁹

Voegelin's embrace of the concept of human being as *imago Dei* may be traced to the beginning of his career. William Petropulos has detailed this fact in his account of the influence of Augustine and Max Scheler on Voegelin's early work. And Voegelin's earliest writings on the subject already show him emphasizing the experiential origins of this concept, as he explains that its critical validation lies in an "opening of the soul," in personal meditation, to a "border experience" of the revelation of transcendent reality.¹⁰ Throughout his career Voegelin continued to insist that only in one's own meditative experiences—in acts of self-discovery that reveal one's consciousness to be a transaction of divine presence and human response—can one verify the substantial truth of the *imago Dei* symbolization. Voegelin repeatedly declared to his readers that such meditative acts are essential to a philosopher's development, since without them the classical Greek and Christian anthropological insights would remain unclear and, more than likely, unconvincing. Without such experiences, and consequent sensitivity to transcendence as "the decisive problem of philosophy," thinkers of influence can easily misunderstand and misrepresent

---

8. Eric Voegelin, *CW*, vol. 17, *The Ecumenic Age*, vol. IV of *Order and History*, ed. Michael Franz (Columbia: University of Missouri Press, 2000), 314–16.

9. Voegelin, *CW*, 31:205 (emphasis added); Eric Voegelin, "The Gospel and Culture," in *CW*, 12:192, 196, 198; "Siger de Brabant," in Voegelin, *CW*, vol. 20, *The Middle Ages to Aquinas*, vol. II of *History of Political Ideas*, ed. Peter von Sivers (Columbia: University of Missouri Press, 1997), 192.

10. William Petropulos, "The Person as *Imago Dei*: Augustine and Max Scheler in Eric Voegelin's *Herrschaftslehre* and *Political Religions*," in *The Politics of the Soul: Eric Voegelin on Religious Experience*, ed. Glenn Hughes (Lanham, MD: Rowman & Littlefield, 1999), 87–114.

the essential character of human existence, particularly in the direction of imagining a purely "immanentist" human nature.[11] So we can readily understand why, as Petropulos states, the themes of "meditation as the basic form of philosophizing, and the person as *imago Dei,* remain of fundamental importance throughout Voegelin's philosophical career."[12]

Voegelin is again emphatic on what happens when the awareness of humankind as *imago Dei* ceases to be effective in personal and social life, whether through inability to grasp its meaning or through a deliberate closing off from the divine. The result is a defection from the truth of human existence as participation in God, and "[this] defection at its core always takes the form of a loss of dignity." To obscure the divine presence in rational and moral consciousness is to debase and degrade the very idea of the human. "The loss of dignity comes about through the denial of the participation in the divine, that is, through the dedivinizing of man ... [and one] cannot dedivinize oneself without dehumanizing oneself—with all the consequences of dehumanization."[13] During the last century, the consequences of this denial of human participation in the divine has extended, most notoriously, to the embrace of immanentist political ideologies leading to policies that have systematically denied to entire groups of peoples—specified ethnicities, "races," nationalities, and economic or social classes—the most basic rights, including the right to be alive. (A comment of Leon Trotsky's is illuminating: "We must put an end once and for all," he wrote, "to the papist-Quaker babble about the sanctity of human life."[14]) The political disasters and barbarisms flowing from twentieth-century ideological mass movements such as National Socialism and Soviet Marxism-Leninism, movements to which Voegelin's work constitutes a monumental retort, are intimately connected with the problem of the eclipse of reverence for the human being as existing "in the form and in the image of God."

---

11. Voegelin describes the problem of transcendence as "the decisive problem of philosophy" in a letter of September 17, 1943, to his friend and colleague Alfred Schütz, in which he also describes as the principal task of the philosophical historian "to penetrate every historical spiritual position to its own point of rest, i.e., to where it is deeply rooted in the experiences of transcendence of the thinker in question. Only when the history of spirit is carried on with this methodological aim can it attain to its philosophical aim, which is to understand the spirit in its historicity or, formulated in another way, to understand the historical forms of the spirit as variations on the theme of experience of transcendence." The letter appears in Peter Emberley and Barry Cooper, trans. and eds., *Faith and Political Philosophy: The Correspondence between Leo Strauss and Eric Voegelin, 1934–1964* (University Park, PA: Pennsylvania State University Press, 1993), 19–34 (29–30, 34).

12. Petropulos, "The Person as *Imago Dei,*" 109.

13. Voegelin, *CW,* 31:87.

14. Quoted in Martin Amis, *Koba the Dread: Laughter and the Twenty Million* (New York: Talk Miramax Books, 2002), 35.

To make this sort of connection apparent, Voegelin states, is part of the duty of a philosopher. A genuine philosopher has the obligation to recognize social disorder and corruption for what it is, to diagnose its causes as far as possible, and to suggest remedial perspectives and insights. Philosophy is always a struggle for true understanding and right order through exposure of the evils and false opinions of society. In this struggle, however, a motivating concern always remains the state of the philosopher's own soul, which cannot help but resonate with the disordering tendencies of the times. "Society can destroy a man's soul because the disorder of society is a disease in the psyche of its members," Voegelin writes. Successful resistance to disorder begins, therefore, with understanding how one's own consciousness manifests contemporary forms of "the tension between existence in truth and the deficient modes of existence."[15] Voegelin was led to the meditative recognition of his own participation in divine transcendence, he makes clear, as part of his effort to resist his own dehumanization under the pressures of forces in his social and political world. His articulation of insights diagnosing the connection between the eclipse of *imago Dei* and forces of degradation had roots in his desire to protect his own dignity.

If one is a child of one's times, however, how does one rise to an existential orientation that allows genuine diagnostic insights into ills of one's own society? It is only possible, Voegelin explains, by virtue of the growth of one's soul through productive encounter with the best of tradition. In opening oneself to the classics, to the most profound that has been thought and said, one encounters through their various articulations the experiences and insights that have founded philosophical and spiritual wisdom. The effective enlargement of one's own horizon through such encounters enables one gradually to advance in critical discernment of the conditions of personal and social order. And this growth is, again, a philosopher's obligation, for an example of which Voegelin could point to his own constant willingness to be educated by the authority of wisdom:

> The study of the classics is the principal instrument of self-education; and if one studies them with loving care... one all of a sudden discovers that one's understanding of a great work increases (and also one's ability to communicate such understanding) for the good reason that the student has increased through the process of study—and that after all is the purpose of the enterprise. (At least it is my purpose in spending the time of my life in the study of prophets, philosophers, and saints.).... The basis of historical interpretation is the identity

---

15. Eric Voegelin, *CW*, vol. 16, *Plato and Aristotle*, vol. III of *Order and History*, ed. Dante Germino (Columbia: University of Missouri Press, 2000), 123–24; "Immortality: Experience and Symbol," in *CW*, 12:66.

of substance (the psyche) in the object and the subject of interpretation; and its purpose is participation in the great dialogue that goes through the centuries among men about their nature and destiny. And participation is impossible without growth in stature (within the personal limitations) toward the rank of the best; and that growth is impossible unless one recognizes authority and surrenders to it.[16]

The vision and understanding of the human as *imago Dei*, and a sensitivity for what its loss has meant for contemporary theory and politics, is available to anyone capable of undergoing the tutelage of culture that, as V. I. Ivanov remarks (in phrasing much like Voegelin's), "is not only monumental but *initiatory* in character, enabling the servants of memory—which is indeed the ruler of all culture—to renew their forebears' experience."[17]

Open and Closed Existence

Voegelin's philosophical growth made clear to him both the extent to which modern thought and political ideology were deficient and destructive through eclipse of the truth of humanity as *imago Dei*, and that his own corrective philosophy of existence would require a sophisticated rearticulation of that truth. Thus his mature work is centered upon a detailed theoretical analysis of human consciousness in its structure as a participation in the divine presence that grounds and transcends the perceivable universe. The "participatory illumination" of human consciousness, he explains, is a gift of luminous self-presence and disclosure of meaning structured by the desire to know; and the divine reality that is the ultimate concern of that desire is always immediately present to consciousness as its ground, inspiration, ordering force, and deepest identity.[18] Human consciousness is thus, in its very constitution, a process of human-divine encounter. It does not have the being of a merely world-immanent thing. It exists, as it were, "in-between" worldly reality and nonspatial, nontemporal divine presence.

Voegelin's adoption of Plato's term *metaxy*, or "in-between," as a stabilizing symbol for his philosophy of existence is meant to keep permanently in view

---

16. From Voegelin's letter of August 22, 1956, to his friend and colleague Robert B. Heilman, in *Robert B. Heilman and Eric Voegelin: A Friendship in Letters, 1944–1984*, ed. Charles R. Embry (Columbia: University of Missouri Press, 2004), 157.

17. V. I. Ivanov and M. O. Gershenzon, *Correspondence across a Room*, trans. Lisa Sergio (Marlboro, VT: Marlboro Press, 1984), 27.

18. Eric Voegelin, *CW*, vol. 18, *In Search of Order*, vol. V of *Order and History*, ed. Ellis Sandoz (Columbia: University of Missouri Press, 2000), 30; "Reason," 265–73.

the truth that a human being exists "in the form and in the image of God," not in the manner of some sort of extrinsic reflection of the divine, but rather through immediate participation and responsive communion. The *metaxy* of consciousness is neither the finite realm of things nor the unconditioned being of divine transcendence, but the non-imaginable "locus" of their co-presence, "the meeting ground of the human and the divine in a consciousness of their distinction and interpenetration." Moved in its questioning by the illumination of meaning that is always already divine presence, and structured by the unrestricted scope and rational norms of questioning, human consciousness consists, ontologically, in its relationship to the fullness of divine meaning in which it participates: "Man's consciousness *is* the reality of tension toward the divine ground of his existence." A person's fulfillment lies, consequently, in fidelity to this relationship. How is this fidelity realized? Through rational and loving thought and action. Innately, a person is already *imago Dei* through the divine presence in consciousness that makes possible such thought and action. This is a person's elemental dignity. But through existentially enacted reason and love, "man *actualizes* his potential to partake of the divine," and so rises to the substantiated freedom, the achieved dignity, of "the *imago Dei* which it is his destiny to be."[19]

Every person is faced with the basic existential choice of either striving to be faithful to the normative directional tension of consciousness, in openness toward the divinely transcendent ground of existence, or avoiding this effort of fidelity and turning away from the divine ground. Adapting Henri Bergson's language of the "open soul" and the "closed soul" (*l'âme ouverte* and *l'âme close*), Voegelin repeatedly analyzes consciousness in terms of "the virtues of openness toward the ground of being" and "the vices of infolding closure," and portrays the impacts of both of these on self and society.[20] Among the virtues of openness Voegelin includes the life of reason properly understood. He explains that human reason can only be realistic in its pursuit of personal

---

19. Voegelin, "On Hegel," 233; "Immortality," 72; "The German University and the Order of German Society: A Reconsideration of the Nazi Era," in Voegelin, *CW*, 12:7 (emphasis added). On the unrestricted scope of human questioning and its intrinsic orientation toward the divine ultimacy that grounds it, see Bernard Lonergan, *Insight: A Study of Human Understanding*, vol. 3 of *The Collected Works of Bernard Lonergan*, ed. Frederick E. Crowe and Robert M. Doran (Toronto: University of Toronto Press, 1992), 372–75, 555–58, 569–70, 659–62.

20. Eric Voegelin, "Equivalences of Experience and Symbolization in History," in *CW*, 12:119. For Bergson's description of the "open soul" and the "closed soul," see Henri Bergson, *The Two Sources of Morality and Religion*, trans. R. Ashley Audra and Cloudesley Brereton, with the assistance of W. Horsfall Carter (Garden City, NY: Doubleday, Anchor Books edition, 1954), 37–39, 52–66.

and political goods if it unfolds with the freedom that comes from acknowledging its own dynamic orientation to an unrestricted and transcendent good. If reason resists the meaningfulness of its own pull toward its divine ground, it will not reason well about the human situation in reality, about human happiness, about the range of values, their pursuit and achievement. Human reason, in other words, cannot effectively be itself unless it is oriented and directed by love for the divine Reason that is its own most fundamental identity. If reason in its dynamic core "is existential *philia* [love], if it is the openness of existence raised to consciousness, then the closure of existence, or any obstruction to openness, will affect the rational structure of the psyche adversely."[21] The achieved dignity of the open soul is indeed located, as Kant emphasized, in the rational exercise of freedom; what Voegelin makes clear is that this exercise will be warped or misguided, to some extent, unless it is nourished by an awareness of itself as a gift of participation in transcendent reason and freedom.

Open existence is difficult to maintain. As a response to the appeal of a transcendent ground of meaning, the open soul must suffer the vicissitudes of faith: of affirming that its own meaning depends upon an intangible, unpossessable, essentially mysterious reality. The difficulties of faith—not faith as a fideistic assent to doctrinal propositions, nor certainly as a fundamentalist or absolutist assumption of the certitude of God's favor, but as an existential faith of loving openness to the divine mystery encountered in illumined conscience and gracious persuasion—are notoriously daunting. Basic to faith is the uncertainty involved in understanding that we cannot understand, in any substantive way, the answers to our most searching questions: why we exist, what our performances in life add up to, the direction of historical process, the mystery of evil and of its longed-for resolution. Also basic to it is anxious awareness of the fragility of genuine commitment, of how easily forgetfulness and self-delusion enter into the effort of openness, and of the unendingness of the task, as long as we remain alive, of recovering and reestablishing our existential orientation through love of transcendent reality. While the dignity of existence only flourishes through the open soul's responsive bond with transcendent meaning, "[this] bond is tenuous, indeed, and it may snap easily," writes Voegelin.

---

21. Voegelin, "Reason," 274. One of the diagnostic terms for the posture of closing oneself off to the normative directionality of one's reason is *stupidity*. See Voegelin, *CW*, 31:89: "Stupidity shall mean here that a man, because of his loss of reality, is not in a position to rightly orient his action in the world, in which he lives. So when the central organ for guiding his action, his theomorphic nature and openness toward reason and spirit, has ceased functioning, then man will act stupidly."

The life of the soul in openness toward God, the waiting, the periods of aridity and dullness, guilt and despondency, contrition and repentance, forsakenness and hope against hope, the silent stirrings of love and grace, trembling on the verge of a certainty that if gained is loss—the very lightness of this fabric may prove too heavy a burden for men who lust for massively possessive experience.[22]

Above all, the difficulty of openness is remaining open to the unpossessable transcendence of transcendence.

For transcendence, although in a sense it can be said to be experienced as the divine presence in the "in-between" of consciousness, is through that same experience disclosed also to be, in its ultimacy, a mystery "beyond" all human experience. *Transcendence* as a symbol expresses the "directional character" of the tension of questioning; and that which we are ultimately directed toward, in the searching and growth of consciousness, is a divine self-sufficiency or perfection that radically transcends all that we can experience or know of it. Ontologically, we experience transcendence as "the Beyond of consciousness which constitutes consciousness by reaching into it," a reality that "incomprehensibly lies beyond all that we experience of it in participation." Epistemologically, we know the ground itself only as "an impenetrable mystery even if it receives the names of *Nous* or God." The challenge of existential openness is to continually long for and grow into fuller participation in a reality beyond anything consciousness could ever experience or understand—a challenge that, as the great religions and wisdom traditions have declared, can only be met through the responding guidance of love. Divine transcendence constitutes, as Voegelin states, a permanent appeal "to which man can lovingly respond or not so lovingly deny himself."[23]

A refusal of loving openness toward transcendence—a refusal to let *amor Dei,* in the Augustinian sense, become the soul's compass and balance—is truly a denial of one's *self.* For a person *is* participation in divine freedom and knowledge—a person is *imago Dei.* The closure of consciousness to its own substantiating ground is the rejection by a person of his or her own personhood,

---

22. Eric Voegelin, *The New Science of Politics,* in *CW,* vol. 5, *Modernity without Restraint: The Political Religions; The New Science of Politics; and Science, Politics, and Gnosticism,* ed. Manfred Henningsen (Columbia: University of Missouri Press, 2000), 187–88.

23. Voegelin, "The Gospel and Culture," 188; "What Is Political Reality?" in Voegelin, *CW,* vol. 6, *Anamnesis: On the Theory of History and Politics,* trans. M. J. Hanak, ed. David Walsh (Columbia: University of Missouri Press, 2002), 396; "Anxiety and Reason," in Voegelin, *CW,* vol. 28, *What Is History? and Other Late Unpublished Writings,* ed. Thomas A. Hollweck and Paul Caringella (1990; available Columbia: University of Missouri Press, 1999), 89, 105; "Remembrance of Things Past," in *CW,* 12:312.

which consists in human-divine relationship. "The denial... of transcending toward divine being destroys the *imago Dei*," Voegelin writes, meaning that a person can "reject his own identity" as *imago Dei* and in doing so "deform his humanity."[24] Closed existence is personal deformation, resulting from the frightened, or despairing, or lazy, or rebellious refusal on the part of consciousness to orient itself on the basis of its innate awareness of its own divine ground and through the cultural legacy that explores the meaning of human-divine relationship.

Closed existence diminishes the psyche, Voegelin asserts, through its chosen posture of imperviousness to divine presence. He describes it as a "contraction" that reduces consciousness "to a self imprisoned in its selfhood," a denial by the soul of its own constitutive depth, resulting in self-excommunication from the divine ground—a "sealing of the spirit by reflection," in V. I. Ivanov's words, "into the solitary cell of individual personality." And from such acts of existential closure there emerge into public discourse deformed images of what a human being is—images that, when accepted and internalized, undermine human dignity by eclipsing its basis in transcendence, by distorting the search for meaning, and by disrupting the sense of human solidarity. Images of the human that publicly replace the participatory *imago Dei* with images of a completely world-immanent or "absolute Self" are not harmless, because from them flow ambitions, decisions, actions, habits, and policies. Dehumanized self-interpretation issues into dehumanizing behavior. As Gabriel Marcel has stated: "Man depends, to a very great degree, on the idea he has of himself and... this idea cannot be degraded without at the same time degrading man."[25]

The deformation of closed existence, Voegelin explains, leads nowhere. The rejection by the self of the divine ground of the self—not as a matter of the avowal or disavowal of concepts, but as a process of existential refusal of attunement and responsive growth—leaves it without convincing and consoling foundation and without rationally persuasive or fulfilling direction. Because consciousness *is* the encounter between immanence and transcendence, any attempt by consciousness to establish its own meaning and value solely on some material basis, or on some world process or dynamism, or on its own knowledge and will, creates a vacuum of substance and purpose at the center of the self, a vacuum typically sensed, Voegelin states, in anxious apprehensions that the existential project has become nothing more than "a confused stirring

---

24. Voegelin, *CW*, 31:263; "The Gospel and Culture," 175; Eric Voegelin, "The Eclipse of Reality," in Voegelin, *CW*, 28:137.

25. Voegelin, "Eclipse of Reality," 111; Ivanov and Gershenzon, *Conversations,* 44; Gabriel Marcel, *Man against Mass Society,* trans. G. S. Fraser (South Bend, IN: Gateway Editions, 1978), 20.

about in the nothingness of abandoned reality." The greatest clarity about this truth has emerged, he insists, in the Christian tradition. "The insight that man in his mere humanity, without the *fides caritate formata* [faith formed by love], is demonic nothingness has been brought by Christianity to the ultimate border of clarity."[26]

And the demonic nothingness of "mere humanity" has revealed itself spectacularly in the political madnesses and intellectual nihilisms of the twentieth century. Analyzing the modern West in light of the realities of open and closed existence, Voegelin explicates the ripening of Western modernity as showing all too clearly the deforming effects of a growing closure toward divine transcendence and an accompanying absolutization of the Self. The centuries of modernity, he relates, have been increasingly dominated by worldviews and ideologies of a reductively "immanentist" character that portray the whole of reality as a world process with no transcendent ground of meaning, with human beings imagined as purely immanent, self-contained entities within that process. The severe irony of modernity, of course, is that it has been the staggering successes of scientific and historical knowledge, together with an intensifying appreciation of human psychological interiority, that have contributed most to a widespread eclipse of the truth of the divinely grounded cosmos. Western modernity has been an astonishing story of technological advance and economic productivity, expansive historical discovery and scholarship, and widening promotion of social and political ideals based on recognition of human liberty as the principle of progress—and at the same time it has produced frenetic aimlessness, irreverent consumption, and totalitarian ambitions propelled by loss of contact with the divine truth and goodness that grounds reality. Drained of an orienting and humbling awareness of the divine measure of action and truth, unable to confront mystery, and charged with the aggressive assurance of its own ultimate value, modernity may be credited, Voegelin writes, with "having unified mankind into a global madhouse bursting with stupendous vitality."[27]

The modern West is the era of the Universal Declaration of Human Rights, and it is likewise the era of Hitler and Stalin and Mao, whose explicit contempt of ideas of the sanctity of human life and of universal human rights and obligations issued into the century's most expansive nightmares of inhumanity and barbarism. The ideas of respect for moral personality, of universal human dignity, and of shared humanity can all too obviously remain ineffective if there is no grounding vision, existentially formative to a sufficiently widespread

---

26. Voegelin, "What Is Political Reality?" 386; *New Science of Politics,* 151.
27. Voegelin, "Immortality," 55.

degree, of the sacral value of the human as a participant in a truth of transcendent being and value. Voegelin's philosophical critique of his own time is driven by his careful and persistent distinction between the formative wisdom in the traditions of Western culture that have given rise to the stable Western democracies and their defense of human dignity and liberties, on the one hand, and the deformative ideas and images of immanentist philosophies and ideologies that have resulted in enforced systems of human degradation unparalleled in their extent and instrumental efficiency, on the other. And he is impeccably clear about the way in which closed existence, with its dreams of absolute Selves in full control of meaning, has fed the forces of deformation. "The deformation of which I am speaking," he writes,

> is the fateful shift in Western society from existence in openness toward the cosmos to existence in the mode of closure against, and denial of, its reality. As the process gains momentum, the symbols of open existence—God, man, the divine origin of the cosmos, and the divine Logos permeating its order—lose the vitality of their truth and are eclipsed by the imagery of a self-creative, self-realizing, self-expressing, self-ordering, and self-saving ego that is thrown into, and confronted with, an immanently closed world.[28]

Closed selves invent the closed world, which, as the imaginary setting of human action, eclipses the transcendent foundation of human dignity and so makes plausible ideologies reliant upon mass dehumanization.

Lamentation and Witness

A contemporary philosopher or anyone else committed to open existence, however, is in no position to condemn the temptations and deformations of existential closure as something in which he or she has no part. Existential *openness* and *closure* do not describe fixed and mutually exclusive postures but rather indicate opposite "ideal types" that help to illuminate a complex field of psychological energies. The terms name what Voegelin would call "poles" or "indices" of a permanent tension of existence. In every person the "flux of existence," he writes, "[has] the structure of a tension between truth and deformation of reality. Not the possession of his humanity but the concern about its full realization is the lot of man." One always remains to some degree shaped by and complicit in the deformative forces of one's society and culture, just as one remains subject to the perennial self-deformations of human bias or sin.

---

28. Eric Voegelin, "On Henry James's *Turn of the Screw*," in *CW*, 12:151.

The virtues of openness toward the ground of being, of thought and action guided by sound reason and genuine love, are, even for the saints and much less for the rest of us, only a partial and precarious accomplishment. To some significant extent one always remains turned away from, unfaithful to, the divine reality that constitutes consciousness by reaching into it. Openness consists in a recurrent struggle to withdraw from that estrangement, a "permanent effort at responsive openness to the appeal of reality."[29]

The dignity that human beings possess, then, is always the dignity of the imperfect and wayfaring creature. Human consciousness has no other existence than that between formation and deformation, morality and immorality, reason and unreason, love and self-excommunication, divine plenitude and demonic nothingness. Voegelin would agree with John Witte, Jr.'s comment that in each person sanctity is blended to some degree with degradation, and that "[a] theory of human dignity that fails to take into account the combined depravity and sanctity of the human person is theologically and politically deficient, if not dangerous."[30] We can understand, and therefore accurately diagnose, the furthest excesses of dehumanizing behavior because the forces of evil live in us, too, however well contained they may be through habits of reason and love. The purpose of such diagnosis, and of every effort at right order, is to bring the *elemental* dignity of our mixed state as far as possible to an *achieved* dignity, toward greater fulfillment of our potential as *imago Dei*, through increasing attunement with the divine ground of being, an effort in which we are always only "on the way."

Open existence, then, is still estrangement from a hoped-for deeper attunement, and in speaking truly for itself must recognize and articulate that estrangement. So Voegelin's philosophical work, as an examination of existence in openness toward divine transcendence, contains abundant remembrance of its own origins in the tension between estrangement and belonging, and to the role played by therapeutic hope and love in the rational unfolding of its own historical and philosophical exegeses. Like the philosophies of Plato, Augustine,

---

29. Voegelin, "Equivalences," 119. On the basic and recurrent forms of human bias, see Lonergan, *Insight*, 223–31, 244–67. Voeglin, "Remembrance," 305. Bernard Lonergan makes the same point in explaining that the authenticity of self-transcendence toward the genuinely true and the good "is ever precarious. Of itself, self-transcendence involves tension between the self as transcending and the self as transcended. So human authenticity is never some pure and serene and secure possession. It is ever a withdrawal from inauthenticity, and every successful withdrawal only brings to light the need for still further withdrawals.... So we are bid to watch and pray, to make our way in fear and trembling." Lonergan, *Method in Theology* (New York: Herder and Herder, 1972), 110.

30. John Witte Jr., "Between Sanctity and Depravity: Human Dignity in Protestant Perspective," in *In Defense of Human Dignity,* 130.

and Kierkegaard, that of Voegelin is a prayer on the part of philosophical reason for deepening communion with the mystery of transcendent meaning and value. And as such, it is a type of lament. For a *lament* in the precise sense, as Voegelin points out in a passage on Thomas Mann's *Doctor Faustus,* is a literary genre that expresses at once an awareness of human distance from the divine, a movement of return in taking up one's destiny as *imago Dei,* and a joy in the hope and dignity of return. One could argue that Voegelin's philosophy as a whole is a majestic *lamentatio*—an often sorrowing, frequently celebratory, recovery of language and vision in philosophical return toward the divine ground of meaning, suffused throughout with "the dignity of the hope to be delivered from ... estrangement."[31]

Finally, Voegelin's philosophy offers itself also as an act of witness. Indirectly, it witnesses to Voegelin's defense of his own dignity through living and writing in conscious acknowledgment of his own existence as *imago Dei.* But most important, it stands as an erudite and profound witness to the modes and meanings of existence in truth and existence in untruth, seeking therapeutic effectiveness by "making people aware of the evil" in social and personal life and by "opening the situation up to public discussion." Perhaps to some degree, Voegelin writes, "its persuasion can help to restore the rule of reason." Nothing is predictable in that regard, but at least the truth of human dignity will have been served to the best of the philosopher's ability:

> Nobody can heal the spiritual disorder of an "age." A philosopher can do no more than work himself free from the rubble of idols which ... threatens to cripple and bury him; and he can hope that the example of his effort will be of help to others who find themselves in the same situation and experience the same desire to gain their humanity under God.[32]

---

31. Voegelin, "The German University," 16–18.
32. Ibid., 35; "The Gospel and Culture," 212; "On Hegel," 231–32.

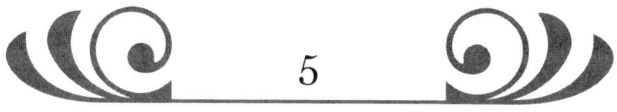

Eric Voegelin and a New Science of Politics

James L. Wiser

In his study of truth and representation, which was published as *The New Science of Politics* in 1952, Eric Voegelin called for a "restored" political science that would be characterized, in part, by its return to a consciousness of principles. In particular he recommended that we seek to "rediscover the rationality of metaphysics in general and philosophical anthropology in particular."[1] In describing what such a rediscovery of rationality would entail, Voegelin specified three elements. First, it would require an adequate understanding of the natural structures of human consciousness. Second, given the temporal character of human existence, it would necessitate the development of an appropriate theory of history. And finally, in order to comprehend the relationship between human order and social order, such a project would include an analysis of those forms of socially relevant irrationality that have emerged throughout history and can be best understood as acts of resistance to the demands of reason itself. In short, Voegelin's project implies much more than what is typically understood to be within the domain of academic political science. As a consequence, his call for a restored political science has produced both confusion and opposition within the discipline. In an effort to address this confusion, I propose to examine Voegelin's understanding of a "renewed" or adequate political science. In doing so, I will focus upon the following:

---

1. Eric Voegelin, *The New Science of Politics* (Chicago: University of Chicago Press, 1952), 23.

1) an analysis of Voegelin's critique of axiomatic or propositional political science;
2) a discussion of Voegelin's appeal to the Classical Greek form of *politike episteme*; and
3) an investigation of his understanding of common sense.

I

Voegelin's best-known criticism of axiomatic or propositional political science is developed within his discussion of positivism in the introduction to his *New Science of Politics*. These arguments are fairly well known and thus do not need to be repeated here. It is important, however, to emphasize the precise nature of his concern. In *The New Science of Politics*, positivism is introduced only as a particular example of a larger intellectual tendency, the roots of which can be traced back to the sixteenth century and whose general principles are operative in such diverse traditions as British empiricism, Cartesian rationalism, and Enlightenment "humanism." Thus in *The New Science of Politics*, Voegelin is not concerned with the specific teachings of such positivists as Henri de Saint-Simon or Auguste Comte[2] but rather with those more general theoretical principles of which positivism is only a particular expression. Positivism is of interest here only inasmuch as it is one example of a more general attempt to realize "the intention of making the social sciences 'scientific' through the use of methods which as closely as possible resemble the methods employed in sciences of the external world."[3]

Voegelin refers to this larger intention as "scientism" and defines it as the doctrine that assumes that the methods of the propositional sciences that investigate the phenomena of the object-world should also serve as the model for all inquiries in general, and for political science in particular.[4] The prob-

---

2. It is interesting to note, however, that when Voegelin does examine the particular teachings of the positivists, he treats them as a total doctrine concerning the nature of God, man, and history. For Voegelin the true importance of positivism becomes apparent only when it is viewed as a comprehensive political theory and not simply as a contribution to the philosophy of science. See his *From Enlightenment to Revolution*, ed. John H. Hallowell (Durham: Duke University Press, 1975), 74–194.

3. Voegelin, *New Science*, 8.

4. A more recent example of scientistic thinking is found in the following statement by David Easton: "In the second place, as part of this [demand for self-conscious attention to empirical theory], the social sciences have been compelled to face up to the theoretical problem of locating stable units of analysis which might possibly play the role in social research that the particles of matter do in the physical sciences." David Easton, *A Framework for Political Analysis* (Englewood Cliffs: Prentice-Hall, 1965), 13.

lem with this doctrine, according to Voegelin, is found in its assumption that political reality is an essentially phenomenal object and thus one that is capable of being understood according to the categories of a propositional or axiomatic science. Voegelin, on the contrary, finds this assumption untenable. Indeed, for him political reality and the tension of consciousness that provides its order "is not a thing about which objective propositions could be formed,"[5] because it is more than simply an external object in the material world. As he writes in *The New Science of Politics:*

> Human society is not merely a fact or an event in the external world to be studied by an observer like a natural phenomenon. Though it has externality as one of its important components, it is as a whole a little world, a cosmion, illuminated with meaning from within by the human beings who continuously create and bear it as the mode and condition of their self-realization.[6]

According to Voegelin an essential aspect of political reality is found in that specific cosmion of meaning that is created by concrete, socially embedded individuals who attempt to ground their existence within the context of their own historical situation. A particular political reality is, among other things, an expression of a specific form of human consciousness. As such, a knowledge of the principles informing that political reality would require an understanding of the sustaining forms of consciousness, and such an understanding, in turn, can only employ those insights that emerge from within the activity of consciousness itself. From Voegelin's perspective, an adequate political science cannot be satisfied with the simple enumeration of objective propositions because the reality it studies transcends the phenomenal order, as such.

II

In his call for a renewed political science, Voegelin repeatedly offers as examples the traditions of Platonic and Aristotelian *politike episteme*. According to his reading, in their approach to political inquiry both Plato and Aristotle understood the prior necessity of developing an adequate theory of human consciousness. In his *Science, Politics, and Gnosticism,* Voegelin described Plato's understanding of scientific political inquiry in a few short paragraphs. Beginning with society's own self-interpretations concerning the principles of a

---

5. Eric Voegelin, *Anamnesis,* trans. Gerhart Niemeyer (Notre Dame: University of Notre Dame Press, 1978), 147.
6. Voegelin, *New Science,* 27.

proper human and social order, Plato sought to pass beyond the realm of image and opinion, which supported such interpretations, and achieve instead a noetic apprehension of the order of Being itself. Of course, each of the various opinions being tested claimed its own intrinsic legitimacy, and the validity of the Platonic challenge presupposed that it was actually possible to gain that noetic insight that would then be capable of validating those subsequent efforts to articulate its meaning. According to Voegelin's interpretation, the eventual validity of Plato's assumption was not established through a prior logical argument. Rather, its correctness was affirmed in the context of an actual event. Thus Voegelin writes:

> And indeed, Platonic-Aristotelian analysis did not in the least begin with speculations about its own possibility, but with the actual insight into being which motivated the analytical process. The decisive event in the establishment of *politike episteme* was the specifically philosophical realization that the levels of being discernible within the world are surmounted by a transcendent source of being and its order. And this insight was itself rooted in the real movements of the human spiritual soul toward divine being experienced as transcendent.[7]

For Voegelin, Platonic *politike episteme* can only be understood in terms of the particular existential event or movement, which Plato experienced as the necessary condition for reason itself. For Plato, reason, or *Nous*, emerged in an act of resistance to disorder. As a response to disorder, it was, at the same time, an articulation of order, inasmuch as it represented the intimation of a noetic coherence beyond the immediacies of time and place. Thus the event of a concrete individual's resistance and response to disorder served to establish the actual criterion of order against which the various opinions about order could then be measured. *Politike episteme* first became possible only when Plato self-consciously engaged in that noetic activity which enabled him to resist the spiritual deformation of his age. To abstract his political principles from their engendering noetic event would not only falsify Plato's teachings, but at the same time obscure the source of their legitimacy. For Plato the principles of political order are an expression of the "clear pattern in the soul"[8] that results from the philosopher's encounter with the Good.

The radical nature of this analysis should be clear. By associating the practice of political science with a particular event in the history of consciousness,

---

7. Eric Voegelin, *Science, Politics, and Gnosticism*, trans. William J. Fitzpatrick (Chicago: Henry Regnery, 1968), 17–18.
8. Plato, *The Republic*, trans. Allan Bloom (New York: Basic Books, 1968), 484c.

Plato establishes the existential prerequisites for any analysis of political order. As Voegelin writes, "Therefore an insight concerning being must *always be really* present."⁹ Without the real presence of such an insight, the political scientist is incapable of achieving that ontological grounding that would allow one to legitimately judge the opinions of others. As the above analysis indicates, however, such an insight is not the logical or necessary result of systematic argumentation. Rather, it is the cognitive and psychological consequence of a particular existential event. In short, for Plato, only the philosopher can actually practice political science, and to be a philosopher is to experience a turning of the human soul away from the realm of appearances and toward that of the transcendent Good.

Much of Voegelin's work has been concerned with an attempt to illuminate the Classical understanding of this turning. To do so, he has written extensively on such symbols as "nous," "ratio," and "metalepsis." Indeed, the secondary literature on Voegelin has focused upon this effort, and thus it is not necessary to repeat his analysis here.¹⁰ Experiencing their own ignorance and drawn by the desire to know the ground of their own Being, individuals seek to encounter that divine presence whose reality is first experienced as the *terminus ad quem* of this search. Participating in both the world and the transcendent, while fully belonging to neither, the open human soul achieves a state of existence-intension in which the very structure of Being itself is revealed.¹¹ This perspective, in turn, is precisely the achievement that allows the philosopher to judge the opinions of others. For Plato, then, *politike episteme* is not the product of a disinterested or universal consciousness-at-large. Rather, it is the political wisdom of one specific form of human consciousness in particular, i.e., the noetic consciousness of the philosopher.

---

9. Voegelin, *Gnosticism*, 17.

10. See, for example, the various essays in Stephen A. McKnight, ed., *Eric Voegelin's Search for Order in History* (Baton Rouge: Louisiana State University Press, 1978), "A Symposium on Eric Voegelin," *Denver Quarterly* 10, no. 3 (Autumn 1975), and Peter Opitz and Gregor Sebba, eds., *The Philosophy of Order: Essays on History, Consciousness, and Politics* (Stuttgart: Klett-Cotta, 1981).

11. Summarizing the "Metaphysical" insight that is gained by achieving existence-intension, Voegelin writes: "Once the fallacies are removed, the hierarchy of being comes into view, not as a number of strata one piled on top of the other, but as movement of reality from the apeirontic depth up to man, through as many levels of the hierarchy as can be discerned empirically, and as the countermovement of creative organization from the divine height down, with the Metaxy of man's consciousness as the site where the movement of the Whole becomes luminous for its eschatological direction." Eric Voegelin, *The Collected Works of Eric Voegelin*, vol. 17, *The Ecumenic Age*, ed. Michael Franz (1974; Columbia: University of Missouri Press, 2000), 409.

III

Although most commentators have focused on Voegelin's appropriation of the Classical Greek form of *politike episteme*, it is, nonetheless, important to realize that Voegelin himself has offered a second possibility for the renewal of political inquiry. Specifically, in his essay "What Is Political Reality?" Voegelin refers to the insights of common sense as providing the essential "propositions" for a true political science. Common sense, in turn, "must be understood in the sense of the Scottish School, especially of Thomas Reid."[12]

Voegelin's attempt to specify the precise tradition of common sense philosophy that he had in mind was necessary inasmuch as the term itself has acquired a variety of meanings that do not serve Voegelin's purpose. For example, within the Enlightenment tradition the term connoted a basic and elemental response to immediate empirical evidence. On one hand, persons of common sense were those who relied upon the information of their senses rather than upon the authority and prejudices of a particular historical—especially theological—tradition. At the same time, such individuals were also portrayed as being characterized by a certain naïveté and simplicity. Thus Voltaire wrote: "'That a man has no common sense' is a coarse insult. 'That man has common sense,' is an insult too; it suggests that he isn't exactly stupid, and that he lacks what is called wit."[13]

Following in the tradition of both Cicero and Reid, however, Voegelin does not intend such a meaning. Indeed for him "common sense ... does not connote a social deadweight of vulgar ideas, nor any *idées reçues* or 'relatively natural world view,' but rather it is the habit of judgment and conduct of a man formed by *ratio*."[14]

It is possible to more fully develop Voegelin's understanding of common sense by referring directly to the work of Thomas Reid. In his *An Inquiry into the Human Mind* (1764), Reid offered his own theoretical alternative to the skepticism presented in David Hume's *Treatise on Human Nature* (1739). Throughout this analysis, Reid presented Hume's work as the logical consequence of those fundamental assumptions that had dominated modern philosophy since the time of Descartes and Locke. Specifically in assuming that the objects of perception, memory, and conception existed essentially as ideas within the human mind, post-Cartesian philosophy was faced with the challenge of jus-

---

12. Voegelin, *Anamnesis*, 211.
13. Voltaire, *Philosophical Dictionary,* trans. Peter Gay (New York: Harcourt, Brace & World, 1962), 467.
14. Voegelin, *Anamnesis*, 212.

tifying its belief in the actual existence of the physical world. Hume's admission that such a challenge could not be met only confirmed the force of those original assumptions which had succeeded in setting the categories for all subsequent analysis. Reid, on the contrary, simply refused to grant the modernist assumption that the objects of the mind's activity were merely mental images and, therefore, proceeded to develop a theory of sensation and perception that acknowledged the intuitive cognition of real principles.

For our purposes, the most important part of Reid's argument is concerned with his understanding of common sense. First for Reid, common sense was not to be understood in contradistinction to philosophy. Whereas the theorist may conceive of common sense as the source of that naïveté against which all philosophy must struggle, Reid described the fundamental common sense apprehension of reality as actually providing the necessary material for all legitimate philosophical speculation.

For Reid, common sense was that particular faculty by which one intuits the nondemonstrable and thus necessarily self-evident first principles as the first moment within a complex act of reason. As such, it provides both the material and the ontological grounding for discursive reasoning. For Reid, the alternative to common sense is found, not in philosophy, but rather in lunacy.[15]

Reid's understanding of common sense was further developed in both his *Essays on the Intellectual Power of Man* (1785) and his *Essays on the Active Powers of the Human Mind* (1788). In the former work, Reid once again refers to common sense as "the first-born of reason" and suggests that reason and common sense are actually inseparable in their nature. Indeed for Reid, common sense is only another name for a specific and necessary operation within reason itself. Thus he writes:

> We ascribe to reason two offices, or two charges. The first is to judge of things self-evident; the second to draw conclusions that are not self-evident from those that are. The first of these is the province and the sole province of common sense; and is only another name for one branch or one degree of reason.[16]

In his *Essays on the Active Powers of the Human Mind*, Reid argued that the ability of common sense to "judge of things self-evident" applies both to the principle of truth and to the principle of goodness. Thus, for him, common sense reason is equally capable of regulating our actions as well as our beliefs.

---

15. Thomas Reid, *An Inquiry into the Human Mind* (Chicago: University of Chicago Press, 1970), 268.
16. Thomas Reid, *Essays on the Active Powers of the Human Mind* (Cambridge: MIT Press, 1969), 567.

Within the realm of action, common sense allows one to grasp those first principles of happiness and duty from which all subsequent moral arguments must proceed. Without such a primary apprehension of the good, all moral reasoning is necessarily without foundation. Unless individuals can agree as to the desirability of happiness and duty, appeals to those principles as standards capable of informing one's moral judgments are without effect. One must first know the good *as good* before one can attempt to resolve what goodness requires at a particular time and in a particular situation.[17] For example, Reid writes:

> It is first a principle in morals, which we ought not to do to another, what we should think wrong to be done to us in like circumstances. If a man is not capable of perceiving this in his cool moments, when he reflects seriously, he is not a moral agent, nor is he capable of being convinced of it by reasoning.... To reason about justice with a man who sees nothing to be just or unjust; or about benevolence with a man who sees nothing in benevolence preferable to malice, is like reasoning with a blind man about color, or with a deaf man about sound.[18]

In emphasizing that common sense is the apperception of self-evident first principles, it is important to distinguish Reid's understanding from that of Descartes. For Descartes, self-evident truth was that truth which was apparent before a truly virgin mind. Thus one was capable of achieving scientific insight only after stripping away all the effects of education, culture, and tradition through a rigorous application of Cartesian doubt. For Reid, on the other hand, the capacity to reason correctly requires both care and nurture. Consequently the power of reason, like all other human powers, must be developed; and the insights of which common sense is capable of achieving are insights that appear not to the a-historical mind, but to the mind "when we come to years of understanding and reflection."[19] Thus Reid wrote:

> The faculties of man unfold themselves in a certain order, appointed by the great Creator. In their gradual process, they may be greatly assisted or retarded, improved or corrupted, by education, instruction, example, exercise, and by the

---

17. Here again there is an obvious similarity between the thought of Reid and of Aristotle. Aristotle introduces his *Ethics* with the warning that the arguments that follow will necessarily be unpersuasive to those who are ethically immature and have not had the benefits of a proper moral education. Aristotle, *Ethics* 1095a–1095a–15. Thus unlike Plato, whose *Republic* is an attempt to demonstrate that justice is a good, Aristotle begins with the assumption that such is the case and proceeds to write about those conditions that will promote its realization.
18. Reid, *Active Powers,* 234.
19. Ibid., 231.

society and conversation of men, which like soil and culture in plants, may produce great changes to the better or to the worse.[20]

Thus it is that when Reid speaks of common sense, he does not intend to suggest that it is a certain spontaneous wisdom that all enjoy simply because of their natural condition. It is rather found in "different persons to different degrees,"[21] and the fact that it requires cultivation and nurture implies that

> (the power of reason) springs up, by insensible degrees, as we grow to maturity. But its strength and vigour depend so much upon its being duly cultivated and exercised, that we see many individuals, nay, many nations in which it is hardly to be perceived.[22]

Common sense, then, is not a given. It is rather a potential that must be developed. In more traditional terms, common sense represents that minimal stage of development in the life of reason which is necessary if there is to be political and social order:

> There is a certain degree of it [common sense] which is necessary to our being subjects of law and government, capable of managing our own affairs, and answerable for our conduct towards others. This is called common sense, because it is common to all men with whom we can transact business, or call to account for their conduct.[23]

In his reading of Thomas Reid, Voegelin reaches a similar conclusion. Rather than contrasting common sense and reason, he refers to the former as "a compact type of rationality."[24] Specifically, it is a form of the rational life that can be differentiated from philosophy in terms of the degree of luminosity with which it comprehends its own situation. Like the philosopher, the person of common sense participates in Being because as a human, he/she is the epitome of Being. Unlike the philosopher, however, the person of common sense has not achieved that degree of self-conscious insight that allows one to articulate a fully differentiated understanding of the noetic experience. In terms of political knowledge, the person of common sense is more like the mature individual (*spoudaios*) of Aristotle's *Ethics* and *Politics* than like the philosopher of Plato's *Republic*.

---

20. Ibid., 247.
21. Thomas Reid, *Essays on the Intellectual Powers of Man* (Cambridge: MIT Press, 1969), 559.
22. Reid, *Active Powers*, 247.
23. Reid, *Intellectual Powers*, 559.
24. Voegelin, *Anamnesis*, 211.

Conclusion

This examination of the Classical Greek *politike episteme* and Thomas Reid's understanding of common sense has attempted to clarify Voegelin's expectations for a renewed political science. Political science is the examination of the problems of political and historical order from the perspective of noetic consciousness.[25] That perspective, in turn, admits of various degrees of development. At the stage of common sense, noetic consciousness allows one to avoid the "lunacy" of attempting to order human existence while ignorant of the encompassing order of reality itself. At the stage of philosophy, however, where one has gained a further insight into the very structure of noetic consciousness, an individual is able to analyze not only those examples where individuals are oblivious to the order of Being, but also those cases where, once having recognized the order of Being, they move to reject it.

According to Voegelin, the first problem, i.e., human ignorance of the order of Being, is best confronted when common sense realism opposes the hardening of rational insight into the tenets of a dogmatic system and refers one instead directly to the participatory experience of reason's first moment. The second problem, i.e., the rejection of the already revealed order of Being, is more difficult. According to Voegelin, inasmuch as the ideological movements of modernity arose after the highly differentiated articulation of the order of Being found in both Greek philosophy and Judaeo-Christian revelation these movements are an example of a self-imposed willful ignorance brought about by a deliberate rejection of historically available insights.[26] Common sense can overcome innocent ignorance by introducing one to the fundamental principles about which he or she was previously unaware. But where such principles have already been acknowledged and then rejected, it is pointless to appeal to their availability in our common sense experience. Something more radical is required to confront the phenomenon of willful ignorance. One must first come to an understanding of why one would reject the structure of Being once

---

25. Of course the entire weight of Voegelin's argument is to insist that the particular perspective available to noetic consciousness is the perspective of the soul as such. In achieving the state of metaleptic existence the philosopher does not leave but rather more fully enters the human condition: "The term *perspective* must not be understood, or rather misunderstood, in a subjective sense. There is not a multitude of perspectives, but only the one perspective that is determined by the place of man in reality." Voegelin, *Anamnesis*, 164.

26. "Rather we are confronted here with persons who know that, and why, their opinions cannot stand up under critical analysis and who therefore make the prohibition of the examination of their premises part of their dogma. This position of a conscious, deliberate, and painstakingly elaborated obstruction of *ratio* constitutes the new phenomenon." Voegelin, *Gnosticism*, 22.

its truth has become historically explicit. What is it about the truth of Being that is so objectionable to some? The analysis of a decision to close a previously open form of consciousness requires a level of self-awareness as to the structure of consciousness itself that is proper only to philosophy. Common sense may allow us to consciously participate in the order of Being by allowing us to apprehend its self-evident principles; but it is only philosophy that seeks to make the very act of participation itself a proper object of inquiry. Plato understood this act of participation as a turning toward the transcendent ground of Being. Only when this is understood can one then understand the decision to reject the principles of common sense as resulting from a prior decision to reject one's participation in Being by turning away from its transcendent ground. According to Voegelin, nothing demonstrates the need to base political science upon an adequate theory of human consciousness more clearly than the peculiar character of modern ideological politics.

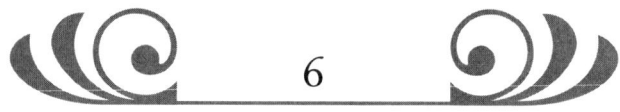

The Big Mystery
Human Emergence as Cosmic Metaxy

Brendan Purcell

Michael Ruse, who has written extensively on evolution and philosophical issues, noted a few years ago that "unfortunately, there is simply nothing in the literature by philosophers on human origins."[1] There are enormous mounds of data, both on prehuman and archaic human materials, all with the capacity for expanding our understanding of human emergence, but philosophy has not kept up. Certainly, Voegelin was concerned with this issue, devoting several pages of notes in the late 1960s to "The Phylogenetic Field," reflecting both on evolution and on the hominid sequence leading up to human emergence.[2] In his "Nachwort" to the German edition of *The Ecumenic Age*, Manfred Henningsen quotes Tilo Schabert's recollection of Voegelin, after his encounter with Marie König's paleolithic studies, remarking that he would need to write a "Volume Zero" to his *Order and History* that would take into account the latest studies in the earliest human symbolizations of order.[3]

---

1. See Michael Ruse, "Philosophy and Paleoanthropology: Some Shared Interests?" in *Conceptual Issues in Modern Human Origins Research,* ed. G. A. Clark and C. M. Willermet (New York: Aldine de Gruyter, 1997), 426 f.

2. Cf. his undated six-page typescript, "Das Phylogenetische Feld—Daten," in Eric Voegelin Papers, box 88, file 1, Hoover Institution Archives, Stanford, CA. There is also his correspondence with Marie König, a specialist in archaic symbolizations, in box 21, file 15, in the same archive, along with his answers to questions on human origins and early symbolizations in *Conversations with Eric Voegelin,* ed. Eric O'Connor (Montreal: Thomas More Institute Papers, 1980), 75–89. *Conversations with Eric Voegelin* now available in Voegelin, *The Collected Works of Eric Voegelin* (hereinafter, *CW*), vol. 33, *The Drama of Humanity and Other Miscellaneous Papers, 1939–1985,* ed. William Petropulos and Gilbert Weiss (Columbia: University of Missouri Press, 2004), 243–343.

3. Tilo Schabert, "Die Werkstatt Eric Voegelins," *Zeistschrift für Politik* 49 (2002): 92.

Perhaps we can take as a starting point toward a philosophy of human origins Voegelin's remark in his foreword to *Anamnesis:*

> Consciousness is the luminous center radiating the concrete order of human existence into society and history. A philosophy of politics is empirical—in the precise sense of an inquiry into the experiences which penetrate with their order the whole area of reality that we express by the symbol "man." The work of this philosophy requires, as we said, the constant exchange between studies on concrete cases of order and analyses of consciousness that make the human order in society and history intelligible.[4]

Some of what is to be discussed in the present essay is simply to present the data required to indicate the emergence of concrete cases of order that can then be analyzed in terms of human consciousness; without that preliminary compilation, the later analysis can be so hindered by methodological confusions that it can hardly be carried out at all. Nonetheless, in recent years I have been struck by the consensus among the most prominent British and American anthropologists that an adequate understanding of the emergence of *Homo sapiens* requires a radical shift in intellectual perspective, although they do not themselves deal with the philosophical implications of that shift.

Drawing particularly on Eric Voegelin's philosophical anthropology and Bernard Lonergan's philosophy of science, what I intend to do here is simply a preliminary mapping of the terrain required for a philosophy of human origins. I would like to begin with what seems to me a magisterial statement of Voegelin's at the end of *The Ecumenic Age*:

> The divine-human In-Between of historically differentiating experience is founded in the consciousness of concrete human beings in concrete bodies on the concrete earth in the concrete universe.... The various strata of reality with their specific time dimensions... are not autonomous entities but form, through the relations of foundation and organization, the hierarchy of being that extends from the inorganic stratum, through the vegetative and animal realms, to the existence of man in his tension toward the divine ground of being.... There is no flux of presence in the Metaxy without its foundation in the biophysical existence of man on earth in the universe. By virtue of their founding character, the lower strata reach into the stratum of human consciousness, not as its cause but as its condition. Only because the strata of reality participate in one another, through the relations of foundation and organization, in the order of the cosmos, can and must the time dimensions of the strata be related to one another, with the time dimension of the universe furnishing the ultimately founding measure.... The physical universe as the ultimate foundation for the higher strata in

---

4. Eric Voegelin, *CW*, vol.6, *Anamnesis: On the Theory of History and Politics*, trans. M. J. Hanak, ed. David Walsh (Columbia: University of Missouri Press, 2002), 34.

the hierarchy of being cannot be identified as the ultimate reality of the Whole, because in the stratum of consciousness we experience the presence of divine reality as the constituent of humanity. In man's consciousness, the foundational movement within reality from the physical depth becomes luminous for the creative constitution of all reality from the height of the divine ground.... Once the fallacies are removed, the hierarchy of being comes into view, not as a number of strata one piled on top of the other, but as [the] movement of reality from the apeirontic depth up to man, through as many levels of the hierarchy as can be discerned empirically, and as the countermovement of creative organization from the divine height down, with the Metaxy of man's consciousness as the site where the movement of the Whole becomes luminous for its eschatological direction.... The Mystery of the historical process is inseparable from the Mystery of a reality that brings forth the universe and the earth, plant and animal life on earth, and ultimately man and his consciousness.[5]

There are two levels discernible here: (1) the intramundane sequence culminating in a human consciousness that articulates the transfinite thrust of the entire sequence; and (2) the reinterpretation of that sequence in the light of our experience of ourselves as occurring within the divine-human In-Between. However, before coming to the Mystery both of the historical process and of its engendering reality, it will be helpful to articulate a philosophical framework for the intramundane sequence of strata. That sequence can be understood in terms of Aristotle's own hylemorphic context, where each "step" represents a new formal organization of the material provided by the previously highest step. So we can give a rough outline of the hierarchy of being, to be read upward from its first to its sixth steps, with a few intermediate stages added in:

> 6TH STEP, c. 45,000 years ago: First *human* life—*Homo Sapiens* skeletal remains in Africa, Europe, Asia, and Australia, accompanied by an explosion of symbolizations of experienced attunement with transfinite reality
> 4.5 million years ago: First hominids
> 5TH STEP, c. 530 million years ago: First multicellular *animal* life—Burgess Shale (Canada), Ediacara (Australia), Tommotian (Russia) fauna
> 4TH STEP, c. 600–550 million years ago: First complex botanical life
> 1.5 billion years ago: Complex eukaryotic cells—algae
> 3RD STEP, c. 3.5 billion years ago: First biological life on earth—prokaryotic (that is, without nucleus) bacterial cells, including archeabacteria, and first eukaryotic cells
> 4.5 billion years ago: Formation of our solar system

---

5. Eric Voegelin, *CW*, vol. 17, *The Ecumenic Age*, vol. IV, *Order and History*, ed. Michael Franz (1974; Columbia: University of Missouri Press, 2000), 407–10.

10 billion years ago: Formation of galaxies
13 billion years ago: Formation of quasars, stars, proto-galaxies
2ND STEP, c. 15 billion years minus 35 minutes ago: First *chemical* elements—helium and hydrogen
15 billion years minus 1/100th of a second ago: First subatomic particles
1ST STEP, c. 15 billion years ago: First *physical* existence: Big Bang

Drawing on Lonergan, we can try to articulate the intramundane sequence. One of Lonergan's criticisms of Darwin is that his notion of scientific explanation depends on a perceptual rather than an intellectual epistemology. Accordingly, Darwin's notion that the basic unit is the species (even if it is changing all the time), rather than the species in interaction with the environment, and his focusing on a gradual accretion of minor changes as an insight into macro-evolutionary development, depend on a notion that scientific knowledge means taking a good look at what is happening rather than employing a notion of explanation in terms of correlations between the data. It is a question, not of looking for visible, gradual changes, but of understanding the relations between various species over time.

In *Insight,* Lonergan has formulated an open framework for dealing with the sequence of levels of being in terms of what he calls "emergent probability." He sees emergent probability as accounting for world processes in terms of six generic notions: (1) spatial distribution; (2) large numbers; (3) long intervals of time; (4) selection; (5) stability; and (6) development. Its openness is a result of its radically nondeductive nature, accepting as a matter of fact that lower aggregates of existence make materially possible the emergence of the next level, but that they neither explain it nor necessitate it. As a heuristic framework, it is not a hypothesis to be verified or falsified within any of the natural sciences, but an intellectual context within which the various findings of the natural sciences can be drawn together. Its theoretical clarity is philosophical, and its greater or lesser relevance to the concrete universe depends on its being in touch with the full range of empirical natural sciences.

The basic building block of emergent probability is what Lonergan calls a "scheme of recurrence": If A occurs, B will occur; if B occurs, C will occur; if C occurs...A will recur. Building on that notion, there can be envisaged a conditioned sequence of schemes of recurrence.

So, we can say that P, Q, R...form a conditioned series, if all the prior members of the series are actually functioning for any later member to become a concrete possibility. Then P (say, the physical and chemical levels of existence) can function without Q (say, the biological level of existence) or R (say, the zoological level of existence); Q can function without R; but Q can not function without P, nor can R function without P and Q.

To tie down intellectually these essentially different steps or levels or strata, we can use Lonergan's notion of the thing, which is a concrete reformulation of Aristotle's notion of substance. For Lonergan, it is an intelligible, concrete unity, differentiated by explanatory parts, implying the possibility of different kinds of things. Since explanatory parts are defined by their relations to one another, there is the possibility of distinct sets of such parts—we have already suggested physical, chemical, biological, botanical, zoological, and intellectual sets. There follows the notion of the explanatory genus, where *genus* here refers in the ontological sense to generically different levels or kinds of being.

Lonergan's example of the set of explanatory genera or kinds is provided by the sciences: where the laws of physics hold for subatomic elements, those of physics and chemistry hold for elements and compounds; those of physics, chemistry, biology, and botany hold for plants, and so on. "As one moves from one genus to the next, there is added a new set of laws which defines its own basic terms by its own empirically established correlations."

Lonergan links the main departments of science with his understanding of successive higher viewpoints and notes that "it is because new insights intervene" that the higher science is essentially, or generically, different from the lower. Correlative to the sequence of strata of things is the series of autonomous sciences as higher viewpoints, physics, chemistry, biology, botany, zoology (at the explanatory level of sensory-perceptual psychology), philosophical anthropology (at the explanatory level of intellectual or rational psychology).

Since the problem of reductionism bedevils discussion of human emergence, it will be useful here to indicate Lonergan's criterion for the relative autonomy of higher from lower sciences: if the laws of a science at a lower level have to regard ranges of occurrences "as mere patterns of happy coincidences" there develops an autonomous higher science. He argues, "Nor does the introduction of the higher autonomous science interfere with the autonomy of the lower; for the higher enters into the field of the lower only in so far as it makes systematic on the lower level what otherwise would be merely coincidental."[6] Lonergan notes that "the contention that things are all of one kind has rested, not on concrete evidence, but on mechanist assumption."[7] Discussing the reductionist fallacy of "things within things," Lonergan points out:

---

6. Bernard Lonergan, *Insight: A Study of Human Understanding* (London: Longmans, 1961), 122–23, 118–19, 255, 257, 256.

7. Ibid., 257. Cf. Voegelin's comment that "the popular assumption that mathematical natural science is the model of science par excellence, and that an operation not using its methods cannot be characterized as scientific, is neither a proposition of natural science, nor of any science whatsoever, but merely an ideological dogma thriving in the sphere of scientism" (*Anamnesis*, 376).

the fact that the laws of the lower orders are verified in the higher genus proves that [correlations] of the lower order exist in things of the higher genus. But it is one thing to prove that [correlations] of the lower order survive within the higher genus; it is quite another to prove that things defined solely by the lower [correlations] also survive. To arrive at [correlations], abstractive procedures are normal; one considers events under some aspects and disregards other aspects of the same events. But to arrive at a thing, one must consider all data within a totality, and one must take into account all their aspects.

One cannot, therefore, conclude from the existence of an aggregate of events, which can be understood in terms of the lower-order laws, the existence of things of the lower order, "for this would be to abstract from the aspect of the aggregate that cannot be accounted for on the lower viewpoint and that justifies the introduction of the higher viewpoint and the higher genus. Accordingly, if there is evidence for the existence of the higher genus, there cannot be evidence for things of lower genera in the same data."[8]

A simple example would be a field of buttercups, showing slight species variation depending on their position in wetter or drier parts of the field. However exhaustively the biochemical changes in the buttercups were registered, no such account would yield the specifically botanical insight into the kind of things buttercups are.[9] Nor are the millions of cells in each buttercup separate "things," since intrinsic to the constitution of each cell is that they are buttercup cells. Voegelin puts this very concretely:

> A plant is a plant. You see it. You don't see its physical-chemical processes, and nothing about the plant changes if you know that physical-chemical processes are going on inside. How these processes will result in what you experience immediately as a plant (a rose or an oak tree), you don't know anyway. So if you know these substructures in the lower levels of the ontic hierarchy (beyond the plant which is organism) and go into the physical, chemical, molecular and atomic structures, ever farther down, the greater becomes the miracle how all that thing is a plant. Nothing is explained. If you try to explain it in terms of some mechanism, you have committed the fallacy of reduction.[10]

(1) From his notion of a thing, Lonergan formulates the logical postulate that if there exist correlations of a higher order, there will exist things of the same higher order.

---

8. Lonergan, *Insight*, 258.
9. I owe this example to Philip McShane's discussion in his *Randomness, Statistics, and Emergence* (Dublin: Gill & Macmillan, 1970), 71–76, and his arguments for the specific difference of botany over biochemistry in his *Plants and Pianos: Two Essays in Advanced Methodology* (Dublin: Milltown Institute, 1971).
10. Voegelin, *Conversations with Eric Voegelin*, 93.

(2) This is followed by the probability postulate that if there exist things differentiated by explanatory correlations and functioning in schemes of recurrence, there exists the possibility, and some probability, of a nonsystematic occurrence of another aggregate of events that would occur regularly only if things of a higher order existed.

(3) A third, evolutionary postulate will be that if nonsystematically there occur suitable aggregates of events, then there will emerge correlations of a higher order to make the recurrence of the aggregates systematic. By the first, logical postulate, there will follow the existence of things of the higher order. By emergent probability there will arise schemes of recurrence that depend upon the classical laws that define the new correlations. This evolutionary postulate is equivalent to the old axiom *materiae dispositae advenit forma* (form accrues to rightly arranged matter). Both the postulate and the axiom have the same components, of "a lower order of things, the occurrence of a suitable disposition in the lower order, and the emergence of a component that pertains to a higher order." The discussion by Stephen Jay Gould and others of what is called below "exaption" or "co-option" is part of this level of analysis.

(4) A fourth, sequential postulate

> would effect the extension of emergent probability to things. It affirms the possibility of a conditioned series of both things and schemes of recurrence realized cumulatively in accord with successive schedules of probabilities. Thus the sequential postulate presupposes the other three; it adds an affirmation of the possibility of applying the other three postulates over and over so that one could begin from the simplest things and proceed to the most complex.[11]

This is not unlike Daniel Dennett's notion of evolutionary algorithms, though without his determinist context.[12] Lonergan notes that the sequential postulate is neither a hypothesis of empirical science nor a scientific theory that can be verified or refuted, but a heuristic assumption that can only be empirically tested through specific determinations and applications. A similar philosophical context is needed for understanding the hominid sequence, including Neanderthals and the emergence of humans, as we shall see.

Lonergan gives examples first of two levels of things in chemistry: both (1) the chemical elements, which means that each of these elements may be seen as roughly equivalent at the chemical level to a biological species, and (2) their compounds. Likewise in biology, where the things are the series of biological

---

11. Lonergan, *Insight*, 260.
12. Daniel C. Dennett, *Darwin's Dangerous Idea: Evolution and the Meanings of Life* (London: Allen Lane, 1995).

species, both (1) at the cellular level, analogous to elements, one finds the three major types of bacteria, and (2) analogous to compounds, one finds multicellular living things: "The things are the series of biological species. They are the higher systems that make systematic the coincidental aggregates at the chemical level. Thus the biological species are a series of solutions to the problem of systematizing coincidental aggregates of chemical processes." Such multicellular organisms would represent plant life, from the simplest algae to the most complex angiosperms.

The third application of the key notion takes the biological organism as its lower level and animal sensitivity as its higher system. The higher correlations now are defined by the laws of psychic stimulus and psychic response, and these correlations make systematic otherwise merely coincidental aggregates of neural events. However, these neural events occur within an already constituted nervous system which, in great part, would have no function if the higher psychic system did not exist to inform it.

Lonergan notes the increasing significance of "immanent intelligibility or constitutive design" as one moves from subatomic entities to animals. Thus subatomic limitations decrease the vast diversity of chemical compounds; the multicellular plant exploits that increasing degree of freedom, since "not only is it an aggregate of cells" but it is "determined by its own laws of development and growth. A third degree of freedom appears in the animal, in which the second degree is exploited to provide the materials for the higher system of biological consciousness."[13]

In each case, there is the evidence that is necessary and sufficient to affirm the existence of a higher set of correlations defining another level or genus of things. And this possibility is recurrent. There can be a series of genera, and within each genus there can be different species, for the things are defined by their correlations or what Aristotle would call their accidental forms, and these differ inasmuch as they systematize differently their different underlying manifolds of lower-order activities.

As we have seen, in things of any higher genus, there survive lower correlations, but there do not survive lower things. The lower conjugates survive, for without them there would be nothing for the higher system of correlations to systematize. On the other hand, lower things do not survive within higher things. Almost as a *reductio ad absurdum* of the notion of things within things, there is Richard Dawkins's *The Selfish Gene,* where he accurately summarizes his argument: "Our genes made us. We animals exist for their preservation and are nothing more than their throwaway survival machines."[14]

---

13. Lonergan, *Insight*, 261, 263–64.
14. Richard Dawkins, *The Selfish Gene* (Oxford: Oxford University Press, 1989), 19–20.

Corresponding to the successive genera, there will be distinct and autonomous empirical sciences. And the successive, distinct autonomous sciences will be related as successive higher viewpoints. Lonergan notes that "if metaphysics [or in other words, a philosophical anthropology] aims at integrating the empirical sciences and common sense to yield a single view of the universe of proportionate being, then it has to deal with facts."

In this nondeductivist philosophical formulation of a cosmological-anthropological view of the world, each level as it were makes a gift of itself to be used by the next highest level, and when we arrive at human existence the entire sequence may be understood as a hylemorphic sequence dynamically oriented beyond itself. Voegelin's notion of a movement of foundational and organizational levels is surely equivalent to Lonergan's, even though Lonergan does not yet make the shift to external causation. Lonergan argues that his evolutionary postulate is to be understood within the limits of empirical science. "As empirical science it prescinds from efficient, instrumental, and final causes, which refer to distinct types of intelligibility and lie beyond the qualifications of empirical method either to affirm or to deny."

With regard to understanding the intelligibility immanent in the universe of data, which considers things no less than events and schemes of recurrence, Lonergan writes: "for things are to be grasped in data; their numbers and differentiation, their distribution and concentrations, their emergence and survival, give rise to questions that require an answer. One does not escape that requirement by appealing to divine wisdom and divine providence, for that appeal reinforces the rejection of obscurantism and provides another argument for affirming an intelligible order immanent in the visible universe."[15]

Since we need a philosophical context to handle the notion of human emergence, it is necessary further to draw on Lonergan's expansion of the Aristotelian heuristic that Voegelin uses when he speaks of the orders of foundation and of organization, which I believe is equivalent to Lonergan's notion of emergent probability. Voegelin asserts that

> as we move from the consciousness of existential tension to the corporeal foundation, we encounter, in the realm of man's being, the synthetic nature of man as defined by Aristotle, with its levels of human-psychic, animal, vegetative, and inanimate being. These levels of the hierarchy of being are related to one another in (a) the grounding of the higher on the lower ones and (b) in the organization of the lower by the higher ones. These relations are not reversible. On the one hand there is no *eu zen*, no good life in Aristotle's sense, without the foundation of *zen;* on the other hand, the order of the good life does not emerge from the

---

15. Lonergan, *Insight*, 438–39, 441, 260–61.

corporeal foundation but comes into being only when the entire existence is ordered by the center of the existential tension.[16]

Lonergan speaks, first, of the principle of emergence, equivalent to Voegelin's order of foundation: "otherwise coincidental manifolds of lower conjugate acts invite the higher integration effected by higher conjugate forms." Second, and equivalent to Voegelin's order of organization, is the principle of correspondence: "significantly different underlying manifolds require different higher integrations." For example, chemical elements differ by atomic numbers and atomic weights, "and these differences are grounded in the underlying manifold." Third, there is the principle of finality, which I would suggest is equivalent to what L. Berg and Colin Groves below call "nomogenesis." The underlying manifold is an upwardly but indeterminately directed dynamism toward ever fuller realization of being. Any actual realization will pertain to some determinate genus and species, but this very indeterminacy is limitation, and every limitation is to finality a barrier to be transcended. Fourth, there is the principle of development itself. It is the linked sequence of dynamic higher integrations. Fifth, the course of development is marked by an increasing explanatory differentiation.

> Sixthly, the course of development is capable of minor flexibility inasmuch as it can pursue the same goal along different routes.... Seventhly, the course of development is capable of a major flexibility that consists in a shift or modification of the ultimate objective. In biology this is the familiar fact of adaptation.... In the light of the foregoing considerations, a development may be defined as a flexible linked sequence of dynamic and increasing differentiated higher integrations that meet the tension of successively transformed underlying manifolds through successive applications of the principles of correspondence and emergence.[17]

Voegelin spoke in his foreword to *Anamnesis* about the constant interchange between the study of concrete cases of order (here represented by a philosophical heuristic for cosmology) and analyses of consciousness. So before going any further in exploring the emergence of the human, it will be helpful to see how the sequence of prehuman levels are in fact implicitly connected to the metaxic issue. In "The Moving Soul," Voegelin noted that

> constructs concerning the structure of the physical universe as a whole cannot be empirically validated. Why, then, do physicists engage again and again in their construction? The only possible answer to this question seems to be that

16. Voegelin, *CW*, 6:407.
17. Lonergan, *Insight*, 451–54.

physicists are men who as human beings feel obliged to develop an image of the universe. They feel obliged to engage in the creation of a mytho-speculative symbol that will satisfy our desire to know the structure of the universe in which we live.[18]

Others working in the area of philosophical anthropology have introduced the notion of "boundary questions," that is, questions that arise within the domain of the natural sciences but cannot be answered by them. Those questions, as Voegelin has noted, are raised by the scientist as human being, even though he may elsewhere, as scientist, appear to sternly deny his own humanity. In fact such boundary questions can easily be tracked as arising on at least four levels: astrophysics, biology, zoology, and anthropology.

Although he has later become notorious for wishing to deny the relevance of the boundary question of astrophysics,[19] Stephen Hawking in an earlier collaboration with George Ellis admitted the key boundary question posed by Big Bang theory. "The creation of the Universe has been argued, indecisively, from early times.... The results we have obtained support the idea that the universe began a finite time ago. However the actual point of creation, the singularity, is outside the scope of presently known laws of physics."[20]

It is beyond my competence to say one way or another that the emergence of the biological level of existence poses a boundary question in biology, equivalent to the question the Big Bang poses to astrophysics. Still, some biologists come close to saying something like this. For example, in 1953, the same year that Stanley Miller and Harold Urey tried to produce life experimentally, James Watson and Francis Crick's discovery of the role of the DNA molecule in all living things indicated an extraordinary complexity in living cells, making their chance emergence from chemicals appear less likely. Nobel Prize–winning biologist Jacques Monod remarked that

> the simplest cells available to us for study have nothing "primitive" about them ... [T]he major problem is the origin of the genetic code and of its transitional mechanism. Indeed it is not so much a "problem" as a veritable enigma. The code is meaningless unless translated. The modern cell's translating machinery

---

18. Eric Voegelin, "The Moving Soul," in *CW*, vol. 28, *What Is History? and Other Late Unpublished Writings,* ed. Thomas A. Hollweck and Paul Caringella (1990; available Columbia: University of Missouri Press, 1999), 168.

19. In his most popular book, Stephen Hawking proposed a view of the universe as having no boundary or edge, no beginning or end (on analogy with a sphere), and remarked of such a world: "It would neither be created nor destroyed. It would just BE." *A Brief History of Time* (London: Bantam Press, 1988), 136.

20. Stephen Hawking and George Ellis, *The Large Scale Structure of Space-Time* (New York: Cambridge University Press, 1973), 364.

consists of at least fifty macro-molecular components *which are themselves coded in DNA: the code cannot be translated except by products of translation.* It is the modern expression of *omne vivum ex ovo.* When and how did this circle become closed? It is exceedingly difficult to imagine.[21]

And Francis Crick, co-discoverer of the structure of DNA, noted that "an honest man, armed with all the knowledge available to us now, could only state that in some sense, the origin of life appears at the moment to be almost a miracle, so many are the conditions which would have had to have been satisfied to get it going."[22]

The emergence of sentient-perceptual, or zoological, life has become a hot issue because of the recently discovered common body plan for all animals dating from around 550 million years ago. What is relevant here, of course, is the psychic life for which that body plan is the foundation. As Lonergan notes of that psychic activity, "elementary knowing vindicates its validity by the survival, not to mention the evolution, of animal species." And he goes on to make the Aristotelian point that

> an explanatory account of animal species will differentiate animals not by their organic but by their psychic differences . . . [T]he animal pertains to an explanatory genus beyond that of the plant; that explanatory genus turns on sensibility; its specific differences are differences of sensibility; and it is in differences of sensibility that are to be found the basis for differences of organic structure, since that structure, as we have seen, possesses a degree of freedom that is limited but not controlled by underlying materials and outer circumstances.[23]

The fact that sentient animal life more or less suddenly appears would seem to underline the issue of the appearance of another, animal-psychological level of being, as a boundary question. While it is not possible here to go into the dramatic shift from nonperceptual life to life that is perceptually organized, it is no secret that the gaps in the fossil record, which Darwin presumed would soon be filled, have remained. As a result, Niles Eldredge and Stephen Gould in 1972 proposed what they saw was an important modification to gradualist Darwinian evolution, in their ground-breaking article, "Punctuated Equilibria: An Alternative to Phyletic Gradualism."[24] Succinctly, Eldredge explains:

---

21. Jacques Monod, *Chance and Necessity: An Essay on the Natural Philosophy of Modern Biology* (London: Collins, 1979), 134 f. (author's emphasis).
22. Quoted in Michael Denton, *Evolution: A Theory in Crisis* (London: Burnett Books, 1985), 268.
23. Lonergan, *Insight,* 252, 265–66.
24. Reprinted in Niles Eldredge, *Time Frames: The Rethinking of Darwinian Evolution and the Theory of Punctuated Equilibria* (London, Heinemann, 1986), 193–223.

if evolutionary change doesn't simply accumulate over the course of time, the question becomes, When and under what conditions does evolutionary change occur?... [N]ew species... tend to show up abruptly in the fossil record as the overwhelming rule.... Punctuated equilibria is a combination of empirical pattern (stasis interrupted by brief bursts of evolutionary change) coupled with preexisting biological theory.[25]

The more recent breakthrough in the early 1990s, called "evolutionary-developmental," or "evo-devo," seems in many ways to correspond at the molecular level to Eldredge and Gould's punctuated equilibrium hypothesis, which in turn is supplemented by the insights of Berg and Groves[26] into nomogenesis as underlying the macro-evolutionary shifts Eldredge and Gould were trying to deal with. Gould's last great work, *The Structure of Evolutionary Theory*, is a massive attempt to marry his revisionist Darwinism with evo-devo.[27]

The basic discovery, made in the early 1990s, was that the sudden emergence of thirty-five phyla or major zoological groups (chordates, crustaceans, mollusks, etc.) around 550 million years ago showed a common deep genetic structure. Each phylum had the same genetic instructions for its top/bottom axis, front/back polarity, head, and sensory organs. Wallace Arthur gives his opinion that

> there was no multicellular animal life prior to 600 million years ago; there was an explosion of body plans in Ediacaran times, with many becoming extinct, and a second body-plan explosion in the early Cambrian; evolution in Vendian and Cambrian times was much more "experimental" than it is now; and internal factors such as developmental constraint (or early lack of it) are important in evolution as well as considerations about niche space and external adaptation.[28]

What is amazing are the jellyfish, or cnidarians, belonging to a thirty-sixth phylum, which may have originated with the first Ediacaran fauna originating 50 million years earlier without the body-plans of the other thirty-five phyla: they still seem to have the same genetic plan for eyes that they share with the other phyla.[29]

---

25. Niles Eldredge, *Reinventing Darwin: The Great Evolutionary Debate* (London: Phoenix, 1995), 94, 104.
26. Cf. L. Berg, *Nomogenesis or Evolution Determined by Law*, trans. J. N. Rostovson (Cambridge, MA: MIT Press, 1969); Colin P. Groves, *A Theory of Human and Primate Evolution* (Oxford: Clarendon Press, 1989).
27. Stephen Jay Gould, *The Structure of Evolutionary Theory* (Cambridge, MA: Harvard University Press, 2002).
28. Wallace Arthur, *The Origin of Animal Body Plans: A Study in Evolutionary Developmental Biology* (Cambridge: Cambridge University Press, 2000), 81.
29. Rudolf A. Raff, *The Shape of Life: Genes, Development, and the Evolution of Animal Form* (Chicago: University of Chicago Press, 1996), 376 f.

Rudolf Raff provides the flavor of evo-devo issues in *The Shape of Life: Genes, Development, and the Evolution of Animal Form*:

> higher taxonomic groups, most notably phyla, possess suites of anatomical features that distinguish them from other groups. Such an underlying anatomical arrangement is called a body plan... [N]o new phyla appear to have originated since the Cambrian.... [B]ecause all bilaterian [two-sided] animals share a common ancestor, they arose from a common bilaterian body plan. The interesting question then becomes whether there is a set of genetic rules that bilaterian animals share. If there is, the diverse body plans of bilaterian phyla have been built upon shared developmental genetic themes, which might constitute a conserved genetic body plan. Slack and co-workers have called this hypothetical Hox gene-centered genetic body plan for most animal phyla the "zootype."...
>
> If each new species required the reinvention of control elements, there would not be time enough for much evolution at all, let alone the spectacularly rapid evolution of novel features observed in the phylogenetic record. There is a kind of tinkering at work, in which the same regulatory elements are recombined into new developmental machines.... Internal rules should not be expected to supersede Darwinian selection, but rather, to complement it in predicting the behavior of evolving ontogenies.[30]

Eric Davidson calls the taking over by a higher level of activity of a lower form "cooption" and notes that "cooptive processes... have been responsible for the evolution of new body parts during the divergence of the Bilateria."[31]

Not only the sudden emergence of sentient-perceptual animal life—focused on by Gould in his *Wonderful Life* study[32]—but the equivalently sudden emergence of the sequence of species within the various zoological genera seems to make "boundary questions" relating to the emergence of each species inescapable. It is no harm to remind ourselves of Voegelin's warning regarding all "emergences" at every level: "the epiphany of structures in reality—be they atoms, molecules, genes, biological species, races, human consciousness, or language—is a mystery inaccessible to explanation."[33]

Since Gould has been fiercely attacked by those he would be driven to call "Darwinian Fundamentalists,"[34] the reason a gradualist, as opposed to a salta-

---

30. Ibid., xiv, 26, 27, 324.
31. Eric H. Davidson, *Genomic Regulatory Systems: Development and Evolution* (San Diego: Academic Press, 2001), 158.
32. Stephen Jay Gould, *Wonderful Life: The Burgess Shale and the Nature of History* (London: HutchinsonRadius, 1990).
33. Eric Voegelin, *CW*, vol. 18, *In Search of Order*, ed. Ellis Sandoz (Columbia: University of Missouri Press, 2000), 31.
34. Stephen Jay Gould, "Darwinian Fundamentalism," *New York Review of Books* 64, no. 10 (June 12, 1997): 34–37.

tory, approach—where boundary questions become more insistent—to evolution was adopted is perhaps, as Thomas Nagel seems to think, because of a *ressentiment* not only against God but against philosophy, that ill serves biology as a natural science:

> My guess is that this cosmic authority problem is not a rare condition and that it is responsible for much of the scientism and reductionism of our time. One of the tendencies it supports is the ludicrous overuse of evolutionary biology to explain everything about life, including everything about the human mind. Darwin enabled modern secular culture to heave a collective sigh of relief, by apparently providing a way to eliminate purpose, meaning and design as fundamental features of the world. Instead they became epiphenomena, generated incidentally by a process that can be entirely explained by the operation of nonteleological laws of physics on the material of which we and our environments are all composed. There might still be thought to be a religious threat in the existence of the laws of physics themselves, and indeed the existence of anything at all—but it seems to be less alarming to most atheists.[35]

As we know, Voegelin too, in his *Hitler and the Germans* lectures, commented on the nonobservational core of Darwin's evolutionary theory.[36] What he has called "the epiphany of structures in reality," accompanied by a pneumopathological fear of the underlying mystery, is at least one of the factors making any debate on biological or zoological emergence such a heated one in our culture.[37] The great claim of Darwinism as an ideology is that it answers the question of existence regarding all living reality. But since there is nothing in biological methodology that can deal with the question of existence as such, a screening device had to be developed to prevent the emergence at the biological and zoological levels of being of Aristotle's-Aquinas's-Leibniz's-Schelling's-Heidegger's question: Why is there something rather than nothing? Why are the things that are the way they are?[38]

---

35. Thomas Nagel, *The Last Word* (New York: Oxford University Press, 1997), 131.
36. Eric Voegelin, *CW*, vol. 31, *Hitler and the Germans,* ed. and trans. Detlev Clemens and Brendan Purcell (Columbia: University of Missouri Press, 1999), 144 f.
37. However, Neal C. Gillespie, in his *Charles Darwin and the Problem of Creation* (Chicago: University of Chicago Press, 1979), amply discusses the anti-intellectualism Darwin had to deal with in certain religious circles, along with his own internal religious struggle—a struggle perhaps more cultural than religious, in fact. The whole issue of closure to scientific inquiry by a school of apologists in the name of a literalizing reading of Scripture makes one on principle sympathetic to the exasperated desire to fend them off, however polemically, by writers like Dennett and Dawkins.
38. Cf. Voegelin's critical discussion of Leibniz's formulation of these questions in *In Search of Order,* 95–101.

In recent books like Stephen Jay Gould's *Rocks of Ages* and Michael Ruse's *Can a Darwinian Be a Christian?* there seems to be a new openness to accepting types of investigation that are different rather than opposed.[39] Typically these types of investigation are natural—scientific and religious; surprisingly, philosophic investigation never seems to be given the same attention. Even so, however limited this breakthrough may be, it does have some cultural importance.

Brooklyn-born Stephen Jay Gould grew up in a secular Jewish, even Marxist, background. But his recent writings have shown him open to religion, even if he considers himself an agnostic. The central idea in his *Rocks of Ages* is that

> science tries to document the factual character of the natural world. Religion operates in the equally important, but utterly different, realm of human purposes, meanings and values. I propose that we encapsulate this central principle of respectful non-interference—accompanied by intense dialogue between the two distinct subjects—by enunciating the principle of NOMA, or Non-Overlapping Magisteria.

Later, Gould justifies NOMA as

> a simple, humane, rational, and altogether conventional argument for mutual respect, based on non-overlapping subject matter, between two components of wisdom in a full human life: our drive to understand the factual character of nature (the magisterium of science), and our need to define meaning in our lives and a moral basis for our actions (the magisterium of religion).[40]

By contrast, Ruse, who comes from a Quaker background, deals with how the content of the theory of evolution should not prevent a Darwinian from being a Christian. He wrote that "natural selection is the only significant cause of permanent organic change.... I am an enthusiastic reductionist." Yet he does not accept that a Darwinian cannot be a Christian and writes that "Saint Augustine and Saint Thomas Aquinas would be appalled at such a presumption." Ruse criticizes writers such as Dawkins and Wilson for an atheism that is "smuggled in [to Darwinian theory] and then given an evolutionary gloss." His rejection of an intrinsic opposition between science and religion indicates a new tone in this whole debate, and a new readiness by Darwinians of reasonably

---

39. Stephen Jay Gould, *Rocks of Ages: Science and Religion in the Fullness of Life* (London: Jonathan Cape, 2001); Michael Ruse, *Can a Darwinian Be a Christian? The Relationship between Science and Religion* (Cambridge: Cambridge University Press, 2001).
40. Gould, *Rock of Ages*, 4–5, 175.

strict observance, such as himself, or the explicitly revisionary Gould to reflect carefully on religious questions. For a philosopher, that is probably as near as they get to a recognition of the mystery of the epiphany of zoological structures in reality.

Furthermore, Ruse agrees with Ernan McMullin's view that "God is not simply forecasting on the basis of what will happen. There is an act of creation which unfurls through time for us, but which is outside time for God and hence for which beginning, middle and end are all as one." Thus Ruse (quoting McMullin) points out that "the contingency or otherwise of the evolutionary sequence does not bear on whether the created universe embodies purpose or not. Asserting the reality of cosmic purpose in this context takes for granted that the universe depends for its existence on an omniscient Creator."[41] To paraphrase Voegelin, the zoologist who constructs the structure of the universe is not satisfied with his role as an observer of zoological reality but exerts his prerogative as man to create symbols expressive of existential tension.[42]

One way of examining the boundary question posed by human emergence is to see whether the Neanderthals,[43] the hominids closest to humans (at least in Europe) in the hominid sequence, require us to move to a level of inquiry generically different from zoology or animal psychology. In his unpublished manuscript "The Phylogenetic Field," Voegelin has jotted down the cheerful note: "History of Mankind v. History of Monkeykind," but could there be a History of Neanderthalkind?[44]

Let us limit our reflections to the issue of symbolization, on the grounds that without a capacity for symbolization it is highly unlikely that Neanderthals were able to think, ask questions, reach out beyond themselves intentionally, or experience what Voegelin calls luminosity. Some have claimed for Neanderthal man the activity of symbolization based upon arguing that the sites indicate ritual burials. In his study "Grave Shortcomings: The Evidence

---

41. Ruse, *Can a Darwinian be a Christian?* ix, 128, 87–88.
42. Voegelin, "The Moving Soul," 169.
43. Recent surveys include: Paul Mellars, *The Neanderthal Legacy: An Archaeological Perspective from Western Europe* (Princeton, NJ: Princeton University Press, 1996); Ian Tattersall, *The Last Neanderthal: The Rise, Success, and Mysterious Extinction of Our Closest Human Relatives* (Boulder, CO: Westview Press, 1999); Ian Tattersall and Geoffrey H. Schwartz, *Extinct Humans* (New York: Westview Press, 2000).
44. He expands on a similar comment in *The Ecumenic Age:* "Without universality, there would be no mankind other than the aggregate of members of a biological species; there would be no more a history of mankind than there is a history of catkind or horsekind. If mankind is to have history, its members must be able to respond to the movement of divine presence in their souls. But if that is the condition, then the mankind who has history is constituted by the God to whom man responds" (377).

for Neanderthal Burial," Robert Gargett examines all the sites at which it is claimed Neanderthal burials took place. At Teshik-Tash he finds no evidence of a deliberate grave, and that so-called "ritual" assemblage of goat horns could be the result of predator activity. "Goat remains make up roughly 85% of the faunal assemblage at Teshik-Tash, and, since horn is the most likely skeletal part to survive, the probability of six horns being preserved in this area of the site by chance is high." At Shanidar, perhaps the most referenced site, he notes that it was only seven years after the original investigation of the site that the conclusion was drawn that Neanderthal remains at Shanidar 4 were buried with flowers, indicating ceremonial activity, although earlier the investigator had considered Shanidar 4, 6, 8, and 9 to have been killed by rockfalls. "No clear evidence for purposeful burial exists in the Shanidar deposits. There are no grave pits, no non-naturally occurring protective strata." Gargett considers that because the investigators were inclined to believe that purposeful burial was a possibility, they thought the presence of an unusually high number of pollen grains indicated that flowers had been buried with the dead. He suggests, rather, that they were blown by the wind. And there seems doubt as to in which level the pollen was found. He concludes that "the removal of mortuary ritual from the behavioral repertoire of Neanderthal may make the observed discontinuity in material culture at the Middle/Upper Paleolithic boundary a little easier to understand." In the "Discussion and Criticism" of the Gargett study, L. P. Kooijmans et al. agree with Gargett and note that "archaeologists must first rule out natural causes for the sediments they recover before concluding that hominids produced them."[45]

Paul Mellars broadly accepts Gargett's demolition of many claimed Neanderthal "burials," but where there are large numbers, seven at La Ferrassie, nine at Shanidar, including the very delicate bones of young children, he still argues that "the case for deliberate interment of most of these skeletons appears virtually beyond dispute." Yet for Mellars, too, the evidence for deliberate grave offerings are much weaker. He concludes: "in the absence of either clear ritual or unambiguous grave offerings associated with the documented range of Neanderthal burials in Europe, it must be concluded that the case for a symbolic component in burial practices remains at best unproven." With regard to claimed symbolism and style in tool manufacture, Mellars finds that the key contrast between Neanderthal and specifically human Upper Paleolithic tools lies in the notion of deliberately "imposed form." Even more telling than the

---

45. Robert H. Gargett, "Grave Shortcomings: The Evidence for Neanderthal Burial," *Current Anthropology* 30 (1989): 169, 175–77; L. P. Kooijmans et al., "On the Evidence for Neanderthal Burial," *Current Anthropology* 30 (1989): 329.

stone tools of Upper Paleolithic are its bone and antler tools, occurring in highly structured living sites, with the recognizable regularity and standardization of Upper Paleolithic art and decorative motifs. Mellars concludes that "it is this dramatic and well defined shift in tool production patterns that suggests that there was indeed a major change in the symbolic and cognitive properties of tool manufacture between the Middle and Upper Palaeolithic periods, which may have equally significant implications for the general mental and cognitive dimensions of the populations involved."

Regarding the claims about Neanderthal symbolization in, for example, rock art, Mellars notes that

> these specimens are very rare. The fact that alleged Mousterian symbolic objects tend to be unique casts further doubt on their actual symbolic content, for they provide no evidence for a shared system of meaning.... Although the persistence of Middle Paleolithic artifact forms is striking, it is not without precedent: relative technological stasis has been the rule in human evolution for 2 million years or more.

On the question of Neanderthal language, Mellars notes the dichotomy between evolutionary and catastrophic views of the emergence of language. For those who argue for a punctuated form of language emergence, such a relatively abrupt shift "might help to explain some of the radical transformations in human behavioral patterns over this period, documented in the archaeological records."[46] We have already discussed Lonergan's view on the need to move to a higher level of explanation when a pile-up of meaningful data exists that is random in terms of a lower level of explanation. This does not arise with the Neanderthal data but it does with regard to these "radical transformations in human behavioral patterns." He agrees with Philip Lieberman on Neanderthal incapacity for language. Lieberman writes:

> The problem arises because the length of the Neanderthal mouth is outside the range of modern human beings.... Neanderthal speech anatomy was more advanced than that of *Homo erectus* or human newborns but still incapable of producing the full range of human speech sounds with the stability and formant frequency structure of sounds like the "supervowel."

Lieberman notes that Neanderthal retention of a primitive face prominently extended about the mouth, typical of earlier hominids where the lower face is positioned in front of the brain, "clearly indicates less efficient speech communication. They represent an intermediate stage in the evolution of human

---

46. Mellars, *The Neanderthal Legacy*, 379, 381–83, 146, 151, 388.

speech. Although their brain was as large as our own, the neural substrate that regulates speech production may also have been less developed.... Neanderthals were inherently unable to produce human speech."[47]

We have already noted that Mellars points out that at the archaeological level there is a "virtual lack of convincing evidence for symbolic behaviour or expression in Neanderthal contexts." Whatever is made of this, no one would question "that elaborate symbolic thought and expression is one of the defining hallmarks of all fully developed languages." For Mellars, the lack of convincing evidence for symbolism in Neanderthal contexts is at least consistent with the lack of a highly developed Neanderthal language, even if it is not concrete proof.

Mellars holds the view "that a radical restructuring of language patterns would not only be consistent with the available archaeological records of behavioral changes over the period of the Middle-Upper Paleolithic transition but might provide the most economical single explanation." He is inclined to agree with linguists such as Noam Chomsky, Steven Pinker, and Derek Bickerton that the emergence of language must have been a catastrophic rather than a gradual process of mental and linguistic evolution. If so, we should expect to find "a fairly dramatic reflection of this transition in the available behavioural records of human development" across whole spectra from technology through subsistence and social patterns to the more overtly symbolic patterns of the human group. Mellars concludes: "The question is where, in the available archaeological records of Europe, might we identify such a watershed, if not over the period to the Middle-to-Upper Paleolithic transition?"[48]

Walker Percy's pungent reflection on the implications of human linguistic (what he calls "triadic" or reflective) activity (as opposed to non-self-conscious "dyadic" activity) brings out the need to explore what grounds the human difference at that "transition" point—where, precisely, the issue of "transition" comes up. "*Thus, there is a sense,*" he argues, "*in which it can be said that, given two mammals extraordinarily similar in organic structure and genetic code, and given that one species has made the breakthrough into triadic behavior and the other has not, there is, semiotically speaking, more difference between the two than there is between the dyadic animal and the planet Saturn.*"[49] Bearing in mind the recent profound, if not fatal, revision of the standard Darwinian evolutionary paradigm, it seems at least likely that a combination of genomic

---

47. Philip Lieberman, *Eve Spoke: Human Language and Human Evolution* (New York: Norton, 1998), 92–97.
48. Mellars, *The Neanderthal Legacy*, 388–89, 391.
49. Walker Percy, *Lost in the Cosmos: The Last Self-Help Book* (New York: Washington Square Press, 1984), 97 (emphasis in original).

regulatory systems with environmental interaction and adaptation will provide the best heuristic for understanding the hominid sequence. That sequence provides a uniquely well-documented series of body plans culminating in our own.[50] And any argument for the kind of anti-human racism that Voegelin opposed in his two so-called race books has been scuttled at the biochemical level over the last twenty years or so.

When Rebecca Cann and her associates at the Department of Human Biology at the University of California at Berkeley studied the mitochondrial DNA variation in different species, they discovered a 5 percent variation between the two slightly different orangutan species in Borneo and Sumatra, a 0.6 percent variation among gorillas, and an astonishingly low 0.3 percent variation among humans of all races. Chris Stringer and Robin McKie remark that

> it is not the gorilla, nor the chimpanzee, nor the orangutan, that is unusual.... Each enjoys a normal spectrum of biological variability. It is the human race that is odd. We display remarkable geographical diversity, and yet astonishing genetic unity.... The realisation that humans are biologically highly homogeneous has one straightforward implication: that mankind has only recently evolved from one tight little group of ancestors.... We are all members of a very young species, and our genes betray this secret.[51]

Moreover, Ian Tattersall and Geoffrey Schwartz have noted that parallel to the maternal mitochondrial DNA sequence is the more recently discovered paternal Y chromosome sequence, with the origin of both now being dated to c. 50,000 BP. They point out that "recent comparative studies of the human Y chromosome (uniquely passed along by men, presumably from an 'African Adam') suggest a pattern similar to that suggested by the maternally derived mtDNA. Even more interesting is that in China, once a hotbed of multiregional thinking, a recent study of microsatellites (repeats of short nuclear DNA segments) has suggested a derivation of the Han Chinese from an ultimately African ancestry."[52]

However, Voegelin's warning of the boundary question posed by human emergence, when he said that the epiphany of structures in reality was a mystery inaccessible to explanation, becomes acute when the "structures" we are dealing with are those of human consciousness and its expression in language. While Lonergan's approach comes at the issue from a different direction, it

---

50. An excellent recent survey can be found in Roger Lewin, *Principles of Human Evolution: A Core Textbook* (Oxford: Blackwells, 1998).

51. Chris Stringer and Robin McKie, *African Exodus: The Origins of Modern Humanity* (London: Pimlico, 1997), 113.

52. Tattersall and Schwartz, *Extinct Humans,* 230.

seems to be in substantial agreement with Voegelin's. He sees inquiry and insight, reflection and judgment, deliberation and choice as "a higher system of sensitive process." But

> inquiry and insight are not so much a higher system as a perennial source of higher systems. There can be in man a perennial source of higher systems because the materials of such systematization are not built into his constitution.... An animal species is a solution to the problem of living, so that a new solution would be a new species; for an animal to begin to live in a new fashion, there would be required not only a modification of its sensibility but also a modification of the organism that the sensibility systematizes.

New developments in humans are based not in a new sensibility, with its corresponding neural basis,

> but inquiring and understanding have their basis, not in a neural structure, but in an [intellectual] structure of psychic contents.... Intelligence is the source of a sequence of systems that unify and relate otherwise coincidental aggregates of sensible contents.... Man, then, is at once explanatory genus and explanatory species. He is explanatory genus, for he represents a higher system beyond sensibility. But that genus is coincident with species, for it is not just a higher system but a source of higher systems. In man there occurs the transition from the intelligible to the intelligent.[53]

We may say that the entire thrust of Voegelin's exploration in philosophical anthropology, where he technically correlates what Lonergan, in terminology that would certainly set Voegelin's teeth on edge, calls the "higher systems" of Myth, Philosophy, Revelation, and Ideology, are in fact systematizations or orderings of ranges of our experience of human, social-historic, cosmic, and divine existence.[54] It is these overarching orders of human experience that express the human specific differences that are grounded in the human generic difference of reason.

---

53. Lonergan, *Insight*, 266–67.
54. Having noted that "mankind," as a universal idea, does not exist, Voegelin suggests that the subject of history "can only be Being in the most general sense, Being itself." He compares the situation of a universal history of mankind to contemporary theoretical physics, where "we have all sorts of relational discoveries, which are so thoroughgoing that the subject matter, the terms of the relations, disappears.... We have found a similar problem in the theory of history: the subject to which all these things happen is disappearing, and we have thus come back practically to a cosmology, a philosophy of the cosmos." See Eric Voegelin, "Equivalences of Experience and Symbolization in History," in *CW*, vol. 12, *Published Essays, 1966–1985*, ed. Ellis Sandoz (1990; available Columbia: University of Missouri Press, 1999), 113, 114.

What we receive from anthropologists, however, is at best a recognition of the singularity of the human. As Tattersall and Schwartz put it:

> our pattern has essentially been one of business as usual for the natural world: a story of repeated evolutionary experimentation, diversification, and, ultimately, extinction. And it was clearly in the context of such experimentation rather than out of constant fine tuning by natural selection over the eons, that our own amazing species appeared on Earth. Albeit, in the end, with a difference: for unlike even our closest relations, *Homo sapiens* is not simply an extrapolation or improvement of what went before it. For reasons we will explore, our species is an entirely unprecedented entity in the living world, however mundanely we may have come by our unusual attributes.[55]

As a result of this valuable but still merely descriptive awareness, we must turn to philosophy for the anthropological articulation that will adequately convey the generic difference of the human. At the material level, Aristotle was aware that human parents could not adequately account for the coming into existence of human children. In *The Generation of Animals,* he writes: "That is why it is a very great puzzle to answer another question, concerning Reason. At what moment, and in what manner, do those creatures which have this principle of Reason acquire their share in it, and where does it come from? This is a very difficult problem which we must endeavor to solve, so far as it may be solved, to the best of our power."[56]

Voegelin has brought out what Aristotle meant by reason, as the basis of mankind, in Aristotle's *Metaphysics* book A.[57] As we all know too well, Aristotle opens his *Metaphysics* with the programmatic: "All men by nature reach out for knowledge," conventionally translated more blandly as "All men by nature desire to know." Voegelin first looked at the second part of this statement, regarding what all men do: *tou eidemi oregontai,* which seems to deserve the more active "*reach out* for knowledge" than the more usual "desire to know." He also refers to 982a32, where Aristotle uses *pursue* or *seize* with regard to knowledge. In *Metaphysics* 981a13–982a20 the knowledge turns out to be questioning, from minor matters to the ground of the cosmos.

In 982b12f, we are told that philosophy begins in wonder, and in 983a14f, he speaks of "a wondering why things should be as they are." So, *thaumazein,* wondering, implies the quest for the ground, a quest undertaken because of

---

55. Tattersall and Schwartz, *Extinct Humans,* 9.
56. Aristotle, *The Generation of Animals* 736b5, trans. A. L. Peck (Cambridge: Harvard University Press, Loeb Classical Library, 1990), 167.
57. Voegelin, "Configurations in History," in *CW,* 28:99–110.

man's consciousness of ignorance, *agnoein,* 982b18. Consequently, Voegelin suggests paraphrasing the first line of the *Metaphysics* as: "All men are by nature in quest of the ground."

Now Voegelin turns to that first part of the opening sentence, "*All men are by nature...*" Aristotle identifies two styles of truth, philosophy and myth. He characterizes what both styles have in common: *wonder* about the ground of being. So he can write, in 982b18f, "the *philomythos* (lover of myth) is in a sense a *philosophos* (lover of wisdom), for myth is composed of wonders." Finally, we know that he could identify with the lover of myth from a letter written in his old age: "the more solitary and isolated I am, the more of a lover of myth (*philomythoteros*) I am becoming."

What is relevant for us is that Aristotle had come to a grasp of what the two cultural forms—myth and philosophy—with which he was acquainted held in common: both were symbolizations of the quest for the ground, which remains an impenetrable mystery. Voegelin could thus see that Aristotle had grasped the key principle of equivalence, that is to say, "the recognizable identity of the reality experienced and symbolized on the various levels of differentiation."[58]

Equivalence refers to this awareness, that in historical reality each person's and each society's quest for the ground is their exegesis of their experience of participation in that ground. However compactly and incompletely they may articulate that experience, and however much in need of further revision their experience and symbolization of reality may be, it has its dignity as a real person's or society's image of the mystery of reality surrounding and embracing them. And it is because of this dignity that the fundamental hermeneutic principle for Voegelin could be stated thusly: "*the reality of experience is self-interpretive.* The men who have the experiences express themselves through symbols; and the symbols are the key to understanding the experience expressed."[59]

It is at this level, characterized by the reflective quest for truth expanded in his magnificent chapter 7, "Universal Humanity" in *The Ecumenic Age,* that Voegelin has developed the core of a philosophical anthropology that will enable our generation to carry out what he himself called "a search of the search"[60] not only of human origins but of the whole of human history.

---

58. Eric Voegelin, *Autobiographical Reflections,* ed. Ellis Sandoz (Baton Rouge: Louisiana State University Press, 1989), 108.
59. Ibid., 81.
60. Voegelin, "Equivalences of Experience," 116.

II
Literature

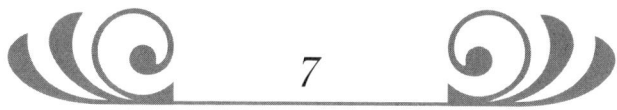

A Discipline of the Mind and Heart
Voegelin and Santayana as Philosophers of Experience

Elizabeth Corey

All serious readers of Voegelin are aware that he considered the philosophy of George Santayana to have been a formative influence on his early intellectual development. In *On the Form of the American Mind,* Voegelin analyzes several aspects of Santayana's philosophy, commenting on his poetry and on his idea of "essence." He sees that Santayana's philosophy is poetic, mystical, and skeptical, and that it is at the same time grounded in commonsense experience. Voegelin might well be describing himself when he writes that "philosophy is not a topic that engages Santayana only on occasion; it is a necessity of life, his daily answer to everything he encounters. He lives by thinking." Voegelin's informal comments in *Autobiographical Reflections* express clearly the reasons for his interest in Santayana. "To me, Santayana was a revelation concerning philosophy, comparable to the revelation I received at the same time through common sense philosophy," writes Voegelin. "Here was a man with a vast background of philosophical knowledge, sensitive to the problems of the spirit without accepting a dogma."[1]

However, students of Santayana will doubtless be aware that he considered himself a materialist. And materialism, as he comments in *Dominations and Powers* is "the most brutal form" of naturalism. Voegelin, of course, is well

---

1. Eric Voegelin, *The Collected Works of Eric Voegelin* (hereinafter, *CW*), vol. 1, *On the Form of the American Mind,* trans. Ruth Hein, ed. Jürgen Gebhardt and Barry Cooper (1995; available Columbia: University of Missouri Press, 1999), 84; Eric Voegelin, *Autobiographical Reflections,* ed. Ellis Sandoz (Baton Rouge: Louisiana State University Press, 1989), 31.

known for his antipathy toward all reductionistic philosophies, materialism featuring prominently among them. So why would Voegelin have been attracted to a thinker who professed such a doctrine, much less have praised him as someone "sensitive to the problems of the spirit"? Moreover, to engage Santayana's critics is to be faced with a mountain of evidence that characterizes Santayana's writings as incomprehensible and unintelligible. William James, at times inclined to be somewhat more indulgent of Santayana, criticized his *Life of Reason* as the "perfection of rottenness in a philosophy."[2] And while his critics admit that Santayana is indeed a poet and a philosopher, most conclude that these two endeavors should remain separate and that Santayana succeeds brilliantly at neither one. So again, what would Voegelin have seen in such a thinker?

"To be great is to be misunderstood," writes Ellis Sandoz in *The Voegelinian Revolution,* and of Santayana it can be said that he was misunderstood by many.[3] But he was not misunderstood by Voegelin, in whom he found a supremely sympathetic audience. And although scholars have often noticed Voegelin's interest in Santayana, no one has yet considered the reasons for this interest. To anticipate my conclusion, I suggest that Voegelin regards Santayana as a model philosopher—someone who understands that philosophy, poetry, and mysticism spring from the same source and apprehend the same reality. This conclusion may not seem immediately apparent, however, for several questions arise for the student of both thinkers: Why did Voegelin so admire a materialist philosopher? How can Voegelin's great admiration for Santayana be reconciled with the overwhelmingly negative criticisms of Santayana's work? And finally: In what specific ways are Voegelin and Santayana engaged in the same quest? The answers to all these questions must begin with a proper understanding of Santayana's conception of materialism.

Santayana's Materialism

Materialism is, of course, a notoriously slippery word. It may signify the Epicurean and Lucretian ideas of atoms falling in a void, conceptions that deny a cosmic organizing principle and aim at alleviating the fear of death. Or it may appear as the "dialectical" materialism of Marx and his followers. In common

---

2. George Santayana, *Dominations and Powers* (New Brunswick: Transaction Publishers, 1995), 18; *The Letters of William James,* ed. H. James (Boston: Atlantic Monthly Press, 1920), 2:122, quoted in Anthony Woodward, *Living in the Eternal: A Study of George Santayana* (Nashville: Vanderbilt University Press, 1988), 6.

3. Ellis Sandoz, *The Voegelinian Revolution* (New Brunswick: Transaction Publishers, 2000), 12.

parlance, it may mean simply the dogged pursuit of wealth and comfort. One thing is certain: Santayana thoroughly rejected this latter variety of materialism. The accumulation of wealth was not something to which he aspired. Santayana stood, indeed, outside the mainstream of an age that concerned itself with progress and prosperity, preferring the pursuit of aesthetic and philosophical endeavors to the workaday occupations of those around him. During his years at Harvard he earned the reproof of his teacher William James, who advised him that his philosophy was a bit "too much like a poem" and too little like the work of the more "serious" philosophers who would be evaluating his doctoral dissertation. But the aesthetic sensibility was primary for Santayana. One may as well call him a poet-philosopher as a philosopher-poet. For Santayana these two disciplines could not be disentangled.

Such aesthetic and philosophical considerations are at the core of the famous criticisms of liberalism that appear throughout Santayana's corpus. Liberalism, he believes, does not elevate the human spirit but brings it down to a low, vulgar level where even the sought-after rewards are ultimately unsatisfactory. It is, to put it quite simply, ugly and inadequate. He writes the following verses in 1896:

> My heart rebels against my generation,
> That talks of freedom and is slave to riches,
> And, toiling 'neath each day's ignoble burden,
> Boasts of the morrow.
> No space for noonday rest or midnight watches,
> No purest joy of breathing under heaven!
> Wretched themselves, they heap, to make them happy,
> Many possessions.

Even the prizes offered by liberal society—wealth, political office, fame—bring with them endless worries. "I hear no laughter among the rich which is not forced and nervous," writes Santayana in an essay from about 1920. "I find no sense of moral security amongst them, no happy freedom, no mastery over anything."[4] The liberal condition could never satisfy Santayana's philosophic and aesthetic longings. Materialism as a phenomenon of liberal society, then, was no part of his constitution.

But while Santayana rejected the vulgar materialism of many of his contemporaries, he nonetheless located his work firmly within the *philosophical* materialist tradition. Indeed, in *Dominations and Powers* he acknowledges that

---

4. *Poems of George Santayana*, ed. Robert Hutchinson (New York: Dover, 1970), 63; George Santayana, *Soliloquies in England and Later Soliloquies* (New York: Scribner's, 1922), 185.

he has repeatedly confessed to being a materialist.[5] This avowal raises two important questions. First, what does Santayana mean by *materialist,* and second (for our purposes), why would Voegelin have been attracted to the thought of such a person? Voegelin, of course, is acutely sensitive to the tendency of modern thinkers to excise various sectors of experience in order to bolster their philosophical apparatus. And materialist philosophers—Hobbes and Marx, for example—are the subjects of some of Voegelin's most incisive attacks. If Santayana is indeed a materialist, why would he capture Voegelin's attention and merit his praise? An answer to this question requires a careful sensitivity to what Santayana means by *materialism.*

Standard definitions of *materialism* describe it as a doctrine that places physical matter in a primary position, relegating concepts such as "mind" or "spirit" to secondary positions or eliminating them altogether. Some such materialism is found in Hobbes, who observes that the origin of all thought is sense: "there is no conception in a man's mind which hath not at first, totally or by parts, been begotten upon the organs of sense." And Marx makes a related point when he writes, famously, that it is "not the consciousness of men that determines their being, but, on the contrary, their social being that determines their consciousness."[6] Material conditions make us entirely who we are.

Materialism would thus seem to be an especially "worldly" philosophy. Since it is concerned with things that can be observed and measured, it lends itself well to empirical studies, promising to provide greater certainty in outcomes and stronger linkages between cause and effect. It falls easily in line with the modern trend toward methodological empiricism. Moreover, in denying or redefining the spiritual realm, materialist philosophies attenuate those fears about death and divine punishment that are such troublesome and persistent parts of the human condition. But all these characteristics—so praiseworthy in the eyes of empiricists and materialists themselves—are of course anathema to Voegelin's conception of philosophy. What is it, then, about Santayana's avowedly materialist philosophy that Voegelin finds so compelling? The answer lies in Santayana's conception of matter, spirit, and essence.

The foundation of Santayana's materialism is not an abstract theory about the nature of matter but rather a simple assumption, made even by children (and poets), that human life takes place "in an existing and persisting world in which there are rocks and trees, men and animals." Matter is "whatsoever in nature, by its motions and tensions, causes all events to take place and all

---

5. Santayana, *Dominations and Powers,* 18.
6. Thomas Hobbes, *Leviathan,* ed. Edwin Curley (Indianapolis: Hackett, 1994), 6; *The Marx-Engels Reader,* ed. Robert C. Tucker (New York: Norton, 1978), 4.

appearances to appear." At the beginning of *Dominations and Powers* Santayana asserts the first presupposition of his inquiry quite frankly: "mankind is a race of animals living in the material world." Therefore nothing can take place entirely outside the realm of matter. A doctor's cure is effective precisely because it is administered, not merely because the doctor possesses the intellectual expertise to know what to do in a given situation. Matter is thus the minimum condition for life, the *conditio sine qua non* of human experience. It determines natural existence, delineating "relations in space and time ... duration and disappearance."[7] Santayana is careful not to say that matter is the only thing that exists, for he believes in a concomitant realm of "spirit." But he does believe that spirit is intimately involved with matter and depends upon it.

With respect to "essence" or "spirit" (the two terms point toward the same kind of experience) Santayana means to demonstrate an ideal form of being—ideal not in the sense of "best" but of "idea." Essences are objects of pure sense or pure thought that flash out in temporary appearances but cannot be captured or held immobile. "By 'essence,'" Santayana writes, "I understand a universal, of any degree of complexity and definition, which may be given immediately, whether to sense or to thought."[8] The crimson of the sunset is an essence, and as such it does not decay with the fading light but simply ceases to be visible. Essences are not themselves material, but human beings can perceive them when they are (temporarily) embodied in matter.

This description of essences sounds remarkably Platonic for an avowed materialist. And yet Santayana breaks definitively from Plato, since he asserts that the existence of essences does not therefore imply that they could be counted or classified in some kind of hierarchy. It is worth quoting in full Santayana's view of essences.

> The quality or function that makes all shepherds shepherds or all goods good is an essence; but so are all the remaining qualities which make each shepherd and each good distinguishable from each other. Far from gathering up the fluidity of existence into a few norms for human language and thought to be focused upon, the realm of essence infinitely multiplies that multiplicity. ... My doctrine lends no countenance to the human presumption that whatsoever man notices or names or loves ought to be more deeply seated in reality or more permanent than what he ignores or despises. ... [Moreover] the realm of essence is no more limited to these few ideals chosen and projected heavenwards by the aspiration of living creatures, than the celestial galaxy is limited to the north star.[9]

---

7. Santayana, *Dominations and Powers*, 19, 18, 6, 12.
8. George Santayana, "Three Proofs of Realism," in Santayana, *Essays in Critical Realism* (New York, 1920), 168 n, quoted in Voegelin, *CW*, 1:73.
9. George Santayana, *Scepticism and Animal Faith* (New York: Dover, 1955), 78–79.

Essences, for Santayana, are infinite in number and have no specific moral content. They never appear "on their own" because they cannot be apprehended at all but for their embodiment in matter. As Santayana continually emphasizes, matter is the precondition for all appearances and events. Thus while Santayana insists that we are always—inescapably—embodied, he also points us toward a realm of permanent, unchanging essences. How exactly does he reconcile these two realms?

In fact Santayana does *not* reconcile materialism and essence in a way that is satisfactory to many philosophers. His work has been described as eloquent but "at bottom unintelligible." Another critic describes his merging of the two realms as "a mystery that no amount of analysis is ever likely to dissolve." Nevertheless, it is clear that Santayana himself found the conjunction of these two realms quite plausible, and it is precisely this intermingling of essence and matter that lies at the center of his thought. For as he writes in *Dominations and Powers*, to deny that spirit could be the efficient cause of something is not to deny spirit altogether: "the materialist does not deny that material agencies may be *at the same time* animated by ideal motives and moral purposes." The doctor whose intelligence alone cannot cure a patient may nevertheless act so that his patient sees him as "bathed . . . in the light of spirit."[10]

Unlike most materialists, therefore, Santayana never denies a realm of "essence" or "spirit." He does, however, assert that these depend upon matter. "Mere" materialism, according to Santayana, is inadequate, since it consists solely in observation of the "hopeless flux and the temporal order of things."[11] Yet from matter there emerges a perception of an immaterial world. Matter affords us glimpses of essences, flashes of illumination. To orient oneself toward essences is "to live in the eternal." It is to forgo our accustomed immersion in practical affairs and to engage in the world of ideas:

> To substitute the society of ideas for that of things is simply to live in the mind; it is to survey the world of existence in its truth and beauty rather than in its personal perspectives, or with practical urgency. It is the sole path to happiness for the intellectual man, because the intellectual man cannot be satisfied with a world of perpetual change, defeat and imperfection. It is the path trodden by ancient philosophers and modern saints or poets; not, of course, by modern writers on philosophy (except Spinoza), because these have not been philosophers *in the vital sense;* they have practiced no spiritual discipline, suffered no change of heart, but lived on exactly like other professors.[12]

---

10. Edward L. Shaughnessy, "Santayana: Latter-Day Janus," *Journal of Aesthetics and Art Criticism* 33 (1975): 310; Woodward, *Living in the Eternal*, 85; Santayana, *Dominations and Powers*, 19.
11. Woodward, *Living in the Eternal*, 2.
12. Santayana, *Soliloquies in England*, 120 (emphasis added).

To be a philosopher "in the vital sense" is thus, according to Santayana, to do much more than engage in empirical or analytic research. It is to take one's own experience as a starting point for reflection, to consider that experience in light of what others have said about the human condition, and to cultivate an openness toward all realms of being. For Santayana, nothing lies outside the bounds of serious reflection. And yet he remains firmly grounded in his conviction that human beings live in a material world and that no one can achieve a wholly contemplative life. It is precisely this intellectual and spiritual openness combined with a grounded matter-of-factness that Voegelin finds so compelling in Santayana's work. Far from viewing him as a garden-variety materialist, Voegelin comments that Santayana's approach may be seen as "an almost mystical skepticism that in fact is not materialism at all."[13]

How exactly does this openness to experience manifest itself in Santayana's corpus? In the first place, it is apparent even from a cursory inspection of Santayana's published work (poetry, essays, philosophical treatises, a novel) that his interests are extraordinarily broad. He takes up such topics as architecture, national character, manners, and poetry, and it seems there is nothing about which Santayana does not have a considered opinion. But it is not just that Santayana had many interests; this, of course, is not unusual and even to be expected of anyone who calls himself a humanist. What is remarkable about Santayana is his intellectual and spiritual depth. Here is no superficial journalist or polemicist, but a first-rank philosopher. Santayana is said to have understood the history of philosophy as well as any of his contemporaries at Harvard—probably better. Yet it was as a *poet*-philosopher that he most effectively conveyed the manifestations of spirit that he observed and felt in the world around him. Voegelin, of course, devotes considerable attention to Santayana's poetry in *On the Form of the American Mind*. Not everyone is as inclined as Voegelin to indulge Santayana's poetic inclinations, but the rewards of such indulgence are profound.

Santayana and His Critics

Many of Santayana's critics complain that his poetic style—eloquent though it is—obscures his philosophy, rendering it at bottom unintelligible and confusing to "layman and professional philosopher alike." It is a dilemma that one of his most sympathetic readers has characterized simply as the "Santayana problem."[14] But a consideration of the substance of these criticisms may provide a

---

13. Voegelin, *CW*, 1:xxxvii, quoting *Autobiographical Reflections*, 31.
14. Shaughnessy, "Latter-Day Janus," 310, 311.

clearer picture of the precise ways in which Santayana departs from orthodoxy and finds his own unique voice. It should also help to explain Voegelin's interest in Santayana. For even the most absurd misrepresentations of Santayana's project may be valuable in bringing particular facets of Santyana's thought to the fore, in the same way that "a caricature reveals the potentialities of a face."[15]

Many critics find Santayana's work difficult to grasp because of what is perceived as an overemphasis on aesthetics. The realm of aesthetics has its place, say such critics, but it must not range too widely. Aesthetic considerations are a delightful holiday from the serious business of philosophizing, but placing aesthetics at the center of one's life is both impractical and irresponsible. "Santayana has had no concentrated continuation in American thought," writes John E. Smith, because a philosophy "so uncompromisingly aesthetic at its core and so filled with Olympian distance from the plane where mere mortals live runs counter to the seriousness and even moralism of the American temper."[16]

Others believe that Santayana's emphasis on spirit and on aesthetics is a purposeful (or perhaps deluded) misrepresentation of his true doctrine: materialism. They simply cannot understand his continual focus on "spirit." And thus Herbert Schneider writes of Santayana that "when his senses and memories began to fail him in his Italian seclusion," Santayana "imagined his 'real' being to be that of his spirit."[17] Schneider's view is that this must be a mistaken self-understanding, for was not Santayana decidedly a "naturalist" and "realist"? Materialism (naturalism) *implies* a denial of spirit; and so if Santayana is a true materialist then this late focus on spirit is either disingenuous or mere confusion.

These criticisms point to what remains a central issue in Santayana scholarship: his tendency to treat philosophy and poetry as symbols of what is fundamentally the same reality. And while some critics (like Voegelin) praise him for this approach, many find him confusing and contradictory. Santayana is eclectic and unorthodox, not clear, logical, and analytical. Like the skylarks he celebrates in *Soliloquies in England*, Santayana is willing to spend "his whole strength on something ultimate and utterly useless, a momentary entrancing pleasure which (being useless and ultimate) is very like an act of worship or of sacrifice."[18]

---

15. Michael Oakeshott, *Rationalism in Politics*, ed. Timothy Fuller (Indianapolis: Liberty Press, 1991), 58.

16. John E. Smith, *Themes in American Philosophy* (New York: Harper, 1970), 128.

17. Sandoz, *The Voegelinian Revolution*, 15–16. For the context of his remarks, see Herbert W. Schneider, *A History of American Philosophy* (New York: Columbia University Press, 1963), 508.

18. Santayana, *Soliloquies in England*, 109.

But one of the most significant criticisms of Santayana, for the purposes of this essay, has to do with the fact that he was inclined to consider "spirit" an integral part of human experience. Herbert Schneider is obviously quite uncomfortable with Santayana's confession late in life that he could identify himself "heartily with nothing... except with the flame of spirit itself."[19] But it is precisely this sensitivity to "spirit" that makes Santayana worthy of Voegelin's attention. Indeed, both Voegelin and Santayana are criticized and misunderstood for their profound interest in transcendent experience. It is worth noting, however, that despite the official philosophical and academic discomfort with Santayana's wide-ranging work, he has always been extraordinarily popular with the educated public. If there is no "Santayana school," millions of people "have read him for pleasure."[20] His readers have never abandoned him; for Santayana captures the diversity and depth of human experience in a way far more compelling than the vast majority of what often passes for philosophy. Santayana himself understands the problem well enough. "Men of the world," he writes, "find [my books] consistent... [and] to the ladies everything is crystal-clear; yet the *philosophers* say that it is lazy and self-indulgent of me not to tell them plainly what I think, if I know myself what it is."[21]

Santayana's poetic sensibility relates to another important affinity with Voegelin. From the point of view of "professional philosophy" Santayana is frustrating above all because of his refusal to use language objectively. In short, his "doctrines" are unclear. In the words of Richard Butler, "the primary intrinsic difficulty in criticizing [Santayana] is his ornamented literary form, a source of artistic charm and scientific conclusion. A scientific thinker cannot afford the luxury of lush, florid prose and hope to express his thought with precision." Moreover, continues Butler, Santayana "unfortunately... preferred fancy to reason and the impulsive flight of imagination to the planned plodding of demonstration."[22]

Santayana's "failing," however, reflects a conscious decision on his part, and his express aim is to use language differently than his fellows. Although he is well aware that words are overwhelmingly used to convey information in practical, everyday endeavors, he is interested in employing them in other, more creative ways, as a poet does. In *Interpretations of Poetry and Religion* he speaks directly to this issue. When we use language, believes Santayana, we are concerned most often with its use as a currency. Words are symbols or counters that convey an agreed-upon value between persons. Most of us are

---

19. Schneider, *History of American Philosophy,* 509.
20. Shaughnessy, "Latter-Day Janus," 313.
21. Santayana, *Soliloquies in England,* 255 (emphasis added).
22. Richard Butler, *The Mind of Santayana* (New York: Greenwood Press, 1968), 133.

accustomed to think entirely in symbols, and never to be interrupted in the algebraic rapidity of [our] thinking by a moment's pause and examination of heart, nor ever to plunge for a moment into that torrent of sensation and imagery over which the bridge of prosaic associations habitually carries us safe and dry to some conventional act.[23]

Yet the language of poetry can do much more than merely keep us safe and dry. Its purpose is often to bring about a vision of just that "torrent of sensation and imagery" that we seek to avoid in ordinary life. Language thus sheds its preconceived symbolic value and takes on new meanings given by the poet.

> A hidden light illumines all our seeing,
> An unknown love enchants our solitude.
> We feel and know that from the depths of being
> Exhales an infinite, a perfect good.[24]

What could a philosophic analysis of this verse add to a reader's intuitive understanding? Very little, and yet the verse clearly contains philosophical ideas. Here is Santayana the philosopher-poet. His language is evocative and affective, not technical and precise, and the function of his poetry is to "build new structures, richer, finer, fitter to the primary tendencies of our nature, truer to the ultimate possibilities of the soul."[25]

I do not mean to dismiss Santayana's critics out of hand, for they ask the most reasonable of all questions: What exactly is Santayana saying? Is it too much to ask that a reader be able to summarize the salient points and "most important doctrines" from what he has read? At least this much is required of all undergraduates who study philosophy. There are, however, certain philosophers whose work emphatically does not lend itself to summary or to abbreviated explanation—indeed, such an endeavor runs counter to the spirit of these thinkers. Such authors must be read in their entirety or, at the very least, in sizable portions. Both Voegelin and Santayana are included among such thinkers.

Admittedly, philosophers *do* at times set out sparklingly clear doctrines: Locke's teaching that "the purpose of government is to preserve property" is such an example, and it helps to categorize him as a liberal theorist in the tradition of other "state of nature" theorists who form a recognizable class. Never-

---

23. George Santayana, *Interpretations of Poetry and Religion* (Cambridge, MA: MIT Press, 1989), 156.
24. *Poems of George Santayana,* 81.
25. Santayana, *Interpretations,* 161.

theless, we will be sorely disappointed if we ask these questions about Santayana or Voegelin. Neither thinker is interested in building a system from the ground up. Instead, both want to explore the ideas that arise as a result of their own encounters with the world and to follow those ideas where they may lead. Santayana has been criticized for beginning his philosophy *in medias res,* but he believes this is the only valid starting point for thought. It is therefore quite legitimate to argue that, from a certain point of view, it matters little if Santayana's readers do not display "a clear understanding of his philosophical doctrine."[26] For Santayana's work is about much more than philosophy, narrowly understood, and it is at a distant remove from the analytic philosophy of his contemporaries.

> My philosophy neither is nor wishes to be scientific; not even in the sense in which, in temper and method, the *Summa* of St. Thomas might be called scientific. My philosophy is like that of the ancients a discipline of the mind and heart, a lay religion.[27]

His philosophy is poetic, and his poetry is philosophical. As Voegelin observes, for Santayana "broad knowledge is indispensable, as is the philosophic stance. Both are used not to teach or persuade but to communicate."[28] True appreciation of Santayana's project requires nothing else but total immersion in his work.

A Discipline of the Mind and Heart: Philosophy as Experience and Participation

Based on the criticisms enumerated above, Santayana might be judged as an imprecise philosopher whose flowery language gets in the way of intelligibility. Alternatively, he could be seen as a thinker inclined toward poetry as a way of expressing the diversity and breadth of experience, having realized early on that the language of modern philosophy has distinct limitations. Voegelin adopts the latter view, perceiving Santayana's merging of philosophy and poetry as one of his greatest virtues. The radical separation of philosophy from all "ordinary" experience is a pathology that Voegelin recognizes as a particularly modern problem. Voegelin remedies this in his own work by emphasizing the experiential springs of philosophy, noting that philosophy properly understood

---

26. Butler, *Mind of Santayana,* xi.
27. George Santayana, *Realms of Being* (New York: Scribner's, 1942), 827.
28. Voegelin, *CW,* 1:85–86.

is the attempt to answer existential questions that arise in the course of a life thoughtfully lived. In *Anamnesis* he writes that

> the radicalism of philosophizing can never be gauged either by the results or the critical framework of a *system* but rather, in a more literal sense, by the radices of philosophizing in the biography of philosophizing consciousness, i.e., by the experiences that impel toward reflection and do so because they have excited consciousness to the "awe" of existence.[29]

Like Santayana, Voegelin understands that emotion and intellect are not categorically distinct parts of experience but exist together in the same reality. Philosophy, for both thinkers, may originate as a response to a flash of intuition, modulate into the key of systematic philosophical inquiry, and ultimately resolve into something poetic or mystical. But the roots of the philosophical quest lie in everyday, commonsense experience. In this vein, Santayana comments that he is "content to stand where honest laymen are standing, and to write as I might talk with a friend in a country walk or sitting at a tavern."[30] His work is meant to appeal to all readers.

Voegelin, however, is most interested in Santayana because of what he regards as Santayana's "open soul," to borrow a term of Bergson. Santayana's philosophical quest is without limit, although it is at the same time grounded in frank self-examination. Above all, it emerges out of concrete, lived experience. Like Voegelin, Santayana engages in anamnetic meditation, recalling the experiences of his early life and the influences that these had upon his ideas and emotions.[31] He considers such reflection essential to understanding other human beings. Moreover, he recognizes quite clearly that actual experiences never take place in neat philosophical categories (one cannot say *this* was a purely intellectual experience and *that* was an emotional one). Experiences come all jumbled up together, and the sorting-out takes place only later, at a suitable distance from the event. Thus everything is potentially fodder for philosophy. Voegelin observes that

> in Santayana's view no realm of being has been assigned to philosophical method as its special field of investigation. Like art, philosophy can use all things for its material.... Every subject matter for philosophical discourse—an artistic or religious experience, a statement in logic or the mathematical sciences of nature—can therefore be a possible starting point for analysis.[32]

---

29. Eric Voegelin, *Anamnesis,* trans. Gerhart Niemeyer (Notre Dame: University of Notre Dame Press, 1978), 36 (emphasis added).
30. Santayana, *Dominations and Powers,* 7.
31. See particularly Santayana's *Persons and Places* (New York: Scribner's, 1944).
32. Voegelin, *CW,* 1:66.

Such analysis may consist in a rigorous, analytic procedure or it may be suggestive and intuitive. But it is clear that dogmatic philosophical systems insist on vocabularies and methods too technical and restrictive for Santayana's tastes. In defending himself against critics he has written:

> You say you find in "Poetry and Religion" no definite statement of a creed. The reason is that I have none, if by a creed we are to understand settled convictions upon matters of which we can have no real knowledge. But my philosophic attitude, if I may call it so, is definite enough, and I should think would have appeared clearly on almost every page. My feeling is that we know and can know nothing but our experience—our experience as it comes.[33]

For Santayana, philosophy is above all a way of life, and it requires active participation in the order of being.

What exactly does this "participatory" character of reality entail? Human beings, Voegelin observes, do not possess the ability to remove themselves entirely from the flux of their own experience. We *participate* in experience; hence "the story cannot begin unless it starts in the middle."[34] *In medias res*: this is also Santayana's fundamental insight. Human beings are embodied creatures living in a material world and participate (potentially) in all levels of being from *apeiron* to *nous*. Most often we approach the world intentionally, thinking in terms of subject and object, but may now and then become aware of the luminosity of It-reality.[35] Santayana was more sensitive to this luminosity than most. His poetic expression, "affective" language, and his refusal to play by the rules of conventional philosophic discourse point to the experiences of luminosity that he attempted, as best he could, to express in words. He recognizes, as does Voegelin, that there is no Archimedean point from which to consider experience, because no human being can ever escape his own nature. No philosopher can theorize as an absolute outsider.

Participation in reality is not a merely individualistic activity. It does not imply a kind of arbitrary self-creation, but is a discovery of a reality that transcends individuality. The substance of philosophical reflection is thus to express truths that are potentially accessible to every person. Its task is to articulate a shared reality, and particularly the higher realms of spirit that are part of this reality.

> The doctrines of philosophers disagree where they are literal and arbitrary,—mere guesses about the unknown; but they agree or complete one another where they are expressive or symbolic, thoughts wrung by experience from the hearts

---

33. Santayana, *Interpretations*, xxiv.
34. Eric Voegelin, *CW*, vol. 18, *In Search of Order*, vol. V of *Order and History*, ed. Ellis Sandoz (1987; Columbia: University of Missouri Press, 2000), 41.
35. See ibid., 28–32, where Voegelin explains the meaning of these terms.

of poets. Then all philosophies alike are ways of meeting and recording the same flux of images, the same vicissitudes of good and evil, which will visit all generations, while man is man.

The quote is from Santayana, who continues in a similar vein elsewhere: "it is not I that speak but human reason that speaks in me."[36]

The difficulty for both Santayana and Voegelin lies in the task of conveying their experiences of luminosity to others. The potential for luminosity to be "deformed" into intentionality is one of Voegelin's most abiding concerns, since he recognizes that contemporary philosophical discourse almost always speaks in terms of "thing-reality." But however such experience is designated—luminosity, "the spiritual life," the apperception of essences—it is supremely difficult to convey. It does not lend itself easily to analytical exposition. It may be better understood in mystical, poetic, or religious terms, all of which modern philosophy would rather avoid.

Here is where Santayana succeeds brilliantly and befuddles his critics. Since the realm of spirit is a vital part of human experience, it is the duty of a thinker to report, as best he can, his experience of these higher realms. Santayana does this poetically, and his poetry reveals the spiritual quest of a concrete consciousness, expressing the quest so that others may share in it, insofar as they are able. "Poetry has its justification in the service of revelation; poetic diction always remains linked with holy, archaic experiences... [T]here is no other expression for tragic finality than poetry," writes Voegelin. Thus the so-called ambiguity of Santayana's language and his "lush, florid prose" are not tokens of Santayana's philosophical failure but of his poetic and spiritual success. At certain moments poetry may offer "a glimpse of the divine and an incitation to a religious life."[37] Santayana believes that poetry enlarges understanding and evokes the fullness of experience in a way that purely analytical language cannot. In his poetry Santayana is "frankly making confession of an actual spiritual experience."[38] Voegelin admires this spiritual sensitivity as well as the attempt to express it to others.

Finally, however, it should be noted that Santayana's interest in poetic expression does not preclude his also being a serious philosopher. It is not that he is primarily a poet and secondarily a philosopher; he is both at once. This, of course, makes him unintelligible to modern philosophy and accounts for the

---

36. George Santayana, *Three Philosophical Poets* (Cambridge: Harvard University Press, 1945), 70; Santayana, *Interpretations*, xvi.

37. Voegelin, *CW*, 1:86, Santayana, *Interpretations*, 171.

38. George Santayana, *Poems: Selected by the Author and Revised* (New York, 1923), 91, quoted in Shaughnessy, "Latter-Day Janus," 318.

widespread criticism of his work. But it does place him firmly within a tradition of philosophy that has its roots in Plato, a kind of philosophy that aspires to the goal of contemplation by whatever means possible. Santayana writes of his own project:

> In philosophy itself investigation and reasoning are only preparatory and servile parts, means to an end. They terminate in insight, or what in the noblest sense of the word may be called *theory*... a steady contemplation of all things in their order and worth. Such contemplation is imaginative. No one can reach it who has not enlarged his mind and tamed his heart. A philosopher who attains it is, for the moment, a poet; and a poet who turns his practiced and passionate imagination on the order of all things, or on anything in the light of the whole, is for that moment a philosopher.[39]

Once again, Santayana emphasizes the close connection between two enterprises that are often separated. While many modern philosophers refuse to accept the view that philosophy and poetry are allied in significant ways, Voegelin recognizes the virtue of such an understanding. He sees, as does the man of common sense, that experience does not organize itself into arbitrary categories imposed from the outside. It tends to come as a great welter of thoughts, emotions, impulses, and intuitions that may often be best expressed in the language of poetry.

Conclusion

In *The Voegelinian Revolution*, Ellis Sandoz eloquently and pointedly addresses the issue of Voegelin's reception by modern philosophers. "Both obscurity and misunderstanding arise from the drift of Voegelin's philosophy," Sandoz writes, "for it firmly addresses the whole history and hierarchy of human existence with special emphasis upon the modes of man's participation in the divine as reflected in documented experience."[40] He observes that the same may be said of Henri Bergson and particularly of Santayana. The present essay has emphasized the particularly negative critical reaction to Santayana as a means of answering the question Why was Santayana—an avowedly materialist philosopher—so important to Voegelin?

The answer to this question has several parts. First, a proper definition of terms is required to clarify the issue of materialism, for Santayana's materialism

---

39. Santayana, *Three Philosophical Poets*, 11.
40. Sandoz, *Voegelinian Revolution*, 15.

is unlike any other. It consists of the commonsense assumption that human beings are fundamentally embodied and that we live in a material world where nothing happens absent some material cause. At the same time, there exist essences that human beings may now and then apprehend. Both matter and essence are vital parts of experience, and despite much philosophical protest, in Santayana's mind they do exist together. One is left with a materialism that—far from denying the perfect and eternal—strives to apprehend it. In short, Santayana is not a garden-variety materialist but may even be, as Voegelin suggests, a "mystical skeptic."

But the question of why exactly Santayana was so important to Voegelin cannot be properly answered until one faces the question of what it is *in particular* about Santayana's work that so appeals to him. Santayana, of course, was no orthodox Christian. Even though he was not orthodox, he nonetheless was intensely spiritual, alive to the higher realms of being, and willing to attempt to express these in his work. Voegelin's own religious views are the subject of some controversy, and yet what is obviously beyond debate is his character as a mystic-philosopher who strives to apprehend and express transcendence in whatever way it may come. In brief, then, Voegelin is attracted by Santayana's openness to experience and by his sensitivity to transcendence.

Finally, Voegelin sees in Santayana someone who is a full-fledged philosopher, not merely an academic, a professor, or, perhaps worst of all, an "intellectual." Santayana is a true lover of wisdom, someone who could not avoid the philosophical quest in every aspect of his life. For most persons who call themselves philosophers, "philosophy is a vocation they profess, a skill or expertise in a job at which they earn their livings, not a life they live." But for Santayana, "his life was his philosophy; his philosophy was his life. In our modern world, there have not been many of whom this could be said."[41] It can, however, also be said of Voegelin, for whom philosophy is "not a body of 'ideas' or 'opinions' but a man's responsive pursuit of his questioning unrest to the divine sources that have aroused it."[42]

In 1928, Voegelin wrote his analysis of Santayana in *On the Form of the American Mind*. At that time he was a young man, just embarking on what was to be a long and extraordinarily productive career. But several observations in this early book prefigure his most mature understanding of philosophy. Perhaps this may be explained by observing, with Michael Oakeshott, that a man's "greatest works differ from his lesser works in degree and not in kind: they may be more perfect, but they express the same idea." In other words, the

---

41. Horace Kallen, "The Laughing Philosopher," *Journal of Philosophy* 61 (1964): 20.
42. Voegelin, *Anamnesis*, 96.

fundamental insights that Voegelin would express over the course of his career were probably present at the very beginning. What is beyond doubt is that Voegelin saw Santayana as a model for the kind of philosopher he himself would become. Voegelin writes admiringly that philosophy is not "a topic that engages Santayana only on occasion; it is a necessity of life, his daily answer to everything he encounters. He lives by thinking, and he is constantly amazed at the oddness of this world and of his person in it."[43] Precisely the same may be said of Voegelin, and of all those who are philosophers in the vital sense.

---

43. Michael Oakeshott, "Shylock the Jew: An Essay in Villainy," *Caian* 30 (1921): 62; Voegelin, *CW*, 1:84.

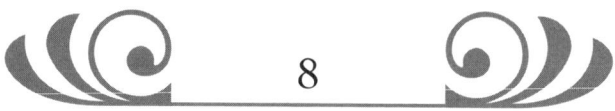

8

Compactness, Poetic Ambiguity, and the Fiction of Robert Penn Warren

Steven D. Ealy

The following episode from C. S. Lewis's *The Silver Chair* provides an entree for a consideration of Eric Voegelin's analysis of symbolization. A gnome by the name of Golg invites the children to come with him to the land of Bism, deep in the center of the earth. "Down there," he tells them, "I could show you real gold, real silver, real diamonds." Jill replies that they are already far below the deepest mines man knows.

Golg responds, "I have heard of those little scratches in the crust that you Topdwellers call mines. But that's where you get dead gold, dead silver, dead gems. Down in Bism we have them alive and growing. There I'll pick you bunches of rubies that you can eat and squeeze you a cupful of diamond juice. You won't care much about fingering the cold, dead treasures of your shallow mines after you have tasted the live ones in Bism."[1] But rather than join Golg on a journey to Bism, the children decide to return to the Overworld—the world of the surface.

One way to understand Voegelin's writing on symbolization suggests that "ideas" are like the dead gold and silver of surface mines, while symbols are the living gems found deep within the earth. Voegelin asserts in *Autobiographical Reflections*, "Ideas transform symbols, which express experiences, into concepts—which are assumed to refer to a reality other than the reality experienced."[2] He

---

1. C. S. Lewis, *The Silver Chair* (New York: Collier Books, 1970), 182.
2. Eric Voegelin, *Autobiographical Reflections*, ed. Ellis Sandoz (Baton Rouge: Louisiana State University Press, 1989), 78.

then adds, "This reality other than the reality experienced does not exist. Hence, ideas are liable to deform the truth of the experiences and their symbolization."

Before continuing I must return to Lewis's children momentarily. Unlike the gnome Golg, Jill and the other children cannot live at the bottom of the world, taking their "diamond juice" straight. The strain of such an attempt perhaps would be too great on them—just as the tension involved in "border experiences" that put us in direct contact with the transcendent is unbearable for most human beings.[3]

In this essay I begin with an examination of Voegelin's discussion of symbols in one of his most important essays, "Equivalences of Experience and Symbolization in History." I then suggest that poetic symbolization has certain advantages over philosophical symbolization, advantages that Voegelin recognized but tended to downplay. Finally, I conclude with a consideration of the cognitive dimensions of poetry in two novels—*All the King's Men* and *World Enough and Time*—by Robert Penn Warren.

Voegelin on Symbolization

Voegelin begins his essay "Equivalences of Experience and Symbolization in History" with the claim that "the search for the constants in human order in society and history is, at present, uncertain of its language." As the essay proceeds Voegelin provides a number of statements and restatements of what those constants are—or what the constant is—and we will begin with a survey of these statements. His first formulation tells us that "what is permanent in the history of mankind *is not the symbols* but man himself in search of his humanity and its order." The next formulation appears to be extremely provisional: "if anything is constant in the history of mankind it is the language of tension between life and death, immortality and mortality, perfection and imperfection, time and timelessness; between order and disorder, truth and untruth, sense and senselessness of existence"—what he calls "tensional symbolisms."[4]

---

3. See Eric Voegelin, *Science, Politics, and Gnosticism* (Washington, DC: Regnery Publishing, Gateway Editions, 1997), 75–77. Available in Voegelin, *The Collected Works of Eric Voegelin* (hereinafter, *CW*), vol. 5, *Modernity without Restraint: The Political Religions; The New Science of Politics; and Science, Politics, and Gnosticism,* ed. Manfred Henningsen (Columbia: University of Missouri Press, 2000).

4. Eric Voegelin, "Equivalences of Experience and Symbolization in History," in Voegelin, *CW*, vol. 12, *Published Essays, 1966–1985,* ed. Ellis Sandoz (1990; available Columbia: University of Missouri Press, 1999), 115 (emphasis added), 119, 120.

Voegelin's third formulation seems to move the focus away from man: "What is constant in the history of mankind... is the structure of existence itself." He then proceeds to enunciate a number of propositions regarding this structure, beginning with the proposition "Man participates in the process of reality." Voegelin adds six more propositions, three positive and three cautionary. The three cautionary corollaries are that reality cannot be observed from the outside, that the experience of reality is never total but always perspectival, and that "the knowledge of reality conveyed by the symbols can never become a final possession of truth" because experience and the symbols it generates "are part of reality in process."[5]

He then attempts to push the search further and deeper: from symbols to the originating experiences, and "from the experiences further back to the depth of the psyche."[6] But there are dangers in treating *psyche* as the constant of mankind's history, most notably the danger of absolutizing it into something that stands outside of history and experience.

Voegelin concludes, in his first conclusion, "There is no constant to be found in history, because the historical field of equivalents is not given as a collective of phenomena which could be submitted to the procedures of abstraction and generalization." But this conclusion is immediately superceded by another, however tentatively it may be stated: "If anything that has turned up in the course of our search deserves the name of a constant, it is the process in the mode of presence... [W]e have not found a constant in history but the constancy of a process that leaves a trail of equivalent symbols in time and space." This appears to be Voegelin's final understanding (in this essay, at least), as he concludes with an affirmation of "the primordial experience of reality as endowed with the constancy and lastingness of structure that we symbolize as the Cosmos."[7]

Voegelin's various formulations of the constants of history are not random but involve a progressive refinement articulating Voegelin's understanding. Thus, as the essay progresses, we seem to be moving closer and closer to the truth of reality until, finally, we have it in our grasp. This grasping of truth, however, is merely an illusion or self-deception, as Voegelin himself has already told us—"the knowledge of reality conveyed by the symbols can never become a final possession of truth." None of those formulations is reality or captures reality; they are all symbolic representations that have developed out of Voegelin's experience of reality—or rather, his participation in reality—and his effort to articulate that experience.

---

5. Ibid., 120, 121.
6. Ibid., 128.
7. Ibid., 131, 132, 133.

The Confusion of Symbol and Reality

Man is not a mere observer of reality; rather, he is an active participant in it. Both man's consciousness of reality and reality itself are tensional and paradoxical. The structure of man's consciousness, as Voegelin conceives it, contains both a dimension of intentionality and a dimension of luminosity. "Intentionality" presents consciousness as embedded in man's bodily existence pointing to or in search of external objects. "Luminosity" presents the self-referential dimension of consciousness that allows consciousness itself to be located as a part of reality, thus placing emphasis on subject.[8] These are not alternative modes of consciousness but structures of consciousness, and both are already and always present. Reality itself also has a dual structure that is in some way related to the poles of human consciousness: "thing-Reality" and "It-Reality." Thing-Reality and It-Reality are not separate realities but two faces of the same coin, two faces always present and always held in tension. These two faces of reality are also related to man's consciousness: intentionality is attuned to "thing-Reality," while luminosity is attuned to "It-Reality." Thus man, while acting intentionally, apart from external reality, is also acting luminously, as a part of reality—reality in process.

One part of man's response to the experience of reality is to articulate its significance, and this he does through the creation of symbols that represent experience and its underlying reality. Symbols are "the language phenomena engendered by the process of participatory experience." There is "a plurality of symbolisms[9] that man has employed, including myth, revelation, science, philosophy, and poetry.

A number of problems may develop in this symbolic activity, and much of Voegelin's analysis is designed to identify these problems. Or perhaps the issues I shall discuss are actually variations on a single theme: the confusion of language symbol with reality. The first problem involves the transmutation of symbol into concept and the confusion of concept with reality. To be vital, symbols must remain tied to their originating experiences; but the transmutation into concepts involves a severing from those experiences and the converting of them into objects that are reified and treated as if they have a life, and a causal power, of their own. This is the ground for Voegelin's critique of his lengthy and, in his own lifetime, unpublished *History of Political Ideas:* "The conception

---

8. Eric Voegelin, "The Beginning of the Beginning," in *CW*, vol. 18, *In Search of Order*, vol. V, *Order and History*, ed. Ellis Sandoz (1987; Columbia: University of Missouri Press, 2000), 28–31. Also see Robert McMahon, "Eric Voegelin's Paradoxes of Consciousness and Participation," *Review of Politics* 61, no. 1 (Winter 1999): 118–29, esp. 119–26.
9. Voegelin, *Autobiographical Reflections*, 74, 79.

of a history of ideas was an ideological deformation of reality. There were no ideas unless there were symbols of immediate experiences."[10]

A second danger is "empty symbols"—"the transformation of original experiences-symbolizations into doctrines entailed a deformation of existence, if the contact with the reality as experienced was lost and the use of the language symbols engendered by the original experiences degenerated into a more or less empty game." Perhaps a fruitful line of investigation in regard to the life of empty symbols would be to consider Husserl's discussion of the sedimentation that takes place in the world of mathematics and science, a phenomenon that separates the science from its originating life experience.[11] This separation does not undermine the ability of science to proceed, however, for the superstructure of science continues to function even if the original foundations of scientific activity are no longer understood. Empty symbols may also continue to have a tremendous impact on social and intellectual life long after the living experiences they were designed to symbolize are lost. In fact, empty symbols become a part of the landscape of human activity and are therefore a part of new experiences that lead to further symbolization.

A third difficulty encountered in the realm of symbolization has to do with man's role as participant in reality and creator of symbols. As Voegelin writes in "The Beginning of the Beginning," "In the depth of the quest, formative truth and deformative untruth *are more closely related than the language of 'truth' and 'resistance' would suggest.*"[12] This is an extraordinary, and an extraordinarily important, statement, for it appears to be at once philosophical analysis and self-disclosure. The reason for the closeness of truth and untruth, Voegelin goes on to argue, is that "truth has its reality in the symbols engendered by the quest," but the agent of creation of those symbols is man's imaginative capacity. What may lead the imaginative capacity astray has been known ever since antiquity as "hybris . . . pride of life, *libido dominandi,* and will to power."[13] Both

10. Ibid., 63.
11. Ibid., 79; Edmund Husserl, "The Origin of Geometry," appendix vi, in *The Crisis of European Sciences and Transcendental Phenomenology,* trans. David Carr (Evanston: Northwestern University Press, 1970), 353–78.
12. Voegelin, "The Beginning," 51, emphasis added. "For 'truth' is not, as the surface language suggests, a something lying around to be accepted, rejected, or resisted; imagining 'truth' as a thing would deform the structure of consciousness in the same manner as does the transformation of the symbols 'reality' and 'Beyond' into things for the purpose of manipulation" (ibid., 51–52).
13. Ibid., 52, 53. Compare Sartre's discussion of why the writer cannot read his own work: "Now the operation of writing involves an implicit quasi-reading which makes real reading impossible. When the words form under his pen, the author doubtless sees them, but he does not see them as the reader does, since he knows them before writing them down. . . . Thus, the writer meets everywhere only his knowledge, his will, his plans, in

resistance to truth and resistance to untruth can thus be traced to the same ground: "the assertive imagination of man as a force in reality." With his usual self-awareness, Voegelin recognizes that his own work is subject to the same temptation to impose "a definite form on reality."[14]

On the Superiority of Poetry

The "old war between philosophy and poetry" was already old in Socrates' time, since that is his characterization of the relationship between them, and it continues in various forms today. One skirmish in this ongoing war—often friendly, often fierce—is found in Voegelin's analysis of the movement from myth to philosophy. The core of this movement, to use Voegelin's own terms, is from a compact articulation of existence to a differentiated articulation. Voegelin is, in many ways, a benign critic of poetry. He assumes that a differentiated symbolization is superior to a compact symbolization, and thus that philosophy is superior to myth or poetry—superior in some ways, but not necessarily in all. The clarity that philosophy achieves, in part through man's self-conscious recognition of himself as both observer and participant in reality, may also become the very ground for confusing symbol with reality itself and thus lead to a deformation of understanding. I call Voegelin a benign critic of poetry because he recognizes, along with Aristotle, that man can use both myth and philosophy equally well as languages to express the truth of reality.[15] Voegelin further understands the value of mythic articulations—symbolizations—of reality as rich lodes of experiential ore that can be mined fruitfully by philosophy, and makes use of mythic and sacred texts in his own work.

However, I would perhaps go further than Voegelin in pointing to a few ways in which mythopoetic symbolism may be actually superior to its philosophical heir. The three points I want to consider are these: first, mythopoetic symbolization is not as susceptible to "ideological deformation" as is philosophy. Second, poetic symbols are more comprehensive than philosophical symbols. Finally, poetry invites openness to experience and an opportunity for enacted experience that philosophy does not. Voegelin, I take it, would be aware of, or at least hospitable to, these concerns, even though they are not stressed in his own work.

---

short, himself." Jean-Paul Sartre, *What Is Literature?* (Routledge Classics, 2001), 30. For an alternative understanding of writing that emphasizes writing as a mode of self-education, see Steven D. Ealy, "The Struggle to Write as the Creation of the Self: Robert Penn Warren on 'A Vision Earned,'" *rWp: An Annual of Robert Penn Warren Studies* 3 (2003): 93–103.
    14. Voegelin, "The Beginning," 54, 47.
    15. Voegelin, "Equivalences," 125.

Philosophical language is differentiated compared to poetry's compact symbolism. Voegelin sees that as an advance, even while acknowledging the earlier mythic symbolization, and sees the philosophical statement as "a differentiated and therefore superior insight."[16] But this move toward differentiation may also be a key weakness in philosophy's activity, in that philosophy's differentiated vocabulary may be more susceptible to the "conceptual subversion"—the transmutation of symbols into concepts, which are then reified—discussed earlier. As Voegelin noted in his discussion of the paradoxical nature of reality and consciousness, "There is no autonomous, nonparadoxic language, ready to be used by man as a system of signs when he wants to refer to the paradoxic structures of reality and consciousness."[17] Philosophical symbols have the rhetorical force of suggesting that the "objects" (concepts) pointed to have an independent life apart from the symbolization itself, that is, these concepts are things that can be manipulated. Mythopoetic symbols, on the other hand, have the rhetorical force of being created and of having their existence only within a created artistic or spiritual world. Thus, the danger of confusing creation and reality is less severe in the world of poetry than in the world of philosophy.

On Voegelin's account reality and human consciousness is inherently, unavoidably, and ineradicably paradoxical in its structure. Paradox, ambiguity, contradictory positions that are equally true, is the world of poetry, and the language of poetry is capable of holding tensional relationships together. The world of logic, clarity, and systematization is the world of philosophy, and the language of philosophy is designed to classify, demystify, and articulate difference. In a paradoxical world a paradoxical mode of symbolization that allows for ambiguity, tension, and incommensurate competing truths may be a better guide and interpreter than a mode of symbolization that organizes and orders.

Voegelin recognizes that differentiation's displacement of compact symbolization may not be an "unqualified good." In his discussion of Egyptian myth, Voegelin writes:

> The very comparison that reveals the limitations of the myth also points toward the source of its strength. For the fact that the speculation on being has differentiated out of the larger complex of cosmogonies suggests that the myth is much richer in content than any of the partial symbolizations derived from it. This richer content may conveniently be subdivided in two classes: The myth, first, contains

---

16. Ibid.
17. Voegelin, "The Beginning," 31. Note that Voegelin does not exempt his own analysis from the paradoxical nature of human existence: "The analysis itself is paradoxic in structure" (ibid., 41). On this point, see McMahon, "Voegelin's Paradoxes," 132.

the various experiential blocs that separate in the course of differentiation; and it, second, contains an experience that welds the blocs into a living whole.[18]

Finally, the mythopoetic enterprise invites openness to and an active participation in experience on the part of its readers through imaginative reenactment in a way that the philosophical enterprise does not; the philosophic mode often moves far too rapidly to challenge and critique. But for a work of art to be a conduit to experience it must be received (attended to on its own terms) rather than used for non-poetic purposes (attempting to fit it into philosophical categories or systems). C. S. Lewis highlights the problem of "using" literature: "To formulate [a work of art, a play] as a philosophy, and regard the actual play as primarily a vehicle for that philosophy, is an outrage to the thing the poet has made for us." Lewis continues,

> What guards the good reader from treating a tragedy—he will not talk much about an abstraction like "Tragedy"—as a mere vehicle for truth is his continual awareness that it not only means, but is. It is not merely *logos* (something said) but *poiema* (something made). The same is true of a novel or narrative poem. They are complex and carefully made objects. Attention to the very objects they are is our first step. To value them chiefly for reflections which they may suggest to us or morals we may draw from them, is a flagrant instance of "using" instead of "receiving."[19]

What and how we learn from works of art revolves around "imaginative enactment." The outcome of this enactment is not a set of concepts or symbols to describe reality but an experience, which is man's fundamental relationship to reality. Robert Penn Warren, quoting Henri Bergson, argues that "fiction 'brings us back into our own presence'—the presence in which we must make our final terms with life and death." The knowledge we gain in this encounter with fiction is not propositional—"does not ordinarily come to us with intellectual labels," in Warren's words—rather "knowledge comes as enactment."[20] Receiving

---

18. Eric Voegelin, *CW*, vol. 14, *Order and History,* vol. I, *Israel and Revelation,* ed. Maurice P. Hogan (1956; Columbia: University of Missouri Press, 2001), 123 (see also 240–41).
19. C. S. Lewis, *An Experiment in Criticism* (Cambridge: Cambridge University Press, 1961), 82–83. In a letter to Robert Heilman in which Voegelin explores the connection between works of art and the inquiry into the nature of man, he recognizes the need for at least a temporary surrender to authority if growth is to take place. See the letter dated August 22, 1956, in Charles R. Embry, ed., *Robert B. Heilman and Eric Voegelin: A Friendship in Letters, 1944–1984* (Columbia: University of Missouri Press, 2004), 156–59, and Embry's comment on this letter in his introduction, 19–20.
20. Robert Penn Warren, "Why Do We Read Fiction?" in Robert Penn Warren, *New and Selected Essays* (New York: Random House, 1989), 60, 61. Warren quotes from Bergson's *Time and Free Will,* trans. F. L. Pogson (1910; rpr. London: George Allen & Unwin, 1959), 134.

a work of literature provides man with an additional mode of participation in reality, but I would emphasize that this participation is not possible when literature is hijacked by philosophers for their ulterior purposes.

The Novels of Robert Penn Warren

Voegelin acknowledges the depth of many ancient texts, both sacred and secular, as sources for mythopoetic symbolism. The real test of the argument I am making, however, would require a discussion, not of a classic text, but of a contemporary work of art. Such a test would also reverse the order with which philosophers tend to approach literary texts—that is, rather than using a philosophical framework as a guide to interpreting and critiquing the work of art, the work of art would be treated as primary. We would listen to the poem, rather than telling the poem what its meaning and significance is. In this regard I will turn to two novels written by Robert Penn Warren as illustrative of the power of modern poetry.

Robert Penn Warren's Jefferson Lectures, published in 1975 under the title *Democracy and Poetry,* are an extended meditation on the diminishment of self in modern America and the possibility of the renewal of selfhood. The core of the self, according to Warren, is "the felt principle of significant unity." This "significant unity" entails two elements: "continuity—the self as a development in time, with a past and a future; and responsibility—the self as a moral identity, recognizing itself as capable of action worthy of praise or blame."[21] The creation of the self is a key component of all of Warren's writings—his protagonists seek to answer the question of self, and on a deeper level, Warren's writing is his own effort at the creation of his self.[22] In this paper I examine two of Warren's novels, *All the King's Men* (1946) and *World Enough and Time* (1950), in relationship to these components of self, continuity, and responsibility. In both novels the protagonists struggle with the perennial human question, "Who am I?"[23]

---

21. Robert Penn Warren, *Democracy and Poetry* (Cambridge, MA: Harvard University Press, 1975), xii, xiii.

22. On the poet's self-creation see *Democracy and Poetry,* especially 67 ff., and "The Use of the Past," in Robert Penn Warren, *New and Selected Essays* (New York: Random House, 1989), 46–53. For Warren's discussion of this notion in relation to other writers, see his *Homage to Theodore Dreiser on the Centennial of His Birth* (New York: Random House, 1971), and "'The Great Mirage': Conrad and *Nostromo,*" in *New and Selected Essays,* 137–61.

23. The opening line of Warren's novel *Band of Angels* (New York: Random House, 1955) is emblematic: "Oh, who am I? for so long that was, you might say, the cry of my heart."

All the King's Men

Jack Burden is the narrator of and an actor in the stories recounted in *All the King's Men*.[24] The first major story relates the origin, rise, and fall of Willie Stark. The second major story of the novel relates the tale of Jack himself. As Jack's narrative of Willie develops we learn about Jack's origin and development as well.

The movement of the novel thus takes place on two levels: the rise and demise of Governor Willie Stark, and the self-discovery of narrator Jack Burden. As narrator, Jack provides an "objective" or external view of Willie Stark in which we are left with the questions about Stark that Burden is left with, and an internal or "subjective" view of Jack Burden as he traces his own psychological/moral development. These two levels are intimately related, for Jack Burden's (internal) journey of self-discovery could never have been made, or at least not made in the same manner, if his story had not at points connected to and overlapped with the (external) story of Willie Stark. As Jack himself says, "The story of Willie Stark and the story of Jack Burden are, in one sense, one story."[25]

The reciprocal relationship between the stories of Willie and Jack is highlighted by the manner in which Jack relates the tale. Jack's narration is presented, not in a straightforward, chronological manner, but through a series of discrete vignettes that are held together in a "medieval interlace structure,"[26] which moves between the stories of Jack and Willie and which ultimately intertwines them. As Jack unfolds his story, we learn about his life and family in a disjointed fashion that requires us to reconstruct the time line of his life. Over the course of the novel, we see Jack as child, adolescent, graduate student, reporter, and political henchman. We also learn of Jack's reflective understanding of his views during these periods of his life.

Throughout the novel Jack characterizes himself, at times seriously and at times facetiously, as a student of history. He recounts two important episodes in his life, which revolve around his "excursion[s] into the enchantments of the past":[27] the story of Cass Mastern and "The Case of the Upright Judge." The first excursion was the subject of his doctoral dissertation, a dissertation

---

24. Robert Penn Warren, *All the King's Men* (San Diego: Harcourt Brace, 1982). Hereinafter this reprint edition will be identified as *AKM*.
25. *AKM,* 157.
26. Lillian Nobles Wooley, "The Medieval Interlace Structure in *All the King's Men*," in *"To Love So Well the World": A Festschrift in Honor of Robert Penn Warren,* ed. Dennis L. Weeks (New York: Pete Lang, 1992), 313–25.
27. *AKM,* 157.

written but never defended because, in Jack's words, "I tried to discover the truth and not the facts. Then, when the truth was not to be discovered, or discovered could not be understood by me, I could not bear to live with the cold-eyed reproach of the facts. So I walked out of a room, the room where the facts lived in a big box of three-by-five-inch note cards, and kept on walking."[28]

Jack's second major piece of historical research, "The Case of the Upright Judge," was a politically motivated job done for Willie, a job that would have both personal and political ramifications. In Jack's own appraisal, "I had every reason to congratulate myself on a job well done. It was a perfect research job, marred in its technical perfection by only one thing: it meant something."[29]

Even though Jack characterizes himself as a student of history, he does not see historical research as a defining part of his life—he does not see asking and answering historical questions to be an essential component of his makeup. Jack does not see anything as an essential component of his makeup, which at an early stage appears to him to be randomly formed through drift and inertia.

Jack contrasts himself to Willie and fails to see in himself the inner compulsion that separates Willie from the masses: people like Willie "are what they are from the time they first kick in the womb until the end. And if that is the case, then their life history is a process of discovering what they really are, and not, as for you and me, sons of luck, a process of becoming what luck makes us."[30] Jack's failure to see a "metaphysical self" when he looked at himself was partly because of the amazing pull that Willie Stark came to have on him.

Ironically, it was through Willie that Jack was given a glimpse of the "metaphysical self" of Jack Burden that Jack had tried not to own. "I had asked the Boss about something else once," Jack recalls, recounting the night that the impeachment attempt against Willie fell through.

> Late that night, back at the Mansion, after he had thrown Tiny and his rabble out of the study, I asked him the question. I asked, "Did you mean what you said?"
>
> Propped back on the big leather couch, he stared at me, and demanded, "What?"
>
> "What you said," I replied, "tonight. You said your strength was their will. You said your justice was their need. All of that."
>
> He kept on staring at me, his eyes bulging, his stare grappling and probing into me.
>
> "You said that," I said.

28. Ibid.
29. Ibid., 191.
30. Ibid., 63.

"God damn it," he exclaimed violently, still staring at me, "God damn it—" he clenched his right fist and struck himself twice on the chest—"God damn it, there's something inside you—there's something inside you."

He left the words hanging there. He turned his eyes from me and stared moodily into the fire. I didn't press my question.[31]

Willie's response to Jack at first sounds as if he were reflecting on that "something inside" every man that motivates his behavior. I think, however, that Willie is making a comment specifically about Jack's inquisitiveness. At times Willie is able to laugh at Jack's characteristic questioning of events. Early in the novel Jack recounts a conversation he had with Willie about the first time they met. Willie shook Jack's hand and then winked at him, or at least Jack thought that he had winked at him, but he was not sure. Years later Jack asked Willie if he had winked at him, and Willie replied, "Boy, if I was to tell you, then you wouldn't have anything to think about."[32] But on the occasion after the speech, Jack is probing Willie's depths, and Willie is irritated by Jack's desire to know.

This reading of Jack's conversation with Willie is reinforced by Jack's later encounter with Sadie Burke at a sanatorium. That "something" in Jack, which Willie pointed to and reacted against, sent Jack to Sadie, Willie's political strategist and sometimes girlfriend, after Willie's assassination. Sadie, too, points Jack to the thing that drives him, and it is not luck: "God damn you Jack Burden, what made you come here? What always makes you mess in things? Why can't you leave me alone? Why can't you? Why?"[33] Jack does not answer Sadie's question, but there is something in him that makes him push on until he has all of the information, all of the facts. Jack has always been good at gathering facts; it is the matter of truth that he finds so confusing. It is the elusive nature of truth that makes Jack's self-characterization as a student of history so tentative. Somehow Jack knows, but will not embrace the knowledge, that history is a quest for something beyond mere facts, whether we call it truth, meaning, or significance.

Jack failed to perceive his metaphysical self partly because of the overwhelming power of Willie's presence and partly because of Jack's desire to avoid responsibility. In the end, Jack learned to point to the inner drive that motivated him, even though he presented it as a universal truth rather than as the inner force in his own life. "The end of man is knowledge," muses Jack, looking back on all that had occurred,

31. Ibid., 261–63.
32. Ibid., 16.
33. Ibid., 410.

but there is one thing he can't know. He can't know whether knowledge will save him or kill him. He will be killed, all right, but he can't know whether he is killed because of the knowledge which he has got or because of the knowledge which he hasn't got and which if he had it, would save him. There's the cold in the stomach, but you open the envelope, you have to open the envelope, for the end of man is to know.[34]

Jack was, then, a natural student of history, driven by a desire to know, a desire that he himself does not completely recognize at the time, and aided by the "luck" of jobs that allowed him to practice his craft of historical research. But Jack's practice of history was informed and tempered by principles that he absorbed in his formal education. Jack learned two things while at State University. The first (acquired as a undergraduate) was the principle of idealism. Jack wryly described himself as a "brass-bound Idealist" while working for Willie and elaborated on the pragmatic importance of the principle of Idealism in his line of work:

> I heard somebody open and shut the gate to the barn lot, but I didn't look around. If I didn't look around it would not be true that somebody had opened the gate with the creaky hinges, and that is a wonderful principle for a man to get hold of. I had got hold of the principle out of a book when I was in college, and I had hung on to it for grim death. I owed my success in life to that principle. It had put me where I was. What you don't know don't hurt you, for it ain't real. They called that Idealism in my book I had when I was in college, and after I got hold of that principle I became an Idealist. I was a brass-bound Idealist in those days. If you are an Idealist it does not matter what you do or what goes on around you because it isn't real anyway.[35]

The second principle Jack learned at State University (acquired as a Ph.D. student in history) was a variation on Nietzsche's reflections in *The Use and Abuse of History*. In Jack's words, "If the human race didn't remember anything it would be perfectly happy."[36]

These principles function together in a way that enables Jack to take up jobs as journalist and political henchmen, and both principles allowed Jack to maintain a tunnel-vision focus on his job without considering the larger implications of what he was doing. In an effort to head off impeachment proceedings against Governor Stark, Jack tracked down the leader of the anti-Stark forces in the House of Representatives. Jack showed Lowdan an envelope full

---

34. Ibid., 9.
35. Ibid., 30, 106.
36. Ibid., 40.

of documents signed by members of the House who had been supporting impeachment but who had changed their minds. "It's blackmail," Lowdan said,

> very quietly, but huskily as though he didn't have the breath to spare. Then, seeming to get a little more breath, "It's blackmail. It's coercion. Bribery, it's bribery. I tell you, you've blackmailed and bribed those men and I—"
> "I don't know why anybody signed this statement," I said, "but if what you charge should happen to be true then the moral strikes me as this: MacMurfee ought not to elect legislators who can be bribed or who have done things they can get blackmailed for."[37]

As journalist and henchman, Jack not only maintained his idealism and presentism as protective devices but he actively sought to limit his knowledge. At one point he cuts off Sadie Burke by averring, "'I don't want to listen. I know too God-damned much now.' And I wasn't joking. I didn't want to listen. The world was full of things I didn't want to know." During an argument with his mother over his job with Willie, Jack told her, "I don't know what those people, as you call them, do. I'm very careful not to ever know what anybody anywhere does any time."[38]

By the judicious application of these principles, Jack was able to describe himself variously as "a piece of furniture," a "hired hand," and an "office boy."[39] He was able to carry out assigned tasks without remorse or even pangs of conscience because he was able to block from his field of vision knowledge about the origins or impact of the items he happened to be working on at the time.

While Jack was able to apply his principles of Idealism and ignorant happiness in such a way as to give himself what today would be called plausible deniability, these principles actually ran counter to Jack's deeper inclination, the necessity to know. Jack's story can be seen, then, as a working out of the tension between his two self-consciously held principles of history and human existence and the demand of his metaphysical self to pursue its end of knowledge. At the practical level, Jack attempted to live his life operating on the basis of these two (related) principles, had to deal with their limitations as a foundation for action and understanding, and then had to find a replacement for them when they failed.

The collapse of Jack's carefully constructed defensive position, which protected him from all responsibility, began with "The Case of the Upright Judge." Judge Irwin, the man who had been more of a father to Jack than Jack's stepfathers,

---

37. Ibid., 149.
38. Ibid., 142, 126.
39. Ibid., 52, 113, 23.

took a position on a political issue in opposition to Governor Stark. Willie ordered Jack to get the dirt on Judge Irwin. Jack denied that there was any dirt to be got, but Jack, the resourceful student of history, got the dirt. The dirt on Judge Irwin had implications that an application of the principle of Idealism could not conceal from Jack. Judge Irwin was a friend of Jack's, and Jack did not want it to be true; additionally, the dirt sullied the reputation of Governor Stanton, father of Jack's friends Adam and Anne Stanton. Finally, the dirt affected Jack's mother and Jack himself, for the Judge committed suicide, and Jack then learned that Judge Irwin, not Ellis Burden, was his father and the man that his mother had always loved.

This knowledge was contained in a metaphorical envelope Jack might never have opened but for Willie Stark. When Jack told us early in the story that man's end is knowledge and that we must open the envelope when it is handed to us, he was speaking from experience and not idle speculation. He had handed envelopes to many people, and they had always opened those envelopes. When Jack wanted to convince Adam Stanton to become director of the new state hospital against his own wishes, Jack gave Adam an envelope with documents relating to his father's complicity in Judge Irwin's one bad act. This material was designed to "change that picture of the world he carries around in his head."[40] In the same way, the knowledge that came from the "envelope" Willie gave to Jack began to change Jack's view of the world.

Willie Stark's story is an archetypal one of the rise, corruption, and fall of a political figure. Jack's is one of more subtle development, of the changes in the picture of the world that Jack carries around in his head, and the effect these changes have on his life and the lives of those around him. Jack had walked away from his doctoral dissertation on Cass Mastern because he could not understand Mastern. Looking back on that decision, Jack reflected on his earlier self:

> I have said that Jack Burden could not put down the facts about Cass Mastern's world because he did not know Cass Mastern.... Jack Burden did not say definitely to himself why he did not know Cass Mastern. But I (who am what Jack Burden became) look back now, years later, and try to say why.
>
> Cass Mastern lived for a few years and in that time he learned that the world is all of one piece. He learned that the world is like an enormous spider web and if you touch it, however lightly, at any point, the vibration ripples to the remotest perimeter and the drowsy spider feels the tingle and is drowsy no more but springs out to fling the gossamer coils about you who have touched the web and then inject the black, numbing poison under your hide. It does not matter whether or not you meant to brush the web of things. Your happy foot or your gay wing

---

40. Ibid., 248.

may have brushed it ever so lightly, but what happens always happens and there is the spider, bearded black and with his great faceted eyes glittering like mirrors in the sun, or like God's eye, and the fangs dripping.

But how could Jack Burden, being what he was, understand that?... They could only be words to him, for to him the world then was simply an accumulation of items, odds and ends of things like the broken and misused and dust-shrouded things gathered in a garret. Or it was a flux of things before his eyes (or behind his eyes) and one thing had nothing to do, in the end, with anything else.[41]

But slowly, over time, Jack came to hold a different picture of the world in his head. The student of history came to see that "if you could not accept the past and its burden there was no future, for without one there cannot be the other, and... if you could accept the past you might hope for the future, for only out of the past can you make the future." Jack came to see this, not because he had been argued into it, but because he had seen too many lives lived in ways that had nothing to do with the determinism of "the Great Twitch." Even his friends who had killed the other, Willie and Adam, "lived [their doom] in the agony of will," not mindless necessity.[42] Jack Burden came to understand the concept of personal responsibility for one's actions, and with that understanding came his acceptance of his own responsibility. Thus was Jack Burden as a "moral identity" born.

World Enough and Time

World Enough and Time[43] tells the story of Jeremiah Beaumont and Rachel Jordan. As in much of Warren's fiction, nothing is presented in a simple and straightforward manner. The story unfolds through the voice of a contemporary historian ruminating over the records, papers, and other ephemera relating to the tale of Jeremiah Beaumont, but supplemented with generous excerpts from the journal of Beaumont himself. The story is thus told by two voices: Jeremiah Beaumont, idealist and participant, and the narrator, skeptical and detached.

The story of Jeremiah Beaumont revolves around his relationship with Rachel Jordan, a maiden he thought had been abused and was in need of a gallant champion, and Wilkie Barron, a friend who (for his own political purposes)

---

41. Ibid., 188–89.
42. Ibid., 435, 436.
43. Robert Penn Warren, *World Enough and Time: A Romantic Novel* (New York: Random House, 1950). Hereinafter cited as *WE*.

sets the trajectory of Beaumont's life. The picture of love painted by Beaumont's relationship to Rachel can be seen as a send-up of the romantic vision of love captured in the world of medieval chivalry and transplanted into the Kentucky backcountry of the 1820s. It is "a tale of selfless passion, innocent trust, and dark betrayal"[44] mixed with generous doses of deception, manipulation, and melodramatic retribution.

Jeremiah Beaumont learned of the plight of Rachel Jordan, a young woman who had been seduced by her late father's attorney, Colonel Fort, from his friend Wilkie Barron. Although Beaumont did not know Jordan, and it happened that Colonel Fort was Beaumont's mentor and benefactor, Beaumont determined that he would punish Fort for his indiscretion. From the beginning Beaumont's reaction was extremely romanticized: he desired to enact in his own life the stories of valor he had learned in his own early study of Rome. He accepted at face value Wilkie Barron's account of events and never sought to confirm the story with Fort, even though he had had a close relationship with Fort up to this point. Instead, he informed Fort by letter that he would not "connive" with his baseness, and that "he would turn from the face of the betrayer, and seek truth in the face of the betrayed."[45] While Beaumont's early efforts to befriend Jordan were rebuffed, he was so persistent in his pursuit that finally she gave in, at least to the point of allowing Beaumont to be in her presence on a regular basis.

Beaumont's actions were motivated by the belief that he "had to create his world or be the victim of a world he did not create. Out of his emptiness, which he could not satisfy with any fullness of the world, he had to bring forth whatever fullness might be his."[46] How one can create a full world out of one's own emptiness is, at best, problematic.

A key part of creating his own world, in Beaumont's mind, was found in establishing a ground for action outside the standards of the world of society. He could only be true to his "deeper self" by acting apart from—or in violation of—the standards of the community. By acting beyond the standards of the community, Beaumont's conduct would set another standard—a standard that would force the world to recognize him. Beaumont decided that he must *act* in order to create his world and thus to create his "deeper self," and

---

44. *WE*, 55.
45. Ibid., 62.
46. Ibid., 115. This is standard romantic fare. Compare Beaumont's attitude with the view expressed by Los in William Blake's *Jerusalem:* "I must Create a System, or be enslav'd by another Mans / I will not Reason & Compare: my business is to Create" (plate 10, lines 20–21). See *The Poetry and Prose of William Blake*, ed. David V. Erdman (New York: Doubleday, 1965), 151.

that the ground for this action must be the "great purpose" that united him with Rachel Jordan. Their "great purpose" was the murder of Colonel Fort.

In trying to sort out the jumbled reasoning that seemed to motivate both Beaumont and Jordan it becomes clear that Beaumont is driven by conflicting images of his relation to the larger society around him. On the one hand, he stood aloof and saw himself (and Rachel Jordan) as the center and creators of his universe. On the other, all of his plans—all of his efforts to achieve the great purpose of the humiliation of Colonel Fort—revolved around the public nature of the action: only if Fort were to be humiliated in public would this great purpose be achieved. Thus Beaumont was dependent on the attention, if not the interest, of the world beyond his control.

Beaumont appeared to be obsessed by the discovery—or creation—of what he variously called "the truth within," "the honesty within," and the "justice within" himself.[47] This truth, or honesty, or justice that Jeremiah Beaumont sought within himself was, in some crucial way, unconnected to the world that swirled around him. The following entry appears in Beaumont's journal: "I seemed to live outside of time, and nothing about me was real but the thought in me. What was real was the moment I strove toward, which was not yet in time. When that moment should fall into the stream of time, I thought that again time and the world would be real to me. But not before."[48]

During his first face-to-face meeting with Rachel Jordan, Jeremiah Beaumont took from her the book she was reading—Plato's *Symposium*—and read aloud from the page she had marked. In Beaumont's own account of this passage he writes: "I began to read in the middle of a sentence at the top of the left-hand page, and I read of love, and how a man of high soul may use the beauties of earth as a ladder by which he mounts for the sake of higher beauties, resting at last in the single Idea of the absolute Beauty in that life which above all others a man should live to be fully man, the contemplation of the Beauty Absolute."[49]

Set against this Platonic idealism is the reality of the trajectory of Beaumont's own life. Rather than moving higher in the contemplation of beauty, Beaumont was involved in a descent. He simultaneously became engaged to marry Jordan and forced a demand from her that he "Kill Fort."[50] When he ultimately carried out this "command," he did so not publicly and in a way

---

47. *WE*, 63, 65, 98, 122, 152, 163.
48. Ibid., 137.
49. Ibid., 69. Compare the story of Paolo and Francesca in *The Inferno* (canto V, lines 73–142), in which the lovers entered into an adulterous relationship while reading the story of Lancelot.
50. *WE*, 114. Beaumont's attitude to the murder resembles that of Raskolnikov in Dostoevsky's *Crime and Punishment*.

that announced to the world the justice of his action, but in disguise and at night. When a reward for the capture of the murderer was offered, Beaumont was selected by a group of people, who did not know that he was actually the murderer, to be the fall guy in their plan to obtain the reward. Thus at his trial Beaumont was caught in a web of lies that he could disprove by telling the truth, with the ironic result that he would condemn himself, for his defense was also built on a web of deceit.

After Beaumont was convicted, his old tutor Dr. Burnham visited him in jail, and Beaumont browbeat Burnham into providing him with laudanum so that he could defeat the executioner by taking his own life. This attempt at suicide failed, and Wilkie Barron affected Beaumont's escape on the day of his scheduled execution. He and Rachel ended up in the lawless kingdom of "The Grand Boz," an old river pirate. With each step along the way Beaumont became more and more degraded, until near the end of the story (both figuratively and literally) he concluded, "The crime for which I seek expiation is never lost. It is always there. It is unpardonable. It is the crime of self, the crime of life. The crime is I."[51]

To understand Beaumont's downward spiral we must reflect on his starting point and on what he affirms and denies in his life. While Beaumont initially saw the passage from Plato as confirmation of his high-toned view of life, he did not start, as Diotima did, with a love of physical beauty, which prepares the ascent to eternal beauty. Rather, Beaumont began with a detached view of "the idea," pure in itself, set apart and in contrast with the evil he found in the world as it existed. Beaumont never experienced the love of the world—or of the beauty of a lover—directly, but only through the veil of his romantic vision. This vision proved to be an inadequate foundation upon which to build either love or a life.

Beaumont's descent, as he himself recounted, involved three stages in the relationship of Idea and World. In the first stage, "the idea is all," and the world will be redeemed by the idea, but this led Beaumont to a scorn of the world. It was during this period that Beaumont talked of the "truth within" and the "justice within." For Beaumont, separation from the world was itself a form of purity, and it was this purity he sought to secure. How Beaumont could enter into the action of the world, and into time, and maintain this detached purity remained unresolved. What in fact happened was that Beaumont was becoming more and more settled into his married life with Rachel, and the reality of this life threatened to displace his "great purpose," the murder of Colonel Fort,

---

51. *WE*, 458.

from the center of his life and thought. In any event, when the idea failed to redeem the world, Beaumont came to believe that "the world must redeem the idea," and this led to the effort to achieve ideal ends through worldly action—in Beaumont's case, the realization of a pure love through the murder of Colonel Fort. Thus we have a reversal from Beaumont's original understanding of idea and world—at this stage, world becomes dominant and idea contingent. In the first stage, somehow, the contemplation of the murder of Fort was sufficient, and in the second it was necessary to actually carry out the murder; only the murder itself could prove the purity of his love for Rachel. This stage is the foundation of most of the political terror we find unleashed in the world. Perhaps this movement can be understood as the movement from a Hegelian position of idea determining material to a Marxian view of material determining the idea. In any event, according to Beaumont, this reversal was followed by a third stage—the denial of the idea and the embrace of the world as all.[52] No longer does Beaumont pursue a noble ideal; rather he wallows in the degraded state he finds himself in the kingdom of the Grand Boz.

Accompanying this changing understanding of idea and world, and key to Beaumont's development—actually, lack of development—is an affirmation and a rejection. The affirmation, time and again, is one of betrayal. He not only believed that he has been continually betrayed by those closest to him, he used this argument to force their compliance to his will. At the same time Beaumont affirmed betrayal, he denied his own responsibility for any of his actions. Thus, when Dr. Burnham came to see him in jail, Beaumont forced Burnham to agree to supply laudanum by blaming Burnham for his situation: "You owe it to me. For it was you that planted the seed of all. If it had not been for you, I would not be here. . . . Under the maple tree, you read me the Greeks and the Romans. You taught me the nobleness of life. And I swear to you, if I have botched and blundered, all began in what you taught. For I yearned to do a thing noble and worthy, and all began in that thought. And it was you."[53]

By the end of *World Enough and Time* Jeremiah Beaumont has come to understand that, rather than creating a world that unfolded out of his "true self," he has been manipulated, for political reasons, by Wilkie Barron. While Beaumont desired to "create his world," in the end he became "victim of a world he did not create."[54] While he desired to achieve the impossible, the creation of a world, Beaumont steadfastly refused the creation that was always

---

52. Ibid., 459.
53. Ibid., 396.
54. Ibid., 115.

within his grasp, the creation of his own self. Beaumont denied both the continuity of his life and the sense of responsibility necessary for a self in Warren's sense. He looked back on his life as a series of discrete episodes, each episode disconnected from all others. Thus, while he longed to understand his "true self," he never connected the dots that would have made his "true self," and then made that self visible, both to Beaumont himself and to those around him. Living "outside time" prevented the continuity necessary to develop a true sense of self. Tied closely to this failure of continuity was his unwillingness to accept responsibility for any of his actions. Beaumont continually sought to shift responsibility for events to external causes—either the nature of the world or the unwillingness of others to support him in his actions. In contrast to Jack Burden, who was ready to act in the world at the conclusion of *All the King's Men,* Jeremiah Beaumont could only ask, at the conclusion of his journal, "Was all for naught?" The narrator of the book immediately concluded by repeating Beaumont's question—"Was all for naught?"[55]

This doubling of Beaumont's final question suggests a doubling of the answer, and the answer is "yes" and the answer is "no." James Justus has argued that "the statements and counterstatements, the assertions and challenges form the heart of the novel. Its life consists neither in the romantic posturing of a deluded young idealist in the early nineteenth century nor in the skeptical, inquiring intelligence of a twentieth-century man of reason, but rather in the engagement between these two sensibilities."[56] This is illustrated by the doubling of the question and the differing answers given by protagonist and narrator. Perhaps Jeremiah Beaumont must answer this question, "No, all was not for naught." What Beaumont finally gained in the end was knowledge—something even better than redemption, he suggests—but knowledge of a particular kind. Beaumont learned how to act by reflecting, not on his experience, but on how he was acted upon by those who desired to use him for their own purposes. The narrator, on the other hand, perhaps must answer, "Yes, Beaumont's frenetic activity was all for naught." The narrator had opened the story of Jeremiah Beaumont by suggesting that perhaps "a man cannot live unless he prepares a drama" and concludes by observing that "all men believe in justice. Otherwise they would not be men."[57] Ultimately, however, from the narrator's perspective, these two claims are perhaps one and the same.

---

55. Ibid., 465.
56. James H. Justus, *The Achievement of Robert Penn Warren* (Baton Rouge: Louisiana State University Press, 1981), 224.
57. *WE,* 5, 463.

Imaginative Enactment and Poetic Cognition

In his essay "The Use of the Past," Warren wrote that "in a way, [the past] 'gives' us nothing. We must earn what we get there. The past must be studied, worked at—in short, created.... In creating the image of the past, we create ourselves, and without that task of creating the past we might be said scarcely to exist. Without it, we sink to the level of a protoplasmic swarm." Through his encounter with his personal history, Jack Burden has begun to create himself, a person able to "go out of the house and go into the convulsion of the world, out of history into history and the awful responsibility of Time."[58]

Jeremiah Beaumont, at the end of his story, stands in marked contrast to Jack Burden. Beaumont has rejected his own family, his own past, his community, and has attempted to create a world out of nothing. In doing so, Beaumont ultimately lost the chance to create his self and to connect both backward and forward in history. Beaumont ends with knowledge of his story, of how he was manipulated by Barron and Skrogg, but it remains unclear that Beaumont even understands his own role in his own story, and thus even his knowledge at the end is limited. Jack Burden finally came to terms with his own past, and thus prepared himself to live in the world of the future. The stories of both these protagonists offer evidence in support of Burden's conclusion that "if you could not accept the past and its burden there was no future, for without one there cannot be the other."[59]

The responsibility that Warren's fictive world leads us to is not a commitment to grand universal principles but rather a challenge that we "accept the past and its burden." This means that we each have our own unique challenge of responsibility; for each of us has a unique past that we must come to terms with. In Warren's world we discover our liberty only in tension with our destiny, not as a fated or predetermined outcome to our life, but as our starting point in the world—the family, community, class and nation and epoch that we are born into. While we have no choice in the matter of our destiny, we are able to decide how to respond to the circumstances we find ourselves in. The polarity of freedom and destiny allows us to mediate between blind obeisance and blind rejection of the past. It is in this field of tension that the possibility of responsible action arises and that each person is given the opportunity to create his own self.[60]

---

58. Warren, "The Use of the Past," 50–51; *AKM*, 438.
59. *AKM*, 435.
60. Warren talks of the poles of life and fiction in "Love and Separateness in Eudora Welty," in *Robert Penn Warren: A Reader* (New York: Vintage Books, 1987), 201, 205. On

There is much in the worlds of Jack Burden and Jeremiah Beaumont that Warren has imaginatively created that resonates with the concerns Eric Voegelin spent his philosophical life investigating—the nature of self, the struggles of life in the metaxy, this in-between existence in which man finds himself, the corrosive desire to construct a "second reality" that then becomes our ground for action. There is a danger, however, in attempting to reduce the "enacted knowledge" of a work of fiction to "a teaching" or a proposition. Such an attempt is an example of the temptation to replace "uncertain truth" with "certain untruth."[61] As Voegelin argued forcefully in "Equivalences of Symbolization and Experience in History," symbols never capture the truth in final form because experience and its symbols are "reality in process." The work of art allows us to imaginatively enter a reality in process, to learn about the motives and experiences of others, and in so doing to learn something about ourselves—or as Warren would put it, to create our self.

Warren offers a description of the "philosophical novelist" that is worth reflecting on. In an essay on Joseph Conrad, he writes:

> The philosophical novelist, or poet, is one for whom the documentation of the world is constantly striving to rise to the level of generalization about values, for whom the image strives to rise to symbol, for whom images always fall into a dialectical configuration, for whom the urgency of experience, no matter how vividly and strongly experience may enchant, is the urgency to know the meaning of experience. This is not to say that the philosophical novelist is schematic and deductive. It is to say quite the contrary, that he is willing to go naked into the pit, again and again, to make the same old struggle for his truth.[62]

Thus for Warren, the "philosophical novelist" is one who keeps in creative tension the various and competing human dispositions that we find in life as we live it, even while recognizing that one of the strongest of those dispositions is to understand the meaning of our existence. The robust work of art is multidimensional, allowing us to examine the competing forces at play within human action, including the competing claims for ultimate significance. Whether through the self-interrogation of Jack Burden or through the on-going debate between Jeremiah Beaumont and the contemporary narrator of his tale, the dialectical tension created by the movement of the story is the path-

---

the polarity of freedom and destiny, see Paul Tillich, *Systematic Theology I* (Chicago: University of Chicago Press, 1951), 182–86. On the role of literature in shaping the individual self, see Steven D. Ealy, "On the Creation of the Self in the Thought of Robert Penn Warren," *Modern Age* 43, no. 3 (Summer 2001): 202–10.

61. Voegelin, *Science, Politics, and Gnosticism*, 75.
62. Robert Penn Warren, "'The Great Mirage,'" 160.

way along which one may begin to glimpse the meaning of the novel. Or, to use terms currently popular in some circles, it is through the dialectical engagement of the novel's competing "teachings" (the "lessons to be learned" from the perspective of each of the novel's major actors) that the novel's meaning may be revealed. For this to occur, the reader must be an active participant in evaluating these competing claims and resolving them in his own mind.

Perhaps both poetry and philosophy make the same old struggle for truth, even as they struggle with each other. As a benign critic of poetry in the battle between philosophy and poetry, Voegelin might see some merit in the argument of this paper, for the advantages of poetry I have discussed are at least tacitly recognized by Voegelin himself. One could make a case that Plato is at least as much a poet as a philosopher—remember that Plato's Socrates had recourse to "likely stories" or myths at key points in the *Gorgias, Phaedrus,* and the *Republic.* Finally, as Voegelin notes, "In a late letter... Aristotle admits to becoming *philomythoteros* the older he becomes."[63]

---

63. Voegelin, "Equivalences," 126.

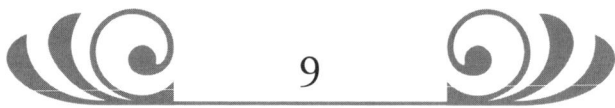

Biographies of Consciousness
Péter Nádas and Eric Voegelin

Charles R. Embry

> A novel is an exceedingly ordinary thing:
> it wades through lived experience.
> —Péter Nádas, "The Novelist and His Selfs"

> Between birth and death the body not only determines, as the sensorium, what part of the world may enter consciousness through it, but also is one of the most important determinants (although not the only one) for the inner tensions and relations of relevance of the world of consciousness.
> —Eric Voegelin, *Anamnesis*

The statement "A novel is an exceedingly ordinary thing: it wades through lived experience" conveys metaphorically the complexity that lies at the heart of any endeavor to explore human consciousness, the body as the sensorium of that consciousness, and the body as the source of the biography of consciousness. To amplify and probe these themes Péter Nádas relies upon his own biographical experiences filtered through his imagination. In the case of *A Book of Memories*, he uses first-person narration voiced by "other selfs." He writes: "This time, with two cuts I divided myself into three. I said I have at least one self to contend with, but in my imagination there may be room for as many as three personae, who will speak concurrently for themselves and for me. . . . The first-person narrative invariably steered me toward confession, so

I had to keep examining the events of my own life, and use only as many of them as these personae would allow."[1] With his creation of these narrative selfs, Nádas explored and amplified what it means to say that consciousness is embodied and that through the sensorium of the body consciousness transcends into the world, especially the world of other human beings. The narrative selfs, thus, wade through that "exceedingly ordinary thing"—"lived experience." The consciousness of these narrative selfs, complete with robust bodies, transcends into the world of other human beings intent upon finding and establishing meaningful relationships that can sustain life and community.

Even though *A Book of Memories* contains, from time to time, discursions on consciousness or internal monologues or accounts of walks through forests and by the sea, the stories told by the narrators are primarily stories that articulate events between and shared experiences of human beings. Discussing the capacity our consciousness has for transcending into the world to find others like ourselves Voegelin asserted: "The fact that consciousness has an experience *at all* of another human being, as a consciousness of the other, is not *a problem* but a given of experience from which one may proceed." Discovering a fellow human being in the world leaves only the problem of finding a symbolic language in which the other person can be acknowledged as such.[2] A solution to this problem of a symbolic language is suggested in the creation by Nádas of "narrative selfs."

Although the obvious connection between Voegelin and Nádas is their emphasis upon recollection and remembrance,[3] I suggest that their treatments of consciousness, especially the embodiment of consciousness that results in a biography of consciousness and the transcendence of consciousness into the world through the body as the sensorium of itself, offer more fruitful material for exploration and comparison. In the "Prefatory Remarks" to "Anamnesis"

---

1. Péter Nádas, "The Novelist and His Selfs," *New Hungarian Quarterly* 33, no. 127 (1992): 20–21. Hereinafter cited as "Selfs."

2. Eric Voegelin, *Collected Works of Eric Voegelin* (hereinafter, *CW*), vol. 6, *Anamnesis*, ed. David Walsh (Columbia: University of Missouri Press, 2002), 71–72. Hereinafter cited as *Anamnesis*.

3. Even though both are engaged in recollecting, Voegelin in order to develop a theory of consciousness and Nádas in order to write a novel that explores relations between human beings, Voegelin limits his recollections to the first ten years of his life and records only memories of those experiences that opened to him sources of excitation leading to further philosophical reflection. See *Anamnesis*, 84. Nádas, on the other hand, remembers "his" biography primarily from the period of his adolescence and young adulthood that was lived during the Hungarian Communist regime. *The End of a Family Story*, translated by Imre Goldstein (New York: Farrar, Straus and Giroux, 1998), by Nádas, may provide a better direct comparison with Voegelin's anamnetic experiments, since that novel focuses on preadolescent childhood.

Voegelin lists the assumptions that underlie his anamnetic experiments, i.e., the remembering of those childhood experiences that excited the "awe of existence" in his consciousness, an excitement that culminated in his philosophical vocation. Two of these assumptions are important for relating Voegelin's work on consciousness to the novel of Péter Nádas. Voegelin argues "that in its intentional function consciousness, in finite experience, transcends into the world, and that this type of transcendence is only one among several and must not be made the central theme of a theory of consciousness; [and] that the experiences of transcendence of consciousness into the body, the external world, the community, history, and the ground of being are givens in the *biography* of consciousness and thus antecede the systematic reflection on consciousness." These assumptions also underlie Voegelin's meditation "What Is Political Reality?" First, consciousness transcends *into the body* as well as the differentiated world that is *external* to the body. Second, "the experiences of transcendence of consciousness" into various levels of reality constitute a *biography* of a consciousness that is always rooted in the consciousness of a particular person. Third, the occasions of the transcendence of consciousness into the various levels of reality are *givens* to consciousness prior to any reflections upon consciousness. A fourth establishes for the body itself a crucial role in the biography of consciousness. In his essay "On the Theory of Consciousness," Voegelin asserts that "the connection [between the body and consciousness] is so intimate that between birth and death the body not only *determines, as the sensorium,* what part of the world may enter consciousness through it, but also is one of the most important determinants (*although not the only one*) for the inner tensions and relations of relevance of the world of consciousness."[4]

In *A Book of Memories,* Nádas focuses the reader's attention on the body very early in the book by using as the epigraph for the novel a passage—"But he spoke of the temple of his body"—from the Gospel of John (John 2:21 KJV). Thereafter, every narrator and every story line affirms the importance of the body for consciousness. Through the voice of Narrator C (to be identified below), Nádas approaches Voegelin's philosophical principles. Calling his father's body "a dark hoax of nature," C asserts that "the body, the human form, however devoutly we may expound in our Christian humility on the externality of the flesh and the primacy of the soul, is so potent a given that already at the moment of our birth, it becomes an immutable attribute."[5]

---

4. *Anamnesis,* 84, 65 (emphasis added).
5. Péter Nádas, *A Book of Memories,* trans. Ivan Sanders with Imre Goldstein (New York: Farrar, Straus and Giroux, 1997), 166. Mihály Szegedy-Maszák refers to the title of this book as *A Book of Memoirs.* See Mihály Szegedy-Maszák, "Péter Nádas," *Hungarian P.E.N.* 27 (1986): 44–45. Hereinafter the book is cited as *Memories.*

A Book of Memories will serve to illustrate the complexities that are involved in exploring "the biography of consciousness" with its dependence upon the body as the sensorium of consciousness. Voegelin recognized the difficulty inherent in the biography of consciousness and its exploration through such anamnetic experiments as he conducted on his own biography of consciousness. Warning that the process of trying to remember early experiences of an elemental nature, experiences that are "only partly transparent," Voegelin suggests "it would be an immense task to investigate the various grades of this complication." The experiences of a time later than the first ten years or so (adding presumably the trauma of adolescence) entail "further complications for an analysis."[6]

A Book of Memories is a novelistic anamnetic experiment. It projected Péter Nádas onto the stage of European literature with publications in German (1991), English (1997), and French (1998) quickly following its Hungarian publication in 1986. Essentially *A Book of Memories* is a novel about a novelist who is writing both a novel (about a novelist writing a novel) and his memoirs. The final version of this novel/memoir cum novel is assembled by Krisztián Somi Tót, a friend of the novelist/memoirist, from a manuscript that he found in the novelist's desk a year and a half after his death. He writes:

> I found the individual chapters of his life story in separate folders. Most of my time was taken up with the careful study of his notes. From the general outline covering the entire manuscript I could determine the sequence of chapters, but even after a thorough review of his notes, I haven't been able to decide in what direction he intended to steer his plot. However, I did find one additional sketchy chapter, a fragment really, that I could not place anywhere. It doesn't appear in any of the repeatedly revised tables of contents. Yet he may have meant it to be the keystone of the whole story.
>
> My work is done. The only thing left for me to do is to append to the text this last fragment.[7]

As noted earlier, Nádas focused the *Book* with the epigraph from the Gospel of John: "But he spoke of the temple of his body." This choice results in at least two discernible emphases. On the one hand, his attentiveness to the "temple of the body" leads to graphic descriptions of the various sensual-erotic activities in which the narrative selfs engage. Through these sensual-erotic components the deceptions and lies of the child-adolescent narrator (C) are linked with the deception and falsity of the historical *Zeitgeist* and the Communist

---

6. *Anamnesis*, 85, 86.
7. *Memories*, 681.

regimes of Mátyás Rákosi (1949–1953 and 1955–1956) and János Kádár (1956–1988) in Hungary[8] via the lies and deceptions that permeate his family relationships, especially with his father and mother. Moreover, the sensual-eroticism permeating the stories (story) in turn directs attention to the human body as the medium of contact with the world of other people, as the sensorium of consciousness in which the experience of the external social world occurs. On the other hand, it leads the "narrative selfs" to include meditations on consciousness that expose connections between the body and the consciousness of the particular narrative self; these meditations elaborate the lived experience of a narrative self.

After he had written this novel, Nádas divulged that he had divided himself into three narrative selfs for *A Book of Memories*. These selfs produce three narratives that alternate regularly by chapter: A, B, C, A, B, C, et cetera. The penultimate chapter introduces a fourth narrative self, Krisztián Somi Tót. The final chapter, told by A, reveals that C was his biographical/historical precursor. The consideration of *A Book of Memories* as an anamnetic experiment necessitates focus on the following: an introduction and brief synopsis of narrative A, written by a thirty-three-year-old man; a lengthier review of narrative C that focuses on the adolescence and early adulthood of narrator A/C with particular emphasis upon C's family and friends and the relationship of both to the regimes of the Hungarian Communists; a quick look at Krisztián, the fourth narrator, and his relationship to A/C; and finally an episode in the biography of A that prompts a description of consciousness in terms of the body and the world external to consciousness.

In "The Beauty of My Anomalous Nature," A begins the novel with a description of the last place that he lived in East Berlin. He reflects on what he is beginning.

> Certainly I don't want to write a travel journal; I can describe only what is mine, let's say the story of my loves, but maybe not even that, since I don't think I could ever talk about the larger significance of mere personal experiences, and since I don't believe or, more precisely, don't know, whether there is anything more significant than these otherwise trivial and uninteresting personal experiences (I assume there can't be), I'm ready to compromise; let this writing be a kind of recollection or reminder, something bound up with the pain and pleasure of reminiscence, something one is supposed to write in old age, a foretaste of what I may feel forty years from now, if I live to be seventy-three and can still reminisce.[9]

---

8. Although Imre Nagy assumed power in 1953, held it until 1955, and resumed power briefly in 1956, he is not mentioned in *A Book of Memories*.

9. *Memories*, 3–4.

Thus we learn that A, now thirty-three, is writing his memoirs. While in Berlin A is also writing a novel, and when he meets Melchior Thoenissen, a poet, through an actress named Thea Sandstuhl, the primary storyline of the A narration is established. The narrator falls in love with Melchior, who is also loved by Thea. Since A comes to believe that Thea can only relate to Melchior through him, he finds it necessary, as the agent that binds together the ménage à trois, to consummate a sexual liaison with Thea.

Melchior and A have an affair that ends in failure. Melchior escapes from East Germany to France, and A returns to Hungary destitute and bereft of emotion and purpose. A's relationship with Melchior failed in part because it was as saturated with lies as the East German political regime. Melchior tells A in one of their conversations that he is tired of living in a place "where a state of emergency had been in effect for fifty years! . . . where for half a century not one honest word had been uttered in public, not one, not even when you were talking with your neighbor." In their hope of "complementing the contact of their bodies with signs beyond the physical," Melchior and A each feverishly tell their stories and eagerly listen to the other's. Yet, Melchior confesses that the "urge to lie, to cover up, to be secretive and sly, was at least as strong as the urge to be sincere, open, and aboveboard, to seek the so-called truth." In fact, he admitted to A that "it was good to lie, it was necessary and pleasurable"; and since he lied all the time, A should not "take anything he said seriously but just as a joke." Beginning his reminiscences, A recalls that his recent past in East Berlin contained only "memories of tastes and smells of a world to which I no longer belong, one I might call my abandoned homeland, which I left to no purpose because nothing bound me to the one I found myself in, either; I was a stranger there, too, and even Melchior, the only human being I loved, could not make me belong; I was lost, I did not exist, my bones and solid flesh turned to jelly."[10]

The final chapter of the novel, "Escape," is also narrated by A. He resumes the story—begun in the first chapter of the novel—of his journey to Heiligendamm after Melchior has fled East Germany and of how he was picked up by the police and taken to Bad Doberan and held until his papers were seen to be in order. After his release by the authorities, and while waiting for a train to return him to East Berlin, he remembers an earlier visit in East Berlin to Mária Stein, his father's former lover. The visit was made by A/C ostensibly to ask Mária whether János Hamar or the man he knew as Father was his father. He remembers that she told him about her imprisonment—along with János Hamar she too was denounced by C's father—and about her life with C's father

10. Ibid., 207, 205–8, 8.

after the death of his mother. Finally, she told him how his father asked her to look at him out the window; when she looked "he shot himself through the mouth." C left, closed the door, and ran out of the building. He never asked who his father was.[11]

Narrative C revolves around the adolescent years of narrator C, the son of a Stalinist state prosecutor in Hungary during the Communist regime of Mátyás Rákosi. This narrative graphically demonstrates a central principle of political theory—discovered by Plato and adopted and amplified by Voegelin in his own work. The Platonic anthropological principle, "the state is man writ large," is premised on the assumption that political theory must be grounded in a philosophical anthropology and a theory of consciousness. Even though only one political event is narrated—the popular demonstration in Budapest on October 23, 1956, in which both C and his friend Kálman were swept up, and during which Kálman is killed—the story told by C demonstrates how the stories of family, friends, and lovers are simultaneously reflections of the story of the deceptions of the Rákosi regime and the *Zeitgeist* itself.

C writes his memoirs at the age of thirty-three, focusing on his adolescence and young adulthood in 1950s Hungary. For the most part C tells the story of his adolescence: (1) the exploits of, and relationships among, his circle of friends, three girls—Hédi Szán, Livia Süli, and Maja Prihoda—and three boys—Krisztián Somi Tót, Kálman Csúzdi, and Prém; (2) his relationship with his father and mother; and (3) his and Maja's spying upon their fathers, who work together. The story begins on the day of Stalin's funeral, with the third chapter, entitled "The Soft Light of the Sun." C is walking home from school through the woods; Krisztián appears and they walk toward each other. The appearance of Krisztián evokes C's "most contradictory and secret feelings":

> "Krisztián!" I would have loved to cry out... [but] saying his name out loud would be like touching his naked body, which is why I avoided him, always waiting until he began walking home with others so I wouldn't walk with him or his way; even in school I was careful not to wind up next to him, lest I'd have to talk to him or, in a sudden commotion, brush against his body; at the same time I kept watching him, tailed him like a shadow, mimicked his gestures in front of the mirror, and it was painfully pleasurable to know that *he was completely unaware of my spying on him;*... in reality, he didn't even bother to look at me, I was like a neutral, useless object to him, completely superfluous and devoid of interest.
>
> Of course, my sober self cautioned me not to acknowledge these passionate feelings; *it was as if two separate beings coexisted in me, totally independent of each other:* at times the joys and sufferings his mere existence caused me seemed like

---

11. Ibid., 692, 700.

nothing but little games, not worth thinking about, because *one of my two selves hated and detested him as much as my other self loved and respected him.*[12]

Krisztián had arranged this tête-à-tête to ask C not to report him to the principal for a derogatory remark about Stalin that C had overheard him make in the school bathroom. The remark increased C's anxiety over his grandfather's derogatory remark the same day about the plan to embalm Stalin's body for public display. The encounter with Krisztián ends with C shouting: "It never occurred to me to do it, believe me!" In answer to Krisztián's "No?" C whispered, "No, not at all." At this point C impetuously kissed Krisztián. C remembers the kiss as very sensual but "free—and this must be emphasized, it was purely free—of any ulterior motives with which adult love, in its own natural way, complements a kiss; *our mouths,* in the purest of possible ways, and regardless of what had gone before or what would follow, *restricted themselves to what two mouths in the fraction of a second could give each other: fulfillment, comfort, and release.*"[13] C walks home alone, sees a strange coat hanging in the hallway, but enters his mother's room anyway—by this time his mother is sick with cancer (which has been hidden from C by his family) and stays in bed most of the time—there to encounter a "stranger" who had earlier disappeared from the family's lives. Later, we learn that the visitor is János Hamar, former intimate friend of his parents who was denounced by C's father and is just returning from a five-year prison term.

In the chapter entitled "Grass Grew over the Scorched Spot," C writes that "a not insignificant detail of our emotional life was the fact that, as a result of our parents' political trustworthiness, we were privileged to live adjacent to the immense, heavily guarded area that contained the residence of Mátyas Rákosi" and reflects that "the whole protected area became something like a focal point, the living nucleus of all my fears." When C refers to "*our* parents' political trustworthiness," he is referring to his adolescent friend Maja Prihoda's father, chief of military counterintelligence, and his own father, a state prosecutor, who sometimes work together. Maja and C agree to conduct regular periodic searches of their fathers' desks to determine if they may be traitors, in

---

12. Ibid., 39–40 (emphasis added).
13. Ibid., 47 (emphasis added). Krisztián, the receiver of the kiss and the reporter of the penultimate chapter of the novel, recalls the kiss: "What should be understood from all this is that no event in my later life could induce me to think that that kiss was really a kiss and not simply the solution to an existential problem I had at the time. I couldn't allow myself to be caught up in dangerous psychological predicaments, I had all I could do to ward off tangible external dangers. I came to appreciate the advantages of psychological self-concealment, and with the years I continued to avoid ambiguous situations and judgments that didn't square exactly with my wishes or interests." *Memories,* 594.

which case they would denounce them to the authorities. C writes, "We were not aware of what we were doing to each other and to ourselves":

> Because it wasn't just official and work-related documents that we came across but all sorts of other material that we did not mean to find, like our parents' extensive personal romantic correspondence; here, the material discovered in my father's drawers was unfortunately more serious, but once we put our hands on it and went over it thoroughly, painstakingly, with the disinterested sternness of professionals, it seemed that by ferreting out sin in the name of ideal purity, invading the most forbidden territory of the deepest and darkest passions, penetrating the most secret regions, we, too, turned into sinners, for sin is indivisible: when tracking a murderer one must become a murderer to experience most profoundly the circumstances and motives of the murder; and so we were right there with our fathers, where not only should we not have set foot but, according to the testimony of the letters, they themselves moved about stealthily, like unrepentant sinners.
>
> There is profound wisdom in the Old Testament's prohibition against casting eyes on the uncovered loins of one's father.

The letters unearthed by the pair of spies reveal that Maja's father is continuing an affair thought by her mother to have been ended some time earlier; thus, Maja becomes an unwilling accomplice in her father's ongoing deception. They also discover that C's father and mother each have lovers they knew before marriage, that these affairs have since continued apace, that their respective lovers are themselves lovers, and finally that all four of them—Mária Stein and János Hamar as well as C's parents—know everything: "my father and mother also wrote letters to each other in which they discussed their feelings about being caught up in this inextricably complicated foursome."[14]

As a thirty-three-year-old adult living and writing in a small Hungarian village, C asks:

> How could we [Maja and I] have known then that our relationship reenacted, repeated, and copied, in a playfully exaggerated form ... our parents' ideals and also their ruthless practices, and to some extent the publicly proclaimed ideals and ruthless practices of that historical period as well? ... [W]e could call ... it ... something real ... more precisely, for us it was turning their activities into a game that enabled us to experience their present life and work—which we thought was wonderful, dangerous, important, and, what's more, respectable.... [W]e loved being serious, we basked in the glory of our assumed political role, not only filled with terror and remorse but bestowing on us a grand sense of power, a feeling that we had power even over them, over these enormously powerful

---

14. Ibid., 270, 271, 341, 342.

men, and all in the name of an ethical precept that, again in their own views, was considered sacred, nothing less than the ideal, self-abnegating, perfect, immaculate Communist purity of their way of life; and what a cruel quirk of fate it was that through it all they were totally unsuspecting, and how could they have guessed that, while in their puritanical and also very practical zeal they were killing scores of real and imagined enemies, they were nurturing vipers in their bosom?

Our secrets carried us into the world of the powerful, initiated us into adulthood by making us prematurely mature and sensible, and of course set us apart from the world of ordinary people, where everything worked more simply and predictably.

These love letters referred openly and unequivocally to the hours in which, by some peculiar mistake, we had been conceived—by mistake, because they didn't want us, they wanted only their love.

C would write later: "I imagine the archangels covered God's eyes while we pored over these letters." This texture of lies and deceptions constitutes the nexus of his relationships, especially at home, "where people living under the same roof grew so far apart, were so consumed by their own physical and moral disintegration, were left to fend for themselves, and only for themselves, that they did not notice, or pretended not to notice, when someone was missing, their own child, from the so-called family nest."[15]

This all-too-brief glimpse of narrative C provides the crucial insights into C's life: that he experiences himself as divided, incomplete, and morally repulsive; that he yearns for the fulfillment, comfort, and release proffered by his kiss of Krisztián—a yearning that thereafter he will seek to fulfill through heterosexual and homosexual love affairs; that he was obsessed with spying and surveillance and that consequently he knew that his relationship to his parents was suffused with lies and deception. C reflected: "If there was a way for me to know when this mutually effective and multifaceted disintegration had begun, whether it had a definite beginning or when and why this commodious family nest had grown cold, I would surely have much to say about human nature and also about the age I lived in."[16]

The characters of the rulers of Hungary during the period of C's pre-adolescent and adolescent years—approximately 1949 to 1958—are mirrored in the character of C/A. And the practices of deceit, spying, denouncement, and lying that characterize such a state saturate the lives of the citizenry, precluding the possibility of *philia politike,* the love of the good between men that creates the community.

15. Ibid., 342–43, 344, 288.
16. Ibid., 288.

While the direct linkage between C and the state is his father, the linkage extends to his mother and to his parents' lovers—Mária Stein and János Hamar. Since that foursome is bound together by the sensual-erotic, and since that sensual-erotic leads to deception (of C) and ultimately betrayal (C's father denounces Mária Stein and János Hamar, who are sentenced to five years in prison), I think that the primary linkage between C's deceptive, divided self and the deceptive nature of the state (through the deceptive family) is the eroticism that permeates the novel.[17] In fact, a large portion of the novel itself is devoted to describing the various erotic activities in which the characters engage and through which they relate to each other. For example, and most important for the development of C's character, C remembers several erotically charged encounters between his pre-adolescent self (these episodes are the only pre-adolescent memories recalled by C) and his father, on the one hand, and his mother, on the other. Early one morning C crawled into bed and fondled his still-sleeping father, who shouted, kicked him out of bed, never touched him again, and was always on the "lookout for any effeminate behaviors" from him. The encounter with his mother seems to be a recurring one in which C sits by his mother's bed and caresses her arm and kisses the crook of her neck and the crook of her elbow. On one such occasion, C's mother dreamily recounts a time when she was picnicking with two men (C's future father and János Hamar), and they (the three of them) could not decide to whom she belonged, which becomes C's question also, but he never asks it.[18]

As we have seen, the adolescent C discovers the layers of lies and deceptions—of forbidden sex and of political denunciation—that permeate the relationships between his parents and their lovers, as well as between his parents and

---

17. Krisztián also engages in promiscuous erotic affairs to find in them a hoped-for satisfaction of his need (and desire) to dominate and maintain authority over others. See note 13. Nádas is not the only novelist to link eroticism with political oppression. Two other Central European novelists who have written creatively and imaginatively about this relationship are Milan Kundera in *The Book of Laughter and Forgetting*, trans. Aaron Asher (New York: Harper Perennial, 1996), and Péter Esterházy in *A Little Hungarian Pornography*, trans. Judith Sollosy (Evanston: Northwestern University Press, 1995). See also Heimito von Doderer, "Sexualität und totaler Staat," in *Die Wiederhehr der Drachen: Aufsätze/Traktate/Reden* (Munich: Biederstein Verlag 1970), 275–98. In *The Demons*, one of the narrators, Kajetan von Schlaggenberg, states: "I had to realize that I had lost my sexual impartiality and was living in a second reality... as everyone who pursues a 'type' becomes the idiotic scarecrow of his own displaced sexuality: a constant anticipation that is never attained.... For sex is the greatest window of our apperception, and if this window clouds, all the others will soon suffer from cataracts. Half blind, you will peer out at all things only through the narrow slit of some program or other, always anticipating what ought to be." Heimito von Doderer, *The Demons*, trans. Richard and Clara Winston (New York: Alfred A. Knopf, 1961), 1077.

18. See *Memories*, 151–71, 342.

himself. Indeed, by engaging in the types of activities that their fathers perform for the Rákosi regime, he and Maja are directly implicated in the characteristics of the regime. Recall C's own description of his and Maja's spying activities: "We could call it aping, but we could also call it something real... more precisely, for us it was turning their activities into a game that enabled us to experience their present life and work—which we thought was wonderful, dangerous, important, and, what's more, respectable."[19]

The deception and lies saturating the society of the Rákosi regime also affected Krisztián's adult life. Living in a loveless marriage, he cheats on his wife. Although he has been quite successful materially, he is not happy. His success has depended upon his skill in deceiving others, and he notes that even as a young child, he had "to think carefully about the ways of thinking, or rather to be careful and not necessarily really think the things I said out loud." A few lines later, he says: "I can't claim that too many people love me, but most consider me a fair-minded person. Yet in view of my friend's poignant analysis, I am compelled by fair-mindedness to ask whether I may not appear to be fair-minded because I always manage to keep my distance from my own endeavors as well as from the people who love me, so that I can avoid having to identify with them while still retaining my control over them."[20]

However, during the three-year period that C lived and wrote in the house of Krisztián's aunts, Krisztián and C have established a friendship based upon neither the pleasures of the body nor mutual utility that leads him to introduce his chapter "No More" with the confession that "I am a rational man, perhaps too rational. I am not inclined to any form of humility. Still, I would like to copy my friend's last sentence onto this empty page. Let it help me finish the job no one's commissioned me to do, which should make it the most personal undertaking of my life, the one closest to my heart." Later in his narrative, but still in a confessional mode, Krisztián tells us that

> after twenty years we did return to that mutual attraction which had once transcended our dissimilarities and which we didn't know what to make of as children. This reversion may have had to do with the fact that slowly but surely my successes were turning into failures, and that he never again wanted to be united with anyone on any level. Not with me, either. He remained attentive, sensitive, but shut up in himself. Turned cold....
>
> My experiences in human relations have made me see everything in this world as temporary and ephemeral. What I perceive today as love or friendship can turn out tomorrow to be nothing but the need to gratify a physical urge, or a move prompted by crass or sly self-interest. I acknowledge this with the greatest

---

19. Ibid., 596.
20. Ibid.

of equanimity.... In the foregoing pages I have already prepared my balance sheet. No loves, no friends.... I haven't yet sunk into total apathy. And that is probably the reason why during those three years it became a vital necessity to have the attentiveness and sensitivity of someone whom I didn't need to, wasn't allowed to, touch. And he himself no longer had such desires. Still, he was closer to me than anyone whose body I could possess.

Both men have become virtually emotionless and cold, and yet penetrating this coldness the mutual attraction—really an allusion to that long since forgotten attraction in childhood—re-emerged. After C's violent death, Krisztián confesses that it took him a year and a half to summon the strength to sit down at C's desk. And in C's desk he found the present manuscript that he carefully prepared for publication. Was it the *Zeitgeist* that had corrupted and emptied Krisztián and C? Was it C's voracious search for human contact—"I wanted everyone to love me," he said, "and I couldn't love anyone"—that left him apathetic and cold?[21] Was C's search for this human contact a result of his parent's obsession with their own "physical and moral disintegration" and the consequent failure to notice the child missing from the so-called family nest? Did Krisztián's success and his ultimate failure derive from the necessity since his youth and C's kiss of his not really thinking the things he said out loud?

Moving from the social-political world of Nádas's narrators, we now turn once again to A and his exploration of his own consciousness after the failure of his relationship with Melchior. In a chapter entitled "Losing Consciousness and Regaining It," A retells his experience of consciousness transcending into the body and through the body into the world. The writing of his memoirs represents a "kind of recollection or reminder" that consciousness has a content derived from the experiences of his body and of the world outside this body; that recollection and remembrance enable the novelist in the voice of A (who is also C) to probe the nature of his consciousness and its contact with the world through his body as the sensorium of that consciousness.

A has traveled to Heiligendamm, a resort on the coast. Walking along the coast on a stormy night, he was knocked unconscious and only remembers regaining consciousness. Describing what *was not there* during the time of unconsciousness and *was there* during the very brief moment of regaining consciousness, he writes that "my consciousness was lacking all those inner flashes of *instinct and habit* that, relying on *experience and desires,* evoke *images and sounds,* ensure the unbroken flow of *imagination and memory* that renders our existence sensible and to an extent even purposeful, enables us to *define our position in the world* and *establish contact with our surroundings,* or to relin-

---

21. Ibid., 592, 672–73, 45.

quish this connection, which in itself is a form of contact."²² This compact statement suggests that for A consciousness is historically, i.e., biographically, constituted in pairs like "instinct and habit," "experiences and desires," "images and sounds," "position in the world" and contact with it, all of which foreground the role of the body in consciousness. Also, one may say that the capacities for imagining and remembering are ensured by these sensual pairs, and that through the flow of this imagination and memory thus ensured our existence is rendered sensible and "to an extent even purposeful." A's remembrance and articulation of "Losing Consciousness and Regaining It" at Heiligendamm illustrates the complexity of the connection between the body and consciousness and the difficulty of understanding the embodiment of consciousness. It is the complexity of this givenness of embodied consciousness that Voegelin includes among the assumptions that underlie his philosophical efforts to recollect the early biographical events that formed his own consciousness.

But as A remembers the mishap on the embankment at Heiligendamm, he remembers something else. The first whispers of returning consciousness made him aware that his body sensed the rocks and the water, but it was, as A writes, "nothing more than sensing existence in pure, disembodied form." Attending to his awakening, he contends that "what little I did perceive of water, stones, my skin, and body, *wrenched as it was from a context or relationship, alluded rather to that intangible whole, that deeper, primeval completeness for which we all keep yearning, awake or in our dreams but mostly in vain;* in this sense, then, what had passed, the total insensibility of unconsciousness, proved to be a far stronger sensual pleasure than the sensation of real things."²³ In his meditation "What Is Political Reality?" Voegelin asserts that "real . . . is the participation of things in one another within the comprehending reality. . . . From the experiences, recollections, phantasmata, and symbolizations of consciousness are compounded the conceptions of reality, in which the termini of participation—i.e., the realities of God and world, of other people and of the concretely participating man—find their place."²⁴ As A strives to articulate the sensual pleasure of "that deeper, primeval completeness" that proved to be far stronger than "the sensation of real things," he seems to symbolize how the consciousness of "the concretely participating man" experiences the unconscious world—source of all the matter from which the body is constituted. Since this sense perception of the world lacks the normal "flow of imagination and memory," lacks the normal "track of remembering and comparing" that is characteristic

22. Ibid., 94 (emphasis added).
23. Ibid., 93–94 (emphasis added).
24. *Anamnesis,* 361.

of consciousness, A can only allude "to that intangible whole, that deeper, primeval completeness for which we all keep yearning." The allusive nature of "that intangible whole," the paradise that is lost with the recovery of consciousness, seems to be an attempt to articulate not only the regaining of consciousness by A but also the beginning or birth of consciousness itself. A laments: "It seemed that by coming back to consciousness, by being able to think and to remember, I had to lose paradise, the state of bliss whose fragmentary effects might still be felt here and there but as a complete whole had gone into hiding, leaving behind only shreds of its receding self, its memory, and the thought that I had never been, and would never again be, as happy as I had been then and there."[25] He cannot stop in that unconscious state, for his body insists that he become conscious again, and with the return of consciousness A returns to the human condition and the attendant realization that the perfection of strength and goodness is no more attainable for him than the possibility of the total freedom to be "infinitely mean and wicked."

Is this symbolization of the regaining of consciousness not a metaphor for the birth of consciousness? Can the *longing for* the paradise of unconsciousness not be associated with the world and with man before the Fall, shrouded as it is in the mists of the beginning? Is not the allusive nature of A's attempt to symbolize the sensual pleasure of unconsciousness a recognition of the mists that shroud the Beginning? Is not the *longing for* the sensual pleasure of unconsciousness and the dream of paradise, "the state of bliss whose fragmentary fragments might still be felt here and there but as a complete whole" that has gone into hiding, the ideologue's dream of "stalling the continual delicate vacillations of reality"?[26] Does not A's longing express the desire for the prelapsarian paradise that is absent the knowledge of good and evil, of consciousness?

A's longing for the "intangible whole," for primeval completeness—experienced at Heiligendamm and articulated shortly after he has failed to sustain a relationship with Melchior—appears to be a longing for the oblivion that characterizes unconsciousness. At the same time it appears as a wish and a dream to renounce his consciousness and thus his humanity. It is indisputable that A has arrived at the point in his life where he wishes to forget, to be absorbed in some vast, primeval oblivion because he failed to find or sustain a meaningful relationship with another human being. In fact, after Melchior escaped from East Berlin to France, A declared, "I was lost, I did not exist." And yet he

---

25. *Memories*, 95.
26. Heimito von Doderer wrote: "People who wished to see the rigid concrete channels of their lives extended into the infinite future were in fact doing nothing but stalling the continual delicate vacillations of reality. And the moment that vibrant equilibrium was halted, a second reality came into being." In von Doderer, *The Demons*, 1237.

also declares in the same sentence that "I could still perceive myself *to be something:* a toad pressing heavily against the earth; a slimy-bodied snail unblinkingly observing my own nothingness."²⁷ And despite the fleeting desire for the "total insensibility of unconsciousness" A's body, with its sensing of the familiarly tangible world, recalls A to consciousness. Ultimately it is the *embodied* consciousness of A that sits at the desk in a small room in the house of Krisztián's aunts in a small Hungarian village that retrieves A from oblivion, which returns him to the world, and saves him to write his memoir and his novel.

But A is crippled. He has become cold. "If I wasn't familiar with the painful reverse side of this coldness," comments Krisztián, "I'd be tempted to say that he became an accurate, intelligently responding, precisely calibrated machine." In his short life spent searching for "fulfillment, contact, and release," split into two selves by the deceits of his childhood, A—aware that there was a self that longed for a "harmonious exterior that shielded strength and goodness . . . in other words, I longed for perfection"—could finally only hope for "a total identification with my true self, for the freedom . . . to be infinitely mean and wicked."²⁸ A has almost lost (it seems) contact with the self that makes possible the human community founded upon the Platonic philia or the *homonoia* of Aristotle, and having lost his contact with the good in himself, he can only long for total identification with what he thinks is his true self, his wicked self. In this passage we witness a transvaluation of the philosophic and political virtues, for the true self becomes associated with the total freedom to be "infinitely mean and wicked." The longing for inner strength and goodness, however, is not destroyed by the infinitely mean and wicked, and A remains a divided self, "shut up in himself."

My intention has been to demonstrate that the assumptions that underlie Voegelin's theory of consciousness can be developed more completely through an examination of *A Book of Memories* by Péter Nádas. In this brief review of selected portions of the novel I have emphasized how the embodied consciousness transcends into the world of other human beings, how the body of the narrators produces a biography of consciousness in its social-political relations, and how the body functions as the sensorium of consciousness and thereby rooting consciousness in the concrete world.

The radicalism of basing the theory of consciousness on the given experiences of an embodied consciousness of a concrete human being, experiences that result in a biography of consciousness, must lead, it seems to me, to charges that these experiences are after all *only* the experiences of a particular human

---

27. *Memories,* 8 (emphasis added).
28. Ibid., 672, 45.

being. How can the explorations by a person of his own biography of consciousness culminate in findings that transcend the particular experiences of a concrete human being? Although they have been called to different types of endeavor—philosophy and fiction—both Voegelin and Nádas have addressed this concern and both finally rely upon their capacity as human beings to imagine.

In the final, posthumously published, volume of *Order and History, In Search of Order,* Voegelin articulated his discovery of "the dimension of consciousness," in which the philosopher becomes "conscious of his participatory role in the process of experience, imagination, and symbolization." He calls this "the reflective distance of consciousness to its own participation in thing-reality and It-reality." This symbol was formulated in the symbolic complex: Reflective Distance—Remembrance—Oblivion. Voegelin wrote that "the power of imagination, however, while assertive of truth, is not necessarily self-assertive. The thinker engaged in the quest for truth can remain, or become, aware of the structure of his quest." When the philosopher becomes aware of the paradox of his consciousness structured by intentionality and luminosity, this awareness may be characterized as a reflectively distancing remembrance. Without summarizing the meditation in which Voegelin expresses these findings of his life-long search, an endeavor that would increase the dimensions of this paper, I will simply point out that the reflectively distancing remembrance and its symbolization depends upon the imagination of the philosopher. This imagination is necessary for both the anamnetic, remembering, search and for the articulation of the results of the search. The imagination of the philosopher must not, in turn, become self-assertive; the philosopher must remember that his imagination alone does not "function automatically as a formative force in the existential quest for truth,"[29] for the philosopher is only human and therefore participates in the various realms of being of which his nature is a composite. The philosopher must remember that "reality... is not a thing confronting man, but the comprehending reality in which he himself is real by participating in it."[30] In the philosopher's symbolic language we find the truth that transcends but is accessible to the individual consciousness of an embodied human being.

Nádas also finds a way to create imaginatively a document that expresses a truth that transcends his own particular biography. In "The Novelist and His Selfs," Nádas asserts that his "first-person narrative invariably steered me toward confession,

---

29. Eric Voegelin, *CW,* vol. 18, *In Search of Order,* vol. V, *Order and History,* ed. by Ellis Sandoz (1987; Columbia: University of Missouri Press, 2000), 54, 55, 54, 55.

30. *Anamnesis,* 361.

so I had to keep examining the events of my own life, and use only as many of them as these personae would allow. In the little openings and crevices between them and my own self, imagination could freely do its work, and it did, pushing my ego aside in the process. The logic of my own life history could remain in the dark, though its contours had to be visible. I didn't know why things happened the way they did, but I could more or less tell what belonged and what didn't.

It was the logic of imagination and not of experience that showed me the way. *The prompts did not come from me.*[31]

The "logic of the imagination," I suggest, is the novelist's equivalent of what Voegelin has called "reflective distance." Both depend upon the "power of imagination," and yet both are dependent upon the biography of a particular embodied consciousness. While Nádas relied upon the "contours" of his own "life history," his "imagination" pushed aside his (self-assertive?) ego. "The logic of imagination" and not his own experiences showed him the way, and "the prompts did not come from me," he wrote.

Eric Voegelin articulated the movement toward anamnetic remembrance in his consciousness and discovered that "the thinker engaged in the quest for truth can remain, or become, aware of the structure of his quest,"[32] while Nádas has simply attempted to tell the story of that most "exceedingly ordinary thing"—"lived experience." Yet is it not the "reflective distance" of the philosopher and the "logic of the imagination" that prevent philosophy and literature from being relevant only to the respective selfs? For as Nádas says, the naïve expression of the imagination—"*Madame Bovary, c'est moi*"—"is the only possible means by which the age-old need to relate events occurring between people can still be satisfied."[33]

31. "Selfs," 20–21.
32. Voegelin, *CW,* 18:54.
33. "Selfs," 20.

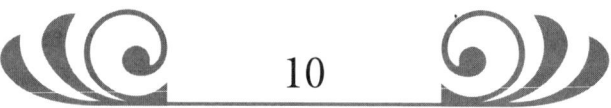

10

Imagining Modern Japan
Natsume Soseki's First Trilogy

Timothy Hoye

"The world was in an uproar; he watched it, but he could not join it. His own world and the real world were aligned on a single plane, but nowhere did they touch. The real world would move on in its uproar and leave him behind. The thought filled him with a great unease."
—Natsume Soseki, *Sanshiro,* 1908

The role of the literary artist in Japan's long history is an honored one in large measure because of the power of language and literature to lift consciousness through imagination. Among Japan's most gifted literary artists is Natsume Soseki (1867–1916), regarded by Nobel laureate Oe Kenzaburo as Japan's "national writer."[1] Soseki[2] resigned his position as professor of English literature at Tokyo Imperial University in 1907 in order to dedicate himself to writ-

---

1. Kenzaburo Oe, "On Modern and Contemporary Japanese Literature," in *Japan, the Ambiguous, and Myself: The Nobel Prize Speech and Other Lectures* (Tokyo: Kodansha International, 1995), 44.
2. Natsume is the family name. Natsume Soseki's given name is Kinnosuke. He chose "Soseki," which means "to rinse one's mouth with stones." It is unusual in Japanese tradition to refer to someone by their given name, but Natsume Soseki is always referred to as simply Soseki. Throughout this essay Japanese names will be presented in the traditional indigenous style of family name first. Also, with respect to putting *hiragana, katakana,* and *kanji* into *romaji,* or English, terms readily identifiable, such as *bushido,* the way of the warrior, will conform to widely accepted usage in which the *o* is not lengthened phonetically

ing fiction in various genres. Among his earliest efforts was a trilogy that first appeared as serialized novels in the *Asahi* newspaper, for which Soseki wrote. The first story in this trilogy is entitled simply *Sanshiro,* which refers to a young man's name. The second in the series is *Sorekara,* which means "and then." The last in the series is called *Mon,* or "gate." What follows is a study of these three novels as representing Soseki's effort to understand and communicate through his unique approach to fiction the rapidly changing dynamics in the "common *nous*"[3] of Japanese society and culture during the Meiji period (1868–1912). Through his "sketches" Soseki explored the mythic, political, and philosophical dimensions of a very well-ordered society rushing perhaps too quickly toward something called modern Japan, a Japan that was for Soseki very difficult indeed to imagine. In his attempt to imagine such a Japan, Soseki saw the erosion not only of fundamental truths as expressed in traditional Japanese myth and zen Buddhist teachings, but also of fundamental truths of the human condition.

The Political Landscape in Late Meiji

In most accounts, the story of modern Japan begins with the arrival of Commodore Matthew C. Perry in Edo Bay in July 1853, and Perry's demands that Japan "open" its ports to American shipping needs and to trade. The subsequent Meiji era (1868–1912) brought enormous changes to Japan, not least of which was a new form of government nominally anchored by the restoration (*go-isshin*) of the emperor and legally defined by the Meiji Constitution of 1889 (*dai nippon teikoku kempou*). The Meiji leadership took as their guiding theme the idea of *fukoku kyohei* (rich country, strong military), a theme inspired by Western models of the modern state. Tokyo, which means "eastern capital," became the new capital of Japan at the beginning of the Meiji era and came to

---

to *ou* to suggest the long "o" sound of the original. In writing names such as Sosuke, in *Mon,* the same approach, used in the official translations, will be followed. When drawing attention to individual characters within names, however, such as *so* in *Sosuke,* the more accurate *sou,* to indicate the long "o" sound, will be used. This is to facilitate those who wish to look up the characters in Andrew Nathaniel Nelson, *The Modern Reader's Japanese-English Character Dictionary* (Tokyo: Charles E. Tuttle, 1994).

3. In a letter to Robert Heilman from Munich in 1959, Eric Voegelin, following Aristotle, defined the "essence of politics" as the "*philia politike,* the friendship which institutes a cooperative community among men." Further, this "friendship is possible among men insofar as they participate in the common *nous,* in the spirit or mind" (Charles R. Embry, ed., *Robert B. Heilman and Eric Voegelin: A Friendship in Letters, 1944–1984* [Columbia: University of Missouri Press, 2004], 194).

symbolize a "westering" Japan. All three of the novels considered here are set in Tokyo, or mostly in Tokyo, and all include numerous references to political events both of the period in which the stories are set, roughly 1908 to 1910, and of the Meiji era as a whole. For one scholar, Soseki's work reflects the very "spirit" of Meiji.[4]

But that spirit was far from one-dimensional. As Joseph Pittau has pointed out, the first few years of Meiji were dominated by a desire for all things Western, "not only techniques but also customs, ideas and values." In a second phase, however, during the 1870s and 1880s, the hunger for reform along Western lines slowed and there was a desire among the leadership for a "new identity in politics" and also "in ideology and morals." During this later phase, the emphasis was more on building, not just a "modern" state, but a "modern *Japanese* state." Three fields of endeavor were given priority during this time: the political, the military, and the educational. Out of the endeavors in these fields, the Japanese leadership wove the framework of a modern Japan that "kept the country united until the end of the second world war."[5]

Among the most important figures in the making of the Meiji Constitution of 1889 were Ito Hirobumi, Inoue Kowashi, and Ikebe Yoshitaka.[6] Ito was Japan's first prime minister and is widely regarded as the principal architect of the constitution. He was among the young men from Choshu in western Honshu who studied with Yoshida Shoin[7] at the famous *shoka sonjuku* school in Hagi. His *Commentaries on the Constitution of the Empire of Japan* is considered essential reading on the political and legal dynamics of the Meiji period. He was among those who went on the famous Iwakura Mission to the West in 1871 to study every aspect of Western civilization in eleven different countries. In 1882, Ito traveled to Europe to study Western constitutionalism, especially in Germany. He was Japanese resident general in Korea when he was assassinated in Manchuria, in 1909, by a Korean nationalist. This event is featured in Soseki's *Mon*. Inoue Kowashi stayed in Japan while Ito was overseas studying constitu-

4. Isamu Fukuchi, "*Kokoro* and the Spirit of Meiji," *Monumenta Nipponica* 48, no. 4 (1993): 469–88.
5. Joseph Pittau, "Inoue Kowashi, 1843–1895, and the Formation of Modern Japan," *Monumenta Nipponica* 20, no. 3/4 (1965): 253–82.
6. There were, of course, many others. Additional notables of the period included Fukuzawa Yukichi, Saionji Kimmochi, Itagaki Taisuke, Okuma Shigenobu, Saigo Takamori, Okubo Toshimichi, Kido Takayoshi, and the German scholar Carl Friedrich Hermann Roessler.
7. Yoshida Shoin (1830–1859) was an enormous influence on the young men of Western Honshu during the early years of Meiji. He early envisioned a Japan with the emperor restored to the center of power and authority. He was tried, convicted, and executed by the Tokugawa shogunate in 1859 and became something of a rallying symbol for dissatisfied samurai who wanted to "honor the emperor, and expel the barbarian" (*sonno joi*).

tionalism so that "the future constitution would not be contrary to the fundamental national polity." In this effort, Inoue was greatly assisted by Ikebe Yoshitaka, who "was a famous scholar of Japanese classics and poetry." Inoue summed up his views on the challenge of forging a modern Japanese state in a poem: "Spinning thread from thousands of foreign herbs to weave it into a fine Yamato dress." For Inoue, the challenge was to accept "modern" ideas "without, however, changing the historical *kokutai*,[8] which was unique and based on a tradition of 2,500 years."[9] The character Sanshiro, in the story of that name and first in Soseki's trilogy, captures the political landscape well: "Meiji thought had been reliving three hundred years of Western history in the space of forty."[10]

Philosophical "Sketches"

Two particularly important characteristics of Soseki's literary art derive from his early dedication both to the philosophical basis of the literary art and to an approach to writing called *shaseibun,* or "sketching." In both respects, Soseki's approach to the modern novel as art was generally counter to the dominant trends among the Japanese writers of his time. He resisted naturalism, for example, that style characteristic of Western writers like Flaubert, Turgenev, Tolstoy, and Dostoevsky so popular among most aspiring Japanese writers of the time. Some consider this naturalist approach to be the real "father" of modern Japanese literature.[11] Soseki, on the contrary, was much taken by Chinese and Japanese classics. According to Thomas Rimer, Soseki grew up during a time when it was "still possible to receive an education that involved the study of traditional Chinese and Japanese literary texts."[12] This is no doubt part of the context of Soseki's resistance to the *genbunitchi,* or the movement to base written Japanese on spoken Japanese. To encourage this was to encourage what Karatani Kojin calls "the invention of a new conception of writing as equivalent with speech." For Karatani, this movement was highly ideological and was always motivated by a desire for "the abolition of *kanji.*" For an artist like Soseki,

---

8. *Kokutai* refers to a mystic bond between the Japanese people and the emperor and is usually associated with the period 1890–1945, that is, the period during the Meiji Constitution.

9. Pittau, "Inoue Kowashi," 266, 267.

10. Soseki Natsume, *Sanshiro: A Novel,* trans., with a critical essay, by Jay Rubin (Seattle: University of Washington Press, 1977), 18.

11. Oscar Benl, "Naturalism in Japanese Literature," *Monumenta Nipponica* 9, no. 1/2 (1953): 1–33.

12. J. Thomas Rimer, *Modern Japanese Fiction and Its Traditions: An Introduction* (Princeton: Princeton University Press, 1978), 38.

however, such a movement could only obscure and perhaps in time destroy what some scholars call the "faded mythologies" imbedded in traditional languages. This is especially true in the highly ideographic style of expression in *kanji* that came to be used for sophisticated expression in the evolution of modern Japanese society. Concerns over such confusion would be especially central to a scholar such as Soseki, who wished to "probe the psychological origins of literature," to understand "what led to its appearance, development, and decline," and also what "social factors" brought literature into the world "and caused it to flourish or wither."[13]

Before Soseki wrote novels, in fact, and continuing throughout his career as a literary artist, he wrote and lectured on such topics as the "Philosophical Basis of Literary Art," "Substance and Form," and "Literature and Morality." At Tokyo Imperial University from 1903 to 1907, Soseki also gave lectures entitled "On Literature," "The General Concept of Literature," and "Eighteenth-Century English Literature." Soseki was especially "earnest" among Japanese writers in his search for "answers to questions on the nature of literature."[14] Among constants for Soseki as artist was his belief that one of the duties of the literary artist was to "impact on the future of the human race." Among technical priorities was to cultivate "character and technique."[15] In his work, Soseki reveals an increasing sensitivity to the ecumenic pressures emanating from the West, a sensitivity that may help to explain his turning to the writing of novels as opposed to his previous theoretical studies in search of the true meaning of literature. Among examples of Western pressure was the *genbunitchi* movement noted above.

Karatani Kojin emphasizes that Soseki was greatly influenced in his style by an approach to writing called *shaseibun*. Soseki was a close friend during his student days with Masaoka Shiki, who had developed this approach to writing. Soseki and Shiki had long practiced composing *haiku* poetry together. Soseki had in fact apparently intended *Wagahai wa neko de aru* (I Am a Cat) as an experiment in "sketching," with publication expected in a *haiku* journal called *The Cuckoo* (*Hototogisu*). This style of writing was "an attempt to revitalize language in all its diversity." For Soseki, this technique meant "the liberation of diverse genres." By this style, for example, writers avoid the past tense and write

---

13. Kojin Karatani, *Origins of Modern Japanese Literature*, trans. and ed. Brett de Bary, with a foreword by Fredric Jameson (Durham, NC: Duke University Press, 1993), 12–51. On the *genbunitchi* movement, see Nanette Twine, "The *Genbunitchi* Movement: Its Origins, Development, and Conclusion," *Monumenta Nipponica* 33, no. 3 (1978): 333–56.

14. Makoto Ueda, *Modern Japanese Writers and the Nature of Literature* (Stanford: Stanford University Press, 1976), 1.

15. Beongcheon Yu, *Natsume Soseki* (New York: Twayne, 1969), 60.

in present and present progressive tenses only. Soseki relied heavily on a narrator in his novels. This is true, according to Karatani, for all of Soseki's novels except the last two—*Michikusa* (Grass by the Wayside) and *Meian* (Light and Darkness). Soseki likened this approach "in every way" to that of *haiku* poetry, making this style distinctive, that is, not borrowed from the West.[16] All three of the stories in Soseki's first trilogy may be considered as "philosophical sketches."

The Woman in the Woods

In *Sanshiro*, the principal focus of the young man protagonist's attention is a young woman named Mineko. She is among an ensemble of characters in Tokyo, around 1908, in late Meiji, all of whom are either in or around Tokyo Imperial University, Japan's most prestigious institution of higher education. Sanshiro first sees Mineko while she is walking with a nurse at the pond in the center of the university campus. As Sanshiro becomes increasingly fascinated by Mineko through a series of mostly unplanned encounters he also learns that she is posing for a certain artist named Haraguchi, whose painting, unveiled at the end of the novel, is called "Woman in the Woods" (*mori no onna*).[17] In the concluding scene of the story, Sanshiro's friend Yojiro asks him what he thinks of Haraguchi's painting. Sanshiro's response is that the title is wrong. And Soseki's last line in the novel reads: "tada kuchi no nai de mayou hitsuji (sutorei shiipu) to kuri kaesu shita."[18] The 1977 English translation is: "to himself he muttered over and over, 'Stray sheep. Stray sheep.'"[19]

There is a world of meaning in Soseki's last line. It is powerfully suggestive of a "cosmion, illuminated with meaning from within by the human beings who continuously create and bear it as the mode and condition of their self realization,"[20] and of the faded mythologies imbedded in language.[21] The language

---

16. Karatani, *Origins*, 179–82.
17. Jay Rubin translates the phrase *mori no onna* as "Girl in the Forest" in the English translation of *Sanshiro* published in 1977. See Natsume, *Sanshiro* (1977), 210. Among the primary arguments in this essay is that there is a particular depth and mystery to the symbol of *mori no onna*, which is captured more by the term *woman* than *girl* and that this depth is clearly intended by Soseki.
18. Soseki Natsume, *Sanshiro* (Tokyo: Shueisha Bunko, 1993), 312.
19. Natsume, *Sanshiro* (1977), 212.
20. Eric Voegelin, *The New Science of Politics: An Introduction* (Chicago: University of Chicago Press, 1969), 28. Available in Voegelin, *The Collected Works of Eric Voegelin* (hereinafter, *CW*), vol. 5, *Modernity without Restraint: The Political Religions; The New Science of Politics; and Science, Politics, and Gnosticism*, ed. Manfred Henningsen (Columbia: University of Missouri Press, 2000).
21. See Ernst Cassirer's comments on F. W. J. Schelling in Ernst Cassirer, *Language and Myth*, trans. Susanne K. Langer (New York: Dover, 1953), 85.

as written by Soseki is particularly transparent in evoking Japan's unique mythic traditions and, indeed, a Japanese *historiogenesis*.[22] Within the story, Soseki's last line points back to two earlier "sketches." The first of these sketches is an encounter with Mineko in a quiet place within Tokyo on the banks of a little river, the Ogawa, which is also Sanshiro's family name. There, Mineko asks Sanshiro if he knows how to say "lost child" (*maigo*) in English. He does not. Mineko instructs him that one would say "stray sheep." And this is exactly how her words are written in the published English translation by Jay Rubin.[23] In the original Japanese version, however, Soseki writes the words "*mayoeru ko*," accompanied by the *katakana* "*sutorei shiipu*." *Katakana* is a phonetic syllabary for foreign terms such as the English *stray* and *sheep*. *Katakana* and the indigenous *hiragana* syllabaries are frequently placed immediately beside particularly difficult, unorthodox, or somewhat archaic Chinese characters (*kanji*). When Mineko first asks Sanshiro if he knows how to say "lost child," Soseki writes *maigo*, which consists of two Chinese characters and clearly means "lost child."[24] But when she answers her own question, noted above, Soseki writes "*mayoeru ko*." The verb *mayou* here is written in the potential form and is best translated "might be lost." And the *katakana* accompanying these words is "*sutorei shiipu*." In other words, as in the English *stray*, the use of the Japanese *mayoeru* places the emphasis on the "potential." Whereas there is a strongly Christian connotation to the English phrase "stray sheep," which evokes the story in Matthew of the one who will be found,[25] that is, saved, there is only the potential "might be lost" in Soseki's Japanese original. At the end of this scene, Mineko is crossing a narrow, shallow brook and loses her footing on a rock. She falls against Sanshiro, and Soseki writes "mayoeru ko (sutorei shiipu) to Mineko ga kuchi no nai de iitta." The published English translation is: "'stray sheep,' she murmured to herself."[26] But Soseki's meaning is clearly "might be a lost child," or, more clearly, "'maybe (I) am a lost child' (*sutorei shiipu*), she

---

22. *Historiogenesis* is a concept developed by Eric Voegelin in his later works, particularly in *The Ecumenic Age*. There, Voegelin defines *historiogenesis* as "a speculation on the origin and cause of social order." It is a "rather complex symbolism" and it includes "historiography, mythopoesis, and noetic speculation" as "components." See Eric Voegelin, *CW*, vol. 17, *The Ecumenic Age*, vol. IV, *Order and History*, ed. Michael Franz (1974; Columbia: University of Missouri Press, 2000), 108, 109.

23. Natsume, *Sanshiro* (1977), 94.

24. Natsume, *Sanshiro* (1993), 136.

25. The parable of the lost sheep reads as follows in the King James Version of the Bible: "How think ye? If a man have an hundred sheep, and one of them be gone astray, doth he not leave the ninety and nine, and goeth into the mountains, and seeketh that which is gone astray?" (Matt. 18:12).

26. Natsume, *Sanshiro* (1977), 95.

murmured to herself." This nuance becomes particularly significant at the novel's end, where Mineko has just married a Christian.

The other, or second, earlier sketch is the narration of Hirota sensei's dream. Sanshiro has gone to visit his friend Hirota sensei, who is taking a nap. Upon waking, Hirota sensei explains that he was dreaming of a girl of maybe twelve or thirteen whom he had only met once twenty years before and to whom he had never spoken. In the dream he is walking in the middle of a large wood ("ooki na mori no naka o aruite iru") when he encounters her.[27] He recognizes her from the funeral in 1889, the year of the Meiji Constitution, of Mori Arinori, who had been assassinated. Hirota sensei was then a student attached to a guard unit for the funeral parade route when the girl passed. In the dream, she says that he has "changed." He replies that she has not. He also says to her, "You are a painting." She replies to him, "You are a poem." Each of these two sketches is critical to the concluding scene in the novel and its meaning.

Regarding the first scene, with Mineko, one needs to be aware both of the meanings suggested by the Chinese characters used in her full name and, also, of a tendency in the Japanese novel in general to portray "types" rather than "living individuals."[28] Mineko's full name is Satomi Mineko, Satomi being the family name. The two characters *sato* and *mi*, together, mean "to see one's home village." Yet, *sato* has a more powerful connotation than the English "home village" and may be translated also as "the country" or "parents' home."[29] There are few images more evocative of strong feeling within Japanese tradition than that of *furusato*, or "old home village." Even today, a popular folk song of that name is sung at virtually any gathering where nostalgic feeling for Japan and Japaneseness is sought. The name Mineko, similarly, evokes deep stirrings of ancient Japan. The three characters mean, respectively, "beauty" (*mi*), "ancestral altar" (*ne*), and "child" (*ko*). So, as a "type," Mineko embodies the archetypal suggestion, something of a "picture," of the founding deity of Japan, *amaterasu omikami*, and of the traditional tale *taketori monogatari*, the tale of the bamboo cutter and his daughter *kaguyahime*, the shining princess. Within the Japanese literary tradition, the tale of the bamboo cutter is considered the "most famous of the early Japanese tales"[30] and the "ancestor of all romances."[31] Mineko symbolizes, in short, nothing less than the common *nous* of traditional

---

27. Natsume, *Sanshiro* (1993), 283.
28. Masao Miyoshi, *Accomplices of Silence: The Modern Japanese Novel* (Berkeley: University of California Press, 1974), xi–xvi.
29. See Nelson, *Character Dictionary*, 902.
30. Rimer, *Modern Japanese Fiction*, 66.
31. Helen Craig McCullough, *Classical Japanese Prose: An Anthology* (Stanford: Stanford University Press, 1990), 28.

Japanese society with a deeply felt aesthetic sense at its center, a sense sometimes conceptualized as *mono no aware* (a kind of deep pathos).

Sanshiro expresses this sense most clearly in his thoughts while one day watching Haraguchi as he paints Mineko's portrait. For Sanshiro, Mineko is herself "a picture" and "sealed in silence." It was as if Haraguchi was "not painting" Mineko at all but "copying a painting of mysterious depth, using all his energy to make a mediocre picture that lacked precisely this depth." And somehow it was as if the second Mineko were slowly merging with the first such that soon, on the verge of "melding into one," the "river of time would suddenly shift its course and flow into eternity."[32] Later, at the museum, with knowledge that Mineko has since married a Christian, Sanshiro tells his friend Yojiro that the title of the painting is wrong, and we read Soseki's last line, quoted above. It is the same "inner" speech as Mineko's at the little river. Sanshiro is talking to himself. But Soseki, for the first time, does not write *mayoeru ko;* instead, he writes *mayou hitsuji,* using two characters that literally mean "lost sheep." There is no doubt in his mind that a "sheep" (*hitsuji*) is "lost." And the powerful suggestion is that it is not only Mineko who is lost but all that she represents in archetypal terms. The radical, or root,[33] in the Chinese character for beauty, the *mi* in Mineko, means "sheep," *hitsuji* in Japanese. The complete character for *mi,* or *utsuku* (*shii*)—the more common (*kunyomi*), traditional Japanese for "beautiful"—is a combination of the characters for "sheep" and "big." So what Sanshiro is really saying to himself is that the picture is surely "big," but without the "sheep." Hence, his title of "lost sheep." When Sanshiro first sees the picture in Haraguchi's studio he says only "naru hodo ooki na mono desu na"(it really is big isn't it.)[34] Not only is the picture not beautiful, it is a depiction of having lost the roots of the very common *nous* that is the unique Japanese aesthetic sensibility. This common *nous* is reflected in numerous concepts that build from the radical for "sheep." For example, in Japanese the concept *gi,* meaning "justice" or "righteousness," is used to create other concepts such as *gijin,* "righteous man"; *gishi,* meaning "loyal retainer" and highly evocative of the famous forty-seven ronin of the *Chushingura* tale; *gimu,* "duty" or "obligation"; *giri,* "sense of duty"; *seigi,* another way of referring to justice; and even *gikai,* the national assembly. This is the context of noted Japan scholar George Sansom's point in the inaugural

---

32. Natsume, *Sanshiro* (1977), 171.
33. A radical is one of 214 basic elements used to classify both Chinese and Japanese characters in dictionaries. It is the basis for looking up characters in these dictionaries. The character for "sheep," *hitsuji,* is radical number 123 in Nelson, *Character Dictionary,* 720.
34. Natsume, *Sanshiro* (1993), 250.

article for *Monumenta Nipponica,* published in 1938. He noted there the great difficulty in finding "equivalence in terminology" when translating between English and Japanese, a difficulty "not only in philosophy but in everyday discussion." He also observed, in the same article, that one of the most interesting problems for the Western student of Japanese history and culture is "how to explain the growth and persistence of a strong aesthetic bent throughout all Japanese history."[35] Donald Richie, noted film critic and longtime observer of Japanese culture, has made the observation that "aesthetic qualifications become moral qualifications in Japan; beauty becomes honesty."[36] In Sanshiro's title for Mineko's portrait, "lost sheep," the reader is reminded of a comment by Hirota sensei, who always seemed to Sanshiro something of a "Shinto priest": "Japan is going to perish."[37]

And this points to a reconsideration of the second earlier scene, in which Hirota sensei had a dream. He said to the young female in the woods, "You are a painting." This is the true picture of the "woman in the woods" for Soseki, and it is the picture of the shining princess archetype deep within Hirota sensei's psyche revealed only in a dream and "shaped" by a vision at a funeral attendant to the birth of a modern Japanese state twenty years earlier. Haraguchi's painting is too "large" and, as symbol, opaque. The girl in Hirota's dream, as symbol, is transparent but deep within the subconscious. The artist Haraguchi has midwifed only the "big" from all that is suggestive in the Chinese character for beauty. The root, or radical, of the character, the "sheep," is "lost." Soseki has taken a Christian parable, that of the "lost sheep" in Matthew 18:12, and given it a distinctively Japanese reading with deeply tragic overtones.

Hirota sensei is a "poet," not a painter, who is "made of philosophy" such that when he smoked he "blew from his nostrils" the "smoke of philosophy." But his nickname reveals a problem. He was known as the "great darkness."[38] The common *nous* shaped by a historiogenesis unique to Japan and evolved over centuries was fading deeper into the subconscious of sensei like Hirota and literary artists like Natsume Soseki. What would the psychic substance of a society without the psychic moorings of Shinto myth to restrain a slide into "bigness" from Western, ecumenic pressure look like? This is the subject of *Sorekara* (And Then).

---

35. George B. Sansom, "Some Problems in the Study of Japanese History," *Monumenta Nipponica* 1, no. 1 (1938): 43–46.
36. Donald Richie, *A Lateral View: Essays on Contemporary Japan* (Tokyo: Japan Times, 1987), 79, 80.
37. Natsume, *Sanshiro* (1977), 10–15.
38. Ibid., 60, 97.

The Man in the Mirror

The Chinese characters in the name for Sanshiro mean, respectively, "three" (*san*), "four" (*shi*), and "person(s)" (*ro*). The clear suggestion is that the young man named Sanshiro is three or four persons and not an integral personality. He is a young man in search of an identity amid the "urgent life force of a changing society."[39] The protagonist in *Sorekara*, by contrast, is a little older, a little more settled, in a material sense, and is called Daisuke. *Dai* means "period" or "generation" and *suke* literally means "assistant" or helper. It is the same character used in "assistant professor" or "assistant director." More importantly, during Meiji, it was a common suffix in men's names and highly suggestive of the rising middle class, or bourgeoisie. The main character in *Mon*, the third novel in the trilogy, is the similarly suffixed Sosuke. Daisuke, then, is somewhat symbolic of everyman in the Japanese society of 1909, and the sense in which he "helps" unfolds in the story. He could be considered an older Sanshiro, according to "type," but narrower according to development. Where Sanshiro is a student with a beginner's mind who explores the common *nous* of Meiji society befitting a student at the country's most prestigious institution of higher education, Daisuke is a bachelor preoccupied with his physical condition, his father's influence, and a certain young lady named Michiyo. The reader is drawn from a collective subconscious of the common *nous* in Sanshiro, to a personal world of the ego in *Sorekara*.

The story begins with a dream sequence in which Daisuke hears the approach of steps to his gate outside and "sees" a "pair of large clogs suspended from the sky." When the footsteps grow dim, the clogs disappear and Daisuke awakes. This is not the dream of sensei. It is the dream of a very self-conscious man. It is the consciousness of a man for whom immediate physical stimuli are all important. There seems to be no particular significance to the vision of the wooden clogs beyond the fact that they are "large." Similarly, a camellia blossom, a "large blossom, which was nearly as large as a baby's head," had fallen to the floor during the night, making a sound like "a rubber ball" that had "bounced off the ceiling." Just to make sure all was well amid these night sounds, Daisuke placed his hand over his heart to feel "the blood pulsing correctly at the edge of his ribs." Then he went back to sleep. Daisuke was obsessed with his physical health. In Shinto, the mirror is a powerful symbol for self-reflection. In literature, in film, in the arts in general, mirrors often signal poignant moments of deep reflection. In Shinto mythology, the sacred mirror

---

39. Ibid., 37.

yata no kagami was used to lure *Amaterasu omikami* out of the cave into which she fled, causing chaos and darkness in the world. This mirror, with some sacred, curved jewels and a sacred sword are the three symbols of authority for the Japanese emperor. In *Sorekara,* however, when Daisuke stands before the mirror, he sees only himself:

> Daisuke peered into the mirror. His motions were precisely those of a woman powdering her face. And, in fact, he took such pride in his body that had there been the need, he would not have hesitated to powder his face. More than anything he disliked the shriveled body and wizened features of a Buddhist holy man, and whenever he turned to the mirror, he was thankful that at least he had not been born with such a face. If people called him a dandy, he was not in the least disturbed. To this extent had he moved beyond the old Japan.[40]

Neither Shinto nor Buddhist influences moved Daisuke beyond his immediate reflection in the mirror.

In traditional Japanese culture, in the "old Japan" of Japanese history, the importation of Buddhism from Korea in the sixth century represented less a rivalry with native Shintoism than a complement. Over time, and through the developments of Tendai, Shingon, Jodoshu, Shinshu, Nichiren, and Zen schools, Buddhism and Shinto became somewhat syncretistic. Even the strong Confucian influence of the Edo period and the *kokugaku* (national learning) movement of late Edo failed dramatically to alter what was called the *ryoubu Shinto,* or "dual Shinto system." Under this system Buddhist priests would often control Shinto shrines. But all of this changed with the Meiji restoration. In 1868, the removal of all Buddhist images from Shinto shrines was decreed. A movement called *haibutsu kishaku*, "abolish the Buddha, destroy Sakyamuni," followed. These events led to the decline of Buddhist influence in Japan during Meiji. These were cultural developments of enormous consequence. As Daisetz T. Suzuki points out in *Zen and Japanese Culture,* the Buddhist tradition in Japan, particularly the Zen influence, was central in shaping Japanese culture, the arts, the development of the *bushido* (way of the warrior), interpretations of Confucius in Japan, and particularly unique artistic traditions such as *sado* (the way of tea) and *haiku* poetry. The Zen influence is also evident in the evolution of distinctively Japanese aesthetic concepts such as *wabi* (subdued taste), *sabi* (elegant simplicity), and *mono no aware* (a kind of deep pathos). Zen teachings, over the centuries, came to permeate religious, moral, aesthetic,

---

40. Soseki Natsume, *And Then,* trans., with an afterword, by Norma Moore Field (New York: Perigree Books, 1982), 1–3.

and epistemological dimensions of Japanese life. For Suzuki, Zen "has entered internally into every phase of the cultural life of the people."[41] For the character Daisuke, none of this is of importance. There is only the "wizened features of a Buddhist holy man."

Similarly, Michiyo, who is the wife of Daisuke's best friend, Hiraoka, personifies nothing of the shining princess archetype rooted in Shinto myth. She is something of an obsession: "Only Michiyo weighed on his mind somewhat." He had failed to acknowledge his feelings for Michiyo years earlier and had helped encourage the wedding with Hiraoka. But when the two of them reenter his life, Daisuke begins to nurture the old feelings for Michiyo. She has a heart problem and, like Oyone in *Mon,* is childless and will probably not have children. Yet, Daisuke is consumed with her love. Everyone else in his life—his father, his brother, his sister-in-law, in fact, "all of society"—were "his enemies." Daisuke was not completely without interest in the larger society. He was conscious of the fact that civilization had taken the "collective we" and "transformed it into isolated individuals." Also, moderns did not "weep." Daisuke "had yet to meet the individual who, as he stood groaning beneath the oppression of Occidental civilization in the seething arena of the struggle for survival, was still able to shed genuine tears for another." In the place of a capacity to weep, the life appetites had grown to prominence. Daisuke understood that "the striking growth of the life appetites was, in effect, a tidal wave that had swept from European shores."[42] But he is unable to make connections with a larger, common *nous.* There is little aesthetic sensibility and no consciousness of a "woman in the woods." Daisuke is representative, instead, of *egophany* and a "refusal to apperceive."[43]

"Sketches" featuring the color red play a large role in both *Sorekara* and *Sanshiro.* In perhaps the most dramatic example, Sanshiro is in his room looking out the window at a fire in the distance. On one level, the fire with its red flare symbolizes anxiety and alarm. But it also signifies for Sanshiro something of a "red destiny." There is a sense that the anxiety and alarm is more deeply rooted and, more specifically, rooted in the long, complex experience in Japan with Mahayana Buddhism. There is an eschatological component to this tradition, according to which there are three ages, that of the Buddha, that

---

41. Daisetz T. Suzuki, *Zen and Japanese Culture* (Princeton: Princeton University Press, 1973), 21.

42. Natsume, *And Then,* 92, 255, 102, 104.

43. This is Eric Voegelin's translation of Heimito von Doderer's *Apperzeptionsverweigerung* in the *Daemonen.* See Eric Voegelin, *CW,* vol. 18, *In Search of Order,* vol. V, *Order and History,* ed. Ellis Sandoz (1987; Columbia: University of Missouri Press, 2000), 46, 47.

of the dharma, and that of decay and destruction. The last period is called *mappo,* and there was a widespread belief during the late Heian and early Kamakura periods that the age of *mappo* had arrived. This is the context for the flowering of Buddhism during the early Kamakura period, a period that witnessed the coming of several reform movements and several heroic leaders in the history of Japanese Buddhism. Among the dominant trends in Kamakura Buddhism was the return to the Lotus Sutra as a source of inspiration and guidance, a trend most pronounced in the teachings of Nichiren (1222–1282). Nichiren also stressed the period in which he lived and taught as representing the last days, *mappo.* There is a famous scene in the Lotus Sutra of a "burning house," which suggests the coming of *mappo.* It is not inconceivable that Soseki was conscious of his own times sharing features with the late Heian, early Kamakura periods and that the burning house in *Sanshiro* symbolizes this connection. At the conclusion of *Sorekara* Daisuke himself is "burning." The "red destiny" of which Sanshiro becomes conscious in the novel *Sanshiro* becomes explicit in the final scene of the sequel, *Sorekara.* There, while riding on a streetcar in Tokyo, Daisuke essentially goes mad, his head burnt away in red visions: "Finally, the whole world turned red. And with Daisuke's head at the center, it began to spin around and around, breathing tongues of fire. Daisuke decided to go on riding until his head was completely burnt away."[44]

Beyond the Temple Gate

The protagonist in *Mon* (Gate) is Nonaka Sosuke. The Chinese characters for Nonaka mean "a field" (*no*) and "inside" (*naka*).[45] The characters for Sosuke are *sou,* meaning "religion," and the same *suke* as in Daisuke in *Sorekara.* As Daisuke is a kind of bourgeois exemplar writ large, Sosuke is a somewhat similar type confronted with religion. Sosuke is a minor civil servant on a modest income who is married with no children and living in Tokyo. As with Sanshiro and Daisuke, Sosuke "breathed the air of Tokyo." Unlike the other two protagonists, however, Sosuke was "always so fatigued in mind and body that he traveled in a daze, completely unaware of his surroundings." When riding the streetcar for Marunouchi every day, where he worked, he would "in his disgust" become the same as those around him, that is, "like a machine." In his

---

44. Natsume, *And Then,* 257.
45. The first character can also be read as *ya,* as in *yajin,* meaning "rustic person" and highly suggestive of "common people." See character 4814 in Nelson, *Character Dictionary,* 903.

earlier days, he used to love books, but that was part of a life "that had passed forever." Sosuke lives with his wife, Oyone, in a house that is set farthest back from the street in the little area of Tokyo where they live. The house also symbolizes their isolation from the larger society, an isolation brought on by an indiscrete act several years before when Sosuke was a student in Kyoto. Every evening they would sit together by a lamp in the light of which "Sosuke was conscious only of Oyone, and Oyone only of Sosuke."[46]

The characters for Oyone's name signify "narrow" and "child." And in the narrowing circle that defined his life and Oyone's, Sosuke became indifferent to the larger political world, of which he and Oyone were a part under the Meiji Constitution, and forgetful even of the most basic elements of a conscious life. With respect to politics, Sosuke was aware of the great statesman Ito Hirobumi's assassination in Manchuria on October 26, 1909, but was "unmoved ... by the whole affair."[47] With respect to consciousness, he sometimes had trouble remembering even basic Chinese characters. He asked Oyone once what the character was for *kin* in *kinrai* (these days; of late). He could not even remember the character for *kon* in *konnichi*, which is the largest part of *konnichi wa*, the most common greeting in Japan, most often translated as simply "hello." This experience with *anoia*[48] did not seem to trouble him or Oyone, who "passed the incident off casually." Oyone was very sickly and had lost three children. She blamed herself, often felt her life one of "tortuous endurance," and "did not reveal these feelings even to her husband." She once went to a fortune-teller, who told her, "You can never have a child." The reason, she was told, was that she had done a "terrible deed" to another and "the sin is still working itself out." Together, Sosuke and Oyone "kept the souls of mountain hermits." Sosuke and Oyone "had no faith with which to recognize a God or to encounter a Buddha." They "kept their eyes fixed on each other instead."[49]

Though Sosuke lived a narrow existence, his younger brother Koroku reminded him of his old, lively self. As a young man, Sosuke was self-indulgent, a "perfect exemplar of the young man of the world of that day." He was "quick witted, but had little inclination to study." He was always seeking some new pleasure and had many friends. His best friend was Yasui, and it was through Yasui that Sosuke met Oyone, the event that changed his life. Sosuke betrayed his best friend to secure Oyone's affections for himself. This experience in

---

46. Soseki Natsume, *Mon* (The Gate), trans. Francis Mathy (New York: Perigree Books, 1982), 11–14, 61.

47. Natsume, *Mon*, 21.

48. *Anoia* "most clearly expresses the state of oblivion as a deformation of noetic consciousness." See Voegelin, *CW*, 18:45.

49. Natsume, *Mon*, 6, 7, 130–34, 169.

Kyoto drained Sosuke of all vitality and changed him into the particularly narrow man described above. Over time, Sosuke developed a sense of "the deep chasm that separates self and other."[50]

One day, totally unexpectedly, the betrayed friend Yasui appears at the house next door to Sosuke and Oyone. Yasui is unaware of this coincidence. Sosuke decides to escape to Kamakura in search of some peace of mind, in search of some religious answer to his torments. The temple to which he goes belongs to the Rinzai sect of Zen Buddhism. It was at the Rinzai temples in Kyoto and Kamakura that the "creative assimilation" of a "new cultural substance and its independent development" (from China) began to take place in Japan during the early Kamakura period.[51] Sosuke's guide at the temple is Gido. Among Gido's gifts to Sosuke is a little book that describes "the stages a man practicing Zen must pass through, from the shallowest to the most profound," as well as the psychological states at each stage. Gido tells Sosuke the story of the monk who was "too sinful ever to reach *satori*," who felt "lower than dung." And yet, Gido adds, "Look at the enlightenment he finally achieved!" Sosuke, however, felt "ignorant and impotent." He had come to the temple to "have the gate opened to him." The only greeting he received, however, was, "It's no use knocking. Open the gate yourself and enter." Sosuke seemed to have been "fated from birth to stand forever outside the gate, unable to pass through."[52]

Exile, Anamnesis, and the Storyteller

In Japanese history, Sugawara no Michizane has symbolized the scholar in exile for a thousand years.[53] As Hirota sensei is exiled, in *Sanshiro*, from the center of intellectual life at Tokyo Imperial University, so also are literary artists like Natsume Soseki exiled from the larger life of Japanese society. As the common *nous* of the larger society quickened in its dissolution in late Meiji, Soseki abandoned his teaching post at the university and began to write serialized novels for the *Asahi* newspaper—an effort, perhaps, to bring the literary art back into the mainstream and the literary artist out of exile. Soseki believed that the artist must always seek through art to render "the beautiful, the true,

---

50. Ibid., 136, 74.
51. Heinrich Dumoulin, *A History of Zen Buddhism*, trans. Paul Peachey (Boston: Beacon Press, 1969), 149.
52. Natsume, *Mon*, 200–204.
53. Sugawara no Michizane (845–903) was a court scholar in the Heian court who was exiled to Kyushu in southern Japan by a jealous member of the Fujiwara family. Today he is revered as a god of scholarship and learning to whom students pray for help on exams.

the good, and the sublime."[54] Among his earliest efforts in this regard were *Sanshiro*, *Sorekara*, and *Mon*, his first trilogy. *Sanshiro* is the most analytical in its exploration of myth and legend, of the origin and cause, or historiogenesis, of Japanese social order. The "woman in the woods" of Hirota's dream is a transparent symbol of the shining princess archetype of Japanese tradition, which expresses the aesthetic center of Japanese consciousness and social order, a center institutionally represented by the emperor and the imperial house. The "woman in the woods" of Haraguchi's art is opaque, except as an oversized corruption of Japanese sensibility. The proper title for the piece is "lost sheep," a precise rendering of the *kanji* character for "beauty" reducing the meaning to simply "big." *Sorekara* is more exploratory than analytical. It probes the corners of consciousness in what is left without the traditional common *nous*. It explores the mind of Daisuke, preoccupied with the nuances of physical existence, political pressures from the West, and pressures from his father as representative of an oppressive Japanese past, and Michiyo, who is representative only of Daisuke's personal lost opportunities. This mind, in the end, burns away in a red destiny, suggesting the coming of *mappo*, the final days of Buddhist teaching. In *Mon*, we have a turn to religion by someone not unlike Daisuke. But there is nothing beyond the temple gate for one who cannot even open it. In the end, Sosuke, like his predecessor in *Sorekara*, remains primarily conscious only of his physical reality. At story's end, he has winter on his mind as he "continued to cut his nails."[55] *Mon*, in its probing of connections between *egophany* and theology is the most philosophic of the three stories. In these stories Natsume Soseki examines the erosion of Japanese civilization's common *nous*, explores the consequences of that erosion, and seeks answers for the future of that civilization. Ultimately, however, Soseki has great difficulty imagining a modern Japan. The prospect seems to lie beyond his imagination. Two years before his death in 1916, Soseki penned his masterpiece, *Kokoro*, an enormously delicate story. There is nothing of "size" in it. In the story, the character Sensei takes his own life; but Soseki leaves just the slightest room to imagine hope. Sensei makes of his young friend a dying request: "My first wish is that her memory of me should be kept as unsullied as possible. So long as my wife is alive, I want you to keep everything I have told you a secret—even after I myself am dead."[56] Perhaps by protecting *ojosan*, Sensei's wife and archetypal symbol in the story, there is the hint of a prospect for re-

---

54. Yu, *Soseki*, 60.
55. Natsume, *Mon*, 213.
56. Soseki Natsume, *Kokoro*, trans. Edwin McClellan (Washington, DC: Regnery Publishing, 1999), 248.

ducing the pressure of the "large" in life and making room, at least, for the "woman in the woods" and the missing "sheep" to be found through *anamnesis,* not forgetting.

Just before the scene in *Sanshiro* in which Mineko says to herself that she "might" be lost, Sanshiro and Mineko are in fact a bit lost in the middle of Tokyo. They have just left a doll show. She asks him, "Where are we now?" He says they are "on the way to Tennoji in Yanaka. It's exactly the opposite direction from home." She says, "I don't feel well," and "Isn't there some quiet place we could go?" They can't go forward and can't go back. And this is where they find a place to rest and speak of "stray sheep." In a later scene, a student stands to make a speech at a large dinner gathering. He says that the youth of today "can no longer endure the new oppression from the West" nor the "oppression of the old Japan."[57] They too cannot seem to go forward or back. These scenes dramatize the primary issue for Soseki: how to preserve the hard-won middle way, or *chuuyou* of Japanese, largely Zen Buddhist, tradition.[58] Sanshiro sees the loss of a common culture, Daisuke goes mad under the pressure, and Sosuke virtually loses consciousness of anything beyond his lengthening nails. What emerges from Soseki's first trilogy is, even for Japan's best storyteller, the virtual impossibility of even imagining such a middle way in a post-Meiji, modern Japan.

57. Natsume, *Sanshiro* (1977), 90, 108.
58. Nelson defines *chuuyou* as "mean, golden mean, moderation, middle path; Doctrine of the Mean." See Nelson, *Character Dictionary,* 57. According to one scholar, Soseki understood this "way" to be one in which man "becomes present to heaven and heaven to man." See Ward William Biddle, "The Authenticity of Natsume Soseki," *Monumenta Nipponica* 28, no. 4 (1973): 393. This concept of *chuuyou* might be favorably compared to Plato's concept of *metaxy.* On the Platonic *metaxy* see Voegelin, *CW,* 18:27, 28.

 # III
Politics

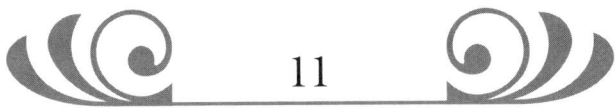

11

The Concept of "the Political" Revisited

Jürgen Gebhardt

On October 1, 1808, the famous encounter of Johann Wolfgang von Goethe and the Emperor Napoleon took place in Erfurt. Napoleon disapproved of dramatic tragedies that hinged upon fate: "Why be concerned with fate today (*Was will man jetzt mit dem Schicksal*)? Politics is fate." No longer the unfathomable gods, as in classical drama, but daimonic personalities such as Napoleon himself weave the threads of human destiny, as Goethe's friend Eckermann opined.[1] This opaque formula of "politics as destiny" with its "tragic" undercurrent became quite popular in German discussions. Hegel explained Napoleon's dictum in more general terms: human beings are no longer subject to the *fatum* of the ancients, because it had been replaced by politics, which brings about a new tragedy insofar as the irresistible forces of circumstances dominate all human individuality.

Both Goethe and Hegel considered Napoleon a "world-historical individual." To Hegel this meant that Napoleon was a manager of the world spirit (*Geschäftsführer des Weltgeists*). Like Alexander or Caesar they were destined to usher in a new era of world history, elevating it to a higher degree of universality. These heroes are great destroyers of old orders, and by the cunning of reason creators of the new. In Hegel's view of world history they are agents of progress, understood in terms of consciousness of freedom, which is the substance of the new *fatum* of politics. It is an emphatic notion of politics

---

1. Jürgen Gebhardt, "Auf der Suche nach dem Politischen," in *Bürgersinn und Kritik,* ed. Michael Th. Greven et al.(Baden-Baden: Nomov Verlag, 1998), 15–27.

transcending the everyday business of governmental and public affairs in that it refers to the movement of the historical process per se. The issue here is not an exegesis of Hegel so much as his insistence on the agency of politics in shaping human destiny. Indeed, Napoleon was fate personified for the whole continent and especially for central Europe.

At the *Fürstentag* of Erfurt Napoleon was at the height of his power. He had reshaped the political landscape of Europe: between 1803 and 1806 the ancient order of the Holy Roman Empire broke asunder, and more than a thousand years of history was overcome and extinguished. People lived through a critical epoch of far-reaching change. The disruption of traditional ways of life forced them to confront the question as to which forces act upon the fate of societies and how to make sense of a seemingly amorphous reality. Napoleon's perfunctory remark brought to the fore the truth of the modern era: politics is destiny.

This comprehensive idea of politics articulates a fundamental experience of the interplay of order and disorder in our time. The reflexive quest for rationality that would dissolve this compact and topical notion of politics as destiny can only be answered in terms of a theoretically grounded concept of the political. Carl Schmitt, under the impact of the postwar crisis of the twenties, set out to rethink the nature of politics. He accorded primacy and autonomy to politics, which is implied in the Hegelian phrase "politics is fate," and he distinguished politics in the sense of "the political" as semantically distinct from the indeterminate meaning of politics prevalent in common parlance and in political discourse.

This terminology was not, however, of Schmitt's making. The semantic coinage, so far as I can see, belongs to Hegel. He seems to have been the first to introduce this expression into the German vocabulary. At least in one case it can be assumed that he gave this figure of speech a specific technical meaning. In his *History of Philosophy* he pointed out that for Aristotle "the political is the highest because its purpose is the highest in respect to the practical.... The political is therefore as in Plato the primordial."[2] Hegel tied the emergence of philosophy to the principle of freedom as it materializes in "the political" of the Hellenic polis-culture. Hegel did not systematically explicate a categorical difference between politics and the political because to him only the "state" is the object of world history, being the divine idea on earth that bestows spiritual reality upon human beings. Hegel remained in his writings under the spell of the tradition of the European state-centered notion of politics.

---

2. Georg Wilhelm Friedrich Hegel, *Vorlesungen über die Philosophie der Geschichte,* vol. 2 (Frankfurt: Suhrkamp, 1971).

One can speculate how Hegel came to speak of the political in reference to the ancient philosophers. Obviously he was very much aware of the Hellenic origin of this neologism. The substantiation of the adjective *politikos* transformed it into an abstract term *to politikon,* which designates an object of thought denoting the essence of the polis-order. This "essentialization" of polis-affairs (*ta politika*) in terms of the concept of *to politikon* signifies the general linguistic turn of Hellenic thought toward a reflexive comprehension of reality, which in turn constitutes the birth of scientific language. This conceptualization can be traced to Herodotus's *Histories* (6.57). In their reflexive, that is, philosophical, inquiry into the world of citizen-man, Plato (*Laws* 757 c–e) and Aristotle (*Politics* 1253b) refer to *to politikon* in order to express conceptually the very substance of human order, namely, justice. This concept of the political blends the analysis of polis affairs with a normative paradigm of human existence in society. Hegel did not explicate this meaning of the political. To him it was superseded by the abstract universality of the state derived from the Roman ideas of *res publica* and *imperium.* In this he remained true to the Roman legacy transmitted to, and absorbed by, late medieval and early modern European state-building.

From the period of state formation onward, European discourses focused on the state- and power-centered notion of politics as represented by the prototypical centralized monarchy. It was to become the foundational concept of political and scientific self-understanding, gaining universal recognition in the science of Max Weber and subsequently in modern social science. Weber's understanding of politics is intrinsically bound up with his notion of the "political association" that successfully claims the monopoly of legitimate use of physical force within a given territory, the state being considered as the sole source of the right to coercion in modernity. "Politically" oriented action is social action insofar as it aims at influencing the leadership of a political association in terms of appropriation, expropriation, redistribution, or allocation of governmental powers.[3] Talcott Parsons helped Weber cross the Atlantic, and the new postwar American political science subjected him to semantic Americanization, although it retained his central idea of political rule: the authoritative command of the ruler over the ruled. In the parlance of functionalistic system-analysis, the political aspect of a social act is contingent upon the relation of the act to the authoritative allocation of values for the whole society as it is influenced by the distribution and use of power.[4]

David Easton's somewhat democratically moderated Weberianism is to date

---

3. Max Weber, *Wirtschaft und Gesellschaft* (Köln: Kiepenheuer and Witsch, 1956), 39.
4. David Easton, *The Political System* (New York: Alfred A. Knopf, 1953), 134–35.

still the theoretical mainstay of conventional American political science. The commitment to liberal democracy required, however, a reintegration of the concept of a self-governing citizenry into the power-centered paradigm of politics. Weber's state was the busy activity of the power-hungry in the face of a blind crowd of subjects; the political agency of citizens remained in a categorical no man's land, and the typology of the legitimacy of the power-holders contains no mention of democratic self-rule. That is why the prevalent paradigm of politics in modern political discourses is Janus-faced: the bottom line is power-based decision-making, but mitigated by a modicum of moral civility. This latter imports the notion of *civil* government, as distinguished from all other modes of rule or domination. It points to a different understanding of what politics is all about and reveals that the discourse of power does not tell the whole story, because another, competing vision of politics came into play in post-medieval political thought.

The idea of politics resurfaced in the manifold modes of neoclassical political thought focusing on the rediscovery of the *scientia civile* of Scholasticism and Renaissance humanism.[5] The self-understanding of republican city-regimes, foremost in Italy, was tuned to the citizen-centered norms of politics in that it legitimized the claim to self-government: "Et si non est civis non est homo, quia 'homo est naturaliter animal civile.'"[6] The "Italianization" of Anglo-Saxon politics in the sixteenth and seventeenth centuries injected a good portion of this understanding of politics into English thought. Already in the fifteenth century Fortescue distinguished between the *regimen politicum* of the consensual agreement of "king in parliament" and the *regimen despoticum* of French monarchy, a distinction taken directly from Tolomeo of Lucca.

In the English Revolution the neoclassical republicans advanced the communitarian notion of politics that finally was linked to constitutionalism. It preserved an anti-statist bias right up to modern thinkers such as Oakeshott, Crick, or Arendt, who all challenged the prevalence of the Weberian paradigm in intellectual discourse. "It is only after one eliminates this disastrous reduction of public affairs to the business of domination that the original data in the realm of human affairs will appear or rather reappear in their authentic diversity."[7]

---

5. Jürgen Gebhardt, "Der bürgerschaftliche Begriff des Politischen: Ursprünge und Metamorphosen," in *Geisteswissenschaftliche Dimensionen der Politik,* ed. Roland Kley and Silvano Möckli (Bern: Paul Haupt, 2000), 146–54.

6. Remigio de'Girolami, "De bono communi," in *La teologia politica communale di Remigio de'Girolami,* ed. Maria Consigliade Matteis (Bologna: Patron, 1977), 3–51.

7. Hannah Arendt, "Reflections on Violence," *Journal of International Affairs* 23, no. 1 (1969): 1–35.

This clash of traditions accounts for the above-stated ambivalence of the modern Western idea of politics: the republican version tends to be consensual and citizen-centered, whereas the monarchical or state version focuses on power and domination. Neither, however, transcended the implied bifurcation of political reality in terms of a reflexive comprehension of the whole of human being and its order, as was the intention of the ancient political scientists. A modern quest for a theoretically grounded concept of the political can no longer begin from definite political points of reference, whether they be the city, the state, or the empire, and then explicate normatively their self-interpretative meaning of order. The historical realm has become global, and the dynamic processes of change unleashed by human agency evoked the question of who is pulling the strings of human destiny in the face of the fading away of unfathomable gods. If the modern tragedy is enacted by human agency wresting order from the chaotic forces of disorder, it must be staged in the arena of politics. It reflects the structural makeup of the socio-historical world in its entirety as it reveals itself in the manifold forms of symbolic self-representation and socio-political modes of order. But the phenomenon of the political thus delineated does not by itself answer the quest for an understanding of forces that shape human destiny in the arena of politics once the symbolic images of the past have been dissolved. The *dramatis personae* of the new tragedy articulate no less than the ones of old tragedy the experiential basis of the motivating experiences at the root of any struggle for order, an issue considered below.

German discourse up to the twentieth century stayed within the state-centered notion of politics. Public semantics insisted on the primacy of the state whenever politics or the political was thematized. And it might be added that no other Western political language generated a semantic equivalent to the German *das Politische* before the twentieth century, which is before Carl Schmitt.

World War I brought more than military defeat to Germany. It meant the breakdown of a political way of life comparable to the downfall of the ancient regime in 1803. The state, that is, cultural and political order incarnate, lost its "political character" and metamorphosed into a blend of state and society that subordinated the political entity to "nonpolitical" societal forces (parties, trade unions, business associations, churches, etc.). This diagnosis was shared by many state-conscious conservative intellectuals in the Weimar republic. But if the state is no longer the epitome of political agency, and if human destiny is determined by a plurality of political powers and actors, where is politics located? This theoretically diffuse situation of a political agency that had turned into an anonymous power operating upon the society at large gave the expression of "the political" a new relevance.

Among the numerous writings on this subject Schmitt's *The Concept of the Political* became the most influential. In retrospect Schmitt observed that "the classical profile of the state was shattered as its monopoly on politics waned. New... political protagonists asserted themselves.... From this followed a new degree of reflection for theoretical thought. Now one could distinguish 'politics' from 'political.' The new protagonists became the core of the entire complex called 'political.' Here lies the beginning and thrust of every attempt to recognize the many new subjects of the political, which become active in political reality, in the politics of the state or nonstate, and which bring about new kinds of friend-enemy groupings."[8] His experiential point of departure is the German condition in 1919—theoretically in that the symbolic unity of state and politics is challenged by the liberalization of politics and politically in that German sovereignty and international status had been grossly diminished by the Treaty of Versailles. This myopic viewpoint along with his underlying anti-liberal perspective and cultural-pessimistic polemics mar the intellectual quality of Schmitt's study considerably. But we are not concerned with an exegesis of Schmitt. The following remarks pertain only to the point of general theoretical relevance.

Sensitive to the crisis, Schmitt reacted to the eroding efficacy of traditional socio-culturally conditioned modes of social integration. He observed that societal existence under modern conditions is determined by political agency representing the society as a whole. It transcends, therefore, state, government, or the political system. Schmitt relocated political agency in any group of actors who act as the ultimate and decisive political entity in determining who is friend and who is enemy. The political denotes the ultimate form of societal existence insofar as "every religious, moral, economic, ethical, or other antithesis is transformed into a political one if it is sufficiently strong to group human beings effectively according to whether they are friend or enemy." This distinction explicates "the utmost degree of friend and enemy of intensity of a union or separation, of an association or dissociation."[9] Thus, community formation is in principle "political," but it is grounded on the existential experience of absolute conflict that is in the last analysis based on the experience of war. The omnipresence of the political reflects the omnipresence of war.

Schmitt is thus the heir of Max Weber's extreme statism, which claimed that the emotional basis of a political association derives from the war fraternity (*Kriegsbrüderlichkeit*) experienced on the battlefield in the sacredness of

---

8. Carl Schmitt, *The Concept of the Political* (Chicago: University of Chicago Press, 1996), 13.
9. Ibid., 37, 26.

sacrificing one's own life for the common cause. Such a phenomenology of the political is based upon Schmitt's theologically grounded crypto-Hobbesian anthropology of the absolute sinfulness of human being. The disjunction of friend and enemy hypostasizes total conflict (spirit against spirit, life against life) thus reducing human affairs to an effective struggle against an effective enemy. The friend is but a comrade in arms, and there is no indication of any community-creating qualities in human beings that let them befriend each other. Schmitt remains firmly attached to the state- and power-centered notion of politics. The political, in his view, is a deadly power game. Whoever refuses to play it loses his societal being. Schmitt's historical and theoretical analysis in principle eclipses the dimension of the political that is reflected in the citizen-centered communitarian notion of politics and the idea of humanity based on human reason. Moreover, his theology of original sin inspires a radical political Augustinianism and prevents him from any philosophical reflection on the ground of order beyond the battleground where the libidinous forces of human self-empowerment clash.

Schmitt's analysis of the political purported to be an inquiry into "the order of human things," but the question of order was dissolved into the question of disorder. In Platonic parlance he investigated the *stasioteia* instead of the *politeia*. He was, however, right to disengage the political from the state. Indeed, the political comprehends and structures the different spheres of life: economics, culture, religion. That is, the politico-historical world is pervaded by the ordering logic of the political insofar as every politico-symbolic form of order represents the existence of human being in its entirety, from the material to the spiritual. For this reason Schmitt's observation is correct: All conflicts, whether ethical, economic, or ethnic-cultural, may turn into "political" conflicts if the order of the society at large is at stake. But when this transformation occurs, conflicts are then motivated by the question of the right order of society; they are struggles for order caused by experiences of disorder. The concept of the political rightly understood expresses the formative principle of human existence in society and history both with respect to political agency in the Voegelinian sense of the existential representation of the society and with respect to its ordering logic in the sense of a comprehensive meaning and truth represented by the whole of society. This argument reflects Voegelin's theory of representation. It does not, however, deal with the question of the political, but rather it can be read as a contribution to the problems raised by the aporetic character of Schmitt's presentation of the political.

In the aftermath of the deep ruptures in the political world of the late twentieth and early twenty-first century, international discussion has turned with a new urgency to reconceptualizing politics. Schmitt and the concept of the political have been added to the intellectual agenda of the contemporary scientific and political community. The semantic differentiation of politics and the political has entered all Western and even many non-Western languages. A rich literary production has arisen, with titles such as the "return of the political," the "challenge of the political," the "invention of the political," the "transformation of the political," the "thinking of the political," and the "permanence of the political." But most of this production does not live up to its titles. The conceptualizations offered are fuzzy. Often "the political" turns out to be a highbrow synonym for "politics."[10] Compared to this literature, the Arendtian restitution of the classical tradition of the political remains theoretically superior. Arendt anamnetically recovered the original meaning of the political in the Greek polis, which in fact unfolded to its fullest only in the classical citizen-polis of Athens. Her paradigm of the political measures political phenomena against the normative standard of the classical citizen-centered idea of politics. But this alleged singularity of authentic politics neglected the whole range of human self-interpretation and actualization as it has emerged in the global ecumene. The omnipresent quest for the political signals an intellectual turn toward a new understanding of politics beyond the confines of power games and governmental agency. The problem is summed up by David Held: "Today the traditional terms of reference of politics as a discipline, and of political theory in particular, appear under strain. More than ever before there are reasons for doubting whether a primary focus on the nature and proper form of politics of government and states can legitimately remain the basic subject matter of political theory. At issue is the coherence of the political."[11]

A coherent concept of the political presupposes a coherent philosophy of the political that substantiates the primacy of the political. In this sense Voegelin's new science of politics, which developed over several decades of theoretical and empirical research, unfolded a concept of the political within the interpretive frame of a science of the order of human existence in society and history. Voegelin himself talked only occasionally of the political, even in those early writings where he argued critically with Schmitt. In his fragmentary *Regierungslehre* of the early thirties he dealt with the first version of *The Concept of the Political* of 1927, but there the issue was not the question of the political but Schmitt's theoretical contribution to the central subject of Voe-

---

10. Armin Nassehi, "Der Begriff des Politischen und die doppelte Normativität der 'soziologischen' Moderne," in *Der Begriff des Politischen,* ed. Armin Nassehi and Markus Schroer (Baden-Baden: Nomos Verlag, 2003), 133–86.
11. Hannah Arendt, *Was ist Politik?* (Munich: Piper, 1993), 36–42; David Held, "Editor's Introduction," in *Political Theory Today,* ed. David Held (Oxford: Oxford University Press, 1991), 16.

gelin's study, namely, the governance of one human being over another and the identification of the source of power. In this respect Voegelin was interested only in Schmitt's description of the substance of power "that is prior to and transcends its phenomenal forms" in that it binds human existence into the whole of the governmental order.[12] Neither here nor in his later review of Schmitt's *Verfassungslehre* did Voegelin take up the issue of Schmitt's conceptualization of the political per se. But we can assume from the tenor of that review that he considered Schmitt's exploration of the political as marred by the author's blending theoretical analysis with his practical political intentions. For this reason, Voegelin abstained from any reference to the concept of the political and approached the political in terms of political reality. Voegelin's far-reaching study of the predicament of humanity extends in scope and subject matter beyond the realm of the political proper. The problem under discussion here addresses the question of whether Voegelin's science of politics introduces a theoretical grounding for a concept of the political that squares with the human experience of order and disorder in its global breadth and temporal depth.[13]

In the *New Science of Politics,* political society denotes a cosmion of meaning, illuminated from within by its own self-interpretation. The types of order and the attendant symbols of self-expression that can be found in historical political societies are the object of study in *Order and History*. These cosmioi are not, however, self-contained and closed political entities. They constitute the historical field that reflects the "patterns of meaning as they revealed themselves in the self-interpretation of persons and societies in history." These patterns of meaning emerge from "man's consciousness of his humanity as it differentiates historically" in that the nature of human being "unfolds its potentialities historically."[14] From this vantage point political reality is no longer limited to politically organized society, be it the city or the state. The whole of human experience of existence in society and history comes into view, which is to say the human search for humanity and its order.

Human self-interpretation is the pivot of this hermeneutical approach to political reality in that it brings forth symbols whereby humans express their

---

12. Eric Voegelin, *The Collected Works of Eric Voegelin* (hereinafter, *CW*), vol. 32, *The Theory of Governance and Other Miscellaneous Papers, 1921–1938,* trans. Sue Bollans et al., ed. William Petropulos and Gilbert Weiss (Columbia: University of Missouri Press, 2003), 361.
13. Jürgen Gebhardt, "Was ist der Gegenstand einer empirisch-hermeneutischen Theorie des Politischen," in *Politische Theorie-heute,* ed. Michael Th. Greven and Rainer Schmalz Bruns (Baden-Baden: Nomos Verlag, 1999), 101–19.
14. Eric Voegelin, *CW,* vol. 17, *Order and History,* vol. IV, *The Ecumenic Age,* ed. Michael Franz (1974; Columbia: University of Missouri Press, 2000), 106, 373.

experiences of order. "These experiences," Voegelin explains, "one could explore only by exploring their articulation through symbols. The identification of the subject-matter, and with the subject-matter, of the method to be used in its exploration, led to the principle at the basis of all my latter work: the reality of experience is self-interpretive."[15] The meaning of this statement is in itself in need of hermeneutical clarification. The reality in question is the experiential field encompassing the realm of human being in its modality of societal existence. It manifests the historical unfolding of the potentialities of human nature articulating the human quest for order and truth in time and space. It is because human beings are self-interpreting animals that the realm of human being is self-interpretive. In this way a hermeneutical science of politics that translates the meaning of self-interpretation into the language of rational discourse becomes possible. What now is called the "hermeneutical turn" in the social sciences has been practised by Voegelin from the beginning of his scholarly work, which was in any case informed by the hermeneutic paradigm of German *Geisteswissenschaft* in general, and especially by its foundation, philosophical anthropology. This philosophical hermeneutics aimed to weld anew the philosophical to the empirical in terms of a modern mode of human self-understanding, and it proclaimed anthropology the philosophical centerpiece of hermeneutical research. While Voegelin's implementation of this program underwent shifts and changes, he remained steadfast in his principled hermeneutics. In order to illuminate the meaningful texture of the socio-historical world, Voegelin focused on the interplay between the cognitive exploration of the phenomena of the experiential world as revealed in human self-explication and the reflexive analysis of the human condition.[16]

Voegelin's empirically oriented hermeneutics of politics has been formulated in his early study of political ideas: "It is our belief that the sphere of politics is the original sphere in which the fundamental changes of sentiments and attitudes occur, and that from the realm of politics new forces radiate into the other spheres of human activity—that is, into the realms of philosophy, the arts, and of literature." He did not postulate a "simplistic causal relationship between political institutions and other civilizational phenomena of an age. But, in keeping with our theory of the evocative character of the political cosmion, it means that in the political evocation on principle man is engaged with the whole of his personality and that all civilizational creations of a com-

---

15. Eric Voegelin, *Autobiographical Reflections* (Baton Rouge: Louisiana State University Press, 1989), 80.
16. Jürgen Gebhardt, "The Vocation of the Scholar," in *International and Interdisciplinary Perspectives on Eric Voegelin,* ed. Stephen A. McKnight and Geoffrey L. Price (Columbia: University of Missouri Press, 1997), 20–28.

munity must bear the imprint of the comprehensive whole."[17] The understanding of political community in terms of a political cosmion brings its main function to the fore, namely, to "assuage the existential anxiety of man by giving to his soul, through the magic evocation of the community, the assurance of having a meaningful place in a well ordered cosmos." In this sense, as Voegelin indicated in the surviving fragment of the introduction to the study, "the problem of politics has to be considered in the larger setting of an interpretation of human nature"[18] as explicated in *Order and History.*

The *condicio humana* remained the reflexive center of Voegelin's inquiry into the problems of human existence in society and history. It provided the anthropological basis of the political in that the meaning of politico-symbolic complexes of order emerge from concrete human experiences. For this reason, all modes of experience have to come within the purview of inquiry. This refers specifically to the methodological practise of excluding so-called religious ideas from political analysis. Voegelin always complained about political scientists lacking "the most elementary knowledge of religious experiences and their expression, they are unable to recognize politico-religious phenomena when they see them; and are unaware of their decisive role in the constitution of political society."[19] "Humans live in political society with all traits of their being, from the physical to the spiritual and religious traits," and human spirituality is the creative spring of any world-building imagination. Empirically, visions of order come from the most fundamental experience of human existence: finiteness and creatureliness. Human beings experience their existence as being creaturely and, therefore, questionable. From this condition arise stages of agitation that vary in form and content but that can be described as the "experience of being bound to a suprapersonal, all-powerful something" articulating "a feeling of simple dependency" on some intangible ground beyond one's own finite existence. Wherever this "beyond" discloses itself as ultimate and sacred in spiritual experiences it becomes the realissimum around which visions of order crystallize.[20] Such an anthropological approach to the meaning-creating agency of human beings has been outlined in the *Political Religions*

---

17. Eric Voegelin, *CW,* vol. 20, *History of Political Ideas,* vol. II, *The Middle Ages to Aquinas,* ed. Peter von Sivers (Columbia: University of Missouri Press, 1997), 107–8.

18. Eric Voegelin, *CW,* vol. 19, *History of Political Ideas,* vol. I, *Hellenism, Rome, and Early Christianity,* ed. Athanasios Moulakis (Columbia: University of Missouri Press, 1997), 81, 231.

19. Eric Voegelin, "The People of God" (I), 50–51, in Eric Voegelin Papers, box 58, file 4, Hoover Institution Archives, Stanford, CA.

20. Eric Voegelin, *CW,* vol. 5, *Modernity without Restraint: The Political Religions; The New Science of Politics; and Science, Politics, and Gnosticism,* ed. Manfred Henningsen (Columbia: University of Missouri Press, 2000), 70, 31, 32.

(1938) as well as in his later writings where Voegelin returned to this key idea of his research.

Since all human existence is necessarily social, all societal order feeds on the visionary imagination of order arising from concrete human consciousness in the ever-present face of chaos. "By the experience of social disorder human mind is provoked to create order by an act of imagination in accordance with its ordering idea of man."[21] Not every experience of the transcendent involves social existence; experience may be *sensu strictu,* apolitical, as in solitary mysticism. But every order is grounded in transcendent experiences of order as explicated symbolically in terms of the "truth" of society. Wherever human beings engage in reflective activity and strive for an ordered community, the "religious" moment in the experience of order has become "political."

All symbolic interpretations of societal order justify their legitimacy in reference to an ultimate ground of order. The various modes of experience, with their multiplicity of symbolic expression, all revolve around the founding of right order through insight into the ground of order. The sociologist Samuel Eisenstadt speaks of the "charismatic vision" at the root of any institutionalization of societal order,[22] which determines the political logic of the order that structures the whole of a political culture, provides it with coherence, and defines its overall identity.

The foundation of all evocation of symbolic forms of self-interpretation is the dialectical interplay of the human capability for self-transcendence with the experienced finite nature of human life. It refers to the mysterious reciprocity of reason and anxiety that Voegelin emphasized in a late fragment: "Anxiety is the response to the mystery of existence out of nothing. The search of order is the response to anxiety." He further generalizes: every symbolization "expressing the tension of existence has its component of truth as it conveys an insight into the Logos of this tension." And every act of symbolization "has the purpose and effect of bringing forth, maintaining, or restoring the order of existence, personal and social." Accordingly, every act of symbolization "expressing the tension of existence has the functions both of assuaging anxiety and preserving order."[23] Since symbolization discloses the logos of

---

21. Eric Voegelin, *CW,* vol. 27, The Nature of the Law *and Related Legal Writings,* ed. Robert Anthony Pascal, James Lee Babin, and John William Corrington (1991; available Columbia: University of Missouri Press, 1999), 108.

22. Samuel N. Eisenstadt, *Power, Trust, and Meaning* (Chicago: University of Chicago Press, 1995), 35–36.

23. Eric Voegelin, *CW,* vol. 28, *What Is History? and Other Late Unpublished Writings,* ed. Thomas A. Hollweck and Paul Caringella (1990; available Columbia: University of Missouri Press, 1999), 71, 87.

this tension between man as an existent thing and the ground of his existence "there is reason in search of order." The human quest for humanity and its order and the historical responses to this quest in the form of symbolic and social creations mirror in their modalities the comprehensive reality of God and human being, world and society in varied states of historical differentiation. The creative articulation of human potentialities expressed in the respective categories of the order of particular human societies are, according to Voegelin, to be studied historically and comparatively on the basis of a "general ontology of order." Such a study would have to deal with the problems of order in historical societies in respect "to general categories of orders of being (*allgemeine Ordnungskategorien des Seins*)."[24]

In the course of his work Voegelin's understanding of the realm of politics expanded from the political cosmion to the historico-political world in its global breadth and temporal depth. But, I suggest, politics remained the central sphere of symbolic and societal evocation. "The tensions in political reality originate," he states in *Anamnesis,* "in the dynamics of trying to find the right articulation of order." To the question What is political reality? he responds: "The order of man's entire existence" is the subject matter of "a theory of politics." Political reality is mapped under the experiential horizon of the essential interrelation between the human and its order. Analytically explicated, it ranges from the order of a concrete human consciousness through the orders of human and social existence in history. From this results the methodological conclusion that a "philosophy of politics is empirical—in the precise sense of an inquiry into the experiences which penetrate with their order the whole area of reality that we express by the symbol 'man.' The work of this philosophy requires, as we said, the constant exchange between studies on concrete cases of order and analyses of consciousness that make the human order in society and history intelligible."[25] Political reality coincides with the realm of human being proper, that is, insofar as it manifests itself in the dimension of spirit and freedom beyond mere animal existence.

Voegelin's concept of politics as sketched out here is not limited to the sphere of power and rulership, whether state- or citizen-centered. This is not to say that political reality is void of power: the struggle for symbolic supremacy, for the truth of order, is beset with power and derails all too often into pure power struggle. Because of the ultimate intangibility of this truth, there is an ongoing

---

24. Eric Voegelin, "Diskussionsbeitrag," in *Das Naturrecht in der politischen Theorie,* ed. Martin Schmölz (Wien: Springer, 1963), 140–41.
25. Eric Voegelin, *Anamnesis* (Munich: Piper Verlag, 1966), 288, 8. My own translation. See also *CW,* vol. 6, *Anamnesis: On the Theory of History and Politics,* trans. M. J. Hanak, ed. David Walsh (Columbia: Missouri University Press, 2002), 345, 399, 34.

competition and struggle over the meanings of symbols and control of the institutions that define and articulate the lead values of public order. Historically and in the present, struggling for the truth of order has often been a question of life and death. But the moment of power and related human drives is not the sole determinant of the social figurations human beings are engaged in.

Carl Schmitt was said to have explored the order of human things in terms of the political, but his investigation focused on the disorders of the modern world. The current and ongoing discussion of the meaning of the political suggests a comprehensive notion of the political that brings to the fore the logic of order inherent in all societal forms as indicated by Voegelin's concept of political reality. The quest for order and the creative responses to it spring from the experiential ground of existence that reveals itself in the tensional structure of human existence in the in-between of life and death, truth and untruth, perfection and imperfection, order and disorder. The omnipresence of this quest is reflected in the phenomenal world of politics and points toward a transcendent point of reference of the political in terms of the common humanity of all humans. Accordingly, political reality is co-extensive with the unfolding of human being and its order so that the political signifies the fundamental modality of human existence: the political is the epitome of human being in the world.

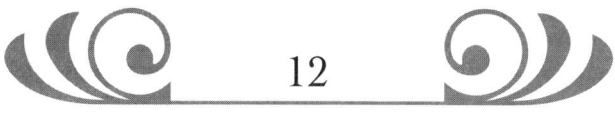

12

Eric Voegelin on the Nature of Law

Timothy Fuller

> Man's existence is *not* primarily an external or phenomenal reality but rather the In-Between existence of participation. He is strung between mortality and immortality. He is capable of virtue and faith but inclined to vice and sin. He aspires to divinity but knows that he is indeed lower than the angels. He is a "mixed bag," we might say. Man is capable of nobility but, as Søren Kierkegaard remarks, he (who can live almost at the level of the angels) more often than not lives like his dog. This pungent statement expresses an understanding of the human condition as the In-Between reality, i.e., as the *permanent* state of man seeking immortality but not finding perfection *in* this world.
> —Ellis Sandoz, *A Government of Laws: Political Theory, Religion, and the American Founding*

We owe a great deal to Eric Voegelin for bringing new light to numerous fields of inquiry. His monograph *The Nature of the Law* in volume 27 of *The Collected Works of Eric Voegelin* is a case in point.[1] What I have to say will be

---

1. Eric Voegelin, *The Nature of the Law,* in *The Collected Works of Eric Voegelin* (hereinafter, *CW*), vol. 27, The Nature of the Law *and Related Legal Writings,* ed. Robert Anthony Pascal, James Lee Babin, and John William Corrington (1991; available Columbia: University of Missouri Press, 1999), 1–70.

based principally on my reflections on that work. First, however, among the many insights we have gained from Voegelin in the study of political and social life, I want to mention two in order to put the discussion of law in context: 1) his identification of Gnosticism, continually present in the tensions of the Christian tradition, as a fundamental, though often unrecognized, feature of the modern situation, and 2) his insistence that the theoretical concepts we employ for analysis must be referable to, and not disconnected from, actual, concrete experience.

Hence, for example, Voegelin remarks that there is an "intrinsic inconsistency" in an "attitude that tends to separate the idea of order from the realities of power.... It seems to be one of the most difficult things for a political thinker to separate clearly the problem of the contents of an order from the problem of enforcing it. The question of right enters into the principles on which an order is built; the maintenance of an order will have always, human nature being what it is, to rely on the instrument of force."[2] There are numerous ways of analyzing modern political life, and of the idea of law and the rule of law, which have been offered to us. Within this variety it is, nevertheless, apparent that modern politics produces a tension between utopianism in varying degrees of intensity, on the one hand, and despair and disillusionment in varying degrees, on the other. Expressions of tension between idealistic aspiration and cynical reduction to struggles for power are obvious and widespread. The dynamics of modern politics show the character they do because the experience is constituted in terms of such tensions. In the remark quoted above, Voegelin speaks of maintaining awareness of the tension between ideas of order and the realities of power, and of accepting the fact of such tension as the context of analysis. Following Voegelin we could say that Gnostic longing to end the tension or resolve it in one direction or another suffuses the modern Western tradition but not without attendant, powerful institutional forms of restraint on the pursuit of those longings. Hence in different times and places utopianism, abstract idealism, rationalism, perfectionism, appear with greater or lesser intensity and activism. In turn, claims to or hopes for enlightenment, when disappointed, are visited by disillusionment and despair.

Among the institutions that offer resistance to, or put restraints upon, these powerful tendencies are constitutions, legal systems, and established practices of the rule of law. The United States is an extraordinary example of all these tendencies and tensions and has thus been described as a, or the, laboratory of modernity. The American polity exhibits both extraordinary aspirations on a global scale—one could mention proclaiming the *novus ordo seclorum,* a cen-

---

2. Eric Voegelin, "Right and Might," ibid., 86.

tury of Wilsonian foreign policy coupled with the urge to economic globalization—along with a constitutional tradition based on limited government, the rule of law, due process, decentralized power, and a realistic estimate of human nature and its limitations. The debate over Nation or Empire is perennially carried on in terms of recovering or restoring our true purpose, recalling us to the founding principles and their meaning for us now. We find ourselves speculating on the "end of history" and also on the "clash of civilizations." We cannot avoid debating the rise and fall of nations and empires, both historically and presently. We relive the antagonism between the ancient Augustinian depreciation of worldliness and Protestant millennialist expectations of the heavenly kingdom on earth. We are compelled to question the Enlightenment claim that the decline and disappearance of religion in favor of secularism must triumph, facing the fact that religion not only has not declined, let alone disappeared, but has shown itself to be a central and powerful presence, and in many places dominant. And so we see that while we may separate church and state, we have no prospect whatever of separating religion from politics. Voegelin provides one of the most satisfactory analyses of this situation.

Since it was prominent among Voegelin's intentions to identify and demystify modern Gnosticism by explaining its sources and dynamics, it is of considerable interest to examine what he has to say about the nature of law in a monograph that relies heavily on the character of the American legal and constitutional experience. His focus on the American experience may not be surprising, since he was lecturing to American students of law, and the essay on which we focus here was originally an informal paper written for the use of students of the law. But it is significant in its implications, as we shall see.

Voegelin knew that we have been living in a revolutionary era of Western history that has been under way for several hundred years. He knew also that the extremes of tyranny and totalitarianism in the twentieth century were to be understood in terms of virulent aspects of our age that were not well understood and often misinterpreted because of defective philosophical and political analyses that had lost connection to ancient sources of inquiry into the human condition or had willfully denied their relevance to our time. Nevertheless, these sources and experiences remain available to us if we know what we are looking for and if we are able to disengage from historical immediacy. Also, we could depend to a degree on the persistence of institutions, as in American constitutional order, which carried forward residual wisdom in our actual practices. Within the Western tradition in general there is a respect for law and the rule of law that is salutary and an indispensable feature of the modern constitutional state and its conspicuous economic success. Many thinkers, in responding to the rise of totalitarianism, two world wars, the advent of the nuclear age and the cold war, and the bipolar division between East and West, sought wisdom in returning to the ancient sources. Voegelin was by no means unique in this respect, even though his project of recovery had distinctive features, which insure that the story of the revival of political science and political philosophy in the late twentieth century cannot properly be told without understanding his role in it. What, then, can we learn from examining Voegelin's reflections on the nature of law?

First, as noted, the essay on the nature of law is a decidedly American document in which Voegelin freely uses American institutions and practices to analyze what law is and what the rule of law may be. He does this while insisting that it is not clear whether law has an essence. The American experience is important but will not turn out to exhaust the sources of insight. There is no doubt that he has Aristotle's political philosophy and Thomas Aquinas's analysis of the essence of law in the back of his mind in this discussion. He knows that it has been a common feature of legal philosophy to try to determine the essence of law, but he resists easy definitions, not questioning the question itself but questioning whether definitiveness is finally possible. But where then does Voegelin end up? That is what remains to be seen.

He points out that there is no simple or convenient way to distinguish between the "essential" and the "non-essential" rules within a legal system, and yet we cannot identify the nature of the law simply by reference to the aggregate of all rules. Moreover, the "essence" or "definition" of law might seem to require a fixed, permanent answer; but if we refer to our actual experience, as we must, we can see that rules come and go and that the interpretation of their meaning changes through time. A legal system gains and loses rules. Legal orders continually transform as laws come and go, constituting what Voegelin calls a "sequence of aggregates." What makes these rules valid? One might answer that question by pointing to the undergirding offered by a consistent rule-making procedure, or a constitutional order, a process and system that structures the content. What then activates the process? That is, how is the rule connected to, derived from, the underlying procedure?

Do we have to say that validity is only momentary or transitory? By focusing on the temporality of law Voegelin tries to show that law is either what *was* valid or what is coming to be but is not yet valid. This would certainly reflect the political/practical experience of always being caught between "what is" and "what ought to be." But this reflection allows Voegelin to pose the question Where is that presence that would reveal the essence of law and not just what has been characteristic of a legal system at different moments?

One might like to say that there is something that persists while other things change. But to distinguish in this way is not easy. The question of how the unchanging, however stipulated, is connected to the changing remains unsettled. But, further, constitutions and procedures also change and can be amended so that even the continuity of process cannot escape the realm of changingness. Essence seems ever to withdraw or retreat in the course of analysis.

One must then look to the larger society of which a legal system is part where one might identify social purpose or direction that informs a legal system as an instrument serving such purpose or direction. But the difficulty here is that we butt up against the distinction between law as a structure for living together *in modus vivendi* and law as binding us to a direction, or an end, defining us as functional contributors to a corporate enterprise. If our experience tells us that as human beings we are real individuals, then we must question whether the purpose of the law is to override our real individuality; but yet we must wonder also if we are merely individuals such that common purpose is illusory. To be sure, we recognize rules and judgments, and we make use of them in our chosen transactions with one another. Voegelin thus suggests that we are all law makers at some level. That is, a legal system cannot function if those subject to it are not somehow able to appropriate the rules to themselves and voluntarily determine their use in specific instances. The nature of law is concerned with this widespread law-acknowledging activity; we must want to be related to each other in certain lawlike ways that we acknowledge to be beneficial. There are, then, common, more or less formal rules for the whole that have to proceed from some recognized authority, and there is the vast array of more or less informal rules for us in particular. In order to flourish, individuals must be oriented to law-abiding conduct. Individuals must want that to be the case—they must choose it—and thus we distinguish between law-abiding and law-breaking conduct. This does not yet tell us if there is an essence of law, but Voegelin seems to be telling us that there are features of human interaction that emerge so as to point toward the desirability of lawfulness, suggesting an as-yet-undefined essence but establishing for sure that the notion of lawlike conduct is continuously accessible to human beings in general. A rule-oriented society reinforces this distinction between abiding by and breaking the law throughout the society to its members: we can describe this as self-regulation and self-rule within a system of rules. One could describe this as a commonality that coheres with a strong sense of the reality of individuality. Self-rule is thus not a liberation from rules but a collaboration in the extension of rule-bound behavior beyond what the general legislative rules can accomplish. Indeed, the law makers are dependent upon this diffusion for their success. That is, a rule-of-law society articulates law-based relationships all the way down and throughout the social order. This also seems to mean that rulers and ruled alike participate in recognizing and instantiating lawlike order. To achieve such an order requires collaboration and not merely imposition. Voegelin sees some version of this requirement as being universal to mankind because there is no natural barrier to increasing differentiation and diversification in human self-awareness. Lawlike conduct cannot then merely be imposed; law is not merely a decree, and the element of recognition and acceptance must be present. So far the argument seems to be compatible with the utter temporality of rules themselves that Voegelin has earlier acknowledged.

But what are all these laws for? Are they for convenience? For maximizing freedom? For securing peace without uniformity of beliefs or values? For seeking salvation? Is there some substantive, common end served by law? Obviously many versions of all these positions are offered to us all the time. One classic example of the tension in this is found in Locke's *Second Treatise*.

Chapter 7 of the *Second Treatise* is called "Of Political or Civil Society." In its first paragraph, paragraph 77, Locke says:

> God having made Man such a creature, that, in his own Judgment, it was not good for him to be alone, put him under strong Obligations of Necessity, Convenience, and Inclination, to drive him into *Society*, as well as fitted him with Understanding and Language to continue and enjoy it.[3]

In the first paragraph of Chapter 8, "Of the Beginning of Political Societies," paragraph 95, Locke says:

> Men being, as has been said, by Nature, all free, equal and independent, no one can be put out of this Estate, and subjected to the Political Power of another, without his own *Consent*. The only way whereby any one divests himself of his Natural Liberty, and *puts on the bonds of Civil Society* is by agreeing with other Men to join and unite into a Community, for their comfortable, safe, and peaceable living one amongst another, in a secure Enjoyment of their Properties, and a greater Security against any that are not of it.[4]

Locke has expressed, first, the idea of natural sociality—a disposition to civility—in terms reminiscent of Aristotle and the Bible, and then later the strong sense of individual liberty, equality, and independence, which are integral to a society that may be called political as opposed to tyrannical. There is a natural disposition to political or civil society, but there is an action of the human will that is required to begin it or realize it. The fulfillment of the dis-

---

3. John Locke, *The Second Treatise of Government*, rev. ed., ed. Peter Laslett (Cambridge: Cambridge University Press, 1963), 361–62.
4. Ibid., 374–75.

position requires conscious consent of individuals to a commonly acknowledged rule of law.

In his essay on law, Voegelin briefly refers to several significant responses to this disposition to lawlike relations. One is the Aristotelian, in which the attempt to define the *polis* shows the tension between focus on the persons who make up the *polis* and the form of the *polis* involving an ideal of citizenship or a shared way of life independent of the particular individual members: form vs. multiplicity. A second is the American approach in which the Declaration of Independence expresses the animating "idea" of proper order, and the constitution instantiates it so that the constitutional form is in-formed by the "idea." Voegelin takes the American approach to represent a conservative version of modernity, which preserves standards that are above procedures while acknowledging the universality of human agency that is protected through a legal system that emphasizes procedure. This establishes the connection between Locke's position and the American combination of revolutionary action with constitution making.

Finally, Voegelin refers to the National Socialist version, which he describes as "intrasystematic proceduralism." In this there is an internal consistency of rules without reference to a substantial order, or transcendent standards of right, from which it insulates itself by denying that there is a substantial unchosen order, or that transcendent standards of right exist.

The Aristotelian and the American responses in acknowledging law are also responses to the question of the meaning or purpose of law, hence implying the reality that law may reflect but that is above and beyond the law. The National Socialist is an inward-looking system that suppresses the question of reality for its subjects. In this third case, the tension between the prevailing law and the idea or ideal of lawfulness is resisted. One might think Voegelin is suggesting that reflection on the experience of law must eventually produce the experience of tension between the changing and the unchanging. Our response to this tension, although not necessarily answering the question of essence, nevertheless impels us to be more thoughtful about how we understand ourselves, and it does so in ways allowing for widespread participation in the deliberation over whether we are yet fully realizing lawfulness. It becomes clearer that all along Voegelin is pointing toward a larger order transcending all regimes, even though legal systems are inadequate to show it in universal terms and may, by proclaiming their autonomy, obscure or deny it. Legal systems cannot be wholly adequate because they must be particular to time and place and they must move with the unavoidable human temporal transitions. But they are perfectly adequate to point to that to which they are inadequate and mutable, but real, responses.

Following Voegelin's reflections so far, we have been led from the legal order to the larger social/political order to the question of the structure of reality. Voegelin's method here is to move from the bottom up, not from the top down. He has avoided using the traditional terminology of natural law theory, but it would be hard to deny that there is an affinity, especially at the point where lawlike relations are seen to be an implication of all human interaction, no matter how well or badly carried out. Political revolutions, for instance, cannot alter the structure of reality but only the expression of and response to that structure within particular orders. The disposition to move toward the lawlike relationship, with all its tension between individual and collective, cannot be eradicated or transformed so that the tension is eliminated. There is a "concreteness of lasting order in the daily actions of every human being."[5] The order does not exist independently but concretely in every human participant. The concreteness of order is found in and amid the multiplicity of conduct. A legal order must somehow be usable, nonarbitrary, compatible with human interaction, and constructive not destructive. Validity, which we noted earlier, is achieved when individuals, as individuals, can actually make the legal order concrete in their interactive conduct. Procedure is necessary but not sufficient. There will always be the question of whether our use of procedures reinforces the sense of rightness or justice that accompanies our acting in accord with the procedures. Technical correctness is not everything.

Thus a collection of persons cannot be ordered merely by the imposition of norms. Rather, there has to be reciprocity between the laws made and the diffused enactment of law by individuals and groups in their varying particular circumstances. Form and content are not independent. The "lasting order" thus both persists and alters in a manner that cannot be captured by analogy to mechanism or organism.[6] Order is discovered through trial and error in the inevitable tension between "what is" and "what ought to be."

And at this point Voegelin introduces the great Ought, which is implied in the daily oughts of life. It would seem that a legal order is to be examined in terms of the degree to which it encourages or discourages attunement to the larger structure of reality that it imperfectly represents. The tension in this quest for attunement, unless suppressed, must lead to reference beyond the rules themselves, and even beyond the mere revision of the rules for temporal, practical purposes. What sort of order do we compose? How best do we express it? How shall we successfully promulgate it? Law thus, for all the reasons given, cannot be reduced to command. Law demands a constant interpretative debate,

---

5. Voegelin, *CW*, 27:40.
6. Ibid., 43.

and individuals must subscribe to the law. At the immediate level of this experience Voegelin finds reason to praise the legal profession. It is lawyers who are trained and attuned to these issues who have necessary expertise, and it establishes their special vocation.

Yet beyond the lawyers there is still a further special category of the philosopher, whose quest is for insight into the Ought above all oughts. The philosopher acutely senses what is present to all in some degree and is potentially the law maker of the true order of things. Voegelin makes these points in part to establish the distinction between what he calls the "true order of society," which is a particular order in fruitful tension with the larger structure of reality, and an ideological or totalitarian order, which seeks to substitute an immanent picture of reality that will close off the tension. No matter how legalistic or procedurally consistent such an order may be, it is not a true legal order. Keeping the distinction alive is the special function of the philosophical man, who allows reflection to lead to encounter with the divine, who knows that there is a *ius divinum et naturale,* and who establishes thereby the required critique of the *ius sociale et historiale.* For while it is true that one must always be in a concrete, actual society, and while it is also true that the truth of order must be sought within particular social orders, and while it is further true that social orders vary with respect to the degree to which persons are enabled to order their lives, nevertheless all these considerations point beyond themselves. At the simplest level, individuals cannot deny the existence of other individuals; societies cannot deny the existence of other societies, of other purposes or, perhaps, of the possible purpose of life.

Voegelin once more distinguishes the Aristotelian from the American approach: For Aristotle the *bios theoretikos* can be pursued in philosophy within the well-ordered city; in America it is "life, liberty and the pursuit of happiness" that establishes the idea of self-development coupled with self-regulation or self-restraint. In both cases, despite obvious differences, there is openness to a larger truth about man, which he did not make and which he cannot avoid. This awareness, which is unsought and unavoidable, always and everywhere is natural. Aristotle had no doubt that individuals are real. The American Founders had no doubt that there is a structure of reality that transcends politics.

The argument allows us to think that there are both ancient and modern modes of recognizing the truth about reality, involving the idea of an Ought that transcends all the oughts but to which all the mundane oughts tend, whether they are acknowledged to be doing this or not. The analysis ascends only to encounter that which the analytical ascent presupposes before it recognizes it. In American terms this means we accept a rule-making authority because we not only need rules to make our multiplicity coherent and safe, but we really want them as factors in human well-being. Convenience and self-interest inevitably play a part, but they are not by themselves adequate to the purpose, nor can they provide the full explanation of what we are about, because there is always more to self-understanding than knowing your momentary interest. We are continually reminded of the informing idea of our order that exists above all processes and procedures, and thus we are not permitted to forget the distinction between "social truth" and "truth as such." Human beings live in tension between the conventional wisdom and wisdom without qualification. The acceptance of the rule-making authority does not imply the superior wisdom of that authority concerning the order of the American polity, since, as we have seen, the instantiation of the order by all of us in our particular circumstances cannot be a matter of speculative wisdom and cannot be in the control of any one person or group. Moreover, no single description of the order is able to describe it in its entirety, and every partial description changes in some degree the picture we have of that which we are trying to understand. Again, there is an affinity between the American approach and Aristotle's recognition that a theory of practical decision-making is never a substitute for adequate judgment in practical decision-making itself. Here Voegelin offers a way to overcome a mere conflict between ancient and modern ideas of law without denying that they have their differences. We must seek the perennial in the interstices of our practices.

By bringing the Aristotelian and American approaches into contact, however, I believe Voegelin is also doing something else of significance for our thinking: If both approaches are valid responses, it may follow that the differences between the ancients and ourselves are not constituted in the greater wisdom of one or the other. In other words, for Voegelin reflection on the nature of law leads to an appreciation of different polities not in terms of earlier or later but in terms of their relative openness to the great Ought. Or, to put it another way, Voegelin is not advocating historicism or progressivism. He is not saying that the American order has simply advanced beyond the Aristotelian, even though he does acknowledge what is different and appropriate to us. This is important because it allows him to defend the rule of law in its modern form without defending modernity altogether, which he certainly would not do, and without suggesting a simple supersession of antiquity, as if we had nothing to learn from that quarter.

His refusal to endorse progressivism is also to be seen in his justification for the continued need of force and enforcement, as we saw at the outset: Perfection is impossible, truth is always in dispute, social order itself is a compulsion to the extent that there is no spontaneous or automatic order. Legal rules are neither mere personal experiences nor the Decalogue. Debate and compromise, procedures such as adjudication and voting, are proper responses to the condition under which we achieve and seek to maintain order, that order in which we all willingly participate without truncating or sacrificing our thought as to what lies beyond it.

Yet there are forces in the soul that disrupt attunement and are ineradicable. Voegelin allows that enforcement of law imposes maturity on the not fully mature, on the not fully thoughtful. Thus law has an educative function, not to replace the tensions of existence, but to bring clarity and manageability to them. We may agree to this while remembering, as Voegelin would want us to, that the tensions between voluntary transaction and self-regulation and "educative" enforcement and punishment are themselves occasions for reflecting on the difference between "social truth" and "truth as such."

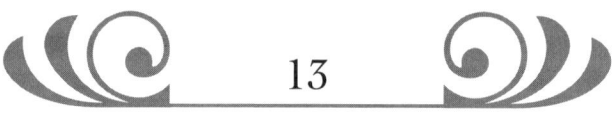

A Classical Prince
The Style of François Mitterrand

Tilo Schabert

Political Classicism

Why do I speak of François Mitterrand as a prince? Why "prince"? And why the epithet "classical"? I am practicing political science, and I reached this appraisal by practicing this activity. At the beginning of my study of Mitterrand, there was only the routine of newspaper reading and, quite preliminary to any scholarly effort, the perception that he was but one politician among many. At the end, everything was different. The "one politician among many" had disappeared. In his person appeared the political figure whom we traditionally associate with the classical notion of a *Princeps, Principe, Prince.* Indeed, princely figures in politics belong to human societies in an essential way. They have appeared at all times and at all places, and they represent in one person the classical features of political leadership or, to use a classical term, of statecraft. Human beings do not live without a *Principe,* even if the person goes by another name, or governs not alone but in conjunction with others. There is even a *Principe* if the "prince" is contorted ridiculously into a caricature, or viciously bent into a monstrous representation.

What happened between the perception of François Mitterrand as "one politician among many" and the insight that in François Mitterrand the classical and paradigmatic figure of the prince had again become real? What took place was that an experiment in political science had been undertaken, in several different laboratories. The experiment was conducted comparatively; laboratories were those fields of human conduct called governments. Political science, too, can be as objective, as "empirical" and as "hard" and experimental as the natural sciences. Strictly considered, political science is even more experimental than natural science because, to use Vico's words, the "political world surely was made by men, and its principles therefore can be found in the constructive life of our human mind."[1]

In government practices can be found the essential features of governments. They were made by people, and the ways by which governments are made therefore can be understood by the ways in which people in principle make a government. The relevant findings are fully objective; something constituted by people is grasped through the forms, through the structures and laws by which people constitute it. A study of the field of governments is, after all, a study of human beings as creative beings. In the laboratory of the researcher, politically creative humans appear in action; the researcher can observe how governing is conducted and how, in this way, a political world is created and sustained. The question sounds simple: What is it that is called government? The answer, however, is anything but simple, because it entails understanding the complexities and surprises of humans engaged in political creativity. This understanding of government was confirmed, experimentally, and in an entirely unintended way. François Mitterrand, the president, was our witness.

The experiment began in an American city: Boston, Massachusetts. I wished to know how this city was governed and what thereby was created in the way of government. The findings, produced by the research undertaken and later presented in a book,[2] converged on this insight: *Governing is creativity,* an encompassing and incessant process of creation. It is the process of creativity that appears as government. The government, however, while being indeed the form of the ongoing creativity, is by no means identical with it. The creativity governs, not the government. The paradigm of governing, I discovered, is a fluid state between chaos and form. At each of these extremes, the creative activity or governing would perfectly be fulfilled if matters could be decided on the basis of logical reasoning alone. Complete as chaos, creative governing would remain utterly free unto itself; complete as form, it would have come into its full reality. The political world, however, organizes itself differently; there, chaos and form fluidly change into each other, They form a *chaosmos,* as I call it, in borrowing the word from James Joyce.[3]

---

1. Cf. Giambattista Vico, *La nuova scienza*, 1.3.
2. Tilo Schabert, *Boston Politics: The Creativity of Power* (New York: W. De Gruyter, 1989).
3. James Joyce, *Finnegans Wake* (London: Faber and Faber, 1971), 118, line 21.

The empirical research in Boston led me to these theoretical conclusions. However, as complete as it was in itself, the study of the creativity of power, based on an analysis of the governing system and the politics in Boston under Mayor Kevin White, was not the end of the matter but only the beginning. The inner world of the world of governing had offered too wide an opening to theoretical curiosity. Now knowing better what there was to explore, my curiosity was directed toward this political world with greater intensity. I tested the paradigm developed in the study on Boston politics by examining the governing styles and practices of four American presidents—Franklin D. Roosevelt, Harry S Truman, Dwight D. Eisenhower, and Lyndon B. Johnson—and two German chancellors—Konrad Adenauer and Helmut Kohl. One of the results was that my interest in François Mitterrand, president of France, became greater and greater.[4]

François Mitterrand knew nothing about the way by which Roosevelt had governed, yet his mode of governing was very similar. François Mitterrand knew nothing about Adenauer's style of governing, yet his style was in many respects the same. And Mitterrand had never heard of Boston's Mayor Kevin White, yet with respect to their art of government, the two could have been twins.[5] Adenauer, again, did not know of the governmental style of Roosevelt, nor did Kevin White know that of Mitterrand. And yet Boston's mayor had shown himself to be a master in governing creatively, at about the time the French politician was beginning to reveal himself as another master in statecraft.

Presidents Truman, Eisenhower, and Johnson could be included into this peculiar configuration of similarities because they were akin to each other in their practice of government as well as to the other leaders already named; and yet each of them, as each of the others, had adopted this practice as his very own and not as a copy. What do these similarities in style that transcended space and time mean?

How did it happen that the same people who made these similarities visible were completely unaware of them themselves? How did they express an equivalent style on the basis of a way of governing that they undoubtedly understood as their *own*? What could Roosevelt and Mitterrand and White and Johnson and Eisenhower and Adenauer have in common, as each of them was

---

4. It led eventually to a study of Mitterrand's leadership and politics undertaken—empirically again (by interviews and archival research)—at the Elysée Palace between 1992 and 1995. See the author's book, *Wie Weltgeschichte gemacht wird: Frankreich und die deutsche Einheit* (Stuttgart: Klett-Cotta, 2002).

5. François Mitterrand, interview with author, at Elysée Palace, June 15, 1993, quoting from author's notes.

entirely for himself *only* Roosevelt, *only* Mitterrand, *only* White, *only* Johnson, *only* Eisenhower, *only* Adenauer?

The Preceding Morphogenetic Structures

What they had in common was that each governed in the way of the classical prince, and each was for that reason original. This is not a contradiction. Mitterrand did not govern in a way similar to Roosevelt because he may have wished to imitate the latter. The astounding similarity came from another source. Mitterrand attained in *his* practice of governing a classicism in the art of government to which Roosevelt had come by *his* practice of governing. Nothing connected Mitterrand with Roosevelt but the common classicism. Viewed from the perspective of this classical understanding of *The Prince*, however, they were similar to each other: in Mitterrand's conduct of government we find Roosevelt's art of governing, and in Roosevelt's conduct of government we find Mitterrand's art of governing.

This statement conveys a structural discovery: to govern is to govern within classical structures. These *morphogenetic* structures are put in action by princes while they govern, and at the same time they themselves may be perfectly unaware that these structures exist. The structures precede political leaders insofar as the leaders enter upon them by actually governing. That is, political leaders execute, with their actual leadership, structures of governing that exist prior to their own government. They produce, in a *general* enactment of forms, the form that is enacted by their *own* conduct of government. This form, their own, is, along morphogenetic lines, structured in a classical way.

There exists, then, for scholarly inquiries into the activity of governing, a coherent field of analysis. This field is constituted by the matter under scrutiny (governments) and not by the inquiry (science). What presents itself, the aforementioned surprising similarities in style, directs the scholar towards his or her field; through the unity of the field a meaningful paradigm emerges that allows us to speak of different things as if they were one. Such an understanding of unity in diversity informs the long, but at present largely forgotten tradition of the *Mirror of the Prince*. Again and again the same mirror was asked: What makes a good prince?[6] Similarly, the field of presidential studies

---

6. Cf. Wilhelm Berges, *Die Fürstenspiegel des hohen und späten Mittelalters* (Leipzig: K.W. Hiersemann, 1938); Hans-Otto Mühleisen and Theo Stammen, eds., *Politische Tugendlehre und Regierungskunst* (Tübingen: M. Niemeyer, 1990).

as pursued in modern American political science, which has nothing equal to it in any European country,[7] focuses upon a constant question: How do American presidents exert *leadership*?[8]

The discovery about which I spoke presented a still greater challenge. It touched upon the process of creativity that produces a government. And it pointed to the field offered by this process in view of an analysis of the activity of governing. With the field of paradigms within which, and according to which, governing occurs as a process of creativity, a science of government finds the field for its inquiries. In short, governing follows laws of creativity. In the analysis of the creativity that all governing is, one can discern a science of government and define the laws of creativity.

By his conduct of government, François Mitterrand produced an ideal model for apprehending in a process of governing the creative nature of this process. In making the model, he was moved by the voice of wisdom: "I have found recently a book by Plutarch whose title, in the Amyot collection, is—in the way, you know, as the ancient Greeks considered: 'Whether man in old age still should care about public affairs and take part in them'. That is the title. And he gives the answer, he, Plutarch . . . He says: 'Yes'. And, do you know on which principle he builds it from the beginning? He says: 'Because old age never was seen to transform a bee into a bumble-bee.'"[9] The French president produced his ideal model by striving toward it using certain strategies for the exercise of power. As will be shown presently, he undertook a practise of exerting power that was already present paradigmatically, *although he did not necessarily know it.*

In the Elysée, Mitterrand maintained his own primacy of power among those who participated in his administration by changing their assignments frequently and so keeping things fluid. He acted as if he repeatedly had said to himself, "Every two or three years the clerks and the vassals ought to be replaced, so that they do not take roots, grow strong or give me reason to worry." This is advice where one can easily recognize the style of Mitterrand; yet, the advice found in this formulation is, not among his statements, but in a book on the art of governing published in Persia in the eleventh century.[10]

---

7. The relevant studies of Wilhelm Hennis in Germany and of Samy Cohen in France still are isolated phenomena.

8. Cf. for instance, the bibliographical data presented in Stephen Skowronek, *The Politics Presidents Make: Leadership from John Adams to George Bush* (Cambridge, MA: Belknap Press, 1993).

9. Interview with François Mitterrand at French Television (TF1), September 17, 1987. I quote after the text of the interview as given in *Le Monde,* September 19, 1987, p. 7.

10. Nizamulmuk, *Siyasatnama—Das Buch der Staatskunst,* trans. from Persian (into German) by Karl Emil Schabinger, ed. Karl Friedrich Schabinger (Zurich: Manesse, 1987), 213.

Mitterrand also knew how to keep people who belonged close to him in a net of complicit understanding. Even though they might have built their own province of partially independent power, still they continued to dangle on his strings. His relevant counsel might have been articulated differently, but its content would hardly have differed from the one given by a chancellor of the Persian Empire in his *Mirror for Princes:* "The ruler ought never to cease to have an eye on the affairs of his administrators. He must continually be informed about all their bearing and doings. Does he entrust someone with an important business, he must have watched him secretly, in a way that the person cannot notice it." And when the pen of this remote prince left us the sentence "Negligence abducts power," he conveyed an insight that Mitterrand in the Elysée conscientiously applied.[11] But, of course, he followed his own wisdom when he preserved by his diligence the foundation of his power on a daily basis.[12]

François Mitterrand created by his own virtuosity an ideal model for the apprehension of the creativity of government. To do this, he did not need an example to emulate; and yet he actualized a pattern of examples. Indeed, it even could be said that he followed such examples. But then, "to follow" would not mean simply to imitate, to continue, to join. Rather, it would have to be understood by way of a law of structural similarity. Mitterrand did not follow examples, but in the creative form of his own practice of government, he followed a general paradigm of governmental creativity that others had followed, too. Hence, they could appear on the surface to have been his examples. The similarity between Mitterrand and other princes emerged from a similar practice of governing (and only on this level of appearances can examples be assumed), but its validity derives only from the unity of the paradigm. Each prince thus created in this general, paradigmatic form his own form of governing and became, in his following the paradigm, similar to others who followed it as well.

Politicians assimilate the figure of the prince by actualizing a creativity within the forms of governmental creativity. They are both creative and not. They are not creative, insofar as they follow antecedents in enacting the forms through which governmental creativity occurs. But they are decidedly creative by producing themselves as the embodiment of forms, by staging and directing themselves and thus making visible what can only become visible through an

---

11. Ibid., 196 f., 193.
12. Mitterrand read every day, when he was working in his office in the Elysée, 200–250 pages of notes, memos on a great variety of subjects, written for him by his aides. Usually, he returned these notes on the same day, often with annotations.

enactment on stage. Mitterrand knew this general law of creativity applied to political creativity as well. He knew that one would be mistaken, as Paul Valéry observed, when one would "go back to the author instead of going back to the machinery that did all the work." We arrive at our own work, Mitterrand said, only by working according to the rules: "I think that a delicacy of style, of expressions, of writing, can be found only, as always, if one respects the rules of language. It's the same in politics." Valéry unequivocally articulated this essential insight. There is therefore a third player in the creative process between work and author that imposes itself upon the author pursuing his work: "One cannot produce the works which one wanted to produce—one obeys something quite other than oneself."[13] Who or what is it, then, whom one obeys? Mitterrand answered for the realm of politics that one obeys the law of creativity. Every creation has its form, and only through form can there be creation: "There is no liberty," Mitterrand said, "without an organization of liberty."[14]

The Three Paradoxes

This sounds paradoxical. Is liberty organized—that is, liberty demarcated and subjugated, not liberty denied? And yet, does not liberty, too, need to come into a form in order simply to exist? Must an order of liberty and the fruition of liberty, although opposite to each other, not necessarily form a union? Was it this that Mitterrand wanted to say? In any case he was referring to the paradoxical way in which the law of creativity in politics becomes manifest. To *homo politicus* applies at all times and at all places this first principle: one is not free to govern as one might wish; one is governed as one sets out to govern.

The Paradox of Power

What happens then to a prince who desires to govern, as he proceeds to do what he desires, namely, *to govern*? The prince will encounter the first paradox in the nature of political government, the paradox of power. Let us imagine the situation more concretely. A single person sits at the desk in the Oval Office

---

13. Paul Valéry, *Cahiers* (1973; rpr., Paris: Gallimard, 1983), 1:253; interview with François Mitterrand, in *Le Point*, no. 970, April 22, 1991, p. 49; Paul Valéry, *Cahiers*, 1:49.

14. Interview with François Mitterrand, in *Libération*, no. 923, May 10, 1984, p. 6. Consider also Mitterrand's similar statement: "Societies exist only by institutions. There is no liberty without institutions" (Interview with François Mitterrand, in *L'Express*, July 21, 1994, p. 22).

in the White House: the American president whose first day in office has begun. Everything here is still quite new for the incoming president. Appropriate to the special moment of a new beginning, the person at the desk harbors great plans and desires to muster as much political energy as possible. Indeed, the American Constitution bestows a great deal of power on the country's president. The person sitting at the desk in the Oval Office is fully willing to exert this power and to start now with the business of governing.

For example, on March 5, 1933, such a situation existed. Franklin D. Roosevelt had taken the oath of office as president and on that day he had come to the Oval Office for his first day of work. He sat down at the desk of the president for the first time, and he desired to begin governing as the new president. However, he was unable to do so. His predecessor, Herbert C. Hoover, had cleared out everything. The drawers in the desk were empty, no piece of paper, no pencil could be found. Roosevelt, with impaired legs that made it impossible for him to walk, alone in the office, called through the open door toward the hallway, demanding that someone bring him something with which to write. It took some time until the yelling of the president of the United States was heard and a staff member arrived to provide the president, this powerful man, with the elementary instruments he needed for governing: paper and pencil.[15] Mitterrand found himself in a similar situation in the first days after his election on May 10, 1981. He was the new president of the French Republic, and he had assumed from his predecessor all the corresponding power. Indeed? All the power? Upon his arrival at the Elysée Palace the offices were empty. All the records and files had departed, too.

When power is assumed—this is the paradox—the power is not there. Rather, the circumstances are designed in such a way that a deployment of power is hampered or even obstructed. This is particularly true regarding the arrangements governing the wielding of political power in modern constitutional states. Constitutional government is erected as the foe of power; it mistrusts power generally and in principle and owes its origin to this mistrust. The object of constitutional government is liberty, so its purpose is to establish the rule of freedom and to secure freedom by constitutional rule. All power therefore is dissolved by the constitutional order and transposed into a play of power so that one power with its natural passion to expand meets another, equally expansive power. Thus each restrains the other and does so as involuntarily as effectively. The logic of this arrangement amounts to a paralysis of

---

15. Cf. Arthur M. Schlesinger Jr., *The Age of Roosevelt: The Coming of the New Deal* (Boston: Houghton Mifflin, 1958), p. 2 f.

power, which is, from the perspective of freedom, precisely the desired result. But what strength, then, is left to the rule and dominion of freedom?

While speaking to journalists whom he had invited for a New Year's celebration, Mitterrand reflected upon his own experience of paradoxical power in the context of constitutionalism. "On the one side," he said, "a President of the French Republic, even under the Fifth Republic, owns much less power than one thinks; on the other he owns more than most of the democratic heads of states." And he raised the question: "How to reconcile these contrasts?" and set out to formulate a response. The French president "owns much less power than one thinks because fortunately there are institutions and traditions; and [for] *a head of state amusing himself with ignoring the institutions and traditions, this would not go on for very long.*" Mitterrand explained that anyone who in holding power—in the office, for instance, of the French president—deems himself powerful makes a mistake: "Power spills out over all edges, like an overfilled casserole. Nothing really is possible in the long term if it stems from fantasy or arbitrariness." Yet, in evoking the black, power-swallowing hole that looms before the eyes of the prince, he is still a prince of power and, Mitterrand continues to explain, should not fool himself into thinking otherwise. There is all the political work that the prince can claim as his own. Even though power escapes, creativity remains: "What is so magnificent about power—always a limited power, in my view—is this: power allows [one] to have an effect on things and life."[16]

The Paradox of Creativity

The prince is bound and the prince is free to produce power. How will the prince do it? The question is put prematurely, for the prince will be obliged before he can do anything to wrestle with a second paradox, the paradox of creativity. Again, creativity results from the problem of governing, because the human beings whom the prince desires to govern have not waited for his desire to govern to manifest itself in order to go about their lives. On the contrary, they have been pursuing their lives all along and they too have been creative with respect to the forms by which they shaped them, and they remain that way even as the prince arrives. The creative intentions of the prince do not encounter an emptiness, a nothingness, from which his intervention for

---

16. Présidence de la République, Service de Presse, Document à usage interne, *Allocution prononcée par Monsieur François Mitterrand, Président de la République, lors de la présentation des voeux de la presse,* January 6, 1995, p. 2.

the first time produces, makes, and constructs something. The condition is precisely reverse. The creative intentions of the prince are opposed by a world full of things already created, full of existent forms and an ongoing creativity entirely independent of the creative intentions of the prince. The room where the creations of the prince are to appear is already occupied. So where is there room for the person called on to govern?

Mitterrand and his administration encountered this difficulty in a most instructive way during the first two years after they came to power. They wished to transform the economy of France according to their ideas on economic policy. However, the room for economic creations was occupied. The economy of France followed other laws than those of socialist planning and proved to be quite resistant to plans of socialist reform. The project of economic socialism encountered, not an empty or unorganized reality, but a replenished and highly organized reality that eluded governmental intervention. Was any creative effect possible? Had it not better be abandoned? On the other hand, did it not originate in a general mandate for creativity, namely, the will of the people to have a socialist government? In fact, it took almost three years for Mitterrand and his administration to find a way beyond this contradiction to devise an economic policy that permitted a creative approach within the paradox of creativity. The difficulties of the socialist project aroused by the conflict it engendered were caused by the same new beginnning that was supposed to have begun with Mitterrand's election. For the crowd celebrating his victory at the eve of his election on the Place de la Bastille, a new political creation was under way. In spite of its passing away as a swiftly shadowy metaphor, there is no other way to understand the chant with which their crowd welcomed the new master: *Mitterrand—Soleil!*

There was a reason for this. Everyone who wants to govern and hence to be elected or to receive under another form the consent of those to be governed, will promise a good government; and thus he promises something false. A government made by human beings (who are not only good but also bad) in a world of human beings (who are not only good but also bad) can at best be a beneficial, but not a good, government. The vision of the good is not an empirical reality; it would not even be needed if the world of humans—despite all their good intentions—were not anything but good. And yet, the person who wants to govern will do very little without arousing the people by a vision—by promises made in electoral campaigns. False things will be said. Without making false promises a candidate for a political office is not real. This matter of everyday politics is evidence of the paradox of creativity. Before his election in May 1981 Mitterrand promised the socialist heaven. At the same time, however, he remained the master in his art who knew "power is not the Lord of all the things that occur in the world and affect every country of which the world exist."[17]

The Paradox of Politics

It suffices to step onto the Champs-Elysées in the early evening after a day of work in the Elysée Palace to recognize the most elementary of our three paradoxes: the paradox of politics. A few strides, and the experience of a transition may be made by which one image of the constitution of the human world abruptly gives way to another, quite different one. One has done no more than leave an office in the palace and it is as if all reality had been overturned. Where still a few moments ago all things in the world had been perceived in the mode of a unity, there appears now a diversity conspicuously evident and split into thousands of parts. What had been thought to be there, as one glanced out of the windows of the Elysée, dissipates like a delusion. That the people out there were governed from inside the Elysée? How was it possible? How could one even have entertained such an idea?

A prince cannot ask himself this question or his actions would lose purpose. It is not possible to govern in the Elysée and be overwhelmed by the truth taught outside on the Champs-Elysées. The reality of politics is that of the many, each of whom has his own will and intentions, his own routes and aims, his own projects for actions and notions of life, personal itineraries and stations in the world, infinite possibilities in an infinitely free play of human connections, engagements, configurations, attachments, dissolutions, agreements, enmity, collisions, conflicts, friendliness, estrangement, dissension. A walk from the Elysée down the Avenue de Marigny to its intersection with the Champs-Elysées is a very short walk, and everyone can perceive the tableau: the chaos of human whirls, forming itself incessantly into a chaos.

This is the tableau the prince needs to behold continuously if he wants to be prince and to govern. And the prince must also behold continuously, willfully and meticulously, another picture, if his goal is truly to govern. Within the image of a prince the actual prince must hold together what otherwise would scatter, namely, the reality of the one and the many, of human beings in community and human beings in dispersion, of the polis and chaos. Since it arises from the diversity of human beings, there exists a world entirely different from the one within which government exists. The latter presents order;

---

17. Ibid., 6.

the former is full of confusion. Here, stability is the principle, there all is everlasting fluidity. This world is destined for a construction of unity. That world is always but a world of parts.

The prince governs in view of a world the reality of which is only assumed. Consider the day of President Mitterrand's inauguration: the world of the president appears to abide within the firm fabric of the ceremonial of the republic. France lives. It finds its incarnation in the new president. Toward him, the summit, and around him, the center, the French state organizes itself, with all its power internally and externally. Of this the ceremonial is the apparent symbolization. As the limousine in which the president is riding proceeds along the *via sacra* of the French Republic, the passenger could be thought to embody the spectacle of a world governed by him. He is the prince of power, and through him France is a great power. France lives, and she is powerful. She lives, yes, and she is also a plaything of the forces of speculation in the international financial markets. Inside the limousine sits a president who was told that speculation against the French franc is taking place and that its value on the markets cannot be maintained unless he does something very quickly. Interventions to support the franc have proven futile, and the reserves of France will be exhausted within one or two days, after which the rate of exchange for the franc will be dictated by international speculators. Such an event would change not only the status of France on the currency markets but its general position in the area of foreign policy as well. In other words, victory of the speculators would mean a defeat of the sovereign state of France.

There are several options for the French government to exercise in response to the monetary crisis, which is in reality a political crisis. However, his advisers have provided President Mitterrand with contrasting, conflicting counsel. Thus, the challenge of the speculation is exacerbated by conflicting opinions among the president's advisers. And time is running out. Outside the presidential limousine everything proceeds as the ceremonial of power has prescribed. Inside sits Mitterrand. He is supposed to capture by an act of will the vanishing sovereignty of France. Outside, the world of the president appears to be stable and ordered. Inside all is fluid, and the president must erect against it the dam of his decision. He may consider what is going on outside and act inside as if he were the *prince of power,* as if France were sovereign. Then he would want to seize in a reality of purely fluid things a firm and fixed power that is not there. He may follow the lead inside and act outside as if he were the prince of power and all France the stage of his might. Then he would want to display his power by pursuing a reality that continues to escape him. What will he do? Supreme power flew toward him today, and he lacked precisely the power of which today he was so much in need. And this was only the first day.

The Logic of Creativity in Politics

In characterizing Mitterrand, one of his former collaborators in the Elysée remarked: "The difficulty in governing is this: You must have a highly developed sensitivity for the complexity of things and you must be able nevertheless to reach a decision. Malraux showed it very well in *L'Espoir:* there he draws a character whose name is Scali and by whom it is maintained that you cannot be a person of action in being an intellectual, for the intellectual has by necessity a sense of complexity, and because a person of action cannot be other than Manichaean, and must be thought of as someone who believes that all others are entirely wrong and he alone is entirely right. That is the reason why people like Mitterrand are so interesting. He is an intellectual who has a highly developed sensitivity for the complexity of things and beings and one who nevertheless makes decisions. That is, you have to overlook the complexity of things at a certain moment."[18]

Mitterrand endured all these paradoxes. He governed by acting within them, and thus he really governed—within chaos, and not against it. And he governed by acting with them. So he governed by being creative, by embracing chaos and producing it himself. Mitterrand resisted the forces of reality that like Machiavelli's *fortuna* threatened to overwhelm him and make him the plaything of its caprices. He resisted fascination with power that, like *eros* in Plato's theory of constitutional cycles, sought to seduce him to a love of the world so great that he wanted it more and more to his liking. He adjusted himself midway, remained in the middle, prepared for reality and ready for power, in the midst of a play between chaos and form. He extracted structures from fluidity and forced structures back into fluidity. He was the French president in the Elysée, and he was the prince of *chaosmos*. For there is in the morphogenesis of governing, in addition to the paradoxes, a logic that the person who wants to govern may follow—will follow—to the degree that the person really wishes to govern. This logic describes the way of creativity in politics. It comes into effect when a person forms with other persons a government that is thought to be a creative goverment that exists in a fluid state between chaos and form. If creativity is intended to occur in politics, it demands a prince who

---

18. Maurice Benassayag, in *Le Cercle des intimes: François Mitterrand par ses proches,* ed. Caroline Lang (Boulogne: Editions La Sirène, 1996), 91.

as a government creates a *chaosmos* and thus the possibility of governing in the mode of creativity.

In Mitterrand's mind there existed no elaborate theory of paradox. When he was asked about it, he answered empirically with observations from a life in politics.[19] He thought in terms of everyday life, not political science, and he trusted what he saw. He felt no need to conceptualize his insights into the reality of human being nor the procedures that account for the operations of government. There was no reason for him to be familiar with the debate on the problem of governing in the tradition of American political thought and no reason for him to have encountered politically like-minded *confrères* who—like James Madison in the *Federalist Papers*—spoke no differently than he of the need to find a mode for the operation of government where contradictory things, things arranged and things fluid, "stability" and "liberty," are mingled. Informed by the literature of Baudelaire, he adopted a line from *Les Fleurs du Mal* to describe his mode of governing. "I hate the movement that shifts the lines," Baudelaire wrote. From this line Mitterrand took up one element. He dropped the verb and thereby imparted a causal, intentional, truly creative power into the noun. This was the power he spoke about, this was the power he referred to when he explained his idea of governing: "The movement shifting the lines."[20]

He defined the nature of governing by simple formulas and offered the advice: "You have to avoid habits." Generally, he behaved in such a way that people could learn from him. Not only the council of ministers was transformed occasionally into an academy of his teaching, but a group of fellow-travelers was transformed into a circle of friends or collaborators as well. He is said usually to have articulated himself with great ambiguity and thus to have practiced an elusive mode of thinking. The echo of his thought in the perception of others suggests, however, that he knew clearly what he thought: "I do not say that there is no ingenuity in Mitterrand—an ingenuity that is so apt that it can hurt. But at the same time and, above all, it shows a certain view of the nature of life: ambivalence.... This makes it so interesting.... This ambivalence induces him to relativize everything and in every regard, to see in every situation but another stage on an interminable way, because nothing is definitive, ever. I have learned from him that you have to judge life at its end and that something can be understood only after having run its course. There is no end, the way is the end."[21]

---

19. François Mitterrand, interview with author, March 17, 1994.
20. *The Federalist*, No. 63; Charles Baudelaire, *Les fleurs du mal*, chap. 17, "La beauté"; Mitterrand interview, in *Libération*, no. 923, May 10, 1984.
21. "Les réflexions de M. Mitterrand entre deux poses," in *Le Monde*, February 4, 1986; Laurent Fabius, in *Le Cercle des intimes*, 105 f.

The Primacy of Persons

Mitterrand not only taught the logic of creativity in politics, he practiced it. He embraced creativity completely, from the first principle. And this principle reads: to govern creatively is to heed the primacy of persons. Mitterrand therefore had very little interest in organizations. What interested him were people.[22] He developed a sense of reality that made him in the ordinary world of politics a phenomenon of a particular kind, bound to be misunderstood and misinterpreted. In this world, artifacts of language like the notions "state" or "government" are paired up with a reality of their own as if there were indeed the state or the government in the mode of realities *sui generis*. Supported and seemingly confirmed by the appearance of reality that effectively surrounds political institutions, this hypostatized view of the political world is very common. A world of institutions is abstracted from the reality of human beings: no one ever actually has seen such an institution as a government, and all who have looked have seen only the persons of whom it is said that they are the persons forming the respective government. As it is hypostatized into a world of institutions, the truth of the human world is perceived only partially. Everyone knows that this world consists of human beings, but few care to consider and to look at this world more closely, to discern the logic inherent in what they see. Those who do consider and look more carefully, and thus stay in touch with political reality in its unfolding *as* political reality, are led to the insight by which the truth of the human world discloses itself creatively. They experience the whole human world and view it then not only in the mode of its constitution—it comprises human beings—but also in the mode of its creation: it is made of human beings in being made by human beings. These, the human beings making it, are in this world the chief creative and world-forming element. Or, formulated in political terms: in a world of human beings, human beings hold the power to create and to form this world (of politics). A gathering of people is a gathering of power. For it constitutes in the human world precisely the element of which this world exists: its formative element. When human beings gather, purposing their political world, they are as creative as they can be: they create the power for the creation of their world.

All governing, then, begins with the people who have gathered to govern. "To have friends, is Power," Thomas Hobbes wrote in the *Leviathan*. A single person has the use of his "Naturall Power," such as extraordinary strength, prudence, eloquence, or nobility. In having friends, however, the natural power of this one person is augmented by the power of his friends: "For they are

---

22. Cf. Jean Védrine, in *Le Cercle des intimes*, 21.

strengths united."²³ In Mitterrand's life friendships were the strongest and most constant element. His life can be read as a book of friendship, to which from his early youth he added chapter after chapter, one circle of friends after the other, ever new throngs of friends woven continually into each other. He was a master in the art of friendship, and he cultivated it with the utmost care. For many years, he maintained friendships from the old days simply out of fidelity. Under the changed circumstances, of living in the Elysée as president of the republic and thus separated from the modest conditions where many of his friends remained, he did not forget them. The president of France remained the friend of his friends. For example, in the midst of meetings with other princes of this world he wrote postcards to his friends in the Morvan (Burgundy), simple people, but the people with whom he had made friends when he had been active among them as mayor of a small village.²⁴

In the course of his life Mitterrand created more and more his own party— the party of his friends. His friends united their strengths into one, namely, the power of François Mitterrand. With the manifold networks and configurations of support and loyalty that he constructed through his friendships, Mitterrand collected, according to a classical pattern, all the power he needed to attain his goal, namely, to ascend to the position of prince. He demonstrated the truth of the doctrine formulated by Thomas Hobbes, and he became similar to other princes who practiced the art of government. He drew his power to govern from the power of the people who had brought their strengths to him. Within a very long tradition, he formed a new example of the paradigmatic relation between government and the associations of friendship. A look into Roland Syme's classic study, *The Roman Revolution,* illustrates the creative logic Mitterrand followed, as did Augustus or Caesar. "The rule of Augustus was the rule of a party," we read there—and the word *party* does not mean a political party organization in the modern sense, but an association of friends. Or we learn that Caesar made "plans and decisions in the company of his intimates and secretaries." Furthermore, we find the statement: "Without a party a statesman is nothing." Concerning the ethos of political interests of friends, Syme tells us: "Loyalty could only be won by loyalty in return. Caesar never let down a friend, whatever his character and station."²⁵

Syme could have found in Mitterrand his Caesar, so identical appear the politics of friendship practiced by the French and the Roman prince. But

---

23. Thomas Hobbes, *Leviathan* (Harmondsworth: Penguin, 1972), part 1, chap. 10, p. 150.
24. Cf. *vsd,* numéro spécial, January 11–17, 1996, p. 68.
25. Ronald Syme, *The Roman Revolution* (1939; rpr., Oxford: Oxford University Press, 1960), 7, 55, 60, 121.

Mitterrand, naturally, did not have such a model in mind, so much as a strategy of power of his own choosing, when he made decisions for France in the "company of his intimates and secretaries" or refused to desert certain friends, "whatever their character or station," to the consternation and bewilderment of others. For he could not distance himself in the slightest degree from the bond of friendship, because bonds of this kind were the stuff of his power: friendship was the highest good, the wellspring and the mode of the creativity of power. From an association of individual persons in this or that constellation arose the power to be powerful, the power to govern; or to put it in one of those terse expressions that characterize the political language of the American political landscape: "Personnel is policy."[26]

The recent history of the American presidency provides additional proof for the wisdom of Mitterrand. Consider the questions Why give unconditional adherence to the primacy of persons? Do interests of friends really pave the way in politics? In the summer of 1979 the *New York Times* analyzed the situation of President Jimmy Carter in the White House. Three years had passed since he had become the president of the United States, and he was still unsuccessful in the power-based play of American politics. He had proven to be a weak actor who ran with his plans and initiatives directly into the power walls erected by other actors, the Congress especially. Why? The answer found by the *New York Times* was simple, significant, and instructive. Carter, yes, was president. But he was no prince. "The response, quite simply, is that he has no friends on Capitol Hill. 'He does not have this capital of loyalty upon which he could draw,' a Senator from the South said. 'If you are in trouble, you need friends for your defense, and that's exactly what he does not have.'"[27]

Creating Political Power: Problems and Strategies

Whoever wants to govern creatively produces creativity, which is to say, his power, by way of other people. They are the elements of the movement by which power swells and becomes the effect that it is. People prolong the movement through which power—creativity—occurs, movements of persons among persons toward persons that are called government. These movements are not, however, free movements undertaken within a vacuum of creativity. The political world which a prince governs is anything but a formless vacuum waiting,

---

26. Edwin J. Feulner Jr., as quoted by Ronald Brownstein, "Jobs Are the Currency of Politics, and the White House Is on Spending Spree," *National Journal* 15, no. 50–51 (December 15, 1984): 2386.

27. Cf. Steven V. Roberts, "Carter Accord with Congress: President Is Apparently Seeking to Ease Strains," *New York Times,* June 5, 1979.

as it were, for the creative acts of the prince. It is moulded, fashioned, carved throughout. It is, to be precise, full of forms: all that is formed here in the mode of power is but one formation of power among many others. The political world is new compared to everything else that has existed already in this world as a firmly entrenched form of power that resists pressure for change. Any organization, any institution, is definitively human: a form made of human beings. Yet, an organization or institution is also like a block that one seems to crash into and hit when one comes upon it from outside. It is a mass of resistance with its own gravity and weight of power that appears to be much stronger than the combined or even the individual strength of the persons who make the respective organization or institution. If one wishes to have an impact on an institution, it is like colliding with a rock. A less forceful but equally discouraging experience is to have any attempt at change be absorbed by the house of power and digested, without any visible consequences. To govern means to create power, through persons, on the one hand, and through forms of power, on the other hand, that allow creativity to break the institutional resistance encountered in the formation of power.

If this is not done, nothing is done. Truman had accumulated the experience of eight years as American president when just before his departure he responded to a question concerning his successor, president-elect Dwight D. Eisenhower. What did he think, he was asked, about the way Eisenhower might go about his new task? "He will sit there," Truman answered, pointing at the presidential desk, "and he will say: Do this! Do that! And nothing will happen." Franklin D. Roosevelt made similar remarks about the frustrations of power.[28] Mitterrand did not escape the problem, either. To exemplify his relevant experiences, he liked to refer to the difficulties he encountered in advancing his architectural projects as the *grands travaux*. He described eloquently the institutional resistance that had built up against the projects.[29] But he surmounted it creatively, by forming within and against the apparatus of the state all the power necessary for the implementation of his projects. "You know," he told journalists, "I had to defend the *grands travaux* like a cat and a dog."[30] Then he elaborated in order to "illustrate the lesson of power" that he had to impart.

"The power of the President of the Republic does not allow him at any time to decide that considerable sums, a billion francs for instance, are to be allocated, without several controls of such a decision." But the prince forms

---

28. Cf. Richard E. Neustadt, *Presidential Power: The Politics of Leadership* (New York: Wiley, 1961), 9; cf. Fred I. Greenstein, *Leadership in the Modern Presidency* (Cambridge, MA: Harvard University Press, 1988), 27 f.
29. In an interview with the author on June 15, 1993.
30. *Allocution prononcée par Monsieur François Mitterrand,* January 6, 1995, p. 7.

power and extracts from this creation of power the necessary power for himself to be more powerful than others in the contest of power.

> I was present and this was my power. It was, above all, a durable power and I prolonged it a bit... and I had the time, thanks to this condition. The administration of the state, undeniably, has its own qualities and in other respects is solid and present all the time too. But those who are politically in charge change continuously. And now I was President of the Republic, elected for seven years. And you multiply this by two and then you will see what you really have in mind! I said then, each time when Jacques Delors or Pierre Bérégovoy [ministers of finance in two succeeding French governments] came and stated: We must reduce the budgetary allotments, we cut them by so many percent.... Then I said, No, not these appropriations. Certainly, this is the power of the prince, I admit it! So what? There never would be an architectural policy in France, if the budget were established on an annual basis. It would be impossible. The necessary billions would always be missing because there is always a deficit. Hence I held my ground.[31]

"I held my ground." This is a plain statement. But precise as it is, it is again inexact. Any story that tells us what power is, draws the veil of the story over power. The transparency to which politics pretends is a mask of politics. How indeed did Mitterrand hold his ground in the contest of power over the *grands travaux*? The image of the cat and the dog is revealingly expressive. He could scratch and bite now and then. But how? With what? Power is not metaphorical, it recognizes only its own kind. There was but one way for Mitterrand: in order to advance the *grands travaux*, as with everything else he wanted to effect, he had to be powerful, he had to be able to exert his power against and within the governmental apparatus of the French state. He controlled paraconstitutional configurations of personal power that formed within the French political system and beyond it his second government, and in terms of power this second government formed his real government.[32] Mitterrand, of course, was not the first to have found as a response to the problem of power the necessity of forming his own governmental power within an existing system of government in order to command it. This response was known in China 1200 years ago.[33] Still, it was discovered in the twentieth century as movements toward central institutions that eventually were normalized and formally estab-

---

31. Ibid., 7, 8.
32. On the mask of politics, cf. Schabert, *Boston Politics,* 171 ff., 261 ff., and Schabert, "Wie werden Städte regiert?" in *Die Welt der Stadt* (Munich: Piper, 1991), 170 ff. On the concept of a second government, cf. *Boston Politics,* 53 f., and *Die Welt der Stadt,* 178 ff.
33. Cf. Tilo Schabert, *Die Architektur der Welt: Eine kosmologische Lektüre architektonischer Formen* (Munich: Wilhelm Fink, 1997), 30 f.

lished under the names the Elysée, the White House, or the *Bundeskanzleramt* (federal chancellery). These official agencies represent the power of the princes who govern us today.

Roosevelt was the first to overcome the resistance with which the existing administrative apparatus opposed his political plans, when he created one new government organ after the other, each designed in line with his projects and each organized around his position of power. He spread over the system of American government an increasing number of personal configurations of executive power, organs of governmental power of which he was the contriving and controlling center. And he expanded beyond himself, the president in the White House, a growing center of his personal government. In the American Constitution nothing is to be found about a White House, nor about the mighty agency of power that operates today in Washington under this innocent name. Originally the American president was supposed to go about his business assisted by a secretary or two, and until the administration of Franklin D. Roosevelt the behavior of American presidents did not contradict this idyllic image. With Roosevelt, however, the nature of the office changed. He expanded it by increasing the number of persons employed in the executive and by the growing net of institutional organs that enlarged it into a complex of power that furnished what he had sought: the power to govern. The successors of Roosevelt in the office of American president took over this heritage, as if it were the most natural thing in the world, and most of them—Eisenhower, Kennedy, Johnson, and Nixon, in particular—made it larger still. The White House today is an enormous agency of power available for the use of the prince; numerically, its size is on the order of 5,000 to 6,000 persons, and institutionally, it ranges over a multitude of organizational units that is as immense as it is unfathomable.

In the Basic Law of the Federal Republic of Germany a federal chancellory is not mentioned either, just as one would look in vain in the Constitution of the French Fifth Republic for any reference to the Elysée. And yet, in both cases, these constitutionally unknown terms denote an essential organ of government, if not the very center of political power. In Germany, the chancellor represents a constitutional organ, but not the chancellery; the French president represents a constitutional organ, but not the Elysée. Yet today both institutions occupy a paraconstitutional status. They shape preeminently the constitution within which Germany and France exist. They are, in Germany as in France, instruments of the prince, agencies of the predominant power reigning in the country.

Mitterrand could not have found a better prearrangement. It suited him exceedingly well. By the nature of his own political existence he was perfectly prepared to assume an office that was preordained to be the center of a second government, of personal configurations of executive power. Employing the power of the president in accordance with the established convention if it seemed useful to him, he did not hesitate to provide a minister with a junior minister whose loyalty did not belong to the minister but to him, the president. Thus he would rule the minister who, in public, would still appear to be his own man. As strategist of a plenitude of power who made his formal prerogatives effective, Mitterrand was continuingly preoccupied with acquiring power. He devoted a considerable amount of his time and energy to the organization of his influence and to the configurations of power that sustained it. He tried incessantly to control to the greatest extent possible the people and institutions of government, in order to extract from his official rule the personal power that alone enabled him to govern with this government indeed. This is what he alluded to but did not say explicitly when he compared himself to a cat and a dog.

Political Power: How Is the Powerful Prince Powerful?

The logic of creativity in politics induces princes to create a party of friends and the paragovernmental configurations of a second government. And it compels them to do something more. As much power as he may accumulate, the prince can never stop and rest; for the power of a prince is anything but constant. It is indefinite, uncertain, fluid. Depending upon the intensity with which the prince creates it, power is more present at one time and much less at another. It is not enough that the prince is powerful or, to put it more precisely, that the prince has become powerful in acquiring power. The prince must do more. The prince must continue to be powerful and maintain all the power accumulated in the state of power. Question: How does the powerful prince remain powerful? Answer: The prince keeps being powerful in ruling the people *with* whom the prince rules.

To compel others to do what one wants them to do, this is the task the prince needs to perform unremittingly, and even more so as he continues to acquire more power. It is a task by which the prince unwittingly reviews the prince in examining his own capacity to create again and again all the power held. The prince is submitted to a test as relentless as it is continuous. Is there still enough of one's own power left to make others do what one wants them to do and thus to have in them sources for power to feed on? There is no choice, because whoever governs can never govern without the help of others. The responsibilities for the conduct of governmental affairs have to be carried by many. But is it not *the prince* who wants to govern? Yes, and consequently the prince must distribute functions of authority in such a way that it is still *his own person* who governs, even if many others govern for this person too. But in which ways can this be arranged?

The German chancellor Konrad Adenauer used to withhold information from the messengers bringing it; in not showing any particular reaction, he refused the informant any opportunity to know what he thought about the information given, or whether it had any effect upon him, and if so, of what kind. In his practice of power Mitterrand applied precisely the same plan. It was one of the modes by which he pursued the preservation of his power.

Also, he seduced whomever he could and thus involved many people in a trust that restrained them, while his own liberty only grew: "He has a knack in talking to people. It's all charm, his way of speaking, his whole manner, his whole language. He says: 'Between us, . . . dear friend. . . .' And the interlocutor always has the feeling to have a special relationship with the President, to be in his confidence."[34] In this way Mitterrand spun, in the Elysée, threads of power by which, knotting variably the net of his rule, he could keep his collaborators in a constant movement; they followed the movement of his designs. He involved his collaborators in the dynamics of a distant intimacy, by which they were both close to and removed from him and thus, in any case, always uncertain as to their exact place in the circle of all his confidants.

Another tool in the practice of power was developed and refined by President Roosevelt when he habitually drew his knowledge from a variety of sources. Frequently he brought several of them to bear on the same policy matter. By this method he received different reports, enabling him to use each report to check the quality of the others. He could also control the collaborators producing the reports and, if necessary, correct and criticize each of them by virtue of the efforts of the others. Mitterrand also systematically arranged the work of his collaborators in this way and thereby avoided what Roosevelt had likewise avoided: becoming the prisoner of one particular view, or of one particular adviser. Since it was impossible to obtain by himself all the data, documents, ideas that he needed (or wished) to know and to consider, he had to rely on others to research and inquire for him. Such a system of delegation, however, brought with it the danger that he would become subordinate to the choices and orientations of subordinates. In order to avoid this possibility, Mitterrand, in the continuing creation of his power, was compelled deliberately to thwart and to confuse the work of his advisers. Thus he remained master unto himself and unto the advisers, being able still to determine what he knew, thought, and decided.[35]

---

34. Roland Dumas, in *Le Cercle des intimes*, 53.
35. Cf. Maurice Benassayag, ibid., 91 f.

Roosevelt drew around himself (to present a further technique in the practice of power) innumerable circles of authority that overlapped, infringed upon each other, and formed a chaotic maze. None of the persons assisting him in governing escaped this maze. To each he assigned an area of authority that encroached upon the responsibility of others, leaving everyone unaware of the overall plan. When his collaborators realized that they had stepped out of bounds, often after quite some time, they still did not know upon how many areas of authority they infringed nor upon whose areas they had encroached. In addition, Roosevelt stated his views quite ambiguously when he charged someone with the responsibility for a certain matter. To be able to act, his collaborators were obliged to define for themselves the range of their actions, and in so doing, they inevitably collided with each other. But this had been precisely Roosevelt's aim: whoever emerged at the top proved they had the talents Roosevelt wished to promote and attract to himself. Furthermore, the conflicts among his aides and advisers enabled him to assume among them the role of the superior mediator and arbiter.

In interviewing the collaborators of Mitterrand (intermittently during the period 1992–1995) I pursued again my experiment in a twofold way. I described in some detail the chaotic maze by which Roosevelt had governed, and at each particular point my interlocutors responded with a mixture of amazement and amendment, exclaiming: "But this, of course, this is Mitterrand! The method of the president, perfectly! That is he who rules this way, and has done it all the time, I know no one else being so good at it." I was corrected, but the correction did not refer to the paradigm of governing that I described so much as the identity of the person of whom I spoke. And I did not talk about Roosevelt, but asked my interlocutors in the way of someone who is ignorant how they would describe Mitterrand's methods of governing. They were the guides, I was the novice. And as I listened and took in the details, certain familiar features were drawn in my mind in the mirror of the statements made about Mitterrand: this was Roosevelt. There he was, in the White House, in the midst of his maze of power. No, this time, it was Mitterrand.

He gathered around him aides, advisers, associates, who, simply because of the diversity of their dispositions, origins, and professional experiences, could not easily get along: the senior diplomat dressed in the discreet suit of a light blue, quite in the style of his caste, perennially punctual, exquisitely courteous and correct; the young social activist in her ragged jeans and washed-out parka, superbly lax in keeping her office hours and appointments, storing her files in her backpack on the floor of her office; the boring fellow from the socialist party, exiled into an office at the Elysée much too big for him, not really knowing what he was supposed to do there; the extremely competent and beautiful woman, expert in economics and gifted with an overpowering analytical intelligence, with which she promoted her own disturbing ambitions; the clownish grassroots politician, subservient to his master, the prince, and otherwise filled to the brim with power, putting on for everyone the masquerade of his jesting. They all were there. Thrown together as they were, they could not help irritating, fascinating, repelling, alienating, captivating, motivating, and fighting each other, organizing through themselves precisely the chaos Mitterrand desired. Into this collection, which can only be sketched here, let us introduce the one person who, owing to a particular character, would constitute a most exemplary element of disorder (and was it), meddling in everything, putting on airs toward everyone, jealously seeking the exclusive favor of the master, commenting incessantly on all the master's words and deeds, soliciting, entreating, posing himself as the mirror of his prince in that figure formerly employed at noble courts, the *Fou du Roi en titre d'office*. Waiting for the self-organization of chaos—the cat!—a new structure (for another stretch of time), that would advance his rule, in having as its constituents people who had endured the chaos and had found in it a place. A demonstration of power in a withdrawal of power. This pleased the prince. It released the power that he sought.

And Mitterrand appropriated the outlines of power thus presented, until the moment invariably arose when he felt the need to have such outlines arranged in a new, different, transforming configuration. Then he agitated the chaos and unhinged its equilibrium. And chaos, organizing itself again, created his rule anew.

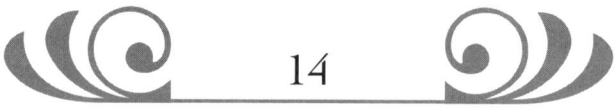

Common Sense and the Rule of Law
Returning Voegelin to Central Europe

Martin Palous

ATHANATOI THNETOI THNETOI ATHANATOI
—Heraclitus

(Mortals are immortals and immortals are mortals.
—John Burnet translation)

An elementary fact in the history of thought is the emergence of philosophical schools around prominent thinkers. The disciples of a master strive to preserve his work for the future, to carry through his basic intention, and to continue in the implementation of the task pursued, but unattained by him, in his lifetime. Such schools do not usually last more than a generation. After a while, the most talented disciples start seeing beyond the limitations of the standpoint from which their teacher approached philosophical problems and come to realize the unattainability of the tasks he had set for himself. At a certain moment, they come to the conclusion that it is no longer possible to continue on the road marked out by him, that they are at a crossroads where they

---

The principal sources of these texts are the drafts of two papers I presented at annual meetings of Eric Voegelin Society in 2000 ("Eric Voegelin, 'Common Sense,' and Central Europe," presented in Washington, DC, 2000, and "The Rule of Law and Common Sense: Returning Voegelin to Central Europe," presented in Philadelphia, 2003).

have to take new decisions, to unveil the open questions and issues behind all the answers the master's philosophical "teaching" contained. Paradoxically, however, this moment of destruction of the teacher's legacy does not necessarily mean its absolute end, its retreat from the human world, and its passage into oblivion. On the contrary, it is exactly here that we can find the key to his potential immortality. Only when he is overcome and problematized, when he is removed from heaven to the earth, does the philosopher gain his place in the dialogue of great, "immortal" thinkers across the borders of civilizations and centuries.

To guess now what place in the overall spiritual context of the twentieth century will belong to Eric Voegelin (1901–1984), whether he will be seen to have affected a fundamental shift in the sphere of political thinking (as his disciples and followers seem to believe) is premature. At the same time, however, it is clear that the open-ended process of Voegelin's possible immortalization has started. Voegelin is undoubtedly one of those contemporary thinkers who, probably against his will and in spite of his own warning that philosophy will not allow itself to be closed into any systematic philosophical teaching, did create a kind of philosophical school. During his academic career in the United States and later in Germany, Voegelin influenced decisively a significant group of philosophers, theologians, political scientists, and cultural anthropologists who now find themselves at the summit of their professional careers and who are convinced that the principal task of their own work is to keep Voegelin's philosophical legacy alive. They have published *The Collected Works of Eric Voegelin*, they organize Voegelin conferences and write studies and monographs on him. They have founded the Eric Voegelin Society, which, since 1985, holds its annual meetings as a part of the conventions of the American Political Science Association.

All this clearly demonstrates that Voegelin was indeed an exceptionally successful and influential teacher and that his legacy represents a very powerful inspiration. In a few years, a global network of Voegelinians has been created, a chain of people as if united by a single philosophical will, sharing Voegelin's fundamental conviction that it is still Plato, Aristotle, and other classical thinkers who should teach us what is (and what is not) philosophy, and that it is philosophy in this classical sense that remains during this time of crisis the single most important weapon to be used "in defense of civilization." The aim these contemporary Platonists (a kind of Platonic Academia operating in the postmodern environment of today's globalizing world) strive for seems to be guided by a single intention: to initiate a Renaissance of classical political thought, to rediscover the liberating power of classical political ideas, to retrieve the dimension of philosophical dialogue for our current political discourse.

Nevertheless, time and tide wait for no man. First-generation Voegelinians have already reached their "acme," and one might raise the question of the future of their project. What will become of Voegelin's legacy in the long term, from the point of view of the dialogue of mankind across the borders of civilizations and centuries? Despite the disciples' efforts at disseminating the ideas of the master, the "Voegelinian revolution" in political thought, as announced in 1982 in a book of the same name by Ellis Sandoz,[1] one of the most prominent American followers of Voegelin, seems yet to be completed. It is realistic and fair to admit that Voegelin's influence on the mainstream of current political thought remains limited. This state of affairs is illustrated by the fact that texts on Voegelinian themes present almost exclusively a positive and accordant interpretation of his teaching. The fact that Voegelin is usually presented as an unrivaled master in matters of political thought demonstrates that the destructive, critical phase of work on his philosophical legacy, which may well be the true test of his actual greatness and key phase of the process of his "immortalization," has not yet begun—or if it has, then it evidently remains at a timid, initial stage. Where will the Voegelinian debate and research be, let us say, thirty years from now? Can we imagine that? Will Voegelin still be recognized as a great, truly "revolutionary" philosopher of the period? Or will this image be reduced by the passage of time, and Voegelin "only" remembered as one of those educated Central Europeans born at a tragic time, uprooted from their domestic environment, living their lives on the periphery of the big world, leaving behind only faded photographs, collected volumes of their works, and gradually disappearing traces of their personal struggles, which were no doubt heroic and respectable but did not make a real difference from the point of view of the universal history of the spirit?

Anamnesis

In raising all these essentially unanswerable questions, I am well aware of the serious limitations of my contribution to any ongoing Voegelinian debate. To clarify my perspective, I will recall my own anamnesis. I will begin in the 1980s in socialist Czechoslovakia, when my own introduction into the world of Western philosophy and my first encounters with Eric Voegelin's thought took place. Then I will focus on the radical change brought by the Velvet Revolution of 1989, which reopened our society, a society that had been kept closed

---

1. Ellis Sandoz, *The Voegelinian Revolution: A Biographical Introduction* (Baton Rouge: Louisiana State University Press, 1981).

for more than four decades, and offered to all its members an opportunity to take part in the political process of rebuilding democracy. In the light of new experience, I have been forced to reexamine my approaches to, and my reading of, the fundamental problems of classical political philosophy, not least of all because I have been able to start communicating with the international Platonic Academia of Voegelinians.

I ran across the name of Eric Voegelin for the first time in the early 1980s, in meetings of "Kampademia," a small group of friends who got together with a bold and somewhat quixotic intention to "revive" the tradition of Socratic/Platonic thought in the midst of a small Czech society stricken in the second half of the twentieth century by the totalitarian plague. Our common teacher was Jan Patočka, one of the last students of Edmund Husserl and undoubtedly the greatest Czech philosopher of the twentieth century. He decided to take a bold, genuinely Socratic step toward the end of his life. Almost seventy years old, he became one of the first three spokespersons of Charter 77.[2] He died only two months after the charter's original declaration, on January 1, 1977, of a heart attack suffered after a series of prolonged police interrogations. Patočka's phenomenological research on the "natural world of human existence" (Husserl's *Lebenswelt*)[3] and especially his philosophy of history, which was elaborated step by step in his private lectures in 1970 and finally sketched in the form of six "heretical essays,"[4] represented the principal points of departure and perhaps the most frequent topic of our disputes and conversations. Through

---

2. Charter 77 was published on January 1, 1977, and publicly asked the government of socialist Czechoslovakia to respect human rights of its citizens, rights guaranteed by two international UN Covenants (the International Covenant on Civil and Political Rights and the International Covenant on Economic, Social, and Cultural Rights) that "were signed on behalf of our Republic in 1968, confirmed in Helsinki in 1975 and came into force in our country on 23 March 1976." Charter 77 was created as "a free, informal, open community of people" that expressed its wish "to conduct a constructive dialogue with the political and state authorities" about various matters of public concern and authorized three people to serve as its first three spokespersons: Jan Patočka, philosopher; Václav Havl, playwright; and Jiří Hájek, international lawyer, who was for a few months in 1968 the Czechoslovak minister for foreign affairs.

3. *The Natural World as a Philosophical Problem* was the title of Patočka's dissertation. First published in Czech as *Přirozený svět jako filosofický problém* (Prague: UNKUČ, 1936); 2nd ed., *The Natural World in Its Author's Reflections after Thirty Three Years* (Prague: Československý spisovatel, 1970), with a new introduction. The English translation does not yet exist. The book is available in German: *Die Naturliche Welt als Philosophisches Problem in Jan Patočka: Ausgewahlte Schriften*, vol. 1, ed. Klaus Nellen (Stuttgart: Klett-Cota Verlag, 1989); and in French: *Le monde naturel comme un problème philosophique*, trans. Jaromír Daněk and Henri Decleve, *Phaenomenologica* 68 (The Hague: Martinus Nijhoff, 1976).

4. The English version is available as Jan Patočka, *Heretical Essays in the Philosophy of History*, trans. Erazim Kohák, ed. James Dodd (Chicago: Open Court, 1996).

Patočka, and under his guidance, we were all introduced not only to the basic ideas of phenomenology formulated by his great teacher but also to the works of many other contemporary philosophers and political thinkers: Hannah Arendt, Eugen Fink, Martin Heidegger, Karl Jaspers, Emanuel Lévinas, Paul Ricoeur, Leo Strauss, and Eric Voegelin. I remember well the lively exchanges after the presentations of Pavel Bratinka, who gave us an introduction to *The New Science of Politics* or of Zdenek Neubauer, who talked about *The Voegelinian Revolution,* inspired by the above-mentioned book by Ellis Sandoz. I also made my own contributions to this debate, being fortunate enough to own the first four volumes of *Order and History*. I received them, thanks to the Jan Hus Foundation, which not only sent us many books during the 1980s but also sponsored visits to Prague of dozens of renowned Western scholars (including Charles Taylor, Roger Scruton, David Levy, Jürgen Habermas, Ernst Tugendhat, Richard Rorty, Norman Podhoretz, Jacques Derrida, Jean-Pierre Vernant, Jean-François Lyotard, Emmanuel LeRoy Ladurie, André Glucksmann, Alain Finkelkraut, Pierre-Jean Labarrière) to give lectures and to challenge our naïve and sometimes uninformed enthusiasm for philosophy, which we conceived following Patočka as a "new possibility of life" in a "shaken situation."[5]

How then did Voegelin's thought fit into our "academic" context at that time? What were we searching for in our ongoing dialogue(s)? What were the main questions with which we were occupied during the last years of European communism? Recently I re-read the publication of some of our seminars from 1983 and 1984 that had been recorded and transcribed.[6] With all the reservations and doubts that such a *recherche du temps perdu* can raise twenty years later, it was, indeed, an interesting experience. To characterize the inquisitive atmosphere of our seminars and the fundamental aim of our "philosophizing," I can use the blunt formulation employed by Voegelin as the title of one of the chapters of his *Autobiographical Reflections:* "Why Philosophize? To Recapture Reality!" We all would have subscribed to Voegelin's equally blunt statement that the motivations of his work arose "from the political situation":

> Anybody with an informed and reflective mind who lives in the twentieth century since the end of the First World War, as I did, finds himself hemmed in, if not oppressed, from all sides by a flood of ideological language—meaning thereby the language symbols that pretend to be concepts but in fact are unanalyzed

---

5. Jan Patočka, "The Beginning of History," ibid., 41. The Prague activities of the Jan Hus Foundation in Prague are described by Barbara Days in her book *The Velvet Philosophers* (London: Claridge Press, 2000).

6. T. R. Korder, "Voegelin a Patočka," *Athanaeum Rozmluvy* 45 (1988).

topoi or topics. Moreover, anybody who is exposed to this dominant climate of opinion has to cope with the problem that language is a social phenomenon. He cannot deal with the users of ideological language as partners in a discussion, but he has to make them the object of investigation. There is no community of language with the representatives of the dominant ideologies. Hence, the community of language that he himself wants to use in order to criticize the users of ideological language must first be discovered and, if necessary, established.[7]

We certainly were resisting not only "a flood of ideological language" but also its political incarnation in the form of an "advanced totalitarian regime."[8] This regime tried desperately to preserve its power in the face of a changing international environment in Europe initiated by the so-called Helsinki process and, after 1985, by the policies of *perestrojka* of the new Soviet leader, Michail Gorbačev. In the Czech context, the regime's attempt to survive meant attempting to destroy our "parallel polis," which had been founded by the declaration of Charter 77.[9] No matter how complicated and even dramatic the circumstances might have been, we were trying to do in our regular academic meetings what Voegelin suggested in the above-quoted passage: to discover and, if necessary, to establish an alternative community of language in order to understand ourselves and our current situation in the world. We did this in order to recover and explore our place on the spiritual map of an emerging global mankind and to connect our personal stories (under the influence of Patočka) to philosophy and philosophy of history.

The reason I threw myself into the study of Voegelin's *Order and History* was clear and simple: I was struck from its opening pages by the power of Voegelin's arguments and found the way he worked with the classical texts and ideas congenial with and complementary to the style of philosophical work of our teacher. Both Patočka and Voegelin pursued their own philosophical projects by summoning all their education and spiritual strength. They both formulated their big questions and proceeded methodically on original paths of thought that ran, nevertheless, parallel to each other. At the same time, thanks to their unusual seriousness and the existential urgency of their respective situations, they moved, in the words of Parmenides, "far from the beaten paths

---

7. Eric Voegelin, *Autobiographical Reflections,* ed. Ellis Sandoz (Baton Rouge: Louisiana State University Press, 1989), 93.
8. The best analysis of how an "advanced totalitarian regime" works and how it keeps the enslaved population under its control can be found in Václav Havel's essay "Stories and Totalitarianism," in Václav Havel, *Open Letters, Selected Writings, 1965–1990,* ed. Paul Wilson (New York: Alfred A. Knopf, 1991), 328–50.
9. More information about the dissidents' "parallel polis" can be found in *Civic Freedom in Central Europe: Voices from Czechoslovakia,* ed. H. Gordon Skilling and Paul Wilson (New York: MacMillan, 1991).

of humans."[10] Nonetheless, as genuine philosophers, they both were excellent interpreters of the history of ideas, true guardians of the authenticity and integrity of philosophical language, which originated in the efforts of concrete men and women in the past to articulate their finite experiences of encounters with the transcendent source of order within their concrete historical societies. Under their guidance, we were being introduced into a philosophy that was less a metaphysical doctrine made up of true propositions about eternal and unmovable Being, and more a way of life and a kind of movement of human existence, the aim of which was to "live in truth," to keep open the possibility of human life to "escape one's own ignorance." Even for a layman or dilettante such as I, both Patočka and Voegelin were able to open the forgotten and largely unnoticed layers of the Western spiritual tradition. They helped me to rediscover the meaning of basic concepts and symbols used in philosophical discourse. They shook me out of my shell of presumed certainties and evoked for me the metaphysical depths that lay beneath the surface of facts and data that had to be explored and known by anyone who wished to understand and to articulate meaningfully our concrete situation within the universal horizon of human history.

Reexamining the contributions I made to our seminars during 1983 and 1984, I have no illusions about their quality or even the originality of their message. On the contrary, their language betrays not only the lack of skill and experience of the contributor, but the power of the Baconian "Idols of the Market Place"—when "the ill and unfit choice of words wonderfully obstructs the understanding"[11]—no matter how strong was my desire to overcome them or at least get them under control. Being inspired and taught by genuine philosophers such as Patočka or Voegelin, we were invited despite the flaws, imperfections, and evident amateurism of our academic conversations, and in the context that was determined by our current political existence in Central Europe, into the society of classical thinkers, including Socrates, Plato, Aristotle, and many others. Thanks to this apprenticeship, we could participate, in our own way, using our modest resources and capabilities, in the never-ending dialogue of mankind initiated in ancient Greece and other centers of the civilized world many centuries ago. The Socratic appeal to care not so much about "money and honor and reputation" but rather about "wisdom and truth and the greatest

---

10. "Parmenides: Peri Fyseos," in Herman Diels, *Die Fragmente der Vorsokratiker,* English, ed. Allan F. Randal, quoted from The Classic Internet Library, http://home.ican.net/~arandall/Parmenides/.

11. Francis Bacon, *The New Organon* (On True Directions Concerning the Interpretation of Nature), 43, in *Selected Works of Francis Bacon,* available, http://www.constitution.org/bacon/bacon.htm.

improvement of the soul"[12] meant in the interpretation of Patočka or Voegelin much more than a superficial invitation to take up "die Moralphilosophie" caricatured by Hegel in his *Vorlesungen über die Geschichte der Philosophie*.[13] What was clearly at stake here for us was the future identity of the heart of Europe and the power of the great ideas and symbols of the past to be mobilized in the concrete situation of our "polis" that was finding itself in the 1980s in one of its worst crises.

The Velvet Revolution of November 1989 brought a radical change to our world. Thanks to the collapse of communism, Central Europe reemerged as an active player in the field of international relations. The decades of the cold war had created a "frozen" system of national societies, which now had given way to a new opportunity to set out on a journey from totalitarianism to democracy. The new situation terminated for obvious reasons the existence of the dissidents' "parallel polis" and brought a new challenge to what I have always considered the most important part of my public engagement: to assist in the rebirth of classical political ideas in our current context and to enhance with their help our capacity to understand our world. While our philosophical "Kampademia" still exists, holding its regular quarterly "conventions," its original pathos of resistance is irretrievably lost, and our aging conversations are taking place in the climate of ideas that is not so conducive to the "remembrance of the things past" as to realizing again and again the dangerously growing gap between past and future.

The new social and political context shaped by our newly gained freedom did not leave my reading of Voegelin untouched. On the one hand, I have had the chance to become acquainted with the activities of a global network of Voegelinians and have benefited greatly from it. I have gained an opportunity to study Voegelin's *Opera Omnia,* volume after volume, to read the abundance of the secondary Voegelinian literature, to participate in the ongoing Voegelinian dialogue within a group of distinguished scholars, and to present my own insights, comments, and eventual discoveries at the regular annual meetings of the Eric Voegelin Society. On the other hand, being pushed forward by the irreversibility of historical time, growing older, and becoming more and more

---

12. Cf. Plato, Ap. 30a–30b, quotation from the English translation by Benjamin Jowett, The Internet Classical Archive, "Apology by Plato," available, http://classics.mit.edu/Plato/apology.html.

13. "Indem Sokrates auf diese Weise der Moralphilosophie ihre Entstehung gab (wie er sie behandelt, wird sie popular), hat ihn Alle Folgezeit des Moralischen Geschwatzes und der Popularphilosophie zu ihrem Patron und Heligen erklart, und ihn zum rechtfertigenden Deckmantel aller Unphilosophie erhoben; wozu noch vollends kamm, dass sein Tod ihm das popularruhmende Interesse des Unschuldig Leidens gab" (G. W. F. Hegel, *Samtliche Werke,* Band 18, Zweiter Band, ed. Hermann Glockner [Stuttgart, 1959], 47).

perplexed, not only by all the difficulties of our own transition to democracy, but by all the intricacies of the New World Order emerging from the ruins of the Old One, I realized that my perception of political ideas has also been changing. I had to admit that in the current situation I am simply unable to read Voegelin in the way I had originally, that I have some difficulties with my original understanding of the Voegelinian project aimed at the "defense of civilization," and that despite the fact that it is among Voegelinians where one can find a living political thought today, there is something problematic, at least from my own point of view, in the prevailing focus and style of current Voegelinian research.

Struggling with my personal loss of direction, I have started looking for a new point of departure. Surprisingly, I did not find it in the realm of ideas, among Voegelin's fascinating insights into their history, that made him without any doubt one of the greatest philosophers of the twentieth century, but in his *Autobiographical Reflections.* The Voegelins' escape from Central Europe, and his encounter with American "common sense," have led me to raise the following questions: Is it not here, in Central Europe, where Voegelin's anabasis, which began in the 1930s when totalitarianism, once characterized by him as a "cadaveric poison of Western civilization,"[14] was on the rise, must come to its end? Is not this potential homecoming rather than all these efforts to summarize the results of Voegelin's Herculean "search for order," and the attempts to compare or confront them with the products of other philosophical schools and traditions, the biggest challenge for the Voegelinian legacy at the beginning of the twenty-first century? Is it not in the midst of singular, passing human matters, and eventually not only in Central Europe, where we should be looking for Voegelin's proverbial Rhodos and where the question of potential immortality of his teaching must be tested?

Having raised these questions, my plan for this essay is to attempt to answer them as follows: in section 3, I will reflect upon how Voegelin's encounter with the pragmatism of William James, with its emphasis upon pluralism and the rejection of the "monistic" epistemology of the neo-Kantian provenance, unconnected with some established European tradition, could inspire Voegelin to rediscover the lost treasure of classical philosophy, tragically absent in the European political discourse of the time. In section 4, I begin by discussing the concrete problem faced by Voegelin in his sixteen-year-long teaching experience at Louisiana State University in Baton Rouge, that is, how to explain what

---

14. Eric Voegelin, "The Origins of Totalitarianism," in *The Collected Works of Eric Voegelin* (hereinafter, *CW*), vol. 11, *Published Essays, 1953–1965,* ed. Ellis Sandoz (Columbia: University of Missouri Press, 2000), 15.

is the nature of law to his American students. I will argue that it is Voegelinian jurisprudence, informed by classical political philosophy and influenced by the American tradition of "common sense," that should inspire the Central European search for a new identity in the world after 11/9 and 9/11.[15]

Escape from Central Europe and Discovery of American Common Sense

Let us begin with the facts of Voegelin's biography. Born on January 3, 1901, in Cologne, Germany, in 1910 he moved with his parents to Vienna, where he received his education: first at the gymnasium and then at the University of Vienna, where he studied political science at the Faculty of Law with Hans Kelsen. International events led to a radical change of the Viennese scene during the course of Voegelin's studies. During the monarchy, Vienna enjoyed the relatively liberal, cosmopolitan atmosphere of a world metropolis. Defeat in war, however, resulted in the disintegration of the empire and in the emergence from its ruins in 1918 of a republic, albeit one lacking the free republican spirit. The liberalism typical of the Viennese imperial era was replaced by petit bourgeois narrow-mindedness and a general sense of grievance about historical injustice. Instead of cosmopolitan tolerance typical of the "world of yesterday" of the former rulers of Central Europe (described so persuasively from a Jewish perspective in Stefan Zweig's autobiography), there was the rise of petty Austrian chauvinism, xenophobia, ideologically motivated encounters of antagonistic social classes, and general spiritual decline and loss of direction. There were, of course, deeper reasons for this transformation; it was not merely the hangover of military defeat and a decline in power; it was also an omen of a deep spiritual and social crisis that in the postwar period began to engulf the whole European continent, culminating in the assumption of power by totalitarian political movements and a second world war. This shift framed Voegelin's political experience and the elementary existential point of departure of his philosophy.

The academic environment (and Voegelin moved around almost exclusively in that environment) was more resistant to the general decline. Reading of the way he planned his academic training, the names of the people who taught

---

15. On November 9, 1989, the fall of the Berlin Wall ended the "short twentieth century," the "age of extremes" (Eric Hobsbawn, *The Age of Extremes: The Short Twentieth Century, 1914–1991* [Harmondsworth: Penguin, 1994]); and on September 11, 2001, Islamic terrorists attacked New York and Washington, reminding mankind what kind of threats and challenges are coming in the dawn of a new globalized age of the third millennium.

him, the places where he studied, and the different disciplines he encountered, one cannot but be amazed by the wide range of possibilities available to the young scholar, by the quality of contemporary spiritual life, and by the high standards of university education in Austria in those days, notwithstanding the political and spiritual decline of the country. Nevertheless, the "decline of the West," as is clearly implied in Voegelin's reflection, was not only felt as a political problem but was becoming increasingly apparent in the intellectual milieu as well. Perhaps that is one reason why Voegelin's intellectual striving was so inseparably linked to the private seminars held among a circle of friends called the *Geistkreis*. It included Alfred Schütz, with whom Voegelin exchanged a written discussion of Husserl's phenomenology, as well as a number of others whom Voegelin later met again in American exile. The *Geistkreis* was a group of young enthusiasts who discussed everything that aroused their inquisitive minds. Even so, the very existence and mission of the group reflected the shifts occurring in the world of Austrian academia. Although its beginnings were inconspicuous, gradually the center of authentic intellectual life moved into the private sphere, where it remained free from manipulation by the state.

Despite Voegelin's receiving his introduction to the world of European learning from an impressive line of German and Austrian professors, a major influence in Voegelin's academic development was his trip to the United States in 1924–1925. As a Laura Spellman Rockefeller Fellow, Voegelin was given his first opportunity to become acquainted with the American university environment and to compare it with his European experience. The encounter with America became his destiny. This is where he encountered "common sense," which "spoiled" him, as he said, to such a degree that from then on he was unable to exist non-problematically within the framework of the venerable and cultivated philosophical traditions of Central Europe. Whereas the European discussion of political and social phenomena moved within a vicious circle of contending philosophies and schools (mainly of neo-Kantian provenance) and thus neglected the increasingly gloomy contemporary political situation, the American way of political thinking was quite different. It did not lean primarily on one or another philosophical school and tradition but was inspired by concrete political events, namely, the foundation of the American republic, the adoption of its Constitution (that henceforth was understood as the source of the "good life" of American citizens), and its further development and protection, which were generally perceived as the basic guarantee of freedom and human dignity. In brief, America presented itself to Voegelin as an amazing synthesis of classical thought, which he had striven in vain to restore in his Central European environment, and the best components of the Christian tradition that, in his view, was also desperately lacking from European modernism. The pragmatism of William James and John Dewey, the philosophy of George Santayana, Whitehead's lectures at Harvard University, and also the solid American theory of law and government, which existed independent of the intellectual heights of philosophy, all that had such a strong impact on Voegelin that he returned to Europe, as he said, a changed man, unable any longer to exist in an increasingly restricted, narrow, and philosophically sterile European environment.

Voegelin's philosophical diagnosis of the crisis of European civilization in the twentieth century transformed him into an uncompromising critic of emerging totalitarian movements and especially of National Socialism. His opposition, however, placed him in immediate jeopardy following the Austrian *Anschluss.* Originally his conversion to Anglo-Saxon "common sense" made Voegelin "unfit for further existence in Central Europe," but German Nazis and their project of the Thousand Year Reich forced him to leave Vienna and become an exile. In March 1938, he fled under dramatic circumstances to Switzerland, and shortly thereafter he left for the United States.

Why did American "common sense" alienate Voegelin not only from contemporary European politics but also from the dominant modern tradition of European political thought? Why was it in the United States of America, in a democratic republic of the New World, which took upon itself more than once in the twentieth century the burden of defending Western civilization against totalitarian barbarity having its origin on the "old continent," that Voegelin rediscovered the liberating power of classical, pre-modern, political thought?

To answer these questions, let us look briefly at the way the problem of "common sense" was approached by one of the great figures of American pragmatism, William James. In his lectures of 1906–1907 (published in 1907 under the title *Pragmatism: A New Name for Some Old Ways of Thinking*),[16] James stated clearly what he understood to be "common sense." It was, he said, "our fundamental way of thinking," discovered already by "exceedingly remote ancestors, which have been able to preserve themselves throughout the experience of all subsequent times," that forms "one great stage of equilibrium in the human mind's development."[17]

The fundamental philosophical question analyzed by James was the problem of *noesis,* the problem of knowledge and knowing. What does it mean to know something? What kind of relationship is established between "knower"

---

16. William James, *Pragmatism: A New Name for Some Old Ways of Thinking* (New York: Longmans, Green, 1907). All quotations in these essays are from *The Writings of William James: A Comprehensive Edition,* ed. with an introduction by John J. McDermott (New York: Modern Library, 1968).

17. Ibid., 420.

and "things to be known"? What ontology is commensurate with the world in which man is able to live as a rational being? Can the classical philosophers, who for the first time formulated the great ontological questions and discovered the fundamental ideas of Western thought, help us in our efforts to understand better our contemporary situation and improve our capacity to use our own "common sense"? According to James, there are two approaches to the problem of noesis: monism, which corresponds to the perennial philosophical quest for the unity of the world, or pluralism. In his lecture "The One and the Many" James says:

> The great monistic *Denkmittel* for a hundred years past has been the notion of the one Knower. The many exist only as objects for his thought—exist in his dream, as it were; and as he knows them, they have one purpose, form one system, tell one tale for him. This notion of an all enveloping noetic unity in things is the sublimest achievement of intellectualist philosophy.[18]

The hypothesis of the "oneness," of the universe, of one world consisting of things seen by an omniscient knower "as forming one single systematic fact," the hypothesis of the actual world being present to the senses of a human spectator always within the finite horizon of his mortality, but "complete eternally," has important implications. Its discovery and conscious acceptance signal a genuine revolution in the historical process of human self-understanding. From this moment on, any theory of knowledge, any plausible answer to all concrete questions emerging from the fact that man is endowed with the capacity of reasoning, that he is able to distinguish in his own noetic activities between pure reason (dealing with matters of truth and untruth), ethical or practical reason (working primarily with the distinction between good and bad), and aesthetic reason (attributing the quality of beautiful and ugly to the things in the human world), has no other choice but simply to take the "monistic" hypothesis into consideration. The "knowing" man must get rid of everything that does not comply with it. He has to leave, as if forced by its coercive power, his pre-critical past behind and enter into a new universalistic era dominated and permeated by modern "science." In short, the necessary consequence of the "Copernican revolution" made in European history by Immanuel Kant is the birth of the modern European spirit with its progressivist understanding of human history, the most important implication of which is the ontological degradation or even the conscious denial of all human knowledge that previously helped man to orient himself in the world, namely, his "common sense."

18. Ibid., 411.

The stance of pragmatic American philosophers must be seen as a gentle and thoughtful rejection, not of the value of Kantian arguments, which were praised highly by William James, but of that absoluteness with which the monistic philosophy was presented. Against the ontological hypothesis that enthrones the one Knower "conceived either as an Absolute or as an Ultimate," the pragmatists raise the counter hypothesis that the widest field of knowledge that ever was or will be still contains some ignorance. Some bits of information always may escape. This is the hypothesis of noetic pluralism, which monists consider so absurd. Since we are bound to treat it as respectfully as noetic monism, until the facts shall have tipped the beam, we find that our pragmatism, though originally nothing but method, has forced us to be friendly to the pluralistic view. It may be that some parts of the world are connected so loosely with some other parts as to be strung along by nothing but the copula "and." They might even come and go without those other parts suffering any internal change. This pluralistic view, of a world of additive constitution, is one that pragmatism is unable to rule out from serious consideration. But this view leads one to the further hypothesis that the actual world, instead of being complete "eternally," as the monists assure us, may be eternally incomplete and at all times subject to addition or liable to loss.[19]

When we adopt a pluralistic view of the world, several fundamental things change. First of all, we lose the systematic and static conception of *noesis* as seen by the one omniscient knower and consisting of individual pieces, the validity of which has been "scientifically" tested and assembled into a coherent and non-contradictory whole. Instead, we focus more on the problem of *noesis* as a process, on the dynamic aspects of the life of mind we are part of in spite of our finite bodily existence. We start discovering the temporal dimensions of a fundamentally human situation that was discovered first by Socrates and two generations later philosophically analyzed by Aristotle, who defined humans as those who do not possess the divine knowledge of the One Knower but are always striving to escape the ignorance they are aware of, because "by nature (they) desire to know."[20]

> Our minds [or our knowledge, as James sometimes stated] thus grow in spots; and like grease spots, the spots spread. But we let them spread as little as possible: we keep unaltered as much of our old knowledge, many of our old prejudices and beliefs, as we can. We patch and tinker more than we renew. The novelty

---

19. Ibid., 418.
20. *Pantes anthrópoi tou eidenai oregontai fysei* (All men by nature desire to know). Aristotle, *Metaphysics* 980a21, trans. W. D. Ross, The Classical Internet Library, available, http://classics.mit.edu/Aristotle/metaphzsics.l.i.html.

soaks in; it stains the ancient mass; but it is also tinged by what absorbs it. Our past apperceives and co-operates; and in the new equilibrium in which each step forward in the process of learning terminates, it happens relatively seldom that the new fact is added raw. More usually it is embedded cooked, as one might say, or stewed down in the sauce of the old.[21]

This figurative description of the process within which human knowledge is acquired, grows, and is altered in the course of time clearly implies a different, and much more positive, attitude of the "pragmatist" toward "common sense" than was the position of monism. At the same time, pragmatism has an incomparably higher appreciation for singular facts that are given in the immediate experience of individual human beings who live in the presence of the known past but who are open toward the unknown future. In short: pragmatism as a noetic stance is much more embedded in the concreteness of human life than in abstract generalities apprehended by those who subscribe to a monistic school of thought. It respects the most fundamental fact of our *noesis*, that the bulk of our knowledge is inherited from our ancestors, from our family or tribe, from the society, culture, and civilization into which we were born. At the same time, however, pragmatism is ready to test the truths we received from the past and still believe in against the changing realities of our life, against all these challenges to which we are exposed, as free human beings, beings who had no choice but to act on their own, to use their own capacity of judgment, and to make, at the right time, the right decisions.

In this regard, the distinction made by James between the use of "common sense" in practical talk, as man's "gumption and good judgment," and in philosophy, which understands by "common sense" the "use of certain intellectual forms and categories" inherited from the past, is not as great as it might seem from his own distinctions and definitions. Pragmatists are indeed interested in and want to explore what may be "our fundamental ways of thinking, which have been able to preserve themselves throughout the experience of all subsequent times," as customs, habits of thought, or beliefs. They are well aware that without these discoveries, sometimes of our "exceedingly remote ancestors," our capacity of good judgment and good action would be damaged and paralyzed. Truth as the supreme noetic category and "good" as the basic orientation point of our practical life come together again in the pragmatic perspective, bridging the gap between them and other transcendentalia (*esse, verum, bonum, pulchrum*) that began in Western civilization with the advent of the modern age.

> Truth is one species of good, and not, as it is usually supposed, a category distinct from good, and coordinated with it. The true is the name of whatever proves

---

21. James, *Pragmatism*, 419.

itself to be good, in the way of belief, and good, too, for definite, assignable reasons. What would be better for us to believe? This sounds very much like a definition of truth. It comes very near to saying what we ought to believe: and in that definition none of you would find any oddity. Ought we ever not to believe what is better for us to believe? And can we then keep the notion of what is better for us, and what is true for us, permanently apart?[22]

In short, the shift from the "monistic" perspective, which has long dominated modern European thought, to the point of view adopted by American pragmatism can heal our contemporary spiritual disease, according to Voegelin. Because the move from monism toward pragmatism opens the door again to classical political thought, it can help to restore the impaired balance of the European political mind. From the pragmatic perspective, one can rediscover under the conditions of modernity the classical Socratic question concerning the human good and the question of humans "giving an account" of their lives, and the question of caring about "the greatest improvement of the soul," to repeat once more the above-quoted passage from Plato's "Apology." One can recapture for contemporary use the meaning of the classical concept of politics as a form of life of free human beings, the meaning of the classical concept of law, that only the ruler is capable of making all citizens equal, and the meaning and scope of natural rights, which are inalienable because they are not the product of human activity but have been established by God.

All this explains why "pragmatism" is a genuine American philosophy and why a pragmatic attitude characterizes more than anything else the frame of the American political mind. There is more: the rediscovery and new "pragmatic" reading of Aristotle and of the other classical political philosophers by the American founding fathers served as one of the major spiritual inspirations for the American Revolution.

Although the fundamental orientation of Voegelin's philosophy remained as it was in his Viennese period, the political circumstances of his work dramatically changed. Voegelin became an American citizen in 1944. The United States, according to him, was the only country that could save Western civilization politically; at the same time, it offered a solution for its spiritual rebirth. Life in crisis-stricken Central Europe may have called for the existence of a Socratic Voegelin, but life in America enabled him to adopt a Platonic perspective. He tried to explore the phenomenon of the crises of European civilization in their full amplitude, taking note of all the ontological implications and penetrating to the very heart of contemporary problems. In order to understand the blind alley where mankind found itself in the middle of the twentieth

22. Ibid., 388–89.

century, and to help cure the disease destroying the European spirit, Voegelin was ready to study the vast amount of material belonging to the discarded spiritual heritage, both European and non-European. He would use not only the instruments he brought with him to America from his Central European past but also the American inspiration of "common sense," which had served him as a beam of light in the Dark Times of the European civilization. His task, however, was enormous. Not being designed as a regular academic project but rather as an emergency operation in defense of civilization, it can evoke in the mind of a pessimist the memory of the eternal punishment of the mythical king Sisyphus, or perhaps, for a more optimistic observer, one of the heroic tasks of Heracles.

Relentlessly and earnestly, Voegelin struggled through the history of mankind in order to complete his work on the new science of politics and the new philosophy of history, the central theme of which is the never-ending struggle within human society between the forces of order and disorder. What we see, however, when we examine the results of his efforts, is not the hero returning victorious from his battles, but a philosopher whose results have the power to generate insights. But alas, when they were erected into an *opus*, they seem to disintegrate in the author's hands. Voegelin returned humbly, again and again, to his point of departure and tried to embrace the accumulated material mastered with such unparalleled effort into his grandiose thought-construction. Instead of the originally planned history of political ideas, he produced a study of the relation between history and order. But even this project remained unfinished. The never-ending search for order grew increasingly distracted by the classical philosophical theme of preparation for death and meditation that aimed beyond the sphere of ephemeral human affairs.

Common Sense and the Rule of Law

Let us reconsider Voegelin's intellectual biography with special focus on the question of the law. I contend that reflection on Voegelin's life experience and his "return" to Central Europe is especially important. It is in the realm of jurisprudence where Voegelin's ideas should first be studied and possibly "applied" if Central Europeans are to understand their totalitarian past, re-examine their historical identity and their vision of the world, and reformulate their political programs for the twenty-first century.

Voegelin studied law at the University of Vienna under Hans Kelsen, undoubtedly one of the most important European jurists of the twentieth century. He was the author of the "pure theory of law" and the founder of an enormously influential school of legal thought, especially in Central Europe.²³ Sharing with Voegelin the fate of the political refugee, Kelsen also spent the second half of his life in America, although intellectually their paths diverged. Kelsen represented for Voegelin the end of a certain European tradition, a tradition that had to be properly understood and seen within its own historical context and also within its own limits. The limitations of Kelsen's "pure theory of law" provide the reasons why, according to Voegelin, we should start the search for the way out of the current impasse. We should start testing our capacity to understand our own situation as far as the idea of law and its place in human society is concerned with Kelsen, and we should be looking to him for "a point of departure for an advancement toward the reconstruction of a complete political science."²⁴

In 1927, Voegelin wrote a small article with the aim of introducing Kelsen's *Allgemeine Staatslehre* to the American public.²⁵ From the American perspective the least comprehensible aspect of Kelsen's legal thought is its foundations in neo-Kantian positivistic logic, although his basic arguments depart from the Marburg school of Simmel and Windelband. What determines the character of the legal materials—legal codes or statutes, procedural rules, case-law, and so on—is not their actual content, but the form in which they are given, their specific a priori, in Kantian terminology, that is antecedent to all forms of experience. Before studying or constructing any positive legal system one must be aware of the fundamental distinction between the "original categories" of *Sein*, Being, or Existence, which refer to the realm of what is, and *Sollen*, ought, or Essence, which refers to the realm of what should be. This basic distinction becomes clearer when we move from the ontological to the epistemological level: the distinction between *Sein* and *Sollen* is translated into the distinction between the causal method of natural sciences, which considers the causal relations among existent things, and the normative method applied in cultural sciences, which deals with all various aspects of cultural objectification.

The basic aim of Kelsen's "pure theory" is to approach the law strictly as a

---

23. In the Czech Republic, Kelsen's students (František Weyr, Ota Weiberger, Václav Chytil, Vladimír Kubeš, Zdeněk Neubauer, Karel English, Jaroslav Kaláb, Jaroslav Krejčí, Josef Kepert, Adolf Procházka, Jaromír Sedláček, just to name the most accomplished ones among them) formed the so-called Brno School of Theory of Law (Brněnská škola právní teorie). Its influence is still remarkable and has a profound effect on our current postcommunist jurisprudence and constitutional discussion. (Cf., for instance, "Brněnská škola právní teorie," Universita Karlova v Praze, Karolinum, 2003.)

24. Eric Voegelin, "Pure Theory of Law and of State," in *CW,* vol. 7, *Published Essays, 1922–1928,* trans. M. J. Hanak, ed. Thomas W. Heilke and John von Heyking (Columbia: University of Missouri Press, 2003), 98–99.

25. Voegelin, "Kelsen's Pure Theory of Law," ibid., 182–91.

positively given normative system, that is, as a structured, hierarchically organized, and complete whole, composed of elementary legal rules (maxims) derived from the basic norm (*Die Grundnorme*), which is the first and supreme legal maxim that articulates the primordial will of the sovereign, namely, the state. The simplest analytical element of this system, the norm, must have a clear formal structure corresponding to the normative a priori of *Sollen*. The norm, *Rechtsatz*, must be, Voegelin explains to his American readers,

> composed of two parts: The first contains a statement concerning unqualified human behavior, the second makes a statement concerning the coercive behavior [*Zwangsakt*] of the state official. The complete rule is a hypothesis making the coercive behavior of the state official dependent on the previous occurrence of the behaviors and events stated in the first part of the rule.[26]

As a result of this formulation, Kelsen's concept of the state, which is developed in his *Staatslehre*, departs from the neo-Kantian paradigm. For Kelsen, the state is fully identified with its law. It is conceived as the materialization of the will of a concrete human society created by raising protective walls of legal order around all the manifold forms of its life. The state should not be built, justified, or explained as a shelter of its national, religious, cultural, or linguistic identity, but only as the sole source of its law and the guarantor of its sovereignty. According to Kelsen, the theory of state has to cope first with the question of its origin and its position within international society under international law; then it proceeds to its basic law, the state constitution, the purpose of which is to provide the overall composition or anatomy of state. Next Kelsen discusses the state organs that perform their diverse functions in the process of the creation of norms and their enforcement; finally he considers all concrete forms and procedures that explain how the principle of *Rechststaat* is realized in all diverse relations between the citizens and the state and among the citizens themselves.

From the beginning, however, it is evident that the reduction of legal orders to "a system of postulates in the realm of *Sollen*" can indeed "surprise the American lawyer who is accustomed to a wealth of rights, duties, privileges, powers, liabilities, and disabilities."[27] It was, moreover, problematic and in a way self-defeating. No matter how purified Kelsen's theory could be of non-normative content and the remnants of state doctrines originating in natural law, it never could be fully dissociated from the reality of the human society

26. Ibid., 185.
27. Ibid., 184, 185.

that it was supposed to form and order. The legal theories of his predecessors, German jurists such as von Gierke, Laband, Gerber, or Jellinek, reflected the rise of Bismarck to power and agreed with his ambition to unify Germany and rebuild it as a modern constitutional federal state. For Kelsen, the main point of reference was the reality of the dismemberment of the Austro-Hungarian Empire, following its defeat in the Great War, 1914–1918. His "pure theory of law" based on the categorical distinction between *Sein* and *Sollen,* which pretended to isolate the normative legal order from any undesirable interference from the higher echelons of "naturally ordered" human society, simply could not remain isolated from real events happening in the human world. Can one imagine a better illustration of the fundamental problem of the neo-Kantian foundations of Kelsen's legal doctrine than the fact that Kelsen, who had been asked to draft the new Austrian constitution and who proceeded to do so as much as possible in conformity with the principles of his "pure theory," saw his finished work influenced, changed, and forced to conform to the empirical, historically determined Austrian political reality?

Nonetheless, no matter whether the Austrian constitution was "pure" or "tainted," in 1927 Voegelin still spoke about it in unambiguously positive terms. He considered Kelsen's practical achievements not only as "the most important event in the modern history of constitutions from the point of view of legal technique," but "with its background of the pure theory of law," as "a remarkable contribution to the development of democracy."[28]

He concluded his article with a kind of summary of Kelsen's position that showed no sign of the approaching spiritual crisis:

> By transferring the legal system into an ideal realm of meanings and reducing it to an instrument, Kelsen destroys any undue respect for existing legal institutions. The content of law is shown to be what it is: not an eternal, sacred order, but a compromise of battling forces—and this content may be changed every day by the chosen representatives of the people according to the wishes of their constituencies without fear of endangering a divine law.... No state entity hides behind the law and issues the legal rules; every rule can be traced back to its origin in a definite governmental agency, which again is but a part in the machinery set up for turning out legal rules in accordance with the desires of different social groups. The pure theory of law thus signifies not only an important progress in legal analysis and technique, but also a development from the half-absolutistic philosophy of the German empire toward the spirit of the new democracy.[29]

28. Ibid., 190.
29. Ibid., 190–91.

"The spirit of the new democracy" that prevailed in the years right after World War I did not, however, long endure. Totalitarian movements seized power first in Italy, then in Germany, and in both countries profound changes in the form of government took place by means of constitutional amendments, and so in continuity with the existing legal order. Austria was first transformed from a democratic republic to an authoritarian state and, a few years later, annexed to Germany. Both Kelsen and Voegelin had to escape from Central Europe and found their new homes in America. Kelsen devoted his time to the new international law initiated by the creation of the United Nations. Voegelin focused on the history of political ideas and elaborated the foundations of his "new science of politics." He returned to the fundamental questions concerning the nature of the law and jurisprudence in his courses taught at Louisiana State University from 1954 to 1957.

The historical events that took place in the world during the three decades that passed between the publication of Voegelin's article about Kelsen in 1927 and the appearance of the mimeographed "temporary edition exclusively for the use of students" registered in Voegelin's course on the nature of the law in 1957 changed substantively the situation of mankind and heavily influenced the development of Voegelin's thought.[30] The world after Auschwitz could not, as was plainly stated by Karl Jaspers, become the same as it had been before the German Reich started implementing its hegemonic plans and waged the war upon anyone who dared to oppose them, eventually against the whole world of Western, Judaeo-Christian civilization. The unprecedented crimes against humanity committed by the Nazi regime, which showed respect neither for elementary human decency nor for "common sense," had a mobilizing effect and catalyzed a strong international response. As Voegelin put it in his famous review of Hannah Arendt's *Origins of Totalitarianism:* "What no religious founder, no philosopher, no imperial conqueror of the past has achieved—to create a community of mankind by creating a common concern for all men—has now been realized through the community of suffering under the earthwide expansion of Western foulness."[31]

But what happened after the war was also far from satisfactory. On the one hand, the main war criminals were tried before an International Court of Justice and a new international organization, the United Nations, was created with the intention of eliminating wars and enhancing peaceful relations among

---

30. "Editors' Introduction," in Eric Voegelin, *CW,* vol. 27, The Nature of the Law *and Related Legal Writings,* ed. Robert Anthony Pascal, James Lee Babin, and John William Corrington (1991; available Columbia: University of Missouri Press, 1999), xiii.
31. Eric Voegelin, "The Origins of Totalitarianism," in *CW,* 11:15.

all nations of the world. The problem, however, was that the Soviet Union, one of the victors in the war, was one of the main vectors of the totalitarian disease. The new internationalism under the aegis of the United Nations, which raised hopes in many people that mankind was finally finding itself on the way to the realization of the Kant's old project of "perpetual peace," was simply not based on a realistic assessment of the emerging international situation because it did not reflect at all its crucial aspect, namely, the Soviet threat. For a political realist, such as George Kennan, who was the first to make this point in his famous long telegram from the American Embassy in Moscow and who was later assigned to formulate the basic principles of U.S. postwar foreign policy, the right response to the emerging challenge was not a utopian belief in the persuasive power of Kantian ideals. He would send a very clear message to the Soviet enemies of American values and Western civilization: the policy of "containment." The result, which was realistically achievable, the "bipolar political architecture" in Europe, had the following implication for Europeans: the inhabitants of the Western half enjoyed freedom and gradually progressed from the painful postwar reconstruction toward prosperity under the American security umbrella. The nations of Europe's Eastern half (including a substantive part of what used to be Central Europe) were deprived of freedom and united with the Soviet Union "forever," as one of the favorite ideological slogans of totalitarian rulers went, and so sentenced to life in the totalitarian prison under Soviet domination.

In short, observing the international developments in the 1950s when Voegelin was teaching in Baton Rouge, there was only one obvious conclusion under pain of renouncing the requirements of "common sense": World War II clearly did not bring the solution to the world crisis caused by the emergence of totalitarianism. Soviet communism was definitely not a partner with the countries of the Free World to be appeased and invited to participate in a dialogue concerning the new world order, a dialogue that had been constituted "through the community of suffering under the earthwide expansion of Western foulness." On the contrary, the rise of the Soviet Union to the position of a world power was an ominous sign, demonstrating how challenging it would be to protect the spiritual foundations of Western civilization in the future.

If in 1924 Voegelin was a young, talented, and well-educated man whose basic aim was to build a bridge between his Central European background and the newly discovered American experience, and who still could believe optimistically after the Great War of 1914–1918 that "the pure theory of law" could provide a historical bridge to "the spirit of the new democracy," thirty years later as an accomplished and respected scholar in the field of political science and philosophy his own life experience had demonstrated more forcefully the depth of the current spiritual and political crisis of European humanity. Voegelin was above all a classicist whose fundamental objective was to reexamine the richness of classical political ideas and symbols and restore them to life, to start with their help a new chapter in the dialogue of mankind. He was in the middle of a successful academic career in America, where he had discovered a "promised land" of pluralistic common sense practiced in American politics and jurisprudence. Being confronted with various aspects of life in his new home, Voegelin gained, he said, "an understanding... of the plurality of human possibilities realized in various civilizations, as an immediate experience, an *experience vécue*."[32] This enlarged understanding of American common sense opened before him a vast and never-ending search for order as it unfolds and exists in human history. When he distributed the mimeographed synopsis of his course among his students, "Voegelin's only comprehensive and systematic text on law," he already had acquired an articulate knowledge of both the method and the objective of his own research. As it is stated clearly in the editors' introduction to volume 27 of Voegelin's *Collected Works*:

> It is a product of the mature Voegelin. He wrote it at a time when he had settled upon the necessity of abandoning his original plan of writing a history of political ideas, published *The New Science of Politics* and the first three volumes of *Order and History,* and taught the course of jurisprudence four years. He had come to realize that ideas do not have a history, that only people do, and that their history consists of their successes and failures in the differentiation of their noetic and pneumatic experience of life under God. For the same reason, he had to come to realize that law cannot have a history apart from the history of the society whose order it articulates, and that its essence, or nature, is precisely the structure of the society whose law it is.[33]

The way Voegelin opened his inquiry into the nature of the law had to be surprising for the average American student unprepared for philosophical arguments and accustomed to the standard pragmatic American jurisprudence, where the meaning and content of all concepts were perceived primarily in relation to their ability to organize the thought of practicing lawyers. Voegelin asked: What makes the law, law? What is its essence, in spite of the fact that there is "a plurality of legal orders accepted as valid in a corresponding plurality of societies"?[34] In order to answer those questions, we do not start by com-

---

32. Voegelin, *Autobiographical Reflections*, 33.
33. "Editor's Introduction," *CW*, 27:xiii–xiv.
34. Voegelin, *The Nature of the Law,* ibid., 7.

paring different laws and legal systems. Rather we must depart from the phenomena of law as they are given in our daily, pre-analytical experience, as they exist in the world in which we live and understand ourselves with the help of our "common sense."

Voegelin started his quest by provisionally accepting Kelsen's view that the law is a system, "an aggregate of rules," enforced in a concrete historical society and characterized by their timeless validity. Observing how a legal system functions, we see immediately that the validity of its rules does not stay the same but "comes and goes," appears and disappears in time. The legal order is not a static system but an entity that finds itself in a permanent process of change. It obviously cannot change all its parts at once. When we say "it changes," we necessarily mean that its own "essence" is of a "historical" nature, that "there remains, from one change to another, an unchanged corpus of rules sufficiently large to retain the identity of the order."[35] Formerly valid rules (rules that have been derogated or abrogated by new ones) and rules that are going to be valid (rules *de lege ferenda*) simply cannot be treated as invalid rules without further qualification, argued Voegelin. The identity of legal order, the source of the validity of its norms is inseparably connected to the fundamental fact that it has not only a presence as "an aggregate of rules," but also a past and a future.

The temporal character of legal order becomes even more obvious when we raise the question of its validity, not in the abstract, but in the context of a concrete legal action, let us say the specific decision of some court. "The court decision is the point at which the law becomes valid for the concrete case." We began with the law as "an aggregate of valid norms" and then had to deal with the problem of change; now we are confronted with the problem that reminded Voegelin of the "Zenonic paradoxa":

> If we remember the aura of uncertainty that surrounds every serious litigation, we must admit that we never know what the aggregate of valid rules really is as long as the court has not handed down its decision in the concrete case. Once the court has reached its decision, the particular aggregate whose validity has become complete with the decision, and thereby incorporates the decision into itself, belongs already to the past. If, therefore, validity is "of the essence of the law," and if every aggregate of rules in the series called legal order belongs either to a past in which it is no longer valid or to a future in which it is not yet valid in the decisive concrete case, then "the law" seems to have disappeared altogether from the realm of existents.[36]

35. Ibid., 12.
36. Ibid., 16–17.

So, what is the law? To summarize again Voegelin's answer to his American students: the law cannot be conceived as a separate entity but must be analyzed and understood in the context of social order. The attention that is usually paid only to the content of norms or eventually to their practical use in concrete situations should be directed also, and perhaps primarily, to those structures within which the law is given to us on the pre-analytical level of our experience. The law in the sense of the aggregate of valid rules that has come into existence in the process of lawmaking defined and regulated by the highest, namely, constitutional, norms must be reconnected with the pre-analytical understanding of the law within a concrete historical society that is being ordered by the law in such a fashion that it respects and guards the law as the very substance of its order, as its fundamental value and *conditio sine qua non* of its own existence.

Such a reconnection between the law and the pre-analytical experiential basis in the context of which the law is originally given opens a new field of inquiry and generates a new set of questions. If the above-mentioned Zenonic argument brings to our attention the temporality of the law, the fact that it is not primarily a static aggregate of norms but a process whose fundamental objective is to order a society and to make its individual members free and equal, the emphasis on the phenomenological approach in the field of jurisprudence points to the problem to be singled out in Voegelin's examination:

> the equivocal use of "the law" in the sense of valid rules made by organs of government and "the law" that somehow pervades the existence of man in society. What is preserved in this pale equivocation of our everyday language is the profound insight, rarely to be found in contemporary legal theory, that "the law" is the substance of order in all realms of being. As a matter of fact, the ancient civilizations usually have in their language a term that signifies the ordering substance pervading the hierarchy of being, from the God, through the world and society, to every single man. Such terms are the Egyptian *maat*, the Chinese *tao*, the Greek *nomos*, and the Latin *lex*.[37]

I do not need to keep following Voegelin's train of thought to point out the central message of his jurisprudence course: to realize that one cannot inquire into the nature of the law without being able to raise the fundamental questions concerning Western history that can be formulated only with the means of Western philosophy. I have no way of knowing how Voegelin's American students reacted to this turn from the realm of experience they could examine with the help of the American brand of "common sense," to the vast area of

---

37. Ibid., 24.

ontological problems that can be identified only within the open field of the universal history of mankind. Nonetheless, what is evident is that their teacher was a genuine philosopher who did not want to miss a single opportunity to challenge the way that the people whom he encountered perceived and understood their own affairs, to shake them out of their shells, to lure them from the *terra firma* of their alleged commonsensical certainties to the depths that open by the virtue of raising fundamental philosophical questions, to tell them that they should "care for their souls," and thus not be satisfied with opinions only, but seek true knowledge if they wanted to act prudently, to serve the "common good" of their societies, and to keep them open to reality and free.

Looking back on what has happened in and with Central Europe in the past fifteen years, one has to admit, first of all, that the situation has grown much more complicated because the impact of the collapse of Communism has been much wider and more far-reaching than it seemed to be during the earlier days of the revolutions that set the whole region on the path of democratization. We certainly need to accept the "rule of law" as the main principle upon which to rebuild our states and the whole region and to complete our return from our Babylonian captivity to Europe, to reintegrate ourselves to the transatlantic community of open societies, respecting unalienable human rights and freedoms, allowing our economies to be regulated by market forces and not by governments, and accepting the culture and form of democracy. We certainly need "common sense" to overcome or at least to reconcile ourselves to all these unfortunate Central European traditions, which are dying hard and changing slowly, that caused us many troubles and much individual suffering in the past century. We desperately need to make the right choices here and now, at the current historical crossroads, in the context of the new threats to Western freedom with which global mankind is confronted in the beginning of the new millennium. However, to absorb and "metabolize" the novelty of our situation we need a renaissance of classical philosophy in Central Europe, as it is gravely needed in the rest of the world.

Above all, we need to listen attentively and respond to the call that is connected with the great Central European philosophers of the twentieth century, such as Jan Patočka and Eric Voegelin. Their greatness and their potential immortalization is based on the fact that both were classicists and understood the message that is conveyed in the fragment of Heraclitus that is used as epigraph in this essay: mortals are immortals and immortals are mortals. How should we understand this cryptic statement? What does it mean? It turns our attention to the middle term between mortality and immortality. It does not turn us away from our transient political matters. It just reminds us, as old Socrates did, that we should care first for something that is more important than "the greatest amount of money and honor and reputation...wisdom and truth and the greatest possible improvement of the soul." Whether this message is persuasive enough to be taken seriously by a sufficient number of Central Europeans today remains to be seen. Socrates himself failed to persuade the Athenians at his trial. But it is certain that if it were missed altogether and fell only on deaf ears, our hopes for freedom and the efforts to reintroduce democracy to our region after the collapse of Communism in 1989 would alike be in vain.

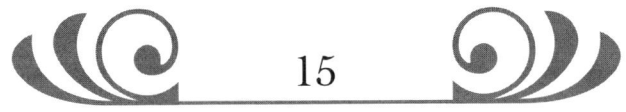

Civilizational Conflict and Spiritual Disorder

Michael Franz

I

During the late 1990s, the clash of civilizations was a debatable possibility. Today, the clash is an ongoing reality that dominates global politics, and indeed the events of 9/11 may someday stand as a tear in the fabric of history dividing two distinct eras. That remains to be established, of course, and since the future is open and unknowable, speculation about its course—much less its end—is not a proper object for philosophical or scientific analysis. Nevertheless, it is clear that the course of future events will be affected in part by how policy makers, political scientists, and the attentive public conceive the configurations of order and disorder surrounding us during the present period of cross-civilizational conflict. Democratic societies act differently under different conceptions of the forces arrayed against them, and conceptions of the forces arrayed against the West are probably in greater flux at the moment than they have been at any time since ideological blocs began to rival individual nation-states as actors in world politics.

If it is difficult to recall a time when conceptions of our political circumstances were both as important and unstable as they are at the moment, it is also difficult to recall a time when such conceptions were influenced as strongly as they are now by a single book, namely, Samuel P. Huntington's *The Clash of Civilizations and the Remaking of World Order*.[1] Huntington's book, published

---

1. Samuel P. Huntington, *The Clash of Civilizations and the Remaking of World Order* (New York: Simon & Schuster, 1996). All citations hereafter are to the Touchstone Books paperback edition, 1997.

in 1996, is a much-expanded treatment of ideas Huntington introduced in a widely read and highly controversial article published in 1993 in *Foreign Affairs* under the (somewhat more tentative) title, "The Clash of Civilizations?"[2] The book became a national bestseller shortly after publication in 1996 (which is already remarkable for a serious work in political science) and then regained bestseller status after the attacks of 9/11. As I write this in April 2004, its phenomenal sales success continues, and it remains the lodestar for discussions of changing political configurations in the wake of the Cold War both within and beyond the academy in the United States, continuing to spur debate around the world.[3]

My objectives here are simple and straightforward: to assess this remarkable book's most prominent strengths and weaknesses and to conclude by suggesting several ways in which its argument can be augmented by Eric Voegelin's work on political disorder and cross-civilizational conflict. As readers acquainted with Voegelin's work are surely aware, he was concerned with these problems in a deep and sustained way. Voegelin often described his lifelong philosophical search for order as having been prompted by the direct experiences of spiritual and political disorder that marked his early years, and he sustained an effort to identify and understand forms of spiritual and political disorder throughout his life. He also analyzed conflicts between civilizations over many years, as in his fascinating early study of the Mongol orders of submission to the European powers and in his late work on the clashes and conquests of "the Ecumenic Age."[4] It will obviously be impossible within the confines of a single chapter to analyze both Huntington's book and Voegelin's related work in a detailed manner, and since I have written extensively on Voegelin's analysis of disorder elsewhere,[5] I will pursue the fairly modest objective here of addressing

---

2. Samuel P. Huntington, "The Clash of Civilizations?" *Foreign Affairs* (Summer 1993): 22–49.

3. The book remains a powerhouse in sales terms. After eight years, it still ranks 820 in sales on amazon.com, showing that the book is not just being assigned to students or purchased from university bookstores, but is still influencing the general, politically attentive public. For a sampling of the early rounds of debate surrounding Huntington's thesis, see *The Clash of Civilizations? The Debate* (New York: W.W. Norton, 1996).

4. See Eric Voegelin, "The Mongol Orders of Submission to European Powers, 1245–1255," in *The Collected Works of Eric Voegelin* (hereinafter, *CW*), vol. 10, *Published Essays, 1940–1952*, ed. Ellis Sandoz (Columbia: University of Missouri Press, 2000), 76–125; *CW*, vol. 17, *The Ecumenic Age,* vol. IV, *Order and History,* ed. Michael Franz (1974; Columbia: University of Missouri Press, 2000), esp. 167–302.

5. Michael Franz, *Eric Voegelin and the Politics of Spiritual Revolt: The Roots of Ideology* (Baton Rouge: Louisiana State University Press, 1992); "Voegelin's Analysis of Marx," Occasional Papers, Eric Voegelin Archive, University of Munich, August 2000; "Brothers under the Skin: Voegelin on the Common Experiential Wellsprings of Spiritual Order and Disorder,"

the strengths and shortcomings of Huntington's book and pointing toward how it can be augmented by Voegelin's work.

II

Huntington's analysis exhibits four important strengths: a sober, clear-sighted philosophical anthropology; a freedom from partisan or ideological attachments; an immunity to "cultural neutrality"; and a willingness to accord an important place to religion in his approach to civilizations. I shall address each of these strengths in turn. *The Clash of Civilizations* is informed by a philosophical anthropology (or at least a set of assumptions about human nature) that is admirably sober and clear-sighted. Huntington's assessments of human beings in their political mode are downright grim and—though abundantly supported by dispassionate historical analysis—are hardly what one expects to encounter in books that become bestsellers. To cite but a few examples, he contends early on that human beings "know who we are only when we know who we are not and often only when we know whom we are against" and that, consequently, "enemies are essential" (21, 20). Continuing along this line, he seeks to explain why cultural differences promote cleavages and conflict by observing that "identity at any level—personal, tribal, racial, civilizational—can only be defined in relation to an 'other'" and that "the civilizational 'us' and the extracivilizational 'them' is a constant in human history" (128–29). Contrary to the pleasantly optimistic but historically baseless views of those who regard warfare as a learned (and therefore eradicable) behavior, Huntington points to "the ubiquity of conflict" and concludes flatly that "it is human to hate" (130). His view of human beings is not cynical, but neither is it prone to pleasing illusions.[6] Huntington's analysis is informed by sober common sense and a healthy appreciation for the constancy of human behavior across historical epochs, enabling him, for instance, to dismiss nonsense like Francis Fukuyama's "end of history" thesis long before it was rendered manifestly nonsensical by world events.[7]

---

in *The Politics of the Soul: Voegelin and Religious Experience,* ed. Glenn R. Hughes (Lanham, MD: Rowman and Littlefield, 1999), 139–61; "Gnosticism and Spiritual Disorder in *The Ecumenic Age,*" *Political Science Reviewer* 27 (1998): 17–43.

6. Note in this connection Huntington's effective criticisms of the notions that world peace and global cultural homogenization may come about by an expansion of trade (67), a spread of Western consumption patterns and popular culture (58), or a widespread adoption of English as a *lingua franca* (59–64).

7. See p. 31. Readers of Voegelin were prepared to see this thesis not only as nonsense but also as a pneumopathological deformation of reality stemming from a revolt against human mortality and the prospect of a mysterious future that will depart from—and

Second, Huntington repeatedly confounds those who would pigeonhole and dismiss him by developing nuanced, balanced positions that are free of partisan or ideological attachments. An example will serve to illustrate the point. Huntington criticizes multiculturalism in the United States in the strongest terms, identifying it as "cultural suicide" (304). Multiculturalists have attacked the identification of the United States with Western civilization (305), thereby threatening the entire civilization with deprivation of leadership from the only nation capable of keeping it cohesive and powerful. In this argument Huntington obviously does not take the part of a disinterested scholarly observer, but rather writes as a Western advocate for the maximal maintenance of Western cohesion and power. However, those who would dismiss him as an American or Western chauvinist must overcome his sharp criticism of Western universalism. Huntington contends that "Western belief in the universality of Western culture suffers three problems: it is false; it is immoral; and it is dangerous" (310).[8] He warns that Western nations cannot simultaneously pursue policies in their own interest while also maintaining "universalist pretensions" without falling into hypocrisy and imposing double standards that will inflame anti-Western sentiment around the globe. I will try to show below that his advocacy in this problem area confronts serious difficulties, but, nevertheless, his balanced criticism of multiculturalism "at home" and universalism abroad stands as an example of the non-ideological character of his approach.[9]

Third, Huntington's work stems from his apparent immunity to the bland "cultural neutrality" that afflicts many scholarly treatments of different civilizations and cultures. He moves unflinchingly from the fact of cultural differences across civilizations to the observation that the peculiarities of cultures are related to the quality and character of life within civilizational zones. Thus,

---

thereby undermine the importance of—every particular present. Huntington presumably developed his immunity to the "end of history" thesis not from a reading of Voegelin but from a commonsense understanding of history.

8. Huntington argues that it is false because global cultural diversity is not giving way to a common, Western-oriented, Anglophone world culture. It is regarded as immoral because the only way non-Western societies could be shaped by Western culture is by a resumption of the bare-knuckle imperialism that accomplished this in prior centuries ("imperialism is the necessary logical consequence of universalism," 310). Finally, universalism is "dangerous to the world because it could lead to a major intercivilizational war between core states and it is dangerous to the West because it could lead to the defeat of the West" (311).

9. Another example is provided by Huntington's even-handed relation to the "realist" theory of international relations, which he adopts when it proves useful and rejects when it shows limitations—sometimes doing both on a single page (e.g., 34).

Huntington contends that "the major differences in political and economic development among civilizations is clearly rooted in their different cultures":

> East Asian economic success has its source in East Asian culture, as do the difficulties East Asian societies have had in achieving stable democratic political systems. Islamic culture explains in large part the failure of democracy to emerge in much of the Muslim world. Developments in the postcommunist societies of Eastern Europe and the former Soviet Union are shaped by their civilizational identities. Those with Western Christian heritages are making progress toward economic development and democratic politics; the prospects for economic and political development in the Orthodox countries are uncertain; the prospects in the Muslim republics are bleak. (29)

Huntington's analysis is enhanced immeasurably in its forcefulness by this aspect of his thinking (which is rather rare among academics, but for which readers of Voegelin will be well prepared). Thus, apropos of our current crisis, Huntington could see in 1996 that

> the underlying problem for the West is not Islamic fundamentalism. It is Islam, a different civilization whose people are convinced of the superiority of their culture and are obsessed with the inferiority of their power. The problem for Islam is not the CIA or the U.S. Department of Defense. It is the West, a different civilization whose people are convinced of the universality of their culture and believe that their superior, if declining, power imposes on them the obligation to extend that culture throughout the world. These are the basic ingredients that fuel conflict between Islam and the West. (217–18)[10]

By dint of his unsqueamish rejection of cultural neutrality, Huntington is often able to move quickly and incisively to the heart of the issue at hand.[11]

---

10. Regarding the propensities of Islam (as opposed to Islamic fundamentalism), Huntington notes that "wherever one looks along the perimeter of Islam, Muslims have problems living peaceably with their neighbors. The question naturally arises as to whether this pattern of late-twentieth-century conflict between Muslim and non-Muslim groups is equally true of relations between groups from other civilizations. In fact, it is not. Muslims make up about one-fifth of the world's population but in the 1990s they have been far more involved in intergroup violence than the people of any other civilization. The evidence is overwhelming.... There were... three times as many intercivilizational conflicts involving Muslims as there were conflicts between all non-Muslim civilizations" (256–57). For Huntington's consideration of possible causal factors behind Islam's propensity for violence, see 262–65.

11. For example, he cuts through the notion that the spread of Western *popular* culture is equivalent to global adoption of Western culture per se, recognizing that non-Western appetites for Western films or fast food simply have no implications for non-Western acceptance of core features of Western civilization such as social pluralism, the rule of law, or

Finally, Huntington is to be credited for his willingness to accord an important place to religion in his approach to civilizations and in his understanding of human psychology and political behavior. This is not to say that his handling of "religious" phenomena is adequate, as we shall see. Nevertheless, he properly recognizes that religion is not only an element in civilizations but usually the most important of the objective elements that define them (42; see also 267). This recognition enables Huntington to avoid the "secular myopia" that can prevent analysts from seeing the volatility that religious differences add to conflicts along the fault lines that separate civilizations:

> While fault line wars share the prolonged duration, high levels of violence, and ideological ambivalence of other communal wars, they also differ from them in two ways.... [C]ommunal wars may occur between ethnic, religious, racial, or linguistic groups. Since religion, however, is the principal defining characteristic of civilizations, fault line wars are almost always between peoples of different religions. Some analysts downplay the significance of this factor. They point, for instance, to the shared ethnicity and language, past peaceful coexistence, and extensive intermarriage of Serbs and Muslims in Bosnia, and dismiss the religious factor with references to Freud's "narcissism of small differences." That judgment, however, is rooted in secular myopia. Millennia of human history have shown that religion is not a "small difference" but possibly the most profound difference that can exist between people. The frequency, intensity, and violence of fault line wars are greatly enhanced by beliefs in different gods. (253–54)[12]

Since Huntington recognizes that myopia that can stem from secularism, he does not follow "twentieth century intellectual elites" who "generally assumed that economic and social modernization was leading to the withering away of religion as a significant element in human existence" (95). Huntington sees a "revanche de Dieu" that has "pervaded every continent, every civilization, and virtually every country" in the second half of the twentieth century (95–96). One can question whether Huntington has drawn the dimensions of this revival accurately, and I will question whether he has adequately understood its well-

---

individualism (see 69–72). Thus, in an illustration that is truly eerie in its closeness to the conduct of the 9/11 terrorists while residing in the United States prior to the attacks, Huntington writes: "Somewhere in the Middle East a half-dozen young men could well be dressed in jeans, drinking Coke, listening to rap, and, between their bows to Mecca, putting together a bomb to blow up an American airliner" (58).

12. The particular analysts Huntington has in mind in this context are Richard H. Schultz Jr. and William J. Olson, and he cites their *Ethnic and Religious Conflict: Emerging Threat to U.S. Security* (Washington, DC: National Strategy Information Center, 1994), 17 ff., as well as H. D. S. Greenway and an article from the *Boston Globe*, December 3, 1992, p. 19.

springs, but there is no question that by taking religion into account Huntington has shown himself a more serious thinker than many of his critics.

III

Despite these admirable strengths, Huntington's treatment of the complex of problems entailed in civilizational clashes is not beyond criticism, for *The Clash of Civilizations* is marred by significant shortcomings, including some involving matters of deep theoretical importance. I will address four of these in particular.

1) First, many specific questions can be raised regarding the existence and boundaries of the civilizations Huntington identifies, which is to say that the basic unit of analysis on which the book is established is questionable. For example, at a "macro" level, it is not clear that Latin America or Africa are self-conscious civilizations at all. In the so-called Orthodox world one might find some centripetal force exerted by religious commonality, but the general cohesiveness and self-consciousness one would expect to find in something properly called a civilization is not clearly evident.[13] Moreover, at the "micro" level, there are many cases of doubtful inclusion on the margins of Huntington's alleged civilizations. Turkey is certainly one of these (as Huntington recognizes), but we might also ask, Is Greece really more meaningfully Orthodox than Western? Where do the Philippines belong? We could multiply examples without much difficulty, but my point is not that Huntington's scheme is imperfect or that his understanding of this or that place is lacking. The real issue has to do with the analytical mode in which Huntington goes about establishing his framework of civilizations, in which the framework itself often seems to take priority over the reality it is supposed to illuminate.

For example, when it turns out that the literature on civilizations shows a consensus on only five contemporary instances (Chinese, Japanese, Indian, Islamic, and Western), Huntington adds three more (Orthodox, Latin American, and African) that enable him to cover virtually all of the globe with his framework. Tellingly, perhaps, these additions are made with the briefest possible justification, involving only one word: Huntington writes that adding

---

13. Conversely, Japan is highly cohesive and intensely self-conscious but does not clearly have a base of any real consequence in religion, as Shinto is more a traditional and ceremonial extension of nationalism than a religion fulfilling the psychological and sociological functions stressed by Huntington.

them is "useful" (45). Useful for what? For understanding political reality, or for lending plausibility to an analytical scheme by achieving seemingly comprehensive coverage of the globe? If reality is too complex and "messy" to support a framework built upon a single unit of analysis, is a thinker not obliged to simply acknowledge this, and to say something like, "My approach works for this place but not that one, and can help explain this phenomenon but doesn't apply to these other phenomena"? At the risk of seeming naïve, are we not supposed to first figure out what is true and then make what use of that we can, rather than adopting approaches because they are useful despite finding that reality resists them? To be fair, Huntington is no ideologist, but the importance that he places upon developing a framework that is "easily grasped" and "intelligible" does put a whiff of the ideologist's procedure into the air (36). And when his treatment seems more attentive to the needs of his framework than to the obstreperous facts that resist it, it is difficult not to recall the operations of ideologists and historiogenetic speculators.[14]

2) Although Huntington should be credited for his willingness to accord an important place to religion in his approach to civilizations and human psychology, he must be faulted for failing to take religion seriously on its own ground. His approach, which is essentially "sociological," is arguably a theoretical shortcoming in its own right; but one must conclude that, beyond methodological disputes, Huntington's external, functionalist approach renders him incapable of illuminating the motivational wellsprings at the core of civilizational conflicts and religiously inspired terrorism.[15]

Huntington never treats religious phenomena as the external manifestations of inward or spiritual experience. He never treats them as a human response to the mystery of existence or regards them as a mode of participation in transcendent reality. Rather, his treatment always approaches religion in a mode that we might call "immanentist functionalism." That is, he always speaks of religion as something that functions in ways that "meet the psychological, emotional, moral, and social needs" of people (65). Religion serves the function of providing an "identity," and, as such, it competes with other sources of identity, including one's tribe or race or occupation or region or ideology or

---

14. In this connection, see Voegelin, *CW,* 17:47.

15. This is true not only of the specifically religious motivational wellsprings but also of secular and political ones. As Barry Cooper has written, "In one way or another, all political orders, including those of the West, are integrated and justified by symbolic narratives that connect political practices in the pragmatic and even secular sense to a larger order of meaning. Thus it is impossible to understand contemporary terrorism without paying close attention to the religiosity or spirituality that terrorists experience as central to their own activities." *New Political Religions, or An Analysis of Modern Terrorism* (Columbia: University of Missouri Press, 2004), 7.

civilization (128–29). His account of "la revanche de Dieu" in the second half of the twentieth century has nothing whatsoever to do with anything beyond the immanent needs addressed by religious communities:

> In times of rapid social change established identities dissolve, the self must be redefined, and new identities created. For people facing the need to determine Who am I? Where do I belong? religion provides compelling answers, and religious groups provide small social communities to replace those lost through urbanization.... More broadly, the religious resurgence throughout the world is a reaction against secularism, moral relativism, and self-indulgence, and a reaffirmation of the values of order, discipline, work, mutual help, and human solidarity. Religious groups meet social needs left untended by state bureaucracies. These include the provision of medical and hospital services, kindergartens and schools, care for the elderly, prompt relief after natural and other catastrophes, and welfare and social support during periods of economic deprivation. (97–98)

He also notes that religion may provide "the most reassuring and supportive justification for struggle against 'godless' forces which are seen as threatening" (267). Nowhere does he address religious belief as a phenomenon that connects to anything beyond the psychological or worldly needs of the believer. And though Huntington looks like he is taking religion seriously when he argues that "millennia of human history have shown that religion is not a 'small difference' but possibly the most profound difference that can exist between people" (254), he is really only saying that religious differences run deep—not that religion itself is something profound.

The immanentist character of Huntington's approach is apparent throughout the book, and it will suffice to exemplify it with regard to a single dimension of the volume. When seeking to get to the "heart: of a thinker, i.e., to see how he or she is most fundamentally oriented toward reality, it is often quite illuminating to examine how he or she conceives history as a whole. To provide a point of comparison, Voegelin writes that "history is not a stream of human beings and their actions in time, but the process of man's participation in a flux of divine presence that has eschatological direction."[16] For Huntington,

1. "Human history is the history of civilizations." (40)
2. "History... consists of changes in human behavior." (56)
3. "Population movements are the motor of history." (198)

The contrast here speaks for itself, and no commentary is required. Of course, to find functionalism and immanentism in a social scientist's approach

---

16. Voegelin, *CW*, 17:50.

to religion is hardly shocking, and my point here is not that I have read Samuel Huntington and have discovered that he is not Eric Voegelin. Rather, the larger point is that Huntington's ability to convey what is happening when violence breaks out along the fault lines running between religions is inherently limited by his failure to address what is really at stake in religion for the authentic believer. Human beings do not launch holy wars because the presence of other religions in the neighborhood threatens their "identities." They do not put infidels to the sword—or fly airplanes into buildings—out of a conviction that their own religion better meets their psychological and social needs. They do these things because the truth of existence is at stake, and an analyst who cannot or will not approach religion in that light is severely limited in what he can teach us about the phenomenon of religiously charged political fanaticism.

We should also note that Huntington's sociological or functionalist approach severely limits our ability to diagnose the disordered activities stemming from such fanaticism. The diagnostic poverty of the functionalist approach is clearly apparent when one considers the events of 9/11. From the standpoint of this approach, one can only judge particular actions as being functional or dysfunctional, not good or evil. Certainly, most observers would find it wholly unsatisfactory to assess the actions of the 9/11 terrorists as merely "dysfunctional." In such a case, we can sense that an insufficient method is preventing us from calling things by their true names. That is a problem of real significance, yet the problems run even deeper. In fact, on closer scrutiny, we can see that the sociological approach forces us to call these actions by names that are false—and appallingly so. If we are limited in our approach to religion to regarding it as a source of personal identity and group cohesiveness, how must we evaluate the actions of the 9/11 terrorists? These actions certainly had a galvanizing effect on the fanatical fringe of Islam, enhancing cohesion within Al Qaeda and enlarging its membership as well as that of associated terrorist organizations.[17] For countless Islamic fundamentalists, the spectacle

---

17. In videotaped remarks from November 9, 2001, Osama bin Laden notes: "Those youth who conducted the [9/11] operations did not accept any law in the popular terms, but they accepted the law that the Prophet Muhammad brought. Those young men [inaudible] said in deeds, in New York and Washington—speeches that overshadowed all other speeches made everywhere else in the world. The speeches are understood by both Arabs and non-Arabs, even by Chinese. It is above all—the media said. Some of them said that in Holland, at one of the centers, the number of people who accepted Islam during the days that followed the operations were more than the people who accepted Islam in the last 11 years. I heard someone on Islamic radio who owns a school in America say: 'We don't have time to keep up with the demands of those who are asking about Islamic books to learn about Islam.'" Translated transcript released by the U.S. Department of Defense and excerpted in the *New York Times,* December 14, 2001.

of the proudest towers of the satanic West being reduced to rubble by a corps of jihadist martyrs was a formidable reinforcement of their personal identities, which are forged in contradistinction to a capitalist, Christian "other." Thus, if we were to adhere to Huntington's approach, we could not even judge the actions of the 9/11 terrorists as "dysfunctional." In fact, we would be compelled to say that the actions functioned very well indeed.

3) Just as Huntington approaches religion in an insufficiently penetrating mode, his account of the ties binding individuals to civilizations is both confusing and confused, as well as psychologically and spiritually superficial. We can point to these shortcomings by considering the following passage:

> Every civilization sees itself as the center of the world and writes its history as the central drama of human history. This has been perhaps even more true of the West than of other cultures. Such monocivilizational viewpoints, however, have decreasing relevance and usefulness in a multicivilizational world. (54–55)

Working backward, one must point out that—by Huntington's own reasoning—the world has *always* been multicivilizational, since he regards civilizations as entities with which humans identify and define themselves in contradistinction to "outsiders." Huntington maintains that

> In the post–Cold War world, the most important distinctions among peoples are not ideological, political, or economic. They are cultural. Peoples and nations are attempting to answer the most basic question humans can face: Who are we? And they are answering that question in the traditional way human beings have answered it, by reference to the things that mean most to them. People define themselves in terms of ancestry, religion, language, history, values, customs, and institutions. They identify with cultural groups: tribes, ethnic groups, religious communities, nations, and, at the broadest level, civilizations. People use politics not just to advance their interests but also to define their identity. We know who we are only when we know who we are not and often only when we know whom we are against. (21)

Thus, there is no reason to believe that "monocivilizational viewpoints" become any more or less "relevant" or "useful" at any particular time. Of course, the "relevance" and "usefulness" of a monocivilizational viewpoint will be different for the social scientist, on the one hand, and for the individual who is absorbed in a living identification with a particular civilization.[18] From

---

18. And, at the risk of belaboring the obvious, we must note that this is almost perfectly analogous to the difference between religion as it exists for the sociological observer, on the one hand, and religion for the individual who is animated by a living faith in God.

Huntington's position as a social scientist, hovering above such particular civilizations, a monocivilizational viewpoint is analytically unsound and therefore neither relevant to nor useful for his purposes. By his own account, however, mere mortals in the civilizational rank and file "are attempting to answer the most basic question humans can face" by identifying with a civilization; and since this attempt can only fulfill the function he ascribes to it if they identify with a *particular* civilization, a monocivilizational viewpoint is profoundly relevant and extremely useful for them. Naturally, this is why it makes sense to say that "every civilization sees itself as the center of the world and writes its history as the central drama of human history." (Strictly speaking, of course, this does not quite make sense, since civilizations neither "see" nor "write" anything; their views and writings flow from particular individuals engaged in a direct, personal encounter with reality, and these views and writings expand from being personally meaningful to being civilizationally constitutive to the extent that they resonate with and render meaningful the living experience of others.)[19]

4) The confusions present in Huntington's understanding of the ties binding individuals to civilizations also afflict his understanding of the implications of his analysis. As he summarizes the upshot of the book:

> The survival of the West depends on Americans reaffirming their Western identity and Westerners accepting their civilization as unique not universal and uniting to renew and preserve it against challenges from non-Western societies. Avoidance of a global war of civilizations depends on world leaders accepting and cooperating to maintain the multicivilizational character of global politics. (20–21)

Given what Huntington has told us about the function that civilizational identifications serve for human beings, is it consistent and reasonable to ask

---

19. Huntington gives us reason to doubt his understanding of how civilizations come into existence, coalesce, and maintain themselves in history against external rivals and internal centripetal tendencies. More specifically, he sometimes seems to imply that civilizational existence is a "bottom-up" rather than a "top-down" phenomenon. Note in this connection his dismissal of the possibility of a universal "Davos Culture" taking root, on the ground that "outside the West, it is probably shared by less than 50 million people or 1 percent of the world's population" (57). He goes on to quote with approval Hedley Bull's observation that "this common intellectual culture exists . . . only at the elite level: its roots are shallow in many societies" (58), and to dismiss the possibility that English will become a global language because its use in many countries is limited to elites (61). Do civilizations originate by the counting of noses or taking of votes? Do civilizations spring from the world with deep roots already set? Do they bubble up from spontaneous groupings of common people who then hire elites to fashion institutions for them?

Westerners to accept their civilization as unique not universal? If "every civilization sees itself as the center of the world," isn't there an important sense in which all civilizations naturally regard their own views and beliefs and mode of life as inherently universal?[20] Specifically, don't members of all civilizations regard their outlook and religion and way of life as being not just optimal *for themselves* but for human beings per se? And even if we were to grant that this may not be characteristic of all civilizations to the same degree, isn't it at a minimum strongly characteristic of Western civilization (with its foundations set in classical philosophy's teaching about human nature and the human good and Christianity's mission of salvation for a single humanity united under God)? It clearly cannot make sense to ask Westerners to "accept their civilization as unique not universal" if its uniqueness consists precisely in its universality.

As noted above, Huntington sharply criticizes any "Western belief in the universality of Western culture" on the grounds that "it is false; it is immoral; and it is dangerous" (310), but none of these points address Western universality in the sense I wish to emphasize here. He contends that Western universality is false because those outside the West are not gravitating toward "a common, western-oriented, Anglophone world culture." This may or may not be true, but it does not mean that Western civilization's key features are not universalistic in the breadth of their scope or in their potential applicability.[21] He contends that Western universality is immoral because it could not become actual except by force, yet non-Western unwillingness to adopt elements like the rule of law or social pluralism does nothing—logically—to invalidate the claims of Westerners who might believe these are optimal arrangements for human beings per se. Finally, while it may be true in an abstract sense that, as Huntington suggests, an attempt to impose Western elements by force upon a

---

20. Huntington seems to wish to deny this when arguing that "the concept of a universal civilization is a distinctive product of Western civilization." He goes on to explain that "in the nineteenth century the idea of 'the white man's burden' helped justify the extension of Western political and economic domination over non-Western societies. At the end of the twentieth century the concept of a universal civilization helps justify Western cultural dominance of other societies and the need for those societies to ape Western practices and institutions. Universalism is the ideology of the West for confrontations with non-Western cultures" (66).

21. This would be true for seven of the eight elements that Huntington identifies as the "distinguishing characteristics of Western society": the Classical legacy, Catholicism and Protestantism, separation of spiritual and temporal authority, rule of law, social pluralism, representative bodies, and individualism. None of these are restricted in scope or applicability as a result of being fundamentally shaped by peculiarities of Europe or North America and, for this reason, unsuitable for potential export and adoption beyond the geographical boundaries of the West. The eighth element, European languages, presents debatable issues.

recalcitrant non-Western world would risk causing a war that the West might lose, this is essentially a straw-man argument. The only person in the world who explicitly advocates doing that sort of thing (e.g., invading Arab countries, killing their leaders, and converting their people to Christianity) is Ann Coulter—and even *National Review* found this sufficiently repellent to fire her for suggesting it.[22]

Huntington's prescription for what should be done on the basis of his analysis (by common people and by leaders) is strikingly bifurcated. Rank-and-file members of Western civilization are called upon to "renew and preserve it against challenges from non-Western societies," which in the broader context of the book (with its emphasis on how civilizational attachment consists in establishment of a personal identity in contradistinction to an "other") means disregarding the siren song of multiculturalism in favor of a proud Western particularism. Leaders, on the other hand, are called upon to accept and cooperate with one another "to maintain the multicivilizational character of global politics." This amounts to calling for a particularistic consciousness among masses and a pluralistic consciousness among leaders, which is quite curious if not quite contradictory or inconceivable. One imagines that a populace engaged in renewing and preserving Western civilization against challenges from non-Western societies might wish to be represented and led by individuals who are also engaged in that effort. If they got their way, Huntington could not get his. For him to get his way, leaders would be required to maintain a two-faced posture, fanning the flames of proud particularism among the people on the domestic front while pursuing a non-judgmental foreign policy that prudently, politely avoids offending other civilizations while cooperating to maintain a multicivilizational order.[23] It is far from clear that Western democracies would—or should—find this an acceptable order of affairs, or that it could prove to be workable, given the realities of human psychology and mass communications.

---

22. Huntington provides no citation to show that *anyone* has actually advocated imposing Western culture on the rest of the world by means of force. See his discussion on p. 310. Regarding the Ann Coulter episode, see the *Washington Post*, August 15, 2002, p. A25.

23. A bifurcated politics of this sort is not quite unknown historically, as nineteenth-century European leaders would sometimes encourage jingoism against a rival while politely playing the game of diplomacy with counterparts from abroad. They were also able sometimes to shift popular antagonisms, affections, and alliances after shifts in the balance of power required an alteration of alliances. However, nineteenth-century European politics were conducted predominantly by aristocrats with relatively weak ties to common people and in the absence of instant mass communications, making such a two-faced procedure much easier to maintain than it would be today.

IV

We have seen that Huntington's analysis is not without its virtues, but also that it is seriously undermined by a truncated treatment of religion and an inadequate understanding of the psycho/spiritual ties connecting individuals to civilizations. These two shortcomings conspire to produce a surprising result: Huntington's book has almost nothing vitally important to say about the horrible events of 9/11 that returned it to bestseller lists. True, the book predicts that global conflict will increasingly occur between civilizational entities rather than nation-states or ideological blocs. And that is indeed what happened in 2001. Also, Huntington points in a not-too-subtle way toward Islamic civilization as the most likely source of serious trouble in the near term, and though this was not quite a feat of clairvoyance, we must say: correct again. While Huntington's book holds some predictive power regarding *what* happened on 9/11, however, it tells us little about *why* it happened. That is, the book does not address—and because of its shortcomings of approach *cannot* address—the core causal issue behind the terrorist attacks: Why would apparently intelligent, competent, and sane people deliberately murder thousands of innocent civilians, and how could they possibly understand this as a heroic act conforming to the will of God?

When I note that the book's shortcomings of approach prevent Huntington from adequately addressing this issue, I mean two things. First, I mean that because the book is built upon a truncated treatment of religion, it does not address authentic religious experience or expression and therefore cannot address religious experience or expression in their deformed modes. By contrast, Voegelin offers a remarkably profound account of spiritual or "religious" experience and expression in all of its main historical forms (i.e., cosmological, philosophical, or theological; mythic, mystical, revelational, and doctrinal, etc.) and, as a direct consequence, was also able to offer accounts of the deformed modes of these forms of experience and expression. Voegelin's unparalleled analyses of spiritual disorder (or Gnosticism) are founded upon his symbolic and historical analyses of authentic spiritual experience, just as his critique of ideology and political religion is founded on his intricate understanding of philosophy and authentic religion. There are several ways to express this in Voegelin's rich terminology: since he has analyzed the various modes of existence in truth, he can specify and diagnose the various modes of existence in untruth; since he has set out the particular aspects of a healthy spiritual order, he can diagnose the symptoms of spiritual disease and disorder; since he records and explicates the symbols historically developed to symbolize spiritual opening to the transcendent Beyond of existence, he can record and explicate the symbols expressing spiritual closure and immanentism; since he elucidates the symbols conveying the experience of "existence-in-tension" toward the ground of being, he can elucidate the symbols that betray "existence-in-revolt" against the contingency and imperfection of a world that cannot be its own ground, and so forth.[24] Conversely, since Huntington is unwilling to press beyond a flat, functionalist, exterior view of religion, he cannot illuminate the vital wellsprings of religious fanaticism in their operations on the level of the human spirit.

Second, when I say that the book's shortcomings of approach prevent Huntington from adequately addressing the "why" of 9/11, I mean that because it is built upon a superficial understanding of the psycho/spiritual ties connecting individuals to civilizations, it cannot illuminate the deep psychic forces that can turn members of one civilization malevolently against those of other civilizations. By contrast, Voegelin shows that societies and civilizations are entities that are much more than collectivities offering individuals an identity and a sense of belonging. Although Huntington approaches them this way, Voegelin shows that a human civilization or society "is not merely a fact, or an event, in the external world to be studied by an observer like a natural phenomenon. . . . [I]t is a whole little world, a cosmion, illuminated with meaning from within by the human beings who continuously create and bear it as the mode and condition of their self-realization."[25] By extension, we can see that an individual absorbed in a living identification with a civilization will perceive threats to it as threats not only to his "identity" but also to the very mode and condition of his self-realization within a particular conception of the order and meaning of divine and worldly reality.[26] Conversely, since Huntington is unwilling or

---

24. That Voegelin's analysis of spiritual disorder can accomplish these objectives has been clear for some time, but it has also been proved recently that his analysis holds great explanatory power for religiously inspired terrorism in particular. Barry Cooper has demonstrated this in his book *New Political Religions, or An Analysis of Modern Terrorism*. Cooper draws upon Voegelin's analysis of pneumopathology (as well as Hannah Arendt's work on ideology and on other sources) to illuminate the characteristics of the consciousness of religiously inspired terrorists, carefully distinguishing the spiritual dimensions of their "moral insanity" from ordinary insanity or madness. His account of the terrorist's imaginative existence within a "second reality" projected by "scotosis" is set forth in general theoretical terms but also applied to specific historical sources and contemporary cases from the Islamic world.

25. Voegelin, *The New Science of Politics: An Introduction*, in *CW*, vol. 5, *Modernity without Restraint: The Political Religions; The New Science of Politics; and Science, Politics, and Gnosticism*, ed. Manfred Henningsen (Columbia: University of Missouri Press, 2000), 109.

26. It is worth noting that Voegelin clearly understood that specific acts and events in the physical world will be perceived as threats to a civilization's provision of personal meaning and a sense of cosmic order to individuals. This is important for understanding

unable to press beyond a flat, functionalist, exterior view of civilizational participation, he cannot illuminate the vital wellsprings of cross-civilizational atrocities.

In closing, we may balance our account somewhat by noting that Huntington's *The Clash of Civilizations and the Remaking of World Order* is an important book marked by significant virtues in approach and execution. It has helped many thousands of citizen readers see past the configurations of power that marked the Cold War era and has helped more than a few political scientists to appreciate the cultural and religious forces at work in world politics. Although the book is marred by significant shortcomings, there is a great difference between coming up short and heading in the wrong direction. Huntington is not, in the main, headed in the wrong direction. Restoring an emphasis on civilizational attachments as actuating factors in political behavior is a move in the right direction, as it helps to restore questions of personal and public meaning, identity, and religious striving to a central place in political analysis. Although we must conclude that Huntington has not shown an adequate approach to such questions, he is not the only guide at our disposal, and we can hope that a modest percentage of the readers he turns in the right direction will try to press beyond the point where he leaves them.

---

how someone might perceive, say, the spread of spoken English or the presence of American troops in Saudi Arabia as an abominable threat requiring terrible retribution. Voegelin writes: "The cosmion has its inner realm of meaning; but this realm exists tangibly in the external world in human beings who have bodies and through their bodies participate in the organic and inorganic externality of the world. A political society can dissolve not only through the disintegration of the beliefs that make it an acting unit in history; it can also be destroyed through the dispersion of its members in such a manner that communication between them becomes physically impossible or, most radically, through their physical extermination; it can also suffer serious damage, partial destruction of tradition, and prolonged paralysis through extermination or suppression of the active members who constitute the political and intellectual ruling minorities of a society." Ibid., 112–13.

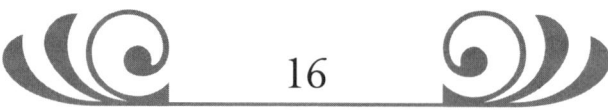

16

Voegelin's Puritan Gnosticism and Bacon's *Great Instauration*

Stephen A. McKnight

Eric Voegelin devoted considerable effort to the analysis of modern historiogenetic myths, which offer a vision of a new, world-immanent order that is the culmination and fulfillment of human history. In *The New Science of Politics* he identifies two primary types of this modern deformation. The better known is his treatment of Marx's revolutionary idea. Less well known, though equally significant, is his analysis of Puritan Gnosticism. While Marx's revolt is a deliberate repudiation of classical philosophy and Christianity, Voegelin saw in Puritan Gnosticism an equally disturbing degeneration within the mainlines of political and religious order, which resulted in the transformation of the transcendent Kingdom of God into a world-immanent Heaven on Earth. Voegelin identified four characteristic elements of Puritan Gnosticism:

1. the successful inversion and transformation of Western religious and political symbols and institutions to create a world-immanent apocalyptic or eschatological fulfillment of history;
2. the systematic formulation of a new doctrine in scriptural terms that sanctified and legitimated the Gnostic call for transformation of the existing political order and the intellectual and institutional foundations on which it rested;
3. an attack on "classic philosophy and scholastic theology, and, since under the two heads came the major and certainly the decisive part of Western intellectual culture," this culture received a destructive blow from which it has been unable to recover;

4. finally, the "Gnostic Revolution has for its purpose a change in the nature of man and the establishment of a transfigured society."[1]

This essay underscores the importance of this second form of historiogenetic deformation through a case study of Francis Bacon's vision of a "Great Instauration" wherein England would be transformed into a utopia through religious reform and the scientific mastery of nature.[2] Before turning to an examination of Bacon, however, it is important to note that Voegelin makes no reference to him in his discussion of Puritan Gnosticism. This essay intends to demonstrate, however, that Bacon's work developed in the religious and political climate that culminated in the Puritan revolution and offers a clear, concise articulation of the features Voegelin identifies as characteristic of Puritan Gnosticism.[3] Moreover, it will argue that an analysis of Bacon makes a fundamental connection with Voegelin's investigation of the transformation of science into scientism, another central theme in *The New Science of Politics*.

The purpose of this case study is twofold. First, it intends to challenge prevailing notions of Bacon as a founding father in the modern rejection of religion in favor of science. Bacon's vision of a great instauration is grounded in his apocalyptic and millenarian interpretation of scripture and of providential signs. The second and broader purpose is to demonstrate that modern forms of disorder do not always have their origin in an "egophanic" rebellion. As Voegelin indicates in *The New Science of Politics* and in many of his subsequent writings, modern dreams of inner-worldly fulfillment also originate within the mainlines of traditional philosophy and theology.

To develop this analysis I will focus on two of Bacon's works, The *Great Instauration* (*Instauratio Magna*) and *The Advancement of Learning*.

The Great Instauration

The *Great Instauration* was published in 1620 when Francis Bacon was lord chancellor and at the height of his political power. Originally, Bacon envisioned a six-part magnum opus. Although the published text falls short of its

---

1. Eric Voegelin, *The New Science of Politics* (Chicago: University of Chicago Press, 1952), 133–61. See esp. 138, 140–41, 152.
2. The term *Great Instauration* is, of course, the title of one of Bacon's key texts; and the Latin terms *instauro* and *instauratio* appear regularly in Bacon's other writings.
3. Voegelin's term *Puritan Gnosticism* would be problematic by contemporary standards. The concept of "Puritanism" has been the subject of extensive debate, and the term *Gnosticism* is problematic. These historiographical and conceptual problems are not directly relevant in this context, however. What is being examined is the correspondence between Bacon's work and the four elements of modern thought, which Voegelin describes.

original design and intent, it nevertheless presents what Bacon regarded as his most essential contribution to launching the rehabilitation of knowledge.

The usual focus of scholarly analysis is Bacon's critique of classical philosophy and scholastic theology. The materials that precede this critique, that is, the title page, the Proemium, and the dedicatory letter, are often ignored. These sections of the text are filled with themes of providential intervention and apocalyptic deliverance and demonstrate that Bacon's instauration has as its primary aim the restitution of humanity to a prelapsarian relation with God and nature. The materials must be closely studied in order to allow these themes to unfold and to establish how the opening sections set a context for understanding the nature of his epistemological revolution. In these compact, concentrated venues Bacon introduces the key image of the instauration of knowledge and establishes its connections to providential design.

The Title Page

Two elements of the title page are important to note. The first is the title of the book, *Instauratio Magna*. Although the term *instauratio* was not in general usage in Bacon's time, his readers, nevertheless, would have known the term and recognized the context for its use in Jacobean England. As Charles Whitney has shown, the primary meaning in Bacon's age derives from the Vulgate edition of the Bible, where the term occurs in more than two dozen passages alluding to the apocalyptic restoration of Jerusalem and the golden age of the Davidic-Solomonic kingship.[4] This theme is particularly significant in the Jacobean period, because King James I was heralded as the new Solomon who would restore Jerusalem. The term is also used in a broader apocalyptic meaning in several Vulgate passages referring to Christ's redemption and restoration of humanity to its prelapsarian condition, prior to Original Sin.[5] So, this title, *Instauratio Magna*, would have signaled to Bacon's readers that this text had to do with apocalyptic restoration and renewal.

The second element of the title page to note is the epigram appearing near the bottom of the page. This inscription reads, "multi pertransibunt et auge-

---

4. Charles Whitney, *Frances Bacon and Modernity* (New Haven, CT: Yale University Press, 1986), and "Bacon's *Instauration*," *Journal of the History of Ideas* 50 (1989): 371–90.

5. The Vulgate also uses the verb *instauro* to describe God's renewal of the world and the apocalyptic Christ's renewal of the world and the fulfillment of time. According to Whitney, "The Vulgate in effect creates a typology or symbolism of *instauration* by lexically connecting the architectural instauration of Solomon's Temple both to a prophetic 'rebuilding' of Israel and to a Christian instauration of all things in the apocalypse." This typological connection does not exist in the Hebrew and Greek originals. Cf. Whitney, "Bacon's *Instauration*," 377.

bitur scientia" (many shall go forth and knowledge will be increased). Bacon's motto is a modification of the Vulgate version of Daniel 12:4. The context is a prophetic vision in which the Archangel Michael reveals God's plan to deliver Israel and install the King of God on earth. Bacon preserves the apocalyptic thrust and relates it to the opening of the new world through the Columbian voyages. But Bacon also transfers the focus from the opening of the terrestrial world to the expansion of the intellectual horizons. The title page, then, signals that the text offers a criticism of the parameters of the current state of knowledge and argues that the boundaries are as false and inhibiting as the ancient prohibition against terrestrial exploration. Knowledge cannot be built upon these old foundations—they are as irrelevant as ancient geography. The foundations must be built fresh, from the ground up.

The title page, then, does indeed signal the subject matter of the text in two important ways. First, the opening of the new world undermines the authority of traditional knowledge by exposing its fundamental errors. At the same time, it shows the extraordinary potential of new, unexpected discoveries. Second, the quotation from the book of Daniel indicates that the pursuit of new knowledge is divinely sanctioned; it is not an act of arrogance or of hubris. The exploration of the new world is not a prideful defiance of the warnings of the gods; it is the fulfillment of divine intent and links human effort to divine design.

The Proemium

The title page is followed by Bacon's Proemium, whose main theme is stated in the first sentence.

> Being convinced that the human intellect makes its own difficulties, not using the true helps which are at man's disposal soberly and judiciously; whence follows manifold ignorance of things, and by reason of that ignorance mischiefs innumerable; he thought all trials should be made, whether that commerce between the mind of man and the nature of things, which is more precious than anything on earth, or at least than anything that is of the earth, might by any means be restored to its perfect and original condition, or if that may not be, yet reduced to a better condition than that in which it now is.[6]

In the very first phrase Bacon contends that the human intellect is responsible for the ignorance and errors that abound. The second phrase asserts that

---

6. Francis Bacon, *The Philosophical Works of Francis Bacon: Reprinted from the Texts and Translations with Notes and Prefaces of Ellis and Spedding*, ed. John M. Robertson (Freeport, NY: Books for Libraries Press, 1970), 241. Subsequent citations are given in the text.

this is because the intellect stubbornly refuses to use resources at its disposal, which could correct the errors that exist. In the next phrase Bacon explains why he has undertaken his present project. "He thought all trials should be made, whether that commerce between the mind of man and the nature of things... might by any means be restored to its perfect and original condition." The reference to restoration is important to note. The Latin *instauro* has the double meaning of building and of rebuilding. According to this statement, Bacon intends to attempt to rebuild the correspondence between the human intellect and its proper object of study—the natural world; and the goal is to rebuild it to its "perfect and original condition." Restitution cannot be accomplished, however, until the current causes of epistemological disorder have been purged and a new starting point or foundation has been established. As Bacon puts it: "There is but one course left, therefore—to try the whole thing anew upon a better plan, and commence a total reconstruction of sciences, arts, and all human knowledge, raised upon the proper foundations" (241).

In the second paragraph of the Proemium Bacon explains why he is chosen to undertake this project. First, it falls to Bacon because no other man seems ready to take on the task. Moreover, Bacon regards this as the most worthy legacy he could leave, because it will provide the most benefit to the human race. Bacon is careful to point out, however, that it is not personal ambition that motivates him; rather it is the worthiness of the goal—charitable service. The emphasis on God's mercy and on humanity's need for charitable concern for others is a theme also found in the dedicatory letter, the next section of the *Great Instauration* to be examined.

Dedication, or Epistle Dedicatory

Bacon, who was lord chancellor at the time, begins his dedication by telling his monarch that the king might feel that Bacon has been neglecting his responsibilities to the state while he has been involved in working on this project. Bacon assures the king, however, that the work itself is a service both to the king and to the nation. While Bacon stresses the importance of the work, which is a suitable project to dedicate to a great king, he claims that the product is not the result of his own wit but is instead "a child of time." Such modesty might be attributed to stylistic convention; but here Bacon minimizes his own role in order to accent the role of divine Providence. Here Bacon indicates that his book "may be ascribed to the mercy and goodness of God, and to the felicity of your Majesty's times." Bacon then adds that because God's hand is in the project, the work that he is dedicating to James I will make the king's reign "famous to posterity" as "times of the wisest and most learned of kings" in which the "regeneration and restoration of the sciences occurred." Bacon then links the reign of James I to the recovery and advancement of learning by associating James with Solomon: "you who resemble Solomon in so many ways" (242). Here Bacon is not only emphasizing God's mercy; he is also identifying the reign of James I with an apocalyptic moment. This apocalyptic period is associated with the restoration of knowledge by linking James I to Solomon, and this, in turn, links God's new mercies to the restoration of knowledge through Bacon's program of instauration.[7]

It should also be noted that Bacon depicts himself as one who has been chosen by God to be the instrument for bringing relief to man's estate through his advancement of knowledge that will correct the ignorance and errors that have accumulated over the course of history. And it should also be remembered that this instauration will restore the correspondence between the mind and the natural world to its "original condition." As we shall see, Bacon is referring to the original condition of Adam before the Fall.

The Preface

In the preface Bacon indicates that he intends to analyze why "the state of knowledge is not prosperous nor greatly advancing." Bacon identifies the first problem obstructing the advancement of knowledge as an undue reverence for the past. Because men have overestimated the value of the arts that they already possess, these arts become "pillars of fate set in the path of knowledge for men have neither desire nor hope to encourage them to penetrate further" (243). The first task then is to break through the barriers that obstruct the advance of truth and prevent the mind's authority over nature. As he begins his criticism of the undue reverence for classical learning, particularly of natural philosophy, Bacon introduces another memorable image when he compares classical philosophy to an adolescent boy: both are sterile and incapable of producing or generating. This is, of course, an inversion of the Renaissance reverence for the classical age as a period of maturity and excellence, which must be recovered and emulated if humanity is to advance. Bacon, by contrast,

---

7. Bacon also links James I to Solomon in *The New Atlantis* and *The Advancement of Learning*. For a discussion of Bacon's equation of James and Solomon, see *The Oxford Francis Bacon*, vol. 4, *The Advancement of Learning* (Oxford: Oxford University Press, 2000), 35 ff.; for a discussion of "Bacon and the British Solomon," see xxxviii ff. The theme of restoration or regeneration was prominent in the iconography of James I court pageantry. See Jonathan Dollimore, *Radical Tragedy: Religion, Ideology, and Power* (Chicago: University of Chicago Press, 1984); Jonathan Goldberg, *James I and the Politics of Literature* (Baltimore: Johns Hopkins University Press, 1983), esp. chap. 2; and Stephen Orgel, *The Illusions of Power* (Berkeley: University of California Press, 1975).

portrays the classical period as humanity's childhood and disparages his contemporaries, who hold such a vaulted opinion of the philosophy of Plato and Aristotle. According to Bacon, the wisdom "which we have derived from the Greeks is but like the boyhood of knowledge and has the characteristic property of boys: it can talk but it cannot generate" (243). As we shall see, Bacon will employ the association of true knowledge with productive knowledge and will contrast sterile, empty knowledge with utilitarian knowledge.[8]

As Bacon reaches the end of his preface, he switches the tone of his narrative and offers a prayer that God will bless the work he is undertaking and through his hands God "will provide the human family with new mercies" (246). This prayer recalls the dedication, where he suggests that his work would provide great blessings for the human race because it is the work of divine Providence. While many works conclude with a petition to God to bless the work that is being offered and use it for some divine purpose, the portion of Bacon's prayer that immediately follows this common motif is not so conventional. He prays that "things human may not interfere with things divine, and that from opening the ways of the sense and the increase of natural light there may arise in our minds no incredulity or darkness with regard to divine mysteries" (246). It would be fairly standard to differentiate natural philosophy from theology or reason from revelation, but Bacon goes further. He is more directly concerned with the equation of knowledge with sin or the equation of the human effort to master nature with prideful rebellion against humanity's creatureliness. In the medieval and early modern periods Original Sin was frequently equated with pride and with rebellion against one's creatureliness. The temptation by Satan was to obtain the knowledge necessary to overcome dependence on God and be able to surpass the creature's debt to the Creator and, thereby, become like God.[9] Bacon takes pains to clarify or redefine the connection between Original Sin, pride, and knowledge by linking pride with seeking knowledge that is properly the province of God alone. He specifically identifies this knowledge with the divine mystery of salvation and grace.

According to Bacon, the desire for knowledge of the natural world is neither forbidden nor sinful; and the proper remedy for sin is in directing the quest for knowledge to its proper subject and in using human reason and art as God intended: "for it was not that pure and uncorrupted natural knowl-

---

8. In the second dedication to James I in *The Advancement of Learning*, Bacon contrasts the barrenness of Elizabeth to James's potency and urges him to create knowledge that can generate benefits for humanity. See the useful discussion in Samuel G. Wong, "Some Baconian Metaphors and the Problems of Pure Prose," *Texas Studies in Literature and Language* 36 (1994): 233–58.

9. Gen. 3:5.

edge whereby Adam gave names to the creatures according to their propriety, which gave occasion to the Fall. It was the ambitious and proud desire of moral knowledge to judge of good and evil, to the end that man may revolt from God and give laws to himself, which was the form and manner of the temptation" (247). This compact statement is pregnant with meaning. It asserts that man's knowledge of nature is not sinful. God charged man with the duty and privilege of "naming" the lesser creatures. "Naming" means defining the essential traits of the created world in relation to human needs and concerns. This brief passage also contains a compact description of the proper task of natural knowledge. Human beings are to be actively involved in exploring the Creation, seeking out its characteristic traits and putting them to use. This brief reference to the Fall and to Original Sin also helps to make clear the full scope of Bacon's program of instauration. Bacon wants to restore knowledge to its original condition before the Fall. He wants to return humanity to its duty of obtaining a true and uncorrupted knowledge of the creation according to its God-given properties.

Further on, Bacon will argue that human beings cannot save themselves from the profound alienation that they have caused. The only way humanity can be saved is if God grants mercy and offers guidance that can lead human beings back to their unalienated state. This is the context for understanding Bacon's project. In Bacon's view, God has chosen the present age for granting new mercies, and Bacon is the means. After this prayer Bacon addresses himself to his readers and exhorts them to join the instauration of the foundations of true knowledge. Then Bacon urges them to have hope and to expect dramatic results. So, the preface concludes with the same emphasis on hope and apocalyptic expectation that is present in the other parts of the *Great Instauration* that we have examined thus far.

As we noted at the outset, the published text is only a small portion of the six-volume work Bacon intended to prepare. Analysis of these sections of the text makes it clear that Bacon thought this abbreviated work deserved to be published immediately, because he was convinced that the time was right and that divine Providence was working through Bacon to bring about a restoration of humanity to its prelapsarian state. Bacon's emphasis on recovery and renewal is grounded in his conviction that God provides guidance that permits recovery and restitution. Bacon is persuaded that God is actively opening new vistas in Bacon's age and that he has been chosen to help point the way toward recovery.

This analysis demonstrates the inadequacies of interpretations of the *Great Instauration* that focus only on Bacon's epistemological critique or the presentation of his own new epistemology. The setting in which these epistemological principles are presented is one of providential intervention that creates an apocalyptic hope of restoring humanity to its proper relation to nature and to God. The root motif of this text is exactly what the title indicates—an instauration. This instauration is more than the rebuilding of knowledge; it is also a spiritual rejuvenation and restoration initiated by God's providential action and by humanity's response to the apocalyptic opportunity that Providence provides. This analysis also demonstrates that Bacon's epistemology is new, a break from Aristotelian and Scholastic epistemology, but also that it is a restoration of the inquiry into nature that began with Adam. So it is wrong to characterize Bacon as a modern who breaks entirely with religion and philosophy. Bacon understands his contribution to be a return of humanity to the condition that God intended. In this condition man lives in harmony with nature, derives benefits from nature through his investigation of the Creation, and learns of God's love and mercy through the discovery of the benefits God provides in the Creation. This analysis has also shown that Bacon is convinced that God is acting to create the conditions under which humanity can be restored to its prelapsarian condition. Only God can create this opportunity; humanity cannot. On the other hand, the instauration requires humanity to be actively involved in the restoration; and this active involvement requires a spiritual regeneration that will cleanse humanity of its arrogance and pride.

This brief analysis of the *Great Instauration* suggests equivalences between Bacon's program and Voegelin's description of Puritan Gnosticism. Bacon is convinced that his age is the appointed time of apocalyptic restoration that would end the long history of human ignorance and error and usher in the millennial age of peace, harmony, and prosperity. Before developing this comparison further, however, it will be useful to examine *The Advancement of Learning*.

The Advancement of Learning

The Advancement of Learning was published in 1605, some fifteen years before the *Great Instauration*. The latter work was treated first because of its compact presentation of Bacon's millenarian vision of a great instauration, which helps to highlight the apocalyptic themes in *The Advancement of Learning*. Scholars usually concentrate on the second part of *The Advancement of Learning*, which offers Bacon's critique of Platonic and Aristotelian speculative philosophy and presents his epistemological reform. Less attention has been given to book 1, and little or no attention has been given to the dedications to James I at the beginning of each of the two books and to their allusions to the Jacobean period as an age of Providence. The analysis offered here will develop as it did with the *Great Instauration* by moving carefully through the text, allowing Bacon's argument to unfold as he himself presented it.

The first thing to note is the full title of the text: *The Two Books of Francis Bacon: Of the Proficiencie and Advancement of Learning Divine and Human.* The abbreviated title, *The Advancement of Learning,* and the analysis usually given focus primarily on a reform of philosophy and ignore Bacon's reference to divine learning. Careful reading of the text, however, makes it clear that Bacon regards both as crucial elements of the instauration. The next feature to note is that both parts of the text are dedicated to James I, who was inaugurated in 1603, two years before it was published. As we have already seen, the court pageantry surrounding James I associated him with Solomon and England with the New Jerusalem, and court iconography associated the rule of James I with the Solomonic virtues—justice, peace, charity—and with Solomonic wisdom. Bacon draws upon these themes and adds his own special emphasis in relation to his project for the advancement of learning.

The First Book

While the entire book is addressed to the king, the first paragraph contains Bacon's actual dedication. Bacon begins by establishing a correspondence between the oblations of a faithful servant of God to the offerings of a faithful subject of a king.[10] A loyal subject must first of all make an oblation in recognition of benefits gained. The second offering is not an extension of his duty; it grows out of the love and affection that a subject has for his lord. Bacon adds that he hopes to discharge the first duty through his direct service through official appointment. The second part of his tribute arises from his high regard for the person of the king, especially for his excellence in learning.

> Leaving aside the other parts of your virtue and fortune, I have been touched, yea and possessed, with an extreme wonder at those your virtues and faculties which the philosophers call intellectual; the largeness of your capacity, the faithfulness of your memory, the swiftness of your apprehension, the penetration of your judgment, and the facility and order of your elocution: and I have often thought that of all the persons living that I have known, your Majesty were the best instance to make a man of Plato's opinion, that all knowledge is but remembrance, and that the mind of man by nature knoweth all things, and hath but her own native and original notions... again revived and restored: such a light of nature I have observed in your Majesty, and such a readiness to take flame employs from the least occasion presented, or the least spark of another's knowledge delivered.[11]

---

10. Bacon is basing this on laws found in Num. 28:3 and Lev. 22:18.
11. *The Philosophical Works of Francis Bacon,* 42. Subsequent citations appear in the text.

This opening is in many ways conventional and formulaic. Parallels were regularly drawn between God's rule of the universe and the king's rule of his terrestrial realm. It was also conventional to associate James I with wisdom, and a book about the state of knowledge would appropriately focus on that reputation. But Bacon's tribute is more subtle and nuanced than this. First, it asserts that true knowledge is remembrance, a concept that Plato develops to explain the difference between the confused state of opinion held by most people and the philosopher's truth. According to Plato, the soul, before being born into the terrestrial realm, participates directly in divine knowledge and has a perfect understanding of reality. This understanding is compromised and fragmented by being immersed into the physical world and distorted by the senses.[12] Through the use of disciplined reason, the senses can be brought under control, and recollection (anamnesis) of the true state of existence can be recalled. Bacon then uses this allusion in order to praise James I as one who has been able to overcome the limitations that plagued most people and to recover true knowledge. This manner of praising James introduces the primary motif of Bacon's text. The advancement of learning depends on being able to move away from the prevailing ignorance and error; moreover, this advance is at the same time a recovery and restoration.

Bacon next turns from the personal virtues of the king to his civil or political virtues, which he links to the portentous circumstances of the time.

> As in your civil estate there appears to be an emulation and contention of your Majesty's virtue with your fortune; a virtuous disposition with the fortunate regiment; a virtuous expectation (when time was) of your greater fortune, with the prosperous possession thereof in that your time; a virtuous observation of the laws of marriage; a virtuous and most Christian desire of peace with the fortunate inclination in your neighbor princes thereunto; so likewise in these intellectual matters, there seems to be no less contention between the excellency of your Majesty's gifts of nature and the universality and perfection of your learning. (42–43)

The implication of this passage is that James's virtues are augmented by providential grace, which creates a time of peace and prosperity. Bacon then returns to his praise of the king's knowledge and asserts that "there has not been since Christ's time any king or temporal monarch which has been so learned in all literature and erudition, divine and human." After delineating the aspects of James's extraordinary learning, Bacon avers that the king's remarkable achievements have to be considered "almost a miracle." This association of James's wisdom with the age of Christ and the claim that this is almost a miracle is

---

12. The myth is found in Phaedo 75e.

another way in which Bacon links the reign of James I with Providence. Continuing his praise of James's erudition in both divine and human spheres of learning, Bacon claims: "there is met in your Majesty a rare conjunction as well with divine and sacred literature as profane and human; so as your Majesty stands invested of that triplicity which in great veneration was ascribed to the ancient Hermes; the power and fortune of a king, the knowledge and illumination of a priest, and the learning and universality of a philosopher" (43). The reference to Hermes Trismegistus serves two purposes. It augments Bacon's emphasis on the recovery and advance of both human and divine learning, but it also identifies the characteristics of the learning to be recovered. Hermes Trismegistus was believed to have had a complete understanding of the workings of nature that allowed him to draw benefits which he gave to his subjects. His kingdom, therefore, lived in peace, harmony, and prosperity. This reference to a theoretical understanding of the foundations of nature that produces useful knowledge, of course, anticipates Bacon's critique of traditional speculative philosophy and his advocacy of a recovery of the understanding of nature that provides useful results.

We find, then, in the opening paragraphs a compact presentation of several key themes. First, Bacon's references to Platonic anamnesis links Bacon's advancement of learning with the recovery of true knowledge. This emphasis on the two aspects of instauration—recovery and advance—is augmented through the reference to both Solomon and Hermes Trismegistus. So, the theme of escaping from the present state of ignorance is prominent in the opening paragraphs. A second prominent theme is the allusion to the beginning of James's reign as an epochal turning point or the beginning of a providential age. Bacon catalogs the characteristics of this providential age: first, the reign is marked by human excellence and divine favor; second, there is both internal stability and international peace; and third, there is a cessation of religious strife both within the country and abroad.

Having offered his extensive praise of James's virtue and wisdom, Bacon returns to his starting point, that is, the gift he wishes to make: "Therefore I did conclude with myself, that I cannot make unto your Majesty a better oblation than of some treatise tending to that end [a lasting memorial to the virtues and wisdom of James]; whereof the sum will consist of these two parts: the former concerning the excellency of learning and knowledge, and the excellency and the merits of the true glory in the augmentation and propagation thereof" (43). Bacon then indicates that the first task of a treatise on learning is to establish the proper scope and boundary of knowledge. While this would be an appropriate beginning for any text of the kind, it is especially appropriate now, because the purpose and the scope of knowledge have been misunderstood for so long. The first step, then, is to "clear the way" so that the "true testimonies concerning the dignity of learning" can be heard without the interruption of tacit objections.

This point in the text marks a transition from Bacon's direct address to his king to the beginning of his philosophical critique. The first objection to be cleared away is the erroneous claim that "the aspiring to over-much knowledge was the original temptation and sin, whereupon ensued the Fall of man; that knowledge hath in it somewhat of the serpent, and therefor where it enterth into a man it makes him swell" (43). Bacon then cites biblical figures, including Solomon and Saint Paul, who have been used to support the view that a preoccupation with knowledge leads to anxiety and to alienation from God. But Bacon maintains that the nature of Original Sin has been misinterpreted and that the cautions of Solomon and Paul against a preoccupation with knowledge have been misused. The Fall from grace was not precipitated by the pursuit of "the pure knowledge of nature and universality, a knowledge by the light whereof man did give names unto the creatures in Paradise, as they were brought before him" (44). The source of man's Fall was the pursuit of "the proud knowledge of good and evil, with an intent by man to give laws unto himself and to depend no more upon God's commandments" (44). This prideful attempt to become autonomous causes man to swell up with pride and to fall from grace. Bacon then returns to claim that God intends humanity to have a full and complete understanding of nature. "God has framed the mind of man as a mirror or glass capable of the image of the universal world... if then such be the capacity and receipt of the mind of man, it is manifest that there is no danger at all in the proportion or quantity of knowledge, how large soever, that should make it swell or out-compass itself" (44). Bacon then affirms that charity—compassion for others—is the corrective against pride. He quotes Saint Paul: "knowledge blows up, but charity builds up" and "if I spoke with the tongues of man and angels, and had not charity, it were but as a tinkling cymbal." According to Bacon, the error is not in speaking with the tongues of man and angels; the error is in pursuing knowledge without charity. Having made this clarification he explains that the cautions of Saint Paul and Solomon are not against pursuing knowledge but in pursuing the wrong kind. At the conclusion of this paragraph, Bacon adds the following statement:

> let no man, upon a weak conceived sobriety or an ill-applied moderation, think or maintain that a man can search for or be too well studied in the book of God's word or in the book of God's works; divinity or philosophy; but rather let man endeavor an endless progress or proficience in both; only let man beware that they apply both to charity, and not to swelling; to use and not to ostentation. (45–46)

These statements reflect a now familiar theme. Humanity has a God-given or God-imposed obligation to know Him and to know the natural world as His creation. The source of sin is not too much knowledge but the rebellion against God and the effort to become a creator rather than a creature, that is, to become autonomous. The safeguard against prideful rebellion is to allow charity to be the motive for the pursuit of knowledge, because the effort to gain knowledge in order to help others prevents a preoccupation with the self.

Bacon devotes the next several paragraphs to an inventory of the fields of knowledge, what is proper to them, and where and how knowledge has become derailed. He identifies three primary sources of error, or "distemper." The first Bacon calls "fantastical learning"; the second, "contentious learning"; and the third, "delicate learning." He takes up the third distemper first, citing as an example the vain learning of the Church, which studies words rather than things. The reference is to Scholastic philosophy and theology, which Bacon contends has lost sight of the truth of scripture and has devoted its efforts to its own elaborate arguments. Proof that Scholastic learning has been preoccupied with "vain imaginations" is found in the recent recovery of ancient scriptural texts and the study of ancient languages of the texts, which make clear the ignorance and errors of the Schoolmen.

> Martin Luther, conducted (no doubt) by an higher Providence but in discourse of reason finding what a province he had undertaken against the Bishop of Rome and the degenerate traditions of the church, and finding his own solitude, being no ways aided by the opinions of his own time, was enforced to awake all antiquity, and to call former times to his succors to make a party against the present time; so that the ancient authors, both in divinity and in humanity, which had long time slept in libraries, began generally to be read and revolved. This by consequence did draw on the necessity of a more exquisite travails and the languages original where and those authors did write, for the better understanding of those authors and the better advantage of pressing and applying their words. (53–54)

The second distemper, contentious learning, is learning that has some basis in empirical analysis, usually by the original thinker or founder of that system of thought, but most of the subsequent effort of the followers of this school are devoted to further system building. That is, more effort is put into the system of argumentation than into additional empirical investigation.

> This kind of degenerate learning did chiefly reign among the school men; who having sharp and strong wits, and abundance of leisure, and small variety of reading; but their wits being shut up in the cells of a few authors (chiefly Aristotle their dictator) as their persons were shut up in the cells of monasteries

and colleges; and knowing little history, either of nature or time; did out of no great quantity of matter, and infinite agitation of wit, spin out unto us those laborious webs of learning which are extant in their books. (55)

Bacon compares such effort to that of the spider, which spins webs out of its own substance. He also describes such effort as sterile and uses the now-familiar reference to Scylla as a monster incapable of the production "so that generalities of the school men are for a while good and proportionable; but then when you descend into their distinctions and decisions, instead of a fruitful womb for the use and benefit of man's life, they end in monstrous altercations and barking questions" (56). The third distemper is a vain fantasy that has no truth. Here Bacon refers specifically to documents that purport to be natural histories but are "fraught with much fabulous matter, a great part not only untried but notoriously untrue, to the great derogation of the credit of natural philosophy" (57). Having identified the diseases that are the causes of the epistemological disorder, Bacon contends that a return to true philosophy requires a return to first principles, or to *prima philosophia.* According to Bacon, the purpose of "primary philosophy" is for "the glory of the Creator and the relief of man's estate." Its aim is to "separate and reject vain speculations and whatsoever is empty and void, and preserve and to augment whatsoever is solid and fruitful; that knowledge may not be as a courtesan, for pleasure and vanity only, or as a bond-woman, to acquire and gain to her master's use; but as a spouse, for generation, fruits, and comfort" (60).

Having proposed the restoration of the dignity of knowledge, Bacon presents a listing of subjects appropriate to *prima philosophia.* Bacon's description of the subjects of human knowledge is arranged in a hierarchy. The highest subject, knowledge of God, is acquired in one of two ways: through the scriptures and direct revelation or through the study of the creation. Next in order of worthiness are spirits, or angels, which Bacon uses as an opportunity to stress the importance of love and charity over power. "To the first place or degree is given to the angels of love which are termed Seraphim; the second to the angels of light, which are termed Cherubim; and the third and so following places to thrones, principalities and the rest which are all angels of power and ministry; so as the angels of knowledge and illumination are placed before the angels of office and domination" (61). From the realm of spirits the next stage or category is the intellectual realm, the realm of forms, and then the creation. Reminding the reader of the primordial state of creation, Bacon next turns to humanity's prelapsarian pursuit of knowledge. "After the creation was finished, it was set down unto us that man was placed in the garden to work therein; which works so appointed to him could be no other work than contemplation;

that is, with the end of the work is but for exercise and experiment, not for necessity" (61). Man's work could be nothing more than contemplation because the creation was perfect and readily revealed its purpose and its benefits to humanity. Humanity carried out empirical investigations and analysis, but this was not labor; it was rather the pleasure of intellectual discovery. After the Fall, however, humanity was alienated from both God and nature and was required to labor in order to discover the benefits of the creation. As a result, humanity's primary task was not simple contemplation but a laborious effort to attain what had been previously readily revealed.

Bacon moves from this account of the primordial state to the history of humanity after the Fall and to a discussion of representative figures who were able to escape human pride and its consequences and to restore—at least in part—humanity's relation to God and nature. Moses is described as the lawgiver and the possessor of "all the learning of the Egyptians," which made him wise in theology, moral philosophy, and philosophy of nature. The second person cited is Solomon, who was "enabled not only to write those excellent parables or aphorisms concerning divine and moral philosophy, but also to compile a natural history of all verdure" (62). Bacon describes the age of Christ as one in which knowledge was perfected. "Our savior himself did show his power to subdue ignorance by his conference with the priests and the doctors of all, before he showed his power to subdue nature by his miracles and in the coming of the Holy Spirit was chiefly figured and expressed in the similitude and gift of tongues, which are but carriers of knowledge." The gifts of the Spirit were continued by "the ancient bishops and fathers of the church who were excellently read and studied in all the learning of the heathen as well as to the scriptures." Bacon then arrives at his own age and the restoration of learning that is under way. "And we see before our eyes, that the age of ourselves and our fathers, when it pleased God to call the church of Rome to account for their degenerate manners and ceremonies, and sundry doctrines obnoxious and framed to uphold the same abuses; at one and the same time it was ordained by the Divine Providence that there should attend withal a renovation and new spring of all other knowledge" (63). Here again the recovery of knowledge includes a restoration of both divine and human knowledge, a topic developed more fully in the *Novum Organum*. In that text Bacon alludes to the restoration of scriptural authority and to overseas exploration, which advances knowledge of the natural world. This compact statement in *The Advancement of Learning* is clearly intended to have the same dual emphasis. Having recited these instances in which recovery of the dignity of knowledge and the proper subjects of study have occurred, Bacon again summarizes the two tasks of knowledge. God has laid "before us two books or volumes to study, if we will be secured from error; first the scriptures, revealing the will of God, and then the creatures expressing his power" (64). Bacon then contends that the historical record demonstrates that the twofold advance in knowledge occurs most often when it is supported by learned princes. Bacon gives six examples, ending the list with Queen Elizabeth, whom he credits with re-establishing the truth of religion, establishing peace and security, the administration of justice, and creating a flourishing state of learning (67). Bacon states that James I has the opportunity to further advance the pursuit of knowledge and create an immortal reputation for himself:

> by learning man ascendeth to the heavens and their motions, wherein the body cannot come; and the like; let us conclude with the dignity and excellency of knowledge and learning and that wherein man's nature doth most aspire; which is immortality or continuance; for to this tendeth generation and the raising of houses and families.... We see then how far the monuments of wit and learning are more durable than the monuments of power or the hands. (73)

Bacon has returned to his starting point. He began by saying that he wishes to offer the king an oblation out of love and devotion. The most enduring gift he can offer is to provide the means for the advancement of learning, which will become a hallmark of the reign of James I.

This analysis makes it obvious that the purpose of the first book of *The Advancement of Learning* is to offer James I the opportunity to create a legacy of the restoration of the dignity of learning. This restoration entails a recovery and advance in theology as well as in natural philosophy. Bacon maintains that spiritual recovery is already under way through the study of ancient languages and the rehabilitation of scriptural texts, and the restitution of natural philosophy has begun through the opening of the terrestrial realm to overseas exploration, which undermines the authority of ancient texts and paves the way for a new beginning. The advance will be accelerated by Bacon's contribution of his new methodology, and this recovery and advance will contribute to the providential restoration of humanity to its proper relationship to God and nature.

The Second Book

Much of the second book is taken up by a plea for the king to provide resources for the advancement of learning. Here Bacon addresses very practical matters of establishing libraries, research laboratories, and funding for scholars. This is followed by a catalog or an inventory of the various divisions of learning, which is the one that is usually given most attention. The analysis provided here will focus briefly on the elements of book 2, which reinforce Bacon's main themes and introduce new or complementary motifs.

Near the end of book 1, Bacon offered high praise for Queen Elizabeth. The opening paragraph of the second book, however, points to a shortcoming of the queen not found in James I. Queen Elizabeth was unmarried and, therefore, could not generate or create a line of descendants. James I, as a respecter of marriage, is capable of generating or procreating. Bacon then notes that the best legacy the king can create is not found in family lines or in governmental administration but in those things that are permanent and immortal. In this context Bacon reminds the king that the advancement of learning would be the most permanent legacy he could create.

> For there is not any more worthy than the further endowment of the world with sound and fruitful knowledge: for why should a few received authors stand up like Hercules's Columns beyond which there should be no sailing or discovering, since we have so bright and benign a star as your Majesty to conduct and prosper us. (75)

Bacon is here repeating the reference to the Pillars of Hercules as a false boundary and now depicts James I as a polestar to serve as the reference or guide to the opening of the intellectual globe. This opening is followed by several paragraphs that outline the practical needs entailed in the advancement of learning. Bacon begins his description of the components of human learning by discussing natural history. He proposes that an inventory be made of texts and inventions, which could serve as the beginning point for assessing the further work that needs to be done. He concludes this discussion with reference to the recent voyages that have opened the terrestrial globe and shown the limitations and errors of ancient teachings, and he once again links the opening of the terrestrial realm with the expansion of the intellectual terrain and associates both with divine Providence.

> And this proficience in navigation and discoveries may plant also an expectation of the further proficience and augmentation of all sciences; because it may seem they are ordained by God to be coevals, that is, to meet in one age. For so the prophet Daniel says of the latter times foretelleth . . . many shall pass to and fro, and knowledge shall be multiplied. (86)

While this is the first appearance in print of the quotation from Daniel, we know that it is repeated several times in his later writings and is one of the key motifs linking overseas expansion with the expansion of knowledge, both of which are the result of human effort and providential design.

Bacon then moves from a description of natural history to ecclesiastical history. On the surface this may appear to be an unusual shift in subject matter, which has no connection to the preceding discussion. Bacon explains that ecclesiastical history has three parts: the history of the church, the history of prophecy, and the history of Providence. It is this third component that ties Bacon's discussion of natural history to his ecclesiastical history. According to Bacon, the history of Providence contains the correspondence between God's revealed will and his secret will. In most instances the working of divine Providence remains hidden from the understanding of philosophers and theologians, although there are extraordinary times and circumstances in which God reveals his secret design in obvious ways. Bacon's meaning is clear in this context. The preceding reference to the providential advancement of learning through overseas exploration is the primary evidence that his is an extraordinary time.

Bacon then turns to a discussion of the three aspects of the one universal science or *prima philosophia:* divine philosophy, natural philosophy, and human philosophy. The three contribute to a unified science because their common purpose is to know God through His revealed word and through His creation. In *prima philosophia* nature is the subject that links God and man. Bacon cautions, however, that natural philosophy cannot broach aspects of the divine that are beyond its scope. Here he has in mind specifically articles of faith, which transcend the reaches of human reason.

The third topic considered part of universal science is the philosophy of human nature or anthropology. Bacon examines the physical and the spiritual components of human nature and discusses the individual and his life in society. He identifies the capacity for language as one of the most distinctive attributes of humanity and contends that language is not a human invention but is rather the result of the recollection of knowledge that humans already possess. This statement would be confusing were it not for the discussion in part 1 where Bacon indicated that all knowledge is remembrance rather than invention. There he made the point that true knowledge and authentic language are an articulation of the proper understanding of nature, which is provided man by God. After the Fall, however, this clear understanding was lost and human language was confounded. Bacon repeats this point here. Because of the Fall, "the mind of man is far from the nature of a clear and equal glass, wherein the beams of things should reflect according to their true incidents; nay, it is rather like an enchanted glass, full of superstition and imposture" (118). Because of his fallen state, man must be reeducated, and Bacon describes various rhetorical means for training the mind and directing the will toward the pursuit of the highest good. While the present state of disorder makes this difficult, it is not an impossible task because humanity can be reawakened to its proper nature and to the proper source of meaning, purpose, and ultimate satisfaction. In this discussion Bacon maintains that the results of misfortune and of humanity's fallen nature can be overcome through hard work or, to be more precise "through suffering," a reference that recalls in the opening sections of part 1 where Bacon describes the consequences of the Fall and identifies hard work as the way for repairing the damage.

Having promoted the benefits of the restoration of true knowledge, Bacon once again cautions against the sin of pride and the attempt to know divine mysteries beyond the scope of human reason.

> We conclude that sacred theology... is grounded only upon the word and Oracle of God, and not upon the light of nature.... This holds not only in those points of faith which concern the great mysteries of the deity, of the creation, of the redemption, but likewise those which concern the law moral truly interpreted: love your enemies: do good to them that hate you; be like to your heavenly Father, that suffers his rain to fall upon the just and the unjust. (168)

Further on in this discussion, Bacon again says that the source of knowledge of matters of faith rests "upon the true and sound interpretation of the scriptures, which are the foundations of the water of life" (171). Toward the end of this discussion, Bacon contends the restoration of divine knowledge has already begun.

> For I am persuaded,... that of the choice and best of those observations upon text of Scriptures which have been made... and sermons within your Majesty's island of Britain by the space of these 40 years... had been set down in a continuance, it had been the best work in divinity which had been written since the apostles' times. (174)

This spiritual renewal offers the prospects for the advancement of divine learning, and Bacon's proposals for the advancement of natural philosophy serves as its complement. The second part of *The Advancement of Learning* ends with this discussion of the recovery of divine truth that serves as a guard against various forms of sin, idolatry, and false religion. It also sets Bacon's work within the context of the providential renewal and restoration of knowledge.

Conclusion

With this analysis in mind we can now turn to the correlation between Bacon's vision of the Great Instauration and Voegelin's characterization of Puritan Gnosticism. The first trait of Puritan Gnosticism that Voegelin describes is the inversion and transformation of religious and political symbols to create world-immanent apocalyptic or eschatological fulfillment of history. Our analysis has shown that world-immanent, eschatological expectation was an integral part of the political and religious climate of Bacon's age. During the Jacobean period, this apocalyptic expectation figured prominently in court iconography, which portrayed James I as the new Solomon and England as the new Zion. Bacon draws upon this millenarian atmosphere and adds an important new element. In Bacon's vision of instauration the new age of peace, harmony, and prosperity requires that humanity become an active agent for inner-worldly fulfillment through the mastery of nature. Bacon, therefore, is an important figure at the threshold of modernity, who provides a vision of humanity's redemptive role in creating paradise on earth. Scholars who have studied the origins of modern disorder have frequently pointed to Joachim of Flora's apocalyptic vision as a key source for a three-stage progressivist construction of history, which is later secularized in the eighteenth and nineteenth centuries. Other scholars have pointed to the Enlightenment as the stage in which salvation history (*Heilesgeschichte*) becomes secularized and man rather than God becomes the agent for redemption. Our analysis has shown that Bacon is another key figure for understanding how apocalyptic yearning becomes immanentized. Apocalyptic expectation is high in Bacon's age, and he adds to this apocalyptic yearning the instrumental means for humanity to create paradise on earth.

The second characteristic feature of Puritan Gnosticism is a systematic formulation of new doctrines in scriptural terms. As we have seen, Bacon repeatedly states that the recovery of spiritual truth is under way in his own age, and he draws comparisons with this spiritual recovery in his own time to that of the period of gospel Christianity. Bacon frequently credits others for this spiritual recovery and says that he is focusing his attention on the other crucial phase of instauration—the reform of natural philosophy. In fact, Bacon frequently offers his own interpretation of key scriptural passages, which he maintains must be properly understood in order for spiritual recovery to be achieved. On several occasions Bacon reinterprets the relation of pride to the concept of Original Sin. Bacon contends that it was humanity's pride and arrogance in seeking inappropriate knowledge of spiritual matters having to do with core doctrines of the faith that alienated man from God. In Bacon's interpretation there is no sinful pride in attempting to master nature and (re)create paradise on earth. Such efforts are in fact divinely commissioned, and humanity would be sinful if it failed to recognize providential intent. We have also seen Bacon's frequent use of the apocalyptic vision of Daniel as evidence for providential action in his own age. In particular, he links it with the dual

to the basic question of the significance of Puritan Gnosticism as a f. modern disorder. As noted at the outset, Voegelin offers, in *The New Scie Politics,* two case studies of modern deformation: the Marxist revolutio idea and Puritan Gnosticism. On the surface it might appear that this is unusual and uneven comparison. Puritan Gnosticism as a political moveme is not comparable to Marxism; it was short-lived and affected only Britaii Voegelin, however, uses Puritan Gnosticism as a case study of the degeneration within the main lines of political and religious order that leads to modern dreams of inner worldly fulfillment that are as corrosive and destructive as the Marxist revolutionary idea. The purpose of this examination of Francis Bacon is to demonstrate that the apocalyptic and millenarian ferment that leads to Puritan Gnosticism is directly connected to the rise of scientism and its core conviction that humanity is capable of mastering nature and perfecting society. The essential point that Voegelin was making in his case study of Puritan Gnosticism is that modern disorder is not always the result of an egophanic revolt of the Marxist type. Disorder also emerges from well-intentioned efforts within the Western philosophical and theological traditions. Francis Bacon is an important case in understanding the links between seventeenth-century apocalyptic and millenarian ferment with the rise of scientism and the secularized vision of salvation history that emerges in the Enlightenment. But Bacon, of course, is not the only source for these modern deformations. Medieval and early modern history is filled with other cases in which disorder emerges from within the main lines of philosophy and theology, and these developments are as destructive as the egophanic revolt against classical philosophy and theology.

advances in the recovery of divine knowledge and in the recovery of natural philosophy. So here again Bacon is formulating his vision of inner-worldly fulfillment in scriptural terms. Finally, we have seen that Bacon's key concept of instauration is itself based on an apocalyptic reading of scriptural passages in order to link James I with Solomon and portray England as the new Zion. Bacon combines these passages with his new interpretation of Original Sin to create his own vision of the restoration of humanity to its prelapsarian state.

The third feature that Voegelin identifies with Puritan Gnosticism is the attack on classic philosophy and Scholastic theology. Bacon repeatedly criticizes classical philosophy and Scholastic theology because these systems are abstract and impotent. They fail to provide useful knowledge that allows humans to transform the world and restore an earthly paradise. Bacon is, therefore, a principal source for the modern notion that knowledge is power and for the claim that the purpose of philosophy is not to understand the world but to change it. While this latter phrase is usually associated with the Marxist revolutionary idea, it is already present in Bacon's writing some two hundred years before Marx.

The fourth characteristic of Puritan Gnosticism is the transformation of the nature of man and the transfiguration of society. The ultimate goal of Bacon's instauration is the transformation of human nature or, more precisely, the restoration of humanity to its prelapsarian condition. This restoration would purge humanity of its pride and create a community that actualizes the Christian virtues of faith and charity (hope is not needed because apocalyptic fulfillment has already begun). The transformation of human nature is also the transformation of society. When humanity recovers its prelapsarian condition, humanity will live together in peace, harmony, and prosperity. While Bacon conceives of his apocalyptic vision in Christian categories, his Enlightenment followers purge the vision of its biblical references. Nevertheless, they retain the fundamental vision of humanity actively transforming the human condition and creating a paradise on earth.[13]

Having identified the correlations between Bacon's vision of instauration and Voegelin's characterization of Puritan Gnosticism, it is apposite to return

---

13. Karl Löwith, *Meaning in History* (Chicago: Chicago University Press, 1949), and others have rightly noted that the Enlightenment is a primary source for a secularized construction of the salvation history in which man rather than God is the agent of salvation, and the transcendent kingdom of God is replaced by a world-immanent paradise. The influence of Bacon on the Enlightenment is unquestioned. While the Enlightenment philosophies purge Bacon's vision of instauration of its religious language, there is no doubt of his influence on the Enlightenment vision of inner-worldly fulfillment through the mastery of nature.

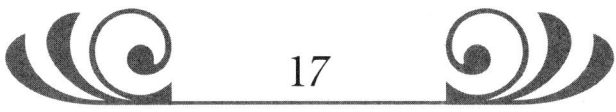

17

History as Open Horizon
Eric Voegelin's Search for a Post-Imperial Order

Thomas Hollweck

I

Thirty years ago, when the fourth volume of *Order and History* appeared under the title *The Ecumenic Age,* seventeen years had passed since the reflection on the skeptic Pyrrho with which Eric Voegelin had concluded *Plato and Aristotle.* His monumental analysis of Platonic-Aristotelian philosophy had ended, somewhat anticlimactically, with a brief chapter, "On Types of Character and Skepticism," which already in 1957 should have raised the question in the reader's mind how the history of order could continue after having reached its culmination in Plato's and Aristotle's *noesis.* Pyrrho's philosophy and that of his school, related centuries later by Sextus Empiricus, himself a denizen of a world shaped by the most successful empire of all, the Roman Empire, was one of the more plausible responses to "the sudden expansion of the civilizational horizon, which swept the polis into a corner of the known world," as Voegelin poignantly formulated it at the time.[1] With the introduction of the "manifold of societies" in the wake of the conquests of Alexander, the "science of skepticism" successfully challenged the "Truth" of the sages as an anachronism in a world that subsequently experienced "the reduction of the whole manifold of societies, with their civilizational content, to a field of appearances

---

1. Eric Voegelin, *The Collected Works of Eric Voegelin* (hereinafter, *CW*), vol. 16, *Plato and Aristotle,* ed. Dante Germino (Columbia: University of Missouri Press, 2000), 427.

that could be neither a source nor a vessel of Truth."² What Voegelin seemed to signal here was the possibility that the two differentiations that occurred in Israel and Hellas might not be followed by another differentiation; that a new situation had been created by the imperial conquests in which later philosophical schools, be they Platonic, Stoic, or Skeptic, could do little else than adjust and adapt to the reality of the new empires. Thus the Skeptic would revert to a "simple conservatism," and he "accepted the customs and convictions prevalent in the society that surrounded him by the accident of his birth, and he let history be transacted over his head, as it befitted the subject of an Empire."³

There was, however, another ending to this story, and that ending happens to be the one with which Voegelin concluded the first of the three volumes of *Order and History, Israel and Revelation*. It is the story of the exodus from the cosmic-divine order of empire as told by the prophets, the story of the Suffering Servant in the "living tradition of Deutero-Isaiah." This story finds its dramatic conclusion in the proclamation of a new beginning in Acts 8, where the Ethiopian eunuch of the queen is reading Isaiah and pondering on the passage: "Like a sheep he was led away to slaughter." The eunuch asks Philip: "'Tell me, of whom is the prophet speaking? of himself, or of someone else?' Then Philip began, reports the historian of the Apostles, and starting from this passage he told him the good news about Jesus."⁴

These two endings form a seemingly unbridgeable gulf opened up by the events of the ecumenic age. Voegelin's attempt to bridge this gulf not only lasted seventeen years but also is marked by a precarious tension, to stay with the image of the bridge, which makes itself felt in every sentence of volume IV of *Order and History*. At the same time, this tension clearly sets it apart not only from the philosophies of history of a Jaspers or a Toynbee but also from a theology of history such as that of Hans Urs von Balthasar, let alone a *Seinsgeschichte* à la Heidegger. The thrust of Voegelin's work goes in a direction that differs from those of his "competitors" in one fundamental way, and it is contained in the famous opening sentence of the preface to *Israel and Revelation*: "The order of history emerges from the history of order." Whatever this emerging order turns out to be, it will most likely not be the order of an "axis time" or the sequence of civilizational courses, or the history of Being (*Sein*) forgotten in the course of the history of being (*Seiendes*), only to reveal itself again in the future of its *parousia*. Nor could it be the order evoked in

---

2. Ibid., 427.
3. Ibid., 428.
4. Eric Voegelin, *CW*, vol. 14, *Israel and Revelation*, vol. I, *Order and History*, ed. Maurice P. Hogan (1956; Columbia: University of Missouri Press, 2001), 570.

Balthasar's theodramatic soteriology, even though there are points of intersection between this work and that of Voegelin. In Voegelin's own account, at the end of those seventeen years of expanding his own historical horizon, history "conceived as a process of increasingly differentiated order" could no longer be placed on the original time-line that was to extend from the imperial civilizations of the Near East to the modern national state, and to the emergence of modern Gnosticism as the symbolic form of order.

Voegelin's abandonment of time-lines as the carriers of the important lines of meaning in history apparently did not occur as a sudden flash of insight but was the result of a series of individual studies further exploring areas of meaning that had occupied him already during the work on the first three volumes of *Order and History*. The visible traces of this process, the papers collected in the volumes *Published Essays, 1953–1965* and *Published Essays, 1966–1985*, as well as in *Anamnesis,* first published in German in 1966, present the most accurate picture of the expansion of this historical horizon, but there is perhaps an even more telling account of the developments leading to *The Ecumenic Age* in the correspondences between Voegelin and the directors of Louisiana State University Press. Here the reader encounters a philosopher and scholar who struggles with the steadily growing recognition that pronouncements about the process of history are always tentative at best and that it is not permissible to take shortcuts in the pursuit of the lines of meaning that constitute what is conventionally called "history."

II

I have given a more detailed description of the genesis of *The Ecumenic Age* elsewhere, as it can be reconstructed from Voegelin's letters to LSU Press and from the papers and drafts published in the *Collected Works*.[5] The process that ultimately led to the publication of volumes IV and V is of far greater significance to the hermeneutics of the project as a whole than the texts themselves reveal to the reader unacquainted with this process. The years between the first three volumes and volume IV can well be called the most productive and—

---

5. See the German translation of parts I and II of *The Ecumenic Age*. Part 1, *Die Legitimität der Antike*, ed. Thomas Hollweck (Paderborn: Wilhelm Fink Verlag, 2004), contains my postscript with a fuller discussion of the frequent changes the volume's conception underwent during the 1960s and early 1970s. The postscript by Manfred Henningsen to part 2, *Das Ökumenische Zeitalter,* ed. Manfred Henningsen (Paderborn: Wilhelm Fink Verlag, 2004), represents an important revisionist reading of the book by someone who had shared many of Voegelin's thoughts at the time during which volume IV evolved.

with some reservations—the happiest of Voegelin's life. *Order and History* had made him an internationally known scholar. The development of the Munich institute with which he was now entrusted presented a welcome challenge to his creative imagination; he was able to surround himself with a group of intellectually alert young scholars; and he was able to spend guest semesters in the United States at such institutions as Notre Dame, Harvard, and the University of Michigan. This is not to say that the biographical changes are in any way responsible for the famous "break" in the program, mentioned in the first sentence of the introduction to *The Ecumenic Age,* but there is sufficient evidence that Voegelin made the fullest possible use of the opportunities for developing all aspects of the question of history and order without regard to the demands of finishing a "work." An additional element that should be taken into account when we look at the evolution of volume IV is that Voegelin's move to Munich enabled him to create his institute's research library in the image of what he considered *Wissenschaft,* as he wrote to Don Ellegood, the director of LSU Press, as early as 1959.[6] (I choose to call the yet to be written sequel "volume IV," because the least certain thing about it was its title, as the correspondence all too clearly reveals.)

In the beginning Voegelin still envisaged a three-volume continuation of *Order and History,* with a fourth volume, under the title *Empire and Christianity,* divided into two parts. The first part was to treat the ecumenic empires, while the second would deal with Jewish apocalypse, Gnosticism, and Christianity up to ca. A.D. 800.[7] As far as his treatment of Christianity was concerned, Voegelin was quite aware of the resonance it would receive, and already in the March letter he had written Ellegood: "We must consider that the volume on Christianity will attract particular attention, and come under fire from all sides. It must be impeccable—or else." This would turn out to be the correct assessment of the issue. The point that needs to be made, though, is that the decision to reduce the number of volumes from six to five was being made already at that time. It would then be only a matter of organizing the materials to be included in such a way that they led up to what he already at that time conceived as the point of destination of the whole process under the title "The Global Expansion of Western Society and the Formation of a Global Society."[8] The years between 1959 and 1961 were also the time when Voegelin, instead of devoting himself to the impeccable treatment of Christianity, made

---

6. Cf. Voegelin to Ellegood, March 9, 1959, in Eric Voegelin Papers, box 23, file 28, Hoover Institution Archives, Stanford, CA.
7. Voegelin to Ellegood, October 27, 1959, ibid.
8. Ibid.

two very important scientific advances, which found their preliminary formulations in the article "Historiogenesis" (1960) and the lecture "World-Empire and the Unity of Mankind" (1961).[9]

"Historiogenesis" is undoubtedly the more important of the two, as is evident from the repeated revisions it underwent. As early as 1960 its author went as far as to write to Ellegood: "I have hit on something like a theory of relativity for the field of symbolic forms, and the discovery of the theoretical formula that will cover all forms to whatever civilizations they belong has made possible an abbreviation of the whole presentation which I had not dreamt of before. Hence, in spite of the enormous amount of materials covered, Volume IV will not be at all fat." Ellegood, in his reply, sounded equally enthusiastic, referring to "your brilliant first chapter" and stating that "this chapter alone should make Volume IV one of the most important in the entire series."[10] Voegelin's assessment of his discovery as "a theory of relativity" should by no means be read as a mere bold metaphor. For the term *historiogenesis* refers to nothing less than a mytho-speculative type that extrapolates pragmatic history backward to mythic, ontological origins in divine reality, a procedure that begins with the Sumerian King Lists and extends as far as the Christian and later modern speculations on the origins of history, summarized in the sentence that recurs in all four versions: "Historiogenesis is one of the great constants in the search of order from antiquity to the present."

The second important statement originating in those early years was the lecture Voegelin gave at the London School of Economics in March 1961. In it he touched upon the major theme of the projected volume, the question of the plurality of the so-called world-empires from antiquity to modernity, and the accompanying problems of ecumene and the representation of mankind through empire. Voegelin already at that time made a convincing case against the instrumentalization of the ideas of world and mankind that had recently reached its grotesque climax in the totalitarian empires of Nazi Germany and

---

9. "Historiogenesis" first appeared simultaneously in *Philosophisches Jahrbuch* 57 (1960): 419–46, and *Philosophia Viva*, ed. M. Müller and M. Schmaus (Freiburg and Munich, 1960). The revised version published in *Anamnesis* (1966), and the draft of a more extensive version under the title "Anxiety and Reason," in Eric Voegelin, *CW*, vol. 28, *What Is History? and Other Late Unpublished Writings*, ed. Thomas A. Hollweck and Paul Caringella (1990; available Columbia: University of Missouri Press, 1999), finally led to chapter 1 of *The Ecumenic Age*. "World-Empire and the Unity of Mankind: The Stevenson Memorial Lecture, no. 11, 1961," *International Affairs* 38, no. 2 (April 1962): 170–83, reprinted in Eric Voegelin, *CW*, vol. 11, *Published Essays, 1953–1965*, ed. Ellis Sandoz (Columbia: University of Missouri Press, 2000).

10. Voegelin to Ellegood, July 21, 1960, in Voegelin Papers, box 23, file 28; Ellegood to Voegelin, August 17, 1960, ibid.

the Soviet Union. He told his audience that both "world" and "universal mankind" are complex symbols rather than things capable of political organization through domination—for "the order of the world is not of 'this world' alone but also of the 'world beyond.'"[11] Likewise, "mankind is the society of man in history, extending in time from its unknown origin toward its unknown future. Moreover, no crosscut at any time represents mankind by virtue of a common power organization. For the living can represent mankind universally only by their representative humanity; and their humanity is representative only when it is oriented toward the eschatological *telos.*" These insights put an end to a five-thousand-year series of "attempts to represent mankind by means of a finite organization in the present," Voegelin concluded, and he called our time "an epoch in the original sense of suspense," when we know that old forms are dying but do not know more than "prefigurations" of the new forms.[12]

By all appearances, Voegelin had established the pattern that volume IV would follow and thus be ready for the anticipated completion in the early 1960s. There was history as the ontological "index" in the equivalence between the modern construction of the Hegelian *Bewußtseinsgeschichte* and the Sumerian King Lists, and then there was the penetrating analysis of the ultimate insufficiency of the ecumenic enterprises that finds its terse expression in the sentence at the end of the first section of chapter 3 of *The Ecumenic Age:* "Philosophically, the ecumene was a miserable symbol."[13] Both analyses were to carry over into the concluding volume V, as Voegelin indicated in his letter to Ellegood of October 1961 where he specifically mentions the lecture on world-empire as the answer to a problem to be raised in volume IV and to be answered in volume V, "that very intricate problem of what makes our time an 'epoch' in politics and history." At the same time, Voegelin expressed his concern that "a gigantic work" such as the concluding volumes of *Order and History,* "with entirely new ideas," cannot be written without "being supported convincingly by the sources, since otherwise the uproar will be unpleasant." In order to underline the point made in this letter, Voegelin sent another letter to Ellegood only three weeks later, accompanied by a synopsis of what was now called *Empire and Christianity.* There he speaks of "four lines of meaning which had to be represented without making a mess of the book." These "lines

---

11. "World-Empire and the Unity of Mankind," 144.
12. Ibid., 155.
13. Eric Voegelin, *CW,* vol. 17, *The Ecumenic Age,* ed. Michael Franz (1974; Columbia: University of Missouri Press, 2000), 230.

of meaning" permit an insight into the structure of the final version of volume IV insofar as they show how Voegelin intended to approach the problem with which he was confronted. They concern (a) the parallelism between the civilizations of the Ecumenic Age, (b) the internal meaning of each civilization, (c) "the line of meaning which starts 2000 years before the Ecumenic Age, runs through it, and goes into the present," and (d) "the main line of historical meaning running from the Ancient Near East through Rome and Christianity into our Western present—a line by which the developments in India and China appear as side lines."[14] This somewhat abstract description of the project was clearly meant to assuage any fears Ellegood may have had about the eventual publication of the remainder of *Order and History*, but we can be certain that the recipient of the letter remained in the dark about the meaning of the lines of meaning, just as any reader would today, unless he made the heroic effort of thinking through these issues for himself. The one thing that does aid us in understanding what Voegelin had in mind is the explicit comparison between his work and that of Toynbee with which he ended the letter. To put it bluntly, Voegelin thought that Toynbee had made a mess of his *Study of History* by pursuing his own "lines of meaning" instead of seeing the main line, the line that "runs from Israel and Hellas into the West." Thus for Toynbee, contemporary civilizations had "no visible meaning" because without that main line the historian will end up indulging in "a happy fraternization with everybody who lives today as equals." It is worth noting that Toynbee's *Study of History* became a kind of countermodel during these years of struggling toward a tenable conception of volume IV and a blueprint of how not to write a philosophy of history.[15]

But this by no means eased Voegelin's own dilemma, as becomes evident from another letter to Ellegood, written in February 1963. Trying to reassure Ellegood that progress is actually being made, Voegelin lists eight problem-complexes he claims to have solved. They were, in Voegelin's order: (1) the question of natural law; (2) the question of "What is the nature of man and society?" (3) the question of "What is history?" (4) the nature of philosophy; (5) the greatest pest of all, i.e., the terminology of Asiatic civilization; (6) the question of "What does reason mean in scholasticism?" (7) the complex of Apocalypse,

---

14. Voegelin to Ellegood, October 21, 1961, in Voegelin Papers, box 23, file 28; Voegelin to Ellegood, November 13, 1961, ibid.
15. What better illustration of my point than Voegelin's contribution to Edward T. Gargan's volume *The Intent of Toynbee's History,* which appeared under the title "Toynbee's *History* as a Search for Truth" in 1961, reprinted in *Published Essays, 1953–1965,* 100–112. The article is a perfect example of deconstruction, before the word had even been invented.

Christianity, and Gnosis; and (8) the continuity of the Gnostic movement from antiquity to the present.[16] Again, as he had already done a few years earlier, Voegelin emphasized the importance of establishing the continuity between the time of the ecumenic empires and "contemporary political problems." The letter ends with an interesting, even revealing sentence: "As a matter of fact, the greatest obstacle has been overcome, that is the obstacle of writing earlier parts without knowing how the story will end." Did Voegelin really believe for a moment that his story could have an ending in any other sense than that of leading to the present and reinterpreting this present in the light of both the ecumenic past and the irreversible differentiations that mark the transition from cosmological to ecumenic empires?

The following two years brought few visible developments as far as volume IV was concerned, even though 1964 saw the very important and successful lectures "Hitler and the Germans," adding to Voegelin's stature as a political scientist in Germany. Later that year and into early 1965 Voegelin had a visiting professorship at Harvard, during which he gave the Ingersoll Lecture on immortality that would be published in the *Harvard Theological Review* in 1967. When Voegelin finally had to respond again to an inquiry from the press, it was the year 1966; *Anamnesis* had appeared, and Voegelin was no closer to a definitive structure of volume IV than he had been in 1963. Whether he would need one or two volumes to conclude *Order and History,* and what the title, or titles, should be, were questions that remained unanswered. At the same time, Voegelin continued his work on questions that he had not even mentioned in his letter to Ellegood of 1963. As the reader of *Anamnesis* knows, Voegelin's primary concern had become the philosophy of consciousness, and so he could comfortably report to Richard Wentworth, Ellegood's successor at LSU Press, that work on the concluding volume *In Search of Order* was progressing "in a most satisfactory manner," but the volume might have to be divided into two, one under the title *The Language of Consciousness* and the other containing the word *Empire* in its title.[17]

Voegelin's other correspondences, especially that with Manfred Henningsen, keep us informed about his research priorities, which elsewhere found their formulation in three other papers, "Configurations in History" (1968), "Equivalences of Experience" (1970), and "The Gospel and Culture" (1971). When Wentworth again raised the question of the unfinished business, it was late 1969, and Voegelin was an emeritus and Henry Salvatori Distinguished Scholar

---

16. Voegelin to Ellegood, February 13, 1963, in Voegelin Papers, box 24, file 1.
17. Voegelin to Richard L. Wentworth, October 14, 1966, ibid.

at the Hoover Institution. "What held up the further volumes of *Order and History* and practically exploded them," Voegelin then wrote in reply, "is, as I have detailed in earlier correspondence, the vast amount of materials that had to be reworked in order to arrive at the theoretical conclusions that would have to form the skeleton of the whole work. During the last 10 years, I have done one such study after another to be sure of my ground."[18] What Voegelin now proposed as the table of contents of *In Search of Order* was nothing less than a list of virtually all the published and unpublished pieces that had been written since "Historiogenesis," comprising a volume that he estimates at about seven hundred manuscript pages. This volume, divided into sixteen chapters and an introduction, was to contain, among the published papers, the "Historiogenesis" published in *Anamnesis,* followed by an expanded version of "Anxiety and Reason" as well as the papers "The Moving Soul" and "The Eclipse of Reality," all published in volume 28 of *The Collected Works,* and, most important, the Schelling chapter from the *History of Political Ideas,* followed by the manuscripts "Nietzsche and Pascal" and "On Henry James's *Turn of the Screw.*"

It is hard to imagine such a volume as the answer to the issues raised in the actual volume IV, but it is equally hard to imagine the latter without precisely all these individual studies, whether they found inclusion in the final text or not. Voegelin himself was only too aware of the whole new slant this proposal gave to the overall conception of *Order and History.* What he suggested to Richard Wentworth was the following: "There should be a volume entitled *In Search of Order,* which I can offer you now for publication as the volume that will conclude the work I started in *Order and History,* though I would not consider it a fourth volume, but an independent work under the title given." This passage seems to say nothing less than that the grand project of *Order and History* would not be concluded at all, that in some way Voegelin found himself in a predicament comparable to that of Toynbee at the end of his *Study of History,* even if for completely different reasons. Voegelin simply seemed to have outgrown the plan of his *opus magnum,* just as twenty years earlier he had outgrown the project of the *History of Political Ideas.* He once again had reached a point of crisis; and just as the younger Voegelin had found a springboard for overcoming the crisis by working on the Walgreen Lectures, "The New Science of Politics," the older Voegelin found a focal outlet in his work on what was to be called *The Drama of Humanity,* begun as the Candler Lectures at Emory University in the spring of 1967. Yet this time, the crisis was of a different nature. Instead of being caused by the theoretical insufficiencies that

---

18. Voegelin to Wentworth, December 12, 1969, ibid.

made themselves more and more felt in the writing of a history of political ideas, the reasons for the delays in finishing *Order and History* are to be sought in the ever-increasing abundance of "the materials," which itself was the result of both a real improvement in the way the latest scholarly research could be communicated (this was 1969, not 1949) and Voegelin's enormously increased ability to tap into this development. Given this new set of conditions, publishers' deadlines became a limitation rather than an opportunity. *The Drama of Humanity* was at last to be his work, as he would tell Wentworth's successor, Charles East, only seven months later with these words: "As far as *The Drama of Humanity* is concerned, I do not want to make any commitments at the moment. The reason why is that my work is always seriously hampered by deadlines, and for once in my life I want to write a book in peace."[19] If one had to characterize the gist of this book, one could perhaps say, and I do so with some trepidation, that it represented Voegelin's Exodus from Empire and—to some degree—from the history represented by empire. For work on this book coincides with the almost youthful interest he began to take in prehistory, the Paleolithic and Neolithic Ages, aided by his most fruitful acquaintance with the independent scholar Marie König, who introduced him to her extensive research on prehistoric symbols and thus gave him evidence of a human dimension before written history that also constitutes a permanent presence in history.[20]

Whatever the uncertainties regarding the final form of volume IV were, as they were being discussed with Leslie Phillabaum, then assistant director of LSU Press, they began to give way to a genuine conception of the book we now know as *The Ecumenic Age*. The idea of the ecumenic age itself began to yield results that Voegelin had not been able to anticipate earlier, for it enabled him to overcome the "departmentalization" of the peoples around the Mediterranean and in the Ancient Near East and to understand fully the issues of that epoch as a developing fundamental struggle between pragmatic expansion and spiritual exodus.[21] Beginning at the latest in 1971, Voegelin's corre-

---

19. Voegelin to Charles East, July, 14, 1970, ibid.
20. Cf. the account given by Tilo Schabert, "Die Werkstatt Eric Voegelins," *Zeitschrift für Politik* 49 (2002), and Manfred Henningsen's postscript to the German edition of part 2 of *The Ecumenic Age,* mentioned above.
21. Cf. a letter Voegelin wrote to Manfred Henningsen, March 24, 1971, while working on the chapter on the Ecumenic Age of volume IV during spring of 1971 at Notre Dame University. There, he points to the fact that the "departmentalization" into Greeks, Persians, and Jews does not help in understanding either Aristotle or Paul, for it was only the pragmatic expansion that began with Cyrus that gave an ecumenic meaning to the idea of the spiritual exodus that had begun in Israel and could now be seen in Plato's and Aristotle's constructions of the paradigmatic polis.

spondences with LSU Press reveal an author working on a book, except that the book he is working on is not *The Drama of Humanity* but the *Ecumenic Age*—or, shall we say, a book that was to be both. For in the relative peacefulness of his new Stanford surroundings, the questions and problems that had to be dealt with in volume IV began to merge into a philosophy of consciousness which would be both a philosophy of history and a philosophy of man. The reader may at this point be spared a further narration of which earlier pieces were to be incorporated into this book, and which were not. Voegelin was now able to synthesize and condense his earlier studies into a coherent summary of the problems he had encountered on the way, and into a succinct statement of which problems were capable of a solution and which were not.

III

In the context of this account of the genesis of *The Ecumenic Age* it would be presumptive of me to give my interpretation of this text, especially after I have tried to argue until now that its structure owes a great deal to the intervening existential and intellectual history of its author. This history, I argue, left indelible traces on both the structure and the content of Voegelin's last book. These traces not only become visible in Voegelin's own introductory remarks about having had to abandon the original plan of *Order and History* in favor of a different pattern "that did not run along lines of time." His admission that "the original list of five types of order and symbolization turned out to be regrettably limited" has been quoted so often that it almost bears no repeating. Almost! For while it makes so much sense to repeat that someone with Voegelin's breadth of knowledge would eventually have to leave behind the unilinear ladder that made his ascent to the revelatory and noetic differentiations of Israel and Hellas possible, one wonders why he did not do so earlier. My suspicion is that we have in these introductory remarks of Voegelin the noetic equivalent to the conclusion of Wittgenstein's *Tractatus* without Wittgenstein's logical purism. Throwing away the ladder that made the ascent possible was not Voegelin's way of doing *Wissenschaft*. He was able to leave the ladder in its place and to move onto the new plateau he had been able to reach by means of the ladder. The reason he was able to do so is to be found in the different natures of the two ladders. While Wittgenstein's ladder was the ladder of logic, Voegelin's was a kind of spiral ladder, that of "eternal-being-realizing-itself-in-time," as he had formulated it in the abandoned chapter "What Is History?" and in the chapter of *Anamnesis* entitled "Eternal Being in Time." My use of Wittgenstein's ladder is by no means a metaphorical whim. On the contrary, I am trying to make sense of something that has preoccupied serious readers of *Order and History* for almost half a century—the question of the differentiation of consciousness and its direction, which may also be the direction of history. But this question was asked not only by Voegelin's readers but was foremost his own question as well. The open ending of *Plato and Aristotle* with its skeptical Pyrrhonic acceptance of the pragmatic situation created by ecumenic conquest, and the hopeful ending of *Israel and Revelation* with the good news about Jesus Christ, might lead even serious readers to ask for a connection between those states of consciousness and their own. And they would, more often than not, be willing to take the shortcuts of skepticism or belief, in order to connect the present with the past of these two endings.

When one looks back at the problems that occupied Voegelin's thinking during the course of the seventeen years leading up to *The Ecumenic Age,* one finds that the concept of the "ecumenic age" and the idea of a "universal mankind" that accompanied the ecumenic age were the catalysts for solutions that Voegelin might not have found had he stubbornly clung to answering the question of the planned opening chapter of volume IV: "What Is History?" This is vividly demonstrated by his reflections on the "Configurations of History," "The Equivalences of Experience and Symbolization," and by his valiant attempt to bring Athens and Jerusalem together in their understanding of theophany, in "The Gospel and Culture." All of these are issues of symbolic equivalences against the backdrop of the primary experience of the cosmos. I suspect that Voegelin owed the ability to penetrate more deeply into the reasons for these equivalences to the seminal discovery of the equivalence between the mythospeculative extrapolation of pragmatic history into a divine origin and the modern systems that try to give meaning to pragmatic history through speculation on the dialectical processes either of *Geist* or of *Produktionsverhältnisse* or even of *Sein*. When Voegelin coined the term *historiogenesis,* he realized that he had found "a millennial constant" as well as an entirely new access to a theory of symbolization in history; hence the already quoted remark about "something like a theory of relativity for the field of symbolic forms." The persistence of the chapter "Historiogenesis" in all tables of contents for volume IV serves as another indication of its overall importance. But what is the connection between a theory that detects the equivalence of arranging heterogeneous elements of reality on a time-line and Voegelin's philosophy of history and consciousness? Voegelin's answers, given in the beginning sections of "Historiogenesis," make the connection abundantly clear, and it is somewhat surprising that it has found relatively little attention so far. "The mythical part of historiogenetic speculation is not a piece of unhistorical fabulation but an attempt to present the reasons that will raise the *res gestae* of the pragmatic part to the rank of history"[22] is only the first in a series of statements establishing the connection, which originates in the experience of history and the anxiety that accompanies experience in cosmological civilizations, as well as in so-called modern ones, when it becomes aware of reality as a tension between existence and nonexistence. Voegelin's discussion of the "cosmological style of truth" in the *Ecumenic Age* should be read together with the even more extended discussion the complex received in the draft of the extended version of "Historiogenesis" known as "Anxiety and Reason."[23]

What emerges from a parallel reading is a much clearer understanding of the importance Voegelin attached in his later years to the symbolism of the "beginning and the beyond." There is a clear shift of emphasis in the early section of the introduction to *The Ecumenic Age*, entitled "The Beginning and the Beyond," where Voegelin makes reference to the connection between abandoning the idea of history as a meaningful course of events on a straight time line as an Israelitic and Christian discovery. The "Beginning and the Beyond" has become the new symbolic formula for the poles of reality that had been slanted all-too-much toward the beginning in historiogenetic speculation. The experience of divine reality is equivalent in both cosmological societies and the Hellenic, Jewish, Christian forms of exodus—but a new direction has been added, that of the horizon of history and the Beyond. How major the long-term reflections on the implications of historiogenesis were is documented in a remark Voegelin made to Henningsen already in 1967, while working on "The Eclipse of Reality":[24] "History must neither be constructed historiogenetically—from the present back to a beginning (ideologically, as with Schiller), nor 'systematically' from an absolute 'Being' through dialectics, as with Hegel. It must rather set out from the existential situation of the historian, provided he has one. The existential situation, however, is not *only* historical, but is also in tension to eternity."[25]

Moreover, Voegelin's discussion of Jesus and the Unknown God in "The Gospel and Culture" as well as the magnificent analysis of the opening of the Gospel of John and the Gnostic possibilities embedded in it, would not have had the precision of thought required for an understanding of the "I am"–relation to the incarnation in the Son of God or Son of Man. As Voegelin wrote to Henningsen during his work on the final version of volume IV: "I am now working on the MS for the 4th volume. Quite a bit of work, since the older

---

22. Voegelin, *CW,* 17:113.
23. Cf. *CW,* vol. 28, esp. 75–78.
24. Ibid., 111–62.
25. Voegelin to Henningsen, September 29, 1967, in Voegelin Papers, box 17, file 14.

pieces have to be brought up to the level of the newer ones. A lot has to be pieced together. I am just now in the process of patching pieces from the later theoretical study ["Anxiety and Reason"—T. H.] into 'Historiogenesis'. On occasion of this work, one comes across some very pleasant finds, such as the older analysis of *anxiety* [original in English—T. H.], which, as I see only now, recognized the problem of the breakthrough from cosmological pluralism to the unity of the Unknown God that had occupied me in the Gospel-Study ["The Gospel and Culture"—T. H.]. By setting a few accents, the connection between the two pieces can be established. A cohesive book will come out of this after all." Henningsen, in his response to "The Gospel and Culture," had picked up on these connections, when he wrote to Voegelin just two weeks earlier: "The last pages of your 'Gospel'-article really make this essay the center of the fourth volume. What comes after that is, in an existential sense, the 'Drama of Humanity'. This, in my opinion, should become one of the main points of the introduction. What I find excellent is the discussion of the 'Unknown God' and the rejection of the attempts at historiogenetic interpretation in it."[26]

Having established the unique position of the historiogenesis "find," there remains for us only the question of how Voegelin managed to bring about the "cohesiveness" to which he aspired in writing the final manuscript. Raising this question returns us to the beginning of this essay and its title. If we accept Voegelin's thesis, volume IV is of course foremost a study of the ecumenic age and its epochal impact on the history of the civilizations that have been within the horizons of that epoch that has now come to an end. Conquest and spiritual exodus were the defining marks of this epoch, and one can of course argue, as did Voegelin, that one of the central events, if not the central event, was "the epiphany of Christ," "the great catalyst that made eschatological consciousness a historical force, both in forming and deforming humanity."[27] The overarching reality of the ecumenic age is found in the breaking up of the cosmological wholeness, symbolized in the experience of the duality of *oikoumene-okeanos* through which "the habitat of man has become the open field of the imperial drive, and the divine mystery that had surrounded the limited territory and its people has become luminous as the divine presence in a transfiguring process in which all men at all times and all places participate." But even more important, the dissociation of the primary experience of the cosmos into expansion and spiritual exodus does not become an unbridgeable gulf when it is under-

---

26. Voegelin to Henningsen, December 6, 1970, ibid.; Henningsen to Voegelin, November 25, 1970, ibid.
27. Voegelin, *CW,* 17:66.

stood that "the bond that prevents the two pieces of reality from falling apart into the two realities of apocalyptic and Gnostic thinkers is found in history."[28]

The history of which Voegelin is speaking here is one that has left its historiogenetic limitation behind and has indeed assumed an "epochal" dimension. This dimension involves the structure of human consciousness itself. "The structure of human consciousness as it becomes luminous for its own historicity is obscured if not destroyed, if one isolates the events of the spiritual exodus from the events of historiography that arise in its wake, and if one ignores the fact that the historians deal with the disturbance of order through the concupiscential exodus in the light of the insight gained by the spiritual outburst—be it Herodotus and Thucydides, or Polybius and Livy, or the Israelite historians from the author of the David Memoirs to the Chronicler, or the Chinese historian Sse-ma Ch'ien." This is Voegelin's final critique of Jaspers's "axis time." Only through an understanding of the unity of ecumene and exodus can we hope to find the open horizon in history and in our consciousness to which the title of this essay alludes. "The 'epoch' involves, besides the spiritual outbursts, the ecumenic empires from the Atlantic to the Pacific and engenders the consciousness of history as the new horizon that surrounds with its divine mystery the existence of man in the habitat that has been opened by the concupiscence of power and knowledge."[29]

One may do well to read this as the good news mentioned at the beginning of this essay. To recite the good news, however, will not be enough; as with all good news, we should strive to live by what it tells us. For the scholar and scientist, this means the practice of genuine ecumenic thinking.

28. Ibid., 380.
29. Ibid., 384–85.

Contributors

Barry Cooper is professor of political science at the University of Calgary. His teaching and research has focused the insights of political philosophers on contemporary issues, including the significance of technology and the media, the constitutional status of Quebec and Alberta, Canadian military policy, and modern terrorism. Cooper's many publications reflect the dual focus of his work. He publishes a weekly column in the *Calgary Herald* and often has hunted with Ellis Sandoz.

Elizabeth Corey received her Ph.D. in political science from Louisiana State University in 2004, under the guidance of Professor Ellis Sandoz. Currently she teaches in the Interdisciplinary Core and Great Texts programs at Baylor University and is working on a manuscript that focuses on the relations among aesthetics, religion, and political philosophy in the work of Michael Oakeshott.

Steven D. Ealy is a senior fellow at Liberty Fund. He is author of *Communication, Speech, and Politics: Habermas and Political Analysis* (1981). Ealy edited "Joseph Conrad: Master of Illusion," a previously unpublished essay by Robert Penn Warren, for publication in the *American Oxonian,* and co-edited the Eric Voegelin–Willmoore Kendall correspondence for the *Political Science Reviewer.*

Charles R. Embry is professor of political science, Texas A&M-Commerce. He was an undergraduate student of Ellis Sandoz at Louisiana Tech University, 1964, and colleague at Texas A&M-Commerce (formerly East Texas State University), 1969–1977. He is the editor of *Robert B. Heilman and Eric Voegelin: A Friendship in Letters, 1944–1984* (University of Missouri Press).

Michael Franz is professor of political science at Loyola College in Maryland. His scholarship focuses on political problems in the philosophy of history. In addition to numerous scholarly articles, he is the author of *Eric Voegelin and the Politics of Spiritual Revolt,* and the editor of Eric Voegelin's *The Ecumenic Age,* vol. 17 of *The Collected Works of Eric Voegelin.*

Timothy Fuller is the Lloyd E. Worner Distinguished Service Professor and professor of political science at Colorado College. He has written on liberal education and on the British intellectual tradition, especially Thomas Hobbes and Michael Oakeshott, and related topics. He has edited several volumes of Oakeshott's papers and is currently at work on a short volume on Oakeshott's thought. He has studied and taught the work of Eric Voegelin for more than thirty years and is a member of the Eric Voegelin Society.

Jürgen Gebhardt, emeritus professor of political science at Friedrich-Alexander University, Erlangen-Nuremberg, completed his dissertation under the direction of Eric Voegelin. He has taught at several universities in the United States as well as in Beijing. He has been active in the German political science community and the Bavaria-America Academy. He has published major studies in European and American politics and political thought.

Thomas Hollweck is professor of German culture and literature at the University of Colorado at Boulder. He is a member of the Editorial Board of the Collected Works of Eric Voegelin. He is the author of a book on Thomas Mann and of numerous publications on German literature as well as the work of Voegelin. Most recently he edited *Die Legitimität der Antike,* part 1 of *The Ecumenic Age.*

Timothy Hoye is professor of government at Texas Woman's University. His doctorate in political science is from Duke University, where he studied with and was an assistant to John H. Hallowell. He has served as a Fulbright exchange scholar at Hiroshima University in Japan and is the author of *Japanese Politics: Fixed and Floating Worlds.* Ellis Sandoz directed his undergraduate and master's level studies in political science.

Glenn Hughes is professor of philosophy at St. Mary's University in San Antonio, Texas. He is the author or editor of several books, including *Mystery and Myth in the Philosophy of Eric Voegelin* (1993) and, most recently, *Transcendence and History: The Search for Ultimacy from Ancient Societies to Postmodernity* (2003). He has published numerous articles on Voegelin's thought as well as on that of the philosopher and theologian Bernard Lonergan.

Stephen A. McKnight is professor emeritus of European intellectual and cultural history at the University of Florida. He is author/editor of seven books, including *Sacralizing the Secular, The Modern Age and the Ancient Wisdom,* and *Science, Pseudo-Science, and Utopianism in Early Modern Thought*. In 2002 he was appointed by President George W. Bush to a four-year term on the National Humanities Council.

Martin Palous, one of the first signatories of Charter 77, served as spokesman for this dissident human rights group in 1986. He is currently ambassador of the Czech Republic to the United States. He has been active in several non-governmental organizations in Europe and taught at Charles University, Prague. He has published extensively on contemporary European politics and political philosophy and translated the works of Hannah Arendt into Czech.

Brendan Purcell is senior lecturer in philosophy at University College Dublin. He is the author to *The Drama of Humanity: Towards a Philosophy of Humanity in History*, and, with Detlev Clemens, he translated and edited Eric Voegelin's *Hitler and the Germans*.

Tilo Schabert, professor at the Friedrich-Alexander University, Erlangen-Nuremberg, has taught and lectured extensively in Europe, America, and Australia. He has been a filmmaker for Bavarian television, the director of the annual ERANOS conferences in Ascona, a member of several academic councils, as well town councillor in Baierbrunn (Munich), and was recently awarded the German-French Parliamentary Prize by the German Federal Parliament and the French National Assembly. He has written extensively on political philosophy, religion, and architecture, and his work has been translated into Portuguese, Croatian, Arabic, Hindi, and Chinese.

David Walsh, professor of politics at The Catholic University in Washington, DC, is the author of a number of works, including *After Ideology* and *The Growth of the Liberal Soul*. He is presently completing a third volume on modernity, *The Luminosity of Existence: An Outline of the Philosophic Revolution of the Modern World*. Ellis Sandoz was the person who welcomed him to the United States when he arrived from Ireland.

Gilbert Weiss teaches political theory and European Union studies at the University of Salzburg. He is the editor of *Theorie, Relevanz und Wahrheit. Eine Rekonstruktion des Briefwechsels zwischen Eric Voegelin und Alfred Schuetz (1938–1959)*, several volumes of *The Collected Works of Eric Voegelin* (with William Petropulos), and, with Ruth Wodak, wrote *Critical Discourse Analysis: Theory and Interdisciplinarity*.

James L. Wiser has been the provost and vice-president of Academic Affairs at the University of San Francisco since 1998. From 1989 to 1998 he served as the senior vice-president and dean of faculties at Loyola University of Chicago. He received his B.A. degree in government from the University of Notre Dame and his M.A. and Ph.D. in political science from Duke University. Wiser has published three books and numerous scholarly articles in the field of political philosophy.

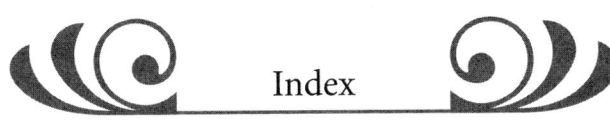

Index

Adenauer, Konrad, 236, 255
Akhenaton (Amenothep VI), 64, 68
Alexander, 325
Al Qaeda, 294
American polity, 224, 225
Amor Dei, 85
Anamnesis (remembrance/recollection or not forgetting), 205; in Bacon, 312; in Freud and Heidegger, 59; in Freud and Voegelin, 60–63; personal (Palous), 260–67; Platonic, 313; principle of investigation (Freud), 59
Anamnetic meditation, 140
Anoia, 202
Anschluss, 269
Apollinaire, Guillaume, 71
Arendt, Hannah, 212, 262; *Origins of Totalitarianism*, 278; on "the political," 216
Aristophanes: *Knights*, 32
Aristotle, 22, 228, 259, 271; *The Generation of Animals*, 124; *homonoia* of, 185; hylemorphic context of, 104; on *philomythos*, 125; as *philomythoteros*, 125, 169; on *philosophos*, 125; *to politikon*, 211
Arthur, Wallace: *The Origin of Animal Body Plans*, 114
Augustine, 79, 89, 117
Augustus, 249
Auschwitz, 278

Bacon, Francis: age of Christ in, 312; apocalyptic vision of Daniel, 322; fall of man, 314; "Great Instauration" compared with Voegelin's analysis of Gnosticism, 321–24; "Great Instauration," 303–21; immanentization of apocalyptic learning, 322; *Novum Organum*, 317; on knowledge as recollection, 312, 320

— *The Advancement of Learning*: apocalyptic themes in, 310; on charity and pride, 314; critique of Platonic and Aristotelian philosophy in, 310; critique of Scholastic learning in, 315; dedication to James I, 310; depiction of James I, 312–13, 319; on fields of knowledge, 315–16; First Book of, 311–18; hierarchy of human knowledge in, 316; history, natural and ecclesiastical, 320; on human nature, 320; on knowledge and sin, 315; Moses, 317; on original sin, 314; *prima philosophia*, 316, 320; Second Book of, 318–21; Solomon, 317; on Solomon and Paul, 314; spiritual renewal, 321; true philosophy, 316

— *Great Instauration*, 303; apocalyptic restoration of Jerusalem in, 304, 310; dedication of, 306–7; knowledge in, 309; preface of, 307–10; title page of, 304–5; restoration of humanity in, 309; working of Divine Providence in, 309
Balthasar, Hans von Urs, 326, 327
Baudelaire, Charles, 247
Being: eternal and unmovable, 264; ground of, 101, 300; hierarchy of, 104–5; human, in tension, 232; mystery of, 21; objectification of, 19; opening of, 12; parousia of, 16; realms of, 135, 186; truth of, 7, 12
Berg, L.: *Nomogenesis or Evolution Determined by Law*, 114
Bergson, Henri, 83, 140, 143, 153
Bickerton, Derek, 121
Big Bang theory, 105, 112
Bismarck, Otto von, 277
Body, 170–73 *passim*, 181, 199, 318; common plan of, 113, 114, 115; and consciousness, 172, 174, 183, 184, 185; and contact with world, 174; and hunting, 34, 35, 42, 43;

mind and, 201; new parts for, 115; as sensorium of consciousness, 170, 185; and soul, 48, 49; of Virtue, 46; well-trained, 49
Bratinka, Pavel, 262
Breton, André: mentioned, 72
Bruell, Christopher: on Xenophon, 29
Butler, Richard: *The Mind of Santayana,* 137

Caesar, 249
Cann, Rebecca, 122
Carter, Jimmy, 250
Cartesian: doubt, 98; rationalism, 92
Central Europe, 265, 266, 267, 268, 274, 278, 283
Chaosmos, 235, 246, 247
Chomsky, Noam, 121
Chushingura, 196
Christ, 304, 312, 317, 336; epiphany of, 338
Christian, 117, 195, 196; anthropological insights, 79; categories, 23; connotation of "stray sheep," 194; discovery, 337; ethics, 54; forms of exodus, 337; "humility," 172; parable, 197; spirituality, 24; teaching, 75; tradition, 87, 224, 268; virtues, 323; vision of existence, 78; vision of *imago dei,* 79
Christianity, 10, 14, 67, 68, 79, 87, 298, 302, 322, 328 329, 331, 332; mission of salvation, 297
Cicero, 96
Civilization(s): boundaries of, 291; clash of, 285; Islamic, 299; literature on, 291; psycho-spiritual ties to, 299; Western, 288, 298
Closure: of existence, 15, 16; spiritual, 300. *See also* Openness
Common *nous,* 200, 203; as collective subconscious, 198; of Japan, 189, 195, 197; of Meiji society, 198
Common sense, 268, 279, 283, 287; American, 266, 267, 269; Anglo-Saxon, 269; compact rationality of, 99; pluralistic, 280; realism, 100; reason and, 97; of Scottish School, 96; and self-conscious insight, 99; tradition of, 96; and Voegelin's restoration, 100; Voltaire on, 96
Communism: collapse of, 265, 283, 284; Soviet, 279
Comte, Auguste, 55, 69, 73, 92
Conflict(s): core of civilizational, 292; cross-civilizational, 285, 286
Conrad, Joseph, 168

Consciousness: biography of, 140, 172; birth of, 184; body as sensorium of, 170; concrete human, 220, 221; of embodied human being, 186; embodiment of, 171; and experience of an other, 171; history of, 94; intentionality of, 149; luminosity of, 149; "modes of," 60, 61; noetic, 95; open form of, 101; paradoxical structure of, 152; particularistic, 298; pluralistic, 298; as process of human-divine encounter, 82; reflective distance of, 186; role of body in, 183; structure of, 101, 339; theory of human, 93, 101; transcendence of, 171
Cosmion: political, 93, 219, 221, 300; society as, 193
Cosmos: primary experience of, 336; dissociation of, 338
Coulter, Ann, 298
Creativity: actualization of, by politicians, 239; general law of, 240; and governing, 243; logic of, in politics, 246–48, 254; paradox of, 242–44; political, 235; process of, 235; as result of governing, 242
Crick, Bernard, 212
Crick, Francis, 112, 113
Czechoslovakia, 260

Darwin, Charles, 54, 105, 113, 116
Darwinian: evolutionary paradigm, 121; fundamentalists, 115; theory, 117
Darwinism, 114, 116
Davidson, Eric H.: *Genomic Regulatory Systems,* 115
Dawkins, Richard, 117; *The Selfish Gene,* 109
De Chirico, Giorgio, 71–72; "Exquisite Corpses" (poem), 73
Deconstruction, 21
Delebecque, Eduard: on Xenophon, 30
Democracies, Western, 298
Dennett, Daniel: notion of evolutionary algorithms, 108
Derrida, Jacques, 18–22, 23, 262; constrictions of language, 18; *différance,* 20; existential turn of, 20; and Heidegger, 21; influence of on postmodern thought, 19; on language, 18–19; language of religion, 20; longing for a presence, 19; religion without God, 20; shift from intentionality to luminosity, 20
Descartes, René, 96, 98
Dewey, John, 269

Dignity, 77, 89. *See also* Human dignity
Disorder(s): of modern world, 222; political, 286; resistance to, 94; spiritual, 286, 299

Easton, David: Weberianism of, 211
Egophany, 200, 204
Eisenhower, Dwight D., 236, 251, 253
Eisenstadt, Samuel, 220
Eldredge, Niles, 114
11/9, 267
Ellis, George, 112
Enactment/reenactment, 153, 167
Enlightenment, 322, 324; claim about religion, 225; "humanism," 92; tradition, 96
Eric Voegelin Society, 259, 265
Existence: authentic spiritual, 299; closure toward, 15, 16; "deficient modes of," 81; deformation of closed, 86; dignity of human, 78; experiential ground of, 222; "flux of," 88; luminosity of, 11, 16; modes of, 90; as mystery, 22, 292; "natural world of human," 261; openness of, 84; primacy of, 26; questions of, 116; "in revolt," 300; "in tension," 300; transcendent ground of, 83; in truth, 299; truth of, at stake, 294; in untruth, 299
Experience(s): biographical, 170; "border," 147; commonsense, 140; concrete, lived, 140, 187, 224; enacted, 151; expressed in poetry, 139; of *helkein*, 69; of *kinein*, 69; of luminosity, 142; modes of, 220; originating, 148, 149; of others, 296; participatory, 149; pre-analytical level of, 282; religious, 69, 299; spirit as part of human, 137; spiritual, 292; transcendent, 220, 137

Faith, 5, 11, 223; articles of, 320; existential, 84; *fides caritate formata* (faith formed by love), 87; leap of, 9; status of, 20; vicissitudes of, 84; and trust, 27; and uncertainty, 84
Fanaticism: religiously charged, 294; wellsprings of, 300
Fink, Eugen, 262
Finkelkraut, Alain, 262
Fortescue, 212
Freedom, 18, 228, 241, 279, 284; consciousness of, 209; dominion of, 242; exercise of, 84; "God, immortality, or," 6; human, 5, 25; and human dignity, 268; increasing degree of, 109; "justice, and peace," 74; longing for total, 185; and obedience, 77; of being, 75; rational, 75, 76; and rationality, 77; spirit and, 221; substantiated, 83; unalienable rights and, 283
Friendship(s), 181; art of, 249; as the highest good, 250; in Mitterrand's life, 249; as object of hunt, 33; politics of, 249; and power, 250
Freud, Sigmund: *Die Traumdeutung* (*The Interpretation of Dreams*), 54, 58; elements of Freudian approach, 55; *Future of an Illusion*, 69; and guilt, 66; and Helmholtz school, 58; history of individual/history of mankind, 55, 56–57; "Jenseits des Lustprizips," 70; *Moses and Monotheism*, 63–69; and "Nirvana principle" (death urge), 70; Oedipus complex, 67; and religion, 55; *Sinnverstehen* (interpretation) as method of psychoanalysis, 57–58; surrealism as Freudian realm of dead, 71; and thanatocracy, 69–73; *Totem und Tabu*, 56; tragic humanism of, 66, 69–70
Functionalism, 292
Fukuyama, Francis, 287

Gargett, Robert: "Grave Shortcomings," 118–19
Gay, Peter, 65
Geist (of Hegel), 336
Geistkreis, 268
Genbunitchi, 191
Gerber, C. F. von, 277
Gierke, Otto Friedrich von, 277
Glucksmann, André, 262
Gnosticism, 299; feature of modernity, 224, 225; Puritan, elements of, 302–3; Puritan, and Bacon's Great Instauration, 310, 322–24
Goethe, Johann Wolfgang von, 29, 209
Gomperz, Theodor: on Xenophon, 29
Good, 94, 98, 204; common, 283; the highest, 320; human, 273, 297; love of the, 179, 185; a perfect, 138; transcendent, 84, 95
Gorbačev, Michail, 263
Gould, Stephen J., 113; on "exaption" or "cooption," 108; *Rock of Ages*, 117; *The Structure of Evolutionary Theory*, 114; *Wonderful Life*, 115
Governing: classical structures of, 237; and creation of power, 251; and friendship, 249; "is creativity," 235; and paradox of power, 240–42; styles and practices of, 236

Government, 235; civil, 212; good, 243
Great War, 1914–1918, 277, 279
Groves, Colin P.: *A Theory of Human and Primate Evolution*, 114
Guthrie, W. K. C.: *A History of Greek Philosophy*, 28

Habermas, Jürgen, 262
Haiku, 192
Havel, Václav: "Stories and Totalitarianism," 263
Hawking, Stephen, and George Ellis: *The Large Scale Structure of Space-Time*, 112
Hegel, Georg Wilhelm Friedriech, 25, 55, 209; *Bewusstseingeschichte* of, 330; *History of Philosophy*, 210; and Schelling, 7–8; *Vorlesungen über die Geschichte der Philosophie*, 265
Heidegger, Martin, 12–18, 25, 262; *Being and Time*, 12; *Daseinsanalyse* of, 59; and modern philosophic revolution, 15; mystery of Being, 21; on Nietzsche, 11; and political misjudgments, 14; postmodern thinkers under shadow of, 16; *Seingeschichte* of, 326
Held, David: *Political Theory Today*, 216
Henningsen, Manfred, 102
Heracles, 274
Heraclitus, 283
Hermes Trismegistus, 313
Herodotus, 339; *Histories*, 211
Higgins, W. E.: *Xenophon the Athenian*, 30
Historiogenesis, 197, 204; Japanese, 194; mytho-speculative type, 329; mythical part of, 336
Hitler, Adolf, 87
Hobbes, Thomas, 132, 248, 249
Homer, 32
Hoover, Herbert C., 241
Human beings: as creative, 235; deformed images of, 86; as equal in dignity, 74; and government, 248
Human dignity: and Christian teaching, 75; as exercise of rational freedom, 76; and Greek philosophy, 75; as *imago Dei*, 75; as spiritual equality, 76; as theomorphic, 78
Human nature: classical teaching on, 297; deformation of, 63; demonizing of, by Freud, 63; fulfillment of, 78; imaginative capacity of, 150; noetic-pneumatic openness of, 62

Hume, David: *Treatise on Human Nature* (1739), 96
Hunting: ancient critics of, 45; art of, 32; of big game, 32; of birds, 33; compared to art of the general, 34; in daylight, of water animals, 32; of hares, 32; and hounds, 34; of human beings, 33; an *icon* of philosophy, 35; induced piety, 35; language of, 33; love of, and gymnastics, 35; at night, 33; of four-footed beasts, 33; on the sea, 33; and philosophy, 33; posthumous (of Orion), 32; and sophism, 47–49; in Xenophon, 35–51. See also *Paideia*
Huntington, Samuel P., *The Clash of Civilizations and the Remaking of World Order*, 285–301; civilizations in, 291; "The Clash of Civilizations?" 286; criticism of multiculturalism, 288; criticism of Western universalism, 297; functionalism in, 293; general assessment of, 301; immanentism of, 293; and monocivilizational viewpoints, 295, 296; philosophical anthropology of, 287; rejection of "cultural neutrality," 287, 288, 289; on role of religion in civilizations, 287, 290, 292, 293; shortcomings of, 291–99
Husserl, Edmund, 58, 150; *Lebenswelt* of, 261; phenomenology of, 268

Identity, 82, 84, 86, 276, 295, 300, 301; at any level, 287; future identity of Europe, 265; and group cohesiveness, 294; of legal order, 281; personal, 298; search for, 198, 267; self as moral, 154, 161; of substance (psyche), 81–82; sources of, 292; Western, 296
Ideologist(s), 292
Ikebe Yoshitaka, 191
Imagination, 170, 171, 205, 220; "assertive," 151; creative (of Voegelin), 328; "flight of," 137; lift consciousness through, 188; logic of, 187; "and memory," 182; modern, 15; "passionate," 143; of the philosopher, 186; "power of," 186; spatio-temporal, 20; world-building, 219
Imago Dei, 78; as participation in transcendent, 75; Christian vision of, 79
Inoue Kowashi, 190, 191
Intentionality: and luminosity, 13, 149, 186; and thing-Reality, 149
International Court of Justice, 278
Islamic fundamentalists, 94

Ito Hirobumi: *Commentaries on the Constitution of the Empire of Japan,* 190
Iwakura Mission to the West, 190
Ivanov, V. I., and M. O. Gershenzon: *Correspondence across a Room,* 82

Jaeger, Werner: on Xenophon, 29
James I (England): compared with Solomon, 307, 311; contrasted with Queen Elizabeth, 319; Epistle Dedicatory (*Great Instauration*) to, 306; linked with Providence, 313; opportunity proffered by Bacon to, 318
James, William, 269, 271–73; "The One and the Many," 270; pragmatism of, 266; *Pragmatism,* 269; on Santayana's *Life of Reason,* 130
Jan Hus Foundation, 262
Japan: mythic traditions of, 194
Jaspers, Karl, 262, 278, 326; "axis time" of, 339; "Die Forderung der Wissenschaftlichkeit," 58
Jellinek, Georg, 277
Joachim of Flora, 322
Johnson, Lyndon B., 236, 253
Jones, Ernest: mentioned, 65
Joyce, James, 235
Judaeo-Christian: revelation, 100; civilization, 278
Judaism, 14, 68; father-religion of, 67; Freud's relation with, 65
Jurisprudence: American politics and, 280; course (of Voegelin), 282; realm of, 274
Justus, James: *The Achievement of Robert Penn Warren,* 166

Kádár, János, 174
"Kampademia," 261, 265
Kant, Immanuel, 25; "Copernican Revolution" of, 270; *The Critique of Judgment,* 6; critique of pure reason, 6; and disclosure of being, 5; on human dignity, 75; on moral autonomy, 75; "perpetual peace" of, 279; and primacy of existence, 5; and rational exercise of freedom, 84; superiority of practical reason, 5
Karatani Kojin, 191
Kelsen, Hans, 267, 276; *Allgemeine Staatslehre,* 275; "pure theory of law," 274, 275, 277; view of law, 281
Kennan, George, 279
Kennedy, John F., 253

Kierkegaard, Søren, 8, 23–26, 54, 90; and the absurd, 23; and Christianity, 10; and contingency, 24; as first postmodern thinker, 10; and irony, 24; and language, 10, 23, 24; participation and existence, 23, 25; and philosophy of existence, 9; postmodern debate around, 10; time and eternity, 23
Knowledge, 60–62, 270, 272, 304–24 *passim;* absolute, 7, 19, 25, 26; correspondence theories of, 6; derivation of, from Being, 14; divine, 271; "the end of man is," 157, 160; as enactment, 153, 168; existence prior to, 16; existential, 8; freedom and, 86; of good and evil, 184; historical, 87; human, 272; as imposition of categories, 6; instauration of, 304; key to, 58; limited, 167; meditative, of participation, 4; "men reach out for," 124; of noumenon, 5; of *paideia* of hunting, 45; participatory requirement of, 23; philosophical, 125; political, 99; power and, 339; prereflective, 8; and pride, 308; problem of, 269; as questioning, 124; of reality, 148; search for, 19; and sensible intuitions, 5; rehabilitation of, 304; of "religious experiences," 219; scientific, 105; and sin, 308; theory of, 270; and will, 86; will for, 59
Kohl, Helmut, 236
Kokutai, 191
Kolakowski, L., 73
König, Marie, 102, 334

Laband, Paul, 277
Labarrière, Pierre-Jean, 262
Ladurie, Emmanuel LeRoy, 262
Language, 263, 264. *See also* Derrida, Jacques; Kierkegaard, Søren; Santayana, George
Law: American, 225; of creativity in politics, 240; educative function of, 233; natural, 276; nature of, 227, 267; pre-analytical experiential basis of, 282; role of individuals in, 227; rule of, 224, 225, 232, 283; and self-regulation, 227; of structural similarity, 239; temporality of, 226, 282
Leadership: political, 234; study of, 238
Lenin, 73; mausoleum, 72
Lévinas, Emmanuel, 23, 262; ethics and ontology, 17; existence as disclosure of philosophy, 17; on Heidegger, 16; and luminosity, 18; and the other, 17; truth of ethics in, 18

Levy, David, 262
Lewis, C. S.: *An Experiment in Criticism,* 153; *The Silver Chair,* 146–47
Liberty, 49, 87, 255; individual, 228; in tension with destiny, 168; and organization, 240; as object of constitutional government, 241; and stability, 247
Lieberman, Philip: *Eve Spoke,* 120–21
Life: animal, 104, 113, 115; biological, 104; botanical, 104; of Christian existence, 78; and community, 171; contemplative, 135; daily oughts of, 230; and death, 73, 147, 153, 222; of fidelity, 10; finiteness of human, 220; good, 107; human, 25, 104, 132; in-between of human, 222; luminosity of, 21; meaning of, 70; minimum condition for, 133; modern political, 224; moral, 5, 17; mysterious fullness of, 11; origin of, 113; Nietzsche exalts, 11; originating experience, 150; philosophical, 51; philosophy as way of, 4, 141; plant, 109; political, 51, 213, 247; possible purpose of, 231; psychic, 58, 63, 113; of reason, 78, 83, 99; religious, 142; sanctity of human, 87; of "soul in openness toward God," 85; spheres of, 215; of spirit, 78, 142; of virtue, 22
Livy, 339
Locke, John, 96, 138; and civility, 228; *Second Treatise,* 228
Logos, 60, 153; divine, 88
Lonergan, Bernard: "emergent probability" of, 105–13; compared with Voegelin, 102–12, 122–23; criticism of Darwin, 105; and notion of explanatory genus, 106; "scheme of recurrence" in, 105; philosophy of science, 103; on reductionist fallacy, 106–7
Love: of divine Reason, 84
Luminosity, 99; and It-Reality, 141, 149; experiences of, 142; of life, 21
Lyotard, Jean-François, 262

Machiavelli, 246
Madison, James, 247
Malraux, André, 246
Mann, Thomas, 90
Mao Zedong, 87
Marburg school, 275
Marcel, Gabriel, 86
Marx, Karl, 54, 55, 69, 73; and Young Hegelians, 9; revolutionary idea of, 302
Marxist philosophy, 9
Materialism: of Epicurus and Lucretius, 130; of Hobbes, 132; and liberalism, 131; of Marx, 130, 132; as naturalism, 129; of Santayana, 130–35
McMullin, Ernan, 118
Meiji: era, 189; "spirit" of, 190
Mellars, Paul: *The Neanderthal Legacy,* 119, 120, 121
Metalepsis, 95
Metaxy (in-between), 103, 168; as symbol in Voegelin, 82–83; Cosmic, 102; of consciousness, 83
Miller, Stanley, 112
Miller, Walter: on Xenophon's *Kyropaideia,* 31
Mirror of the Prince: tradition of, 237
Mirror for Princes (Nizamulmuk), 239
Mitterrand, François: on ambiguity and ambivalence, 247; and art of friendship, 249, 254; and art of governing, 237–40; as classical Prince, 234–57 *passim;* compared with Roosevelt, 255–56; and creation of chaos, 256–57; creativity of, 243, 254; and the Elysée, 253; governing, 245, 246, 255; on paradox of power, 242; as prince of *chaosmos,* 246; second government of, 252
Modernity, 232; and technology, 3; Gnosticism as feature of, 224; irony of, 87; Western, and progress, 87
Monism, 270
Monod, Jacques: *Chance and Necessity,* 112–13
Mori Arinori, 195
Multiculturalism, 288, 298
Mystery: of engendering reality, 104; of epiphany of structures, 118, 122; of historical process, 104; of transcendence, 85
Myth: as articulation of existence, 151; Egyptian, 152; and philosophy, 151; Plato's "likely stories," 169

Nádas, Péter, *A Book of Memories,* 170–87; compared with Voegelin, 185–87
Nagel, Thomas: *The Last Word,* 116
Napoleon, Emperor, 209
National Review, 298
National Socialism, 269
Natsume Soseki, 188–206 *passim;* Meian (*Light and Darkness*), 193; Michikusa (*Grass by the Wayside*), 193; *Mon* (*Gate*), 189, 190, 201–3; Sanshiro, 189, 193–97; Sorekara (*And Then*), 189, 198–201

Nazi Germany, 74
Neanderthals, 108, 118
Neubauer, Zdenek, 262
Neumann, Harry: on Xenophon, 29
New World Order, 266
Nichiren: teachings of, 201
Nietzsche, 54, 55, 69; and existential truth, 11; *The Use and Abuse of History,* 158; *Zarathustra,* 11
9/11, 267, 285, 286, 294, 299, 300
Nixon, Richard M., 253
Noesis, 269; of Plato and Aristotle, 325; as process, 271
Nous: transcendent divine, 76, 78

Oakeshott, Michael, 144, 212
Oe Kenzaburo, 188
Openness: toward Being, 14; challenge of loving, 85; existential, and closure, 88; to experience, 144, 151; to great Ought, 232; intellectual and spiritual, 135; to larger truth, 231; logic of, 11; in Lonergan's "emergent probability," 106; loving, to divine mystery, 84; as mode of human existence, 22; of mythopoetic enterprise, 153; noetic-pneumatic, 62; as struggle, 89; to transcendent ground of being, 83; virtues of, 83, 89
Order(s): of Being/being, 94, 100, 221; concreteness of, 230; configurations of, and disorder, 285; of existence, 220; forces of, and disorder, 274; grounded in transcendent experience, 220; humanity and, 221; idea of, 224; larger social/political, 230; multicivilizational, 298; political quest for, 222; right, 220; totalitarian, 231; transcendent source of, 264; truth of, 221, 231

Paideia, 31, 37, 46; and hunting, 32–35, 40–42, 43, 45, 50; and war, 42
Parmenides, 263
Parsons, Talcott, 211
Participation, 4, 26, 85, 141; active, in experience, 153; active, in order of being, 141; being, 7; of beings in Being, 13; in deliberation (on lawfulness), 229; denial of, in divine, 78; in the divine, 75, 76, 77, 82, 143; in divine freedom and knowledge, 85; in the eternal, 24; in existence, 25; in God, 78; gift of, 84; "in great dialogue," 82; in the ground, 125; as object of inquiry, 101; perspective of, 16; in reality, 148, 154; and responsive communion, 83; termini of, 183; in thing-reality and It-reality, 186; of things in one another, 183; and transcendent ground, 75, 101; in transcendent reality, 292
Patočka, Jan, 261, 263, 264, 265, 283; "The Beginning of History," 262
Percy, Walker: *Lost in the Cosmos,* 121
Perestrojka, 263
Perry, Matthew C., 189
Petropoulos, William, 79
Philia, Platonic, 185
Philia politike, 179
Philosophical anthropology, 112; and Voegelin, 103, 123
Philosophical schools, 258; Platonic, Stoic, Skeptic, 326
Philosophy: in classical sense, 259; as differentiated articulation of existence, 151; as experience and participation, 139–43; experiential springs of, 139; and hunting, 42–45; and instrumentality, 3; and paradox, 22; as participation 4; philosophizing about 5; of Plato and Aristotle, 308; and poetry, 151, 169; postmodern, 11; return of, 5; as struggle for true understanding, 81; as way of life, 141
Philotheros (lover of the hunt), 35
Pinker, Steven, 121
Pittau, Joseph, 190
Plato, 21, 89, 169, 176, 246, 259, 264, 312; *Apology,* 273; *Euthydemus,* 34; *Gorgias,* 169; *Laws,* 33, 35; *Nous* or reason of, 94; *Phaedrus,* 169; *Republic,* 34–35; *Sophist,* 32; *Symposium,* 163; *to politikon,* 211
Platonic anthropological principle, 176
Plotinus, 60
Pluralism, 270; cosmological, 338; noetic, 271; social, 297
Plutarch, 238
Pneumopathological: fear, 116; vacuum, 73; criterion in Voegelin, 62, 63
Podhoretz, Norman, 262
Poiema, 153
Politics: global, 285, 298; ideological, 101; as destiny, 209, 210; monarchical version, 213; paradox of, and the Prince, 244–46; and power in Elysée Palace, 244; reality of, 244; republican version, 213
Politike episteme, 92–96 *passim;* 100

Politische, das, 213
Polybius, 339
Pragmatism, 271; as noetic stance, 272; as genuine American philosophy, 273; of John Dewey, 269; of William James, 266, 269
Presence, 18, 19, 21, 153, 226, 281; in consciousness, 60, 62, 78, 80; divine, 76, 77, 79, 82, 83, 85, 86, 95, 338; of divine Nous in ordering existence, 78; of divine reality, 104; flux of, 103, 293, 334; of knowledge, 60; language of, 20; metaphysics of, 14, 16, 18; mode of, 20, 25, 148
Produktionsverhältnisse (of Marx), 336
Pyrrho, 325

Raff, Rudolf: *The Shape of Life,* 115
Rákosi, Mátyás, 174
Reality: of absolute reason, 54; Austrian, 277; deformation of, 150; of experience, 125; of humanity as *imago Dei,* 77; mystery of, 84, 125; of natural world, 54; participation in transcendent, 292; participatory character of, 141, 148, 154; personal encounter with, 296; philosophy, poetry, and mysticism rooted in, 130; of polis and chaos, 244; political, 92, 221, 248; primordial experience of, 148; tensional and paradoxical, 149, 152; transcends individuality, 141; transcends politics, 231; truth of, 148, 231
Rechtsatz, 276
Reid, Thomas: on common sense, 96–99 *passim; Essays on the Active Powers of the Human Mind* (1788), 97; *Essays on the Intellectual Power of Man* (1785), 97; and goodness, 97; *An Inquiry into the Human Mind* (1764), 96; and truth, 97
Reik, Theodor, 57
Richie, Donald: *A Lateral View,* 197
Ricoeur, Paul, 262
Rights: human, 74–90 *passim;* natural, 273
Rimer, Thomas: *Modern Japanese Fiction and Its Traditions,* 191
Roman Empire, 325
Roosevelt, Franklin D., 236, 241, 251; and art of governing, 237; compared with Mitterrand, 255; and the White House, 253
Rorty, Richard, 262
Ruse, Michael, 102; *Can a Darwinian Be a Christian?* 117

Saint Augustine. *See* Augustine
Saint Paul, 67, 68; and Solomon, 314
Saint-Simon, Henri de, 92
Saint Thomas Aquinas, 117, 139, 226
Sandoz, Ellis: *The Voegelinian Revolution,* 130, 143, 262
Samsom, George: "Some Problems in the Study of Japanese History," 197
Santayana, George, 269; aesthetic dimensions of, 136; criticisms of liberalism, 131; and critics, 135–39; *Dominations and Powers,* 129, 131, 134; *Interpretations of Poetry and Religion,* 137; and language of poetry, 138; man of common sense, 143; materialism of, 130–35 *passim,* 143; matter, spirit, and essence in, 132–35; merging of philosophy and poetry, 139; mystical skepticism of, 135, 144; philosophy begins *in medias res,* 139; and Plato, 133; as poet-philosopher, 135–37, 138; and poetic expression, 142; *Soliloquies in England,* 136; and use of language, 137; Voegelin's view of, 130; within tradition of materialism, 131
Schabert, Tilo, 102
Schneider, Herbert, 136, 137
Scheler, Max, 79
Schelling, Friedrich Wilhelm Joseph von, 116, 333; and existential turn, 7; and philosophy, 8
Schmitt, Carl, 210, 213, 222; *The Concept of the Political,* 214–16; influence of, 215
Schopenhauer, Arthur, 54, 69
Schütz, Alfred, 268
Schwartz, Geoffrey, 122, 124
Scruton, Roger, 262
Sein (Being, Existence), 275, 277, 336
Self: and "other selfs," 170; and "significant unity," 154; creation of, 154
Sextus Empiricus, 325
Shaseibun, 191–93
Shinto: shrines, 199; myth and shining princess archetype, 200; mythology and mirror imagery, 198–99
Simmel, Georg, 275
Sisyphus, 274
Smith, John E.: *Themes in American Philosophy,* 136
Socrates, 264, 271, 284
Socratic question, 273
Sollen (ought, Essence), 275, 277
Soviet Union, 279, 289, 330

Spinoza, Baruch, 134
Sse-ma Ch'ien, 339
Stalin, Joseph, 87
State, the, 176, 180, 211, 213, 214, 215, 217, 248, 251, 252, 268, 276, 306
Statecraft, 234
Strauss, Leo, 262; on Xenophon, 29, 30
Stringer, Chris, and Robin McKie: *African Exodus,* 122
Sumerian King Lists, 330
Surrealistic Papillons (co-production around Breton), 72–73
Suzuki, Daisetz T.: *Zen and Japanese Culture,* 199, 200
Symbol(s): creation of, 149; empty, 150; equivalent, 148; and ideas, 146; language, 149, 150; philosophical, 152; poetic, 151
Symbolism(s): compact, of poetry, 152; mythopoetic, 151; tensional, 147
Symbolization: issue of, 118; mythic, 152; mythopoetic and "ideological deformation," 151; paradoxical, 152
Syme, Roland: *The Roman Revolution,* 249

Tattersall, Ian, and Geoffrey Schwartz: *Extinct Humans,* 122, 124
Taubes, Jacob, 65
Taylor, Charles, 262
Tension(s): in "border experiences," 147; creative, of "philosophical novelist," 168; of existence, 88, 220, 233; "existence in," 300; existential, symbols of, 118; Gnostic longing to end, 224; in political reality, 221; logos of existential, 220; of questioning, 85
Terrorism/terrorists: 9/11, 294, 295; religiously inspired, 292
Thaumazein (wondering), 124
Thaumazo (I wonder), 47
Thomas Aquinas. *See* Saint Thomas Aquinas
Thucydides, 339
To phantastikon, 60
Totalitarianism, 225, 265, 266, 279
Toynbee, Arnold, 326; *Study of History,* 331; Voegelin's assessment of, 331
Tragic humanism, 69–70
Transcendence: as decisive problem of philosophy, 79; sensitivity to, 144
Transcendent: Beyond, 300; divine nature, 75; divine Nous, 76; divine presence, 77; experience, 137; experiences of order, 220; foundation of human dignity, 88; good, 84, 95; ground of being, 101; ground of existence, 83; ground of meaning, 84; Kingdom of God, 302; mystery of, 90; point of reference, 222; reality, 79, 292; reason, 84; source of being, 94; source of order, 264; standards of right, 229; the, 13, 21, 95, 147; value of divine nature, 76
Trotsky, Leon, 80
Truman, Harry S., 236, 251
Truth: "cosmological style of," 337; formative, and deformative untruth, 150; of human existence, 80; reflective quest for, 125; "social," 233; to "live in," 264; and untruth, 150
Tugendhat, Ernst, 262

United Nations, 278, 279
Universal Declaration of Human Rights, 74; era of, 87
Universalism, 288, 297
Urey, Harold, 112

Valéry, Paul, 240
Velvet Revolution of 1989, 260, 265
Vernant, Jean-Pierre, 262
Vico, Giambattista, 235
Voegelin, Eric, 90, 96, 264, 265, 269, 273, 281, 282, 283, 300; anabasis of, 266; on Aristotle's *Metaphysics,* 124–25; biography of, 267; and boundary question, 122; and commitment to human dignity, 77; concept of political reality, 222; correspondence with East, 334; correspondence with Ellegood, 328–29, 330–31, 331–32; correspondence with Henningsen, 332; correspondence with Wentworth, 332–33; critique of ideology of, 299; on dehumanization, 80; Herculean "search for order" of, 266; hermeneutical science of politics, 218; and *imago Dei,* 78–82; influence of Augustine and Schelling on, 79; Ingersoll Lecture of, 332; intellectual history of, 335; interest in Paleolithic and Neolithic Ages, 334; legacy of, 260, 266; letter to Heilman quoted, 81–82; life experience of, 274; and meditative recognition of participation, 81; on mystery, 115; and philosophical anthropology, 218; philosophical legacy of, 259; philosophical search for order, 286; on pragmatic expansion and spiritual exodus, 334; and Santayana's poetry, 135;

and Schmitt, 216–17; science of politics, 217; on symbolization, 147; theory of consciousness, 77, 171–73, 183, 185–86; theory of representation, 215; *Wissenschaft* of, 328
—Writings: "Anamnesis," 171; *Anamnesis,* 60, 103, 110–11, 140, 327, 332, 335; "Anxiety and Reason," 220, 337; *Autobiographical Reflections,* 129, 146, 149–50, 218, 262–63, 280; "The Beginning and the Beyond," 337; "The Beginning of the Beginning," 150; Candler Lectures, 333, 334; *Collected Works,* 259; "Configurations of History," 336; "Conversations with Eric Voegelin," 107; "Diskussionsbeitrag," 221; *The Drama of Humanity,* 333; *The Ecumenic Age,* 104, 217, 286, 293, 325–40; *Empire and Christianity,* 328, 330; "Equivalences of Experience and Symbolization in History," 123, 147, 168, 169, 336; "The Gospel and Culture," 336, 337; *Hitler and the Germans,* 116; "Hitler and the Germans," 332; "Historiogenesis," 329; *History of Political Ideas,* 149, 333; *In Search of Order,* 186, 332–33; *Israel and Revelation,* 326, 336; "The Moving Soul," 111–12; *The Nature of Law,* 223–33, 280–82; *The New Science of Politics,* 91–101 passim, 193, 217, 262, 300, 302–3, 321–24; *On the Form of the American Mind,* 129, 145; "On Henry James's Turn of the Screw," 88; "On the Theory of Consciousness," 172; *Order and History,* 217, 262, 263, 336; "The Origins of Totalitarianism," 266, 278; "The People of God," 219; *Plato and Aristotle,* 325–26, 326; "The Phylogenetic Field," 102, 118; "The Pure Theory of Law and of State," 275, 276, 277; *Political Religions,* 219; *Published Essays,* 327; *Regierungslehre* (fragmentary) 216; *Science, Politics, and Gnosticism,* 93; "What Is Political Reality?" 87, 96, 183; "World-Empire and the Unity of Mankind," 329
Voegelinians, 266; global network of, 259, 260; Platonic Academia of, 259, 261

Waldberg, Patrick, 71
Warren, Robert Penn: *All the King's Men,* 154–61; *Democracy and Poetry,* 154; "The Great Mirage," 168; "The Use of the Past," 167; "Why Do We Read Fiction?" 153; *World Enough and Time,* 161–66
Watson, James, 112
Weber, Max, 58, 211; statism of, 214
White, Mayor Kevin (Boston), 236
Whitehead, Alfred North, 269
Whitney, Charles: cited, 304
Windelband, Wilhelm, 275
Witte, John, Jr.: "Between Sanctity and Depravity," 89
Wittgenstein, Ludvig, 335
Wood, Neal: on Xenophon, 30

Xenophon: *Anabasis,* 31, 36, 39; and hunting, 35–49; *Constitution of Lacedemonians,* 31; *Hipparchikos,* 36; *Kynegetikos,* 31–53 passim; *Kyropaideia,* 31, 36; *Kyrou Anabasis,* 31; life of, 31, 39, 50; *Memorabilia,* 31, 44; modern writers on, 28–31; *Oikonomikos,* 36; *Peri Hippikes,* 36; reasons for low estimations of, 29; *Tyrannikos,* 36

Yerushalmi, Y. H.: *Freud's Moses,* 65–66
Yoshida Shoin, 190

Zen Buddhism, 199–201
Zweig, Arnold: cited, 69
Zweig, Stefan, 267